Y0-CDH-348

Dimensions of Contemporary Japan

A Collection of Essays

Series Editor

Edward R. Beauchamp
University of Hawaii

A Garland Series

Series Contents

Japan's Role in International Politics since World War II

Edited with an introduction by

Edward R. Beauchamp
University of Hawaii

GARLAND PUBLISHING, INC.
A MEMBER OF THE TAYLOR & FRANCIS GROUP
New York & London
1998

Library of Congress Cataloging-in-Publication Data

Japan's role in international politics since World War II / edited with
an introduction by Edward R. Beauchamp.
p. cm. — (Dimensions of contemporary Japan ; 6)
Includes bibliographical references.
ISBN 0-8153-2733-1 (alk. paper)
1. Japan—Foreign relations—1945–1989. 2. Japan—Foreign
relations—1989– 3. World politics—1945- I. Beauchamp, Edward
R., 1933– . II. Series.
DS889.J365 1998
357.52—dc21 98-51523
CIP

Printed on acid-free, 250-year-life paper
Manufactured in the United States of America

Contents

Introduction

The single, most fundamental goal of the Japan postwar occupation (1945–1952) was nothing less than the complete and total transformation of Japan from an aggressive, militaristic power into a peaceful, democratic member of the family of nations. All of the policies of the occupation authorities were designed to accomplish this goal. One of the most important ramifications of this policy, in the international realm, was the famous article nine of the American-imposed Constitution of November 3, 1946.

> Aspiring sincerely to an international peace based on justice and order, the Japanese people forever renounce war as a sovereign right of the nation and the threat or use of force as a means of settling international disputes.
>
> In order to accomplish the aim of the preceding paragraph, land, sea and air forces, as well as other war potential, will never be maintained. The right of belligerancy of the state will not be recognized.

This statement of pacifism has remained part of Japan's basic law to this day, and has from time-to-time been the subject of heated domestic political debate in all discussions of planning for Japan's national defense. This constitutional structure has been very useful to the Japanese government throughout the postwar years. It has been an expedient tool to point to as a means of resisting American pressures to rearm and to place all of the nation's resources into economic reconstruction and expansion. The great irony is, however, that the article has not proven to be an obstacle in persuading the Japanese people that their rather robust "self defense" forces are not in violation of the constitutional restriction on military forces.

Even without an official, formal military establishment, however, Japan was not without defenses. A very close political, economic, and military alliance between that country and its patron, the United States, has well served the interests of both powers. These defense arrangements, and the strong sense of pacifism resulting from the disaster of World War II has allowed the Japanese, in a sense, to have their cake and eat it too for almost half a century. As world conditions are changing rapidly because of the fall of the Berlin wall, the breakup of the old Soviet Union, and the American rapproachment with a rising China, these old arrangements are beginning to be examined in ways that would have been unthinkable a generation ago. Virtually all

Japanese international activities from 1945 to the present have been shaped by article nine and its ramifications.

This volume recounts the major postwar events and controversies in the realm of Japan's international relations. These include Samuels insightful article on how Japan has dealt with security issues from Meiji (1868–1912) to the early 1990s. It is followed by Dore's speculation of Japan's future security in the twenty-first century, and should it lean to the East or to the West in pursuing national security interests? Two other analyses of the more generalized context are found in Itoh's examination of the persistance of a "sankoku" mentality in Japanese foreign policy, and in Hein's analysis of Japanese relations with the West, particularly the United States.

Other contributions deal with specific issues and the influence of Japan's strong sense of pacifism on those issues. Inoguchi discusses Japan's role in United Nations peacekeeping operations while Woolley describes the agony of the debate over whether or not minesweepers should be sent to assist in Gulf War operations. Leitenberg's analysis of possible Japanese military participation in United Nations operations opens up this issue to serious discussion. Vogel speculates on whether a "pax Nipponica" is on the horizon, and Orr casts a critical eye on Japan's rather extensive foreign aid program. Maddock's explication of Japan's role in the global environmental movement is an example of a relatively safe international issue that is harmonious with the nation's declared peaceful approach.

Major issues that resulted from Japan's prewar and wartime policy are also still with us. Among them are Soh's discussion of the emotional issue of Korean "comfort women" and their efforts for redress, and Japan's dispute with her neighbor over who owns the Spratly Islands, discussed by Er. Japan's relations with her Russian neighbors have always been contentious and this theme continues, as illustrated in Kimura's essay on Boris Yeltsin's visit to Japan.

The key element in Japan's relations with the world is still that of sometimes rocky relations with the United States. This large topic is discussed by Shimizu in his analysis of the different views of the U.S. and Japan over recognition of the People's Republic of China. Hurst muses about the strains in the U.S.-Japan alliance, and Vogel expresses a strongly held position on post Cold War relations between the two allies. The Japan-U.S. relationship is summed up in a series of short articles from a major Japanese English-language publication, *Japan Echo*. Finally, Masataka presents a useful view of the general topic of security and diplomacy in U.S.-Japanese relations in the next century.

* * * * *

This collection of articles on modern Japanese society contains over one hundred scholarly pieces that have been written by leading academics in the field. It is drawn from distinguished scholarly journals, as well as from other select sources not as well known. Many readers, however, may be struck by the absence of material from the *Journal of Japanese Studies*. This is due to our inability to secure the necessary permissions from that journal to use their materials.

Richard J. Samuels

Reinventing Security: Japan Since Meiji

SINCE THE MID-NINETEENTH CENTURY, Japanese security planners have had to navigate the Scylla of technological backwardness and the Charybdis of foreign dependence. From 1868 to 1945, the national response of the Japanese to their situation included the use of military force. After 1945, Japan's security was allowed to rest much more heavily on the nation's commercial and technological achievements.

The Japanese saga however is far from closed. For as Japan has reduced its condition of technological vulnerability and dependence, other nations have begun to ask how Japan proposes to use its newly achieved technological autonomy. Even among the Japanese there have been signs of questioning on whether the nation's postwar policies of maintaining low levels of defense-related production, prohibiting the export of military goods, and living under the protection of the US security umbrella still make sense in light of its technological and economic performance. To gain a sense of how that question is likely to be answered, one has to begin with history.

In the nineteenth century, Japan's policies toward its technological backwardness were unambiguous, Japanese leaders exhorted the nation to "revere the Emperor and expel the barbarian," (*sanno jōi*), to "catch up and surpass the West, (*oitsuki oikose*), and to combine "Western technology with Japanese spirit," (*wakon yōsai*)—in short, to sacrifice for national security in a hostile world. The struggle for technological independence has been a feature of Japanese strategy ever since.

Japanese military and industrial strategies have been built on a fusion of industrial, technology, and national security policies. This

Richard J. Samuels is Professor of Political Science at the Massachusetts Institute of Technology.

fusion, dubbed technonationalism, has persisted both in the prewar era, when Japan used military means to achieve its national objectives, and in the postwar period, when its policies were more completely commercial. Undergirding the policies in both eras has been a consistent and powerful belief that national security is enhanced as much by the ability to design and to produce as by the actual deployment of sophisticated equipment.

MILITARY TECHNONATIONALISM

Japanese arms production, particularly swords and armor, was an advanced art long before the establishment of the Tokugawa shogunate in 1600. Firearms were introduced in the mid-sixteenth century by European merchants blown off course to Tanegashima, on the island of Kyushu. The "Tanegashima gun," as it came to be known, promptly was back-engineered for domestic manufacture. The diffusion of Tanegashima gunsmithing technology (and indeed of guns themselves) was so complete that by the late sixteenth century, the Japanese reportedly fought their civil wars with more firearms than any European nation.[1]

The civil wars ended with the Pax Tokugawa, officially isolating Japan from the rest of the world for the next two and a half centuries. But the Japanese continued to monitor foreign developments. In the 1780s, Hayashi Shihei, a Sendai nobleman, attempted to build artillery, but could find only 150-year-old gunpowder. His "Treatise on the Affairs of an Insular Country" first articulated concerns about the backwardness of Japanese arms manufacture and the urgent need to protect Japan, and its manufactures, from foreign domination.

Almost simultaneously with the publication of the Hayashi treatise, one foreign power after another began to call upon Japan for trade and other concessions. The shogunate quickly heeded Hayashi's advice and resumed arms manufacturing. By the 1850s, each local domain (*han*) had begun manufacturing arms, though at widely disparate levels of technological sophistication. The best of the *han* arsenals, such as the Ishikawajima Shipyards and the Hyogo Iron Works, like the best of the shogun's own defense plants, such as the Nagasaki Works, are today among Japan's largest industrial enterprises and defense contractors.

Although arms manufacture was the most advanced manufacturing industry in pre-Meiji Japan—having been the first to introduce modern tools and power systems—even the largest and most modern arsenals in Japan were far short of world standards. In the years before the Meiji restoration in 1868, the Krupp shipyards, Germany's largest, produced ten times the number of steamships with more than forty times the horsepower of those produced by the Nagasaki shipyards, Japan's largest.[2]

To protect Japan from rapacious foreign powers and to stimulate economic development, the Meiji government sought to standardize and modernize the manufacture of munitions. Through acquisition and direct management of existing arsenals, the government quickly assumed the strategic heights of the economy. In the view of the young Meiji oligarchy, modern transportation, communication, and heavy industrial technologies were all necessary to secure the national welfare. The slogan "rich nation, strong army" (*fukoku kyōhei*) was the first official embrace of military technonationalism; it captured well the ideological appeal of modernization.

Thus, arms manufacturing, the most modern industrial sector before the Meiji restoration, led Japan's forced march to industrialization. By 1877, nearly two-thirds of the central government's investments were directed toward the military, and throughout the 1880s the proportion remained above one-half.[3] Military demand and technology were both key stimuli to the rest of the economy;[4] military equipment dominated the exhibits at Japan's first international Industrial Promotion Fair in 1877.

If the institutional center of the early Meiji industrial strategy was the rapidly expanding national arsenal system, the intellectual center was technology borrowed from abroad and made Japanese. Foreign tutelage for national strength was enshrined in the Charter Oath of the Emperor Meiji in 1868: "Intellect and learning would be sought throughout the world in order to establish the foundations of Empire."[5] Japan developed its military-technological intelligence system before completing its military-industrial infrastructure. Japanese engineers went abroad to identify and to acquire advanced technology; foreign experts came to Japan to teach. Within two decades young engineers had mastered a considerable body of foreign design and manufacturing technology, much of it for the military at the Imperial University. This practice served as a template for technology monitoring and indigenization for the rest of the Meiji economy, and soon became standard commercial practice as well.

This indigenization strategy, however, was costly and took time to bear fruit. Although the army largely achieved independence in weapon production by the time of the Russo-Japanese War in 1905, the navy was dependent upon Western technology (British cruisers, for example) until nearly World War I. In a period of large trade deficits, imports of war materiel were nevertheless sustained.

In the evolving view of Meiji strategists, national power and industrial autonomy were interdependent. So, consequently, were military and civilian technologies: the first machine tools for mining were manufactured in 1869 in a government arsenal; the telegraph first was used to suppress the Satsuma Rebellion in 1877; in 1880 the Yokosuka armory produced most of Japan's motors for advanced looms, as well as helping to provide lighthouses, harbor facilities, and other critical infrastructure.

From the beginning, the manufacturing facilities dedicated to civilian production in Japan benefited in myriad ways from government investment in military production and technological leadership. In the 1880s, government armories and other government factories were transferred to private hands. Three successive war mobilizations—in 1905, 1914, and the 1930s—added greatly to the strength of the private sector. By the end of the 1930s, the military output of private factories would exceed that of government arsenals, even though private entrepreneurs were producing overwhelmingly for commercial markets. Most of this production nominally centered in the technologically sophisticated and highly integrated manufacturing and financial conglomerates (*zaibatsu*).

While the Japanese economy had been stimulated by demand for military production, it had not been captured by such production.[6] For instance, although by 1937 the *zaibatsu* accounted for more than half of Japan's total production of war materiel, arms manufacture comprised less than one-fifth of their total production.[7] Impatient with the caution of the *zaibatsu,* the military found it necessary to nurture "new entrepreneurs," such as Nakajima Aircraft and Nissan Motors, as well as other small firms.[8]

Although Japanese planners badly miscalculated the ultimate consequences of military technonationalism, their underlying strategy helped to guide the creation of domestic institutions in manufacturing and research that would persist and flourish in the second half of the twentieth century.[9]

COMMERCIAL TECHNONATIONALISM

The dominant characteristic of Japan's military production in the postwar period was how little there was of it. But contrary to much contemporary mythology, Japan did not achieve its technological position of the 1990s by ignoring the arms industry. Arms production attracted considerable attention by economic planners and businessmen in the early 1950s. US military procurement was an engine of Japan's early postwar reconstruction and continued as an important source of advanced technology into the 1990s.

Article Nine of the 1947 Japanese constitution prohibits Japan from maintaining a "war potential," and renounces Japan's "right of belligerency," but neither that article nor anything else in the constitution precludes the production or export of Japanese arms. In 1948, it is true, the United States reversed its Asian security policy and the intent of Article Nine, which it had authored, in order to establish Japan as a military-industrial bastion—what one Japanese prime minister much later dubbed its "unsinkable aircraft carrier" in the Far East. Procurement of Japanese goods by the US military and other forms of economic aid represented the price paid by the United States for Japanese bases and for Japanese participation in the United States's Cold War rearmament program.[10]

Nearly 70 percent of Japanese exports between 1950 and 1952 comprised US military "special procurement," (*tokujū*), which contributed significantly to the rehabilitation of the Japanese economy. Once the United States granted Japan the permission to resume arms and aircraft manufacture, Japanese industry wasted no time expanding capacity and shifting to munitions production. Weapons sales of 7 million yen in 1952 grew to 15 billion yen in 1954.[11] During the Korean War, 60 percent of the sales of Komatsu, which made Japan's first postwar artillery mortars, represented sales to the military.[12] In 1952 there were 160 separate firms manufacturing ammunition in Japan.[13]

Yet, despite new entrants, the industry was dominated again by former *zaibatsu* firms and their subsidiaries. The top four firms accounted for more than 70 percent of US orders. Few of them had anything like Komatsu's dependence on military markets. Besides, most large firms hedged their bets further by assigning about half the processing of their finished products to subcontractors, who thereby assumed much of the risk that the military boom might eventually fizzle.

This hedging reflected the intense ambivalence of Japanese industry and the Japanese public toward any overt dependence on military activities. The ambivalence could be seen in early postwar Japan in a split between industrial and finance capital. The former, representing the heavy industrial firms of the old *zaibatsu,* such as Mitsubishi, used former high-ranking military officers to generate ambitious rearmament plans and optimistic projections for the arms industry as the engine of postwar redevelopment. "Defense production"—a euphemism promoted by both industry and government—gained the Ministry of International Trade and Industry's support as a key element in Japan's technology strategy.[14] According to MITI aircraft and ordinance director Akazawa Shōichi, the industrial development of the Japanese arms industry was part of Japan's "technology lust."[15]

But in the early 1950s, the bankers and the Ministry of Finance (MOF) were not convinced of the wisdom of expanding the production of arms. They argued that arms production would divert scarce resources from sectors with greater (and more stable) prospects for growth. Former *zaibatsu* bankers, now assuming greater power in the postwar economic restructuring, refused financing to firms that were planning to commit more than 20 or 30 percent of their output to defense products.[16] Bureaucrats in the Ministry of Finance clearly recalled the pressures from militarists to which they had succumbed during the wartime. With fiscal stability having been only recently restored in accordance with the recommendations of a mission headed by a prominent US banker, Joseph M. Dodge, Japanese bankers and MOF officials feared a return to deficit budgeting.

The debate came to a head during the preparation of the 1954 fiscal budget. MOF firmly opposed MITI efforts to introduce fiscal support to the arms industry; MOF was quietly abetted by some MITI officials, who doubted the efficacy of support for the arms industry and instead wanted to secure support for the electric power industry, which they considered to be more strategic. MITI had to settle for limited regulatory power through the Arms Manufacturing

Law (*Buki nado Seizō Hō*) passed by the Diet in July 1953. Unlike other pieces of legislation of the period which granted special support to a number of key industries, this law signaled to the capital markets that arms production would *not* be targeted for special assistance. Defense contractors exited in large numbers, in some cases not to return for thirty or forty years.

The impact of this shakeout persists to the present day. In the early 1990s, the Japanese defense industry is very small; Japanese defense production amounts to barely one half of 1 percent of total Japanese industrial production. Barred from export markets since 1976 by a decision of the Japanese government, Japan's arms sales are equivalent to those of the nation's sushi shops. Despite the best efforts of defense industrialists and some bureaucrats, the Japanese defense industry, as defined by the production of weapons systems, has been the laggard in Japan's "economic miracle."

Nevertheless, despite Japan's limited production of weapons systems, its technological capabilities have positioned Japan as a formidable player in the global defense economy. Japanese firms have emerged as world leaders in the design and manufacture of materials, components, and essential subsystems. According to a foreign ministry report:

> Japanese manufacturers of fiber optics, avionics systems, and other leading edge technologies could build up substantial defense-related businesses without violating the weapons export embargo.[17]

Japan's technological capabilities and its strategy of commercial technonationalism have depended significantly upon its Cold War relationship with the United States. American firms have been the principal source of both military and commercial technology for Japan. Although the transfer of military technology has contributed less to Japan's postwar industrial development than has the transfer of commercial technology, military technology transfers have not been insubstantial.

To gain access to both US military and commercial technology, Japan followed the example of other US allies and ratified a Mutual Defense Assistance Agreement. First, however, Japan had to create a military to which technology could be transferred. In one of the most controversial moves in postwar Japanese politics, despite Article Nine of the constitution prohibiting the maintenance of "war potential," Japan in 1954 established the Japan Defense Agency (JDA) and the Japanese "Self-Defense Forces"(SDF). Although most of the US allies focused the resources they received under the assistance agreement on the development of their arms industry, Japan negotiated to maximize its freedom to diffuse the technology to civilian applications.[18]

As a result, although the mutual defense agreement with the United States was designed to transfer arms and military technology, the Japanese were granted "untied" mutual defense assistance for purposes of "economic development." Indulgent US Army engineers taught Japanese mechanical and civil engineers from Japan's construction engineering firms, such as Kumagai-Gumi, how to use and repair the heavy machinery employed in the construction of Japan's first postwar hydroelectric power plants.[19] Komatsu used military assistance funds to build bulldozers. Under license to provide Japan's first postwar military aircraft, the F-86 and T-33, the Japanese aircraft industry secured training and equipment that it applied for its first foray into commercial aerospace.

But one must not overstate the importance of the mutual defense program. Over the longer postwar period, American military transfers to Japan were dwarfed by the transfer of US commercial technology through the private sale of licenses and joint ventures. These were of far more consequence in nurturing both the military and the general industrial base in Japan, and hence Japanese national security. Between 1951 and 1984, according to one compilation, more than forty thousand separate contracts were signed by Japanese firms to acquire foreign technology; over that thirty-four-year period, Japan paid $17 billion in royalties—a small fraction of *annual* US R&D costs. With nylon from DuPont, nuclear power from General Electric and Westinghouse, the transistor from Bell Laboratories, and the television tube from Corning, US technology licenses were "the technological basis for nearly all of Japan's modern industries."[20] With US and European firms eager to sell their know-how and with US foreign policy aimed at maintaining a politically stable and economically viable ally in the Pacific, Japanese firms identified, acquired, and subsequently indigenized foreign know-how; yet, successive generations of Japanese products have routinely depended less than preceding ones on foreign technology.[21]

In general, therefore, Japan drew upon the US government's support for allies' military projects and the US public's appetite for commercial products to speed the transfer and indigenization of foreign technologies. By the 1990s, the country achieved the status of a technological superpower.[22]

CONSEQUENTIAL ENDOWMENTS

Japan's mid-century shift to commercial technonationalism from military technonationalism has proved to be especially supportive for Japanese industry for several different reasons.

Dual-Use Technologies

Japan's industrial growth was especially rapid in sectors closely linked to the materials and technologies that enhance the battlefield capabilities of modern weapons: data processing, telecommunications, optoelectronics, and lightweight materials. For example, by making integrated circuits in large volumes for consumer electronics and graphite fiber in large volumes for tennis rackets and golf clubs, Japanese manufacturers were able to accumulate knowledge and experience for military aerospace applications. By the late 1970s, Japanese suppliers had become an important source of technology for the US Department of Defense and were advertising their technical ability to provide "ruggedized" products to the military market at bargain prices.[23]

This ability to "spin-on" civilian technologies to military applications was the fruit—the unintended fruit—of a predominantly commercial strategy. Unlike in the United States where most research was funded by the government and where most government-funded research was undertaken for the Department of Defense and the weapons program of the Department of Energy, nearly four-fifths of Japanese R&D spending comprised corporate research funded by commercial firms overwhelmingly for civilian markets.

But the actual level of Japanese military R&D was surely higher than the official budget of the Defense Agency's Technical Research and Development Institute (TRDI). In the early 1990s, reported R&D expenditures were only 1 or 2 percent of Japan's defense budget. The TRDI was the only government agency officially engaged in defense research; but MITI, the Science and Technology

Agency, and the Japan Key Technology Center were all funding large scale R&D projects led by private firms in areas with significant dual-use applications, such as jet engines, microelectronics, and materials processing. These private firms, rather than the TRDI, were taking the responsibility for all prototype manufacturing and testing of defense systems. As a consequence, they informally subsidized defense R&D, and they routinely spread research costs across military and civilian projects.[24] Said one senior TRDI official:

> There is no black versus white, military versus civilian technology. All technology is gray. It becomes military or civilian in application. Today 81% of Japan's R&D efforts are focused on the commercial side. Our R&D base is like Mt. Fuji; the civilian R&D provides a bottom that is very broad.[25]

Japanese dual-use capabilities were first formally acknowledged by a study team of the US Defense Science Board in 1984, which concluded that Japanese technology was at or ahead of the most advanced US capabilities in sixteen different dual-use technologies. These technologies were widely acknowledged as the "key" or "base" technologies for advanced manufacturing in the next century, including gallium arsenide devices, microwave integrated circuits, fiber optic communications, image and speech recognition, flat displays, and ceramics.[26]

Industrial structure

The Japanese system includes both a strategic commitment to the diffusion of innovation and the use of organizational and ideological infrastructures that facilitate such diffusion. As a consequence, technology travels readily between the military and civilian sectors of the economy.

Japan's leading defense contractors have also been Japan's most innovative commercial firms. As elsewhere, the top defense contractors have been among the largest firms in the economy. But unlike in the United States and much of Western Europe, these firms have been highly diversified and have depended little upon sales to the military.

In 1990 only two of the ten largest defense contractors in Japan were dependent upon defense procurement for more than 20 percent of their total sales; half had less than a 5 percent dependency (see Table 1).[27] Only the ammunition and aircraft manufacturing industry depended for more than 5 percent of its total sales upon the Defense Agency; of the remaining industries, only shipbuilding was dependent upon the military for more than 1 percent of total sales.

TABLE 1 Japanese Defense Firms 1990

Firm	Defense Sales (in billion yen)	Share of Defense Sales (percent)	Defense Sales as Percent of Total Firm Sales (percent)
Mitsubishi Heavy Industries	440	28.0	21.0
Kawasaki Heavy Industries	146	9.3	17.0
Mitsubishi Electric	100	6.4	4.1
Ishikawajima-Harima Heavy Industries	78	5.0	12.0
Toshiba Corporation	59	3.8	1.9
NEC Corporation	54	3.5	2.6
Japan Steel Works	34	2.2	28.0
Komatsu, Ltd.	22	1.4	3.5
Fuji Heavy Industries	21	1.4	3.1
Hitachi, Ltd.	20	1.3	0.5

Note: Figures from fiscal 1990

Source: Japan Defense Agency

By the 1980s, however, many Japanese firms, although primarily committed to serving civilian markets, began to realize that considerable potential for growth existed in defense production. In 1980, the four defense-related industry associations joined together with the Japan Electronic Machinery Association to create the Defense Technology Association of Japan (*Bōei Gijutsu Kyōkai*) in order "to strengthen, by public-private cooperation, the ability to independently conceive, research, and build the highest level of equipment." As if to underline Japan's dual-use competence and to punctuate these corporate shifts, Honda Shoichiro, founder of Honda Motors, was made Honorary Chairman, and Ibuka Masaru, founder of Sony, was made a special advisor.

In the years that followed, numerous firms that were well established in nondefense areas took tangible steps to reflect their interest in defense production. Hitachi, for example, established a Defense Technology Promotion Division in 1980. Fujitsu established a subsidiary devoted exclusively to defense systems development and set a corporate goal to bring its defense business up to 20 percent of total sales. Nissan revised its corporate charter to include "manufacture and sale of weapons."[28]

The firms involved in these policy shifts are especially well endowed to manufacture components for the global arms industry. Their activities in nondefense areas have ensured that components, already produced in volume, would be cost competitive and meet high-performance requirements. Their breadth also has endowed them with flexibility in the development and application of new technologies and products. Both scale and scope were enhanced by the *keiretsu* structure, in which a family of firms strengthened their capacity for strategic coordination through cross-holdings of equity, mutual directorships, and intragroup financing by a common bank. All but one of Japan's largest defense contractors are members of *keiretsu* networks, within which it is routine for firms to be guided (and technology to be diffused) as much by relationships as by price.[29] Moreover, Japanese firms have already demonstrated considerable expertise in the organization of production centered on small- and medium-lot batch manufacturing—a skill especially appropriate for producing the components, subassemblies, and subsystems that constitute a considerable portion of defense procurement needs.[30] Indeed, it is likely that the firms that have benefited most from the ambitions of Japan's *keiretsu* firms in the defense sector have been Japan's small- and medium-sized subcontractors. As in the 1950s, the larger firms depend upon their subcontractors for a considerable portion of the value-added in military systems.[31]

The Ability to Partner

Japanese firms that perform as the final assemblers in the defense industry have long enjoyed a set of stable relationships in markets in which they operate, notwithstanding that such markets are characterized by a small number of sellers. There have rarely been clear-cut winners and losers in Japanese defense procurement. Firms that fail to be designated as prime contractors often are assigned a significant subcontracting role, and are rewarded the next time around with a prime contract.[32] In the process, technology is more widely diffused to the benefit of the economy as a whole.

By the 1980s, the global defense industry outside Japan was undergoing changes in directions familiar to Japanese industry.

Whereas "winner-take-all" competitions for contracts among single firms had been typical in earlier years, competitions among "teams" of partner firms were becoming more common. These collaborations extended upstream to domestic research as well, as the United States and the European Community began experimenting with research consortia, such as Sematech and Esprit, to reduce costs and to diffuse innovation of precompetitive, generic technology.

This sort of cooperative R&D has been ubiquitous in Japan's leap from a position of technological backwardness to one of world leadership. Collaborative research has become the defining feature of Japanese research practice and the sine qua non for competitiveness in many technology-intensive sectors. Every major Japanese firm has participated in a large number of consortia, ranging from basic to applied research, and including manufacturing as well. Partnerships have included competitors in the same industry as well as suppliers and customers. In the 1980s, there was a startling acceleration in the creation of new institutions to generate knowledge in Japan, which uniformly involved competing firms. Reliance upon such collaboration, pioneered by the Japanese, seemed likely to transform the landscape of the technology process elsewhere as well.[33]

The Strategic Use of Foreign Partners

As we have seen, Japan's industrial development and national security have depended upon the capacity of the Japanese to identify, assess, acquire, and "indigenize" foreign technology. We are reminded, therefore, that from the Japanese viewpoint the licensing of production has never been an end in itself; it has been in the twentieth century, as it was in the nineteenth century, a means toward learning the processes that underlay the design and production of the products under license.

Foreign licensing has served to close gaps in Japanese manufacturing technology. It has made possible a "learning by doing" process that has enhanced domestic capabilities in military as well as in civilian areas. In the military areas, a pattern has emerged, as Japan has transformed itself from buyer to developer of weapons systems. First, foreign weapons were purchased with foreign funds. Soon, Japan paid for these weapons with its own funds. Within a very short time, Japan negotiated licenses to coproduce these systems. As if following some inexorable law of indigenization, the portion of foreign design and foreign components declined in each subsequent project at the same time that the portion of "dual-use" technology increased. Within a decade or so of having procured foreign licenses, domestic Japanese firms were usually in a position to produce the equipment on their own. By the 1980s, Japan was poised to build its own defense systems with its own technologies, largely generated in the civilian sector.

Yet Japan chose to pursue an intermediate strategy, largely for political reasons. It opted to codevelop these new weapons systems with the United States, its military ally and commercial competitor. Moreover, as Japanese firms moved upstream to R&D, virtually all their new initiatives in aerospace, materials science, and manufacturing technology made provisions for international collaboration in their research activities and invited foreign participation in their efforts.

Of course, there have been limits to the process of learning through the licensing of foreign technology. Since 1952, Japanese firms have coproduced nineteen different US airplanes and helicopters, yet Japan has not succeeded in developing a significant domestic aircraft industry. Although licensed production provides technological insight, equipment, and training from which a determined manufacturer can proceed, it does not routinely teach everything a firm needs to know in order to carry on production of its own. Here, the contrast between civilian and military applications is instructive. Both have depended upon "international cooperation." Both have sought indigenization as a goal. But after the 1950s, the transfers of key technologies for commercial applications was more uniformly successful than the transfers for military applications. It is ironic that this imbalance eventually enhanced Japan's potential to compete in the defense market, as the military use of commercial technologies increased.

Coherent Ideology and Strategic Commitment

Japanese planners have embraced and promulgated a vision of national security that elevates local control and national learning over the more conventional procurement criteria of cost, performance, and delivery dates. It was first articulated in the *Kaikoku Heidan* of Hayashi Shihei in the 1780s, and has been repeatedly invoked across several centuries of Japanese economic development and security planning. Nevertheless, although indigenization has been the unequivocal preference of some business and bureaucratic elites, it has not always been the formal policy of the Japanese government. In the postwar era, Japanese politicians have had to tread carefully around public opinion, which has remained suspicious of military industry, and the Japanese government has had to adapt to the changing designs of its security partner, the United States.

The experience of Nakasone Yasuhiro is instructive. In 1970 the new defense agency chief and future prime minister boldly sought to reduce dependence upon the United States and to introduce a more "autonomous defense" policy (*jishu bōei*). He proposed that indigenization be accepted as the formal centerpiece of JDA procurement policy. (Until then, the JDA would commit itself only to pursuing that policy "as appropriate.") His new "Basic Policy for the Development and Production of Defense Equipment" stated clearly that

> a nation's ability to equip itself for self-defense centers on its industrial capacity. The JDA will consider the nation's industrial capacity and promote the domestic development and production of equipment.[34]

Despite the strong support of the Defense Production Committee of Keidanren, Nakasone was rebuffed by his more cautious colleagues in the Liberal Democratic Party (LDP). Concerned that the public would not accept such a change and that the LDP could not survive further erosion of support, the cabinet opted instead to reaffirm its commitment to the US-Japan Mutual Security Treaty, to articulate a policy of "defensive defense," to tighten legal restrictions on arms exports, and to cap Japanese defense spending at 1 percent of Japan's GNP. To be sure, indigenization would be pursued more vigorously in practice than in law, and much more completely in commercial than in military markets. In the meantime, the official vision of "comprehensive security" would suffice to communicate to the world and to the Japanese people that national security was more a matter of economic advantage than of maintenance of a "war potential."

But a major question remained: how would Japan use its expanding capabilities for producing items desired by military establishments, including dual-use components and military end products?

WHITHER THE JAPANESE DEFENSE INDUSTRY?

Ishihara Shintaro, a member of the Japanese Diet, made headlines by arguing in 1989 that Japan could shift the balance of global power if it diverted shipments of microchips from the United States to the Soviet Union. Ishihara was of course engaging in hyperbole; but there was substance in his metaphor. Japan *had* achieved global power, and as its wealth grew, and as its investment in invention accelerated, Japan surely would have more of it.

In the short run, it seemed certain, Japan's alliance with the United States would continue to constrain Japanese defense spending and its military-industrial development. Even after the Persian Gulf crisis erupted in August 1990, Japan's defense industry was following the US and Soviet leads by scaling down its plans for growth. The 1990 Defense Agency White Paper, anticipating the 1991 visit by President Gorbachev and negotiations over the reversion of the northern territories to Japan, purged all reference to the Soviet Union as a threat to Japan.[35] Japan's new five-year defense program, announced in early 1991, called for a slower rate of growth in the military budget. Weapons R&D spending, however, would rise to 3 percent of total defense spending, two to three times the previous level.

Still, Japan was hedging its bets. While reducing the rate of increase in defense spending, Japan nonetheless was planning to increase defense spending in absolute terms. While firms abroad faced the need to reduce excess capacity and to convert defense plants to civilian production, Japanese firms were expanding their dual-use capabilities, as many firms made significant defense sales for the first time.

Moreover, with the Japan-US relationship under great strain since the 1980s, and with the original raison d'être of this alliance obliterated by the end of the Cold War, both nations were beginning to recalculate the costs and benefits of the relationship.[36] For many Japanese, it seemed high time to wean Japan from its dependence on the United States, and Japanese public opinion seemed ready finally to agree. Yet there was still no obvious replacement for the US consumers or for the US security guarantees on which Japan was heavily reliant, and there was no public support for rearmament—or, as the Gulf crisis demonstrated, for any bold departure from established constraints on force deployments.[37] For many Americans, there was no obvious replacement for Japanese capital or products, despite a growing conviction in the US public that Japan's success had come as a "free ride," unfairly and at the United States's expense.

In fact, in the months before Saddam Hussein's invasion of Kuwait and the Gulf war, Japan had replaced the Soviet Union in US public opinion as the greatest threat to the United States.[38] After the war, another dimension was added to US views of Japan. Japanese hesitations over a contribution to the anti-Iraq coalition and the unwillingness of some Japanese firms to supply the US military with key components during the war left an image of an economic giant which was but a political pygmy.[39] The effect among Americans was to accelerate a growing mistrust of Japanese intentions toward the United States.

These developments went hand-in-hand with new developments in US policy toward Japan. For one thing, the United States intensified its efforts to acquire Japanese military technology. In addition, as the FS-X controversy illustrated, more consideration was given to the possibility of restricting Japanese access to advanced US technology. Predictably, the threat of new restrictions has been seen as the beginning of a "technology blockade" in Japan. It has fueled a national backlash and emboldened advocates of autonomous defense. The respected *Asahi Jānaru* published an article in 1988, for instance, that claimed the United States was adopting a "Nazi-style" attitude toward technology transfer to Japan.[40]

The new emphasis in US policy also increased the desire of the Japanese to accelerate their defense research in order to protect themselves from unilateral US action. One way to contribute to this objective was to accelerate Japanese investments in the US-based defense industry, including firms engaged in R&D. Naturally, this created political difficulties. The Fujitsu acquisition of Fairchild in 1987 was aborted under significant political pressure. And in January 1991, the Bush administration was criticized for refusing to block the purchase by Japan's Fanuc Company of Moore Special Tool, the only US firm that manufactures precision machine tools meeting the Defense and Energy departments' specifications for nuclear weapons production.[41] As Japanese firms continued to seek advanced technological competencies in the United States, it seemed likely that sporadic US efforts to block such transactions would increase in frequency, and that development, in turn, would accelerate Japanese efforts at indigenous development.

In light of these developments, it is ironic that one of the factors contributing to the growth of Japan's defense industry has been US exhortations to "burden share." The Japanese public support for Article Nine of Japan's constitution has meant that any expansion of the country's weaponry must always be justified as "defensive" rather than "offensive" in character; the acquisition of items such as cameras for mounting on military aircraft, therefore, can generate raging debates in Japan. Such problems, however, have not prevented the JDA from responding to US pressures for more defense spending.[42] In the 1980s, Japan's defense budget grew faster than any other area of government spending except for foreign aid. And defense R&D was consistently the fastest growing line item within the defense budget. The predictable result is that today Japan's largely defensive "war potential" is among the largest and most technologically sophisticated in the world.

The rancorous dispute between the United States and Japan over the well-publicized FS-X in 1989 further abetted these developments. Under pressure from Congress and fearful that Japan would use transferred technology to compete in the commercial aerospace industry, the Bush administration decided to renegotiate a bilateral agreement to codevelop a new fighter aircraft for Japan.[43] Japanese defense industrialists used the opportunity to accelerate defense spending, particularly in R&D, and to look for ways of withholding Japanese advanced technologies from the United States.[44] Keidanren issued its first formal endorsement of arms production, and within three months, the Keidanren Defense Production Committee was made a standing committee, a move that for forty years had been judged too politically sensitive to merit Keidanren's support.

Other reactions occurred as well. For its part, the JDA announced several large-scale development programs, including programs to replace imported US missiles, jet engines, and helicopters with Japanese models. During the FS-X dispute, France offered Japan all the jet fighter technologies that the United States was withholding. In March 1990, Mitsubishi Heavy Industries stunned the industry by announcing an omnibus aerospace cooperative relationship with Daimler-Benz that will involve dual-use technologies, especially jet propulsion. Contracts to purchase European aircraft in late 1990, the first of such purchases by Japan, were linked to these European initiatives and to the "hangover" from the FS-X dispute.[45]

Japan will continue to fortify its defense technology base and to expand its alternatives in the global economy. But it is unlikely to take the initiative in greatly modifying or abandoning its alliance with the United States. Unless rejected by the United States, therefore, Japan can be expected to continue its restrained but increasingly flexible approach toward defense planning and military programs, while the Japanese industry remains poised to succeed by creating dependencies in a global market that requires its dual-use products and process technologies. Japanese technonationalism has guided the nation to reinvent security in war and in peace.

ACKNOWLEDGEMENTS

I am grateful for the financial support this project received from the MIT Japan Program and from the MIT Center for International Studies Japan Energy Endowment, the congenial facilities provided by the Science Policy Research Unit at the University of Sussex and the Faculty of Oriental Studies at the University of Cambridge, and comments from the participants in the planning conference for this volume, convened at the Harvard University Center for International Affairs. Conversations with Michael Chinworth, a former colleague at MIT, were also extremely helpful.

ENDNOTES

1 Noel Perrin, *Giving Up the Gun: Japan's Reversion to the Sword—1543–1879* (Boston: David R. Godine, 1979), 4.

2 Koyama, Kōken, *Nihon Gunji Kōgyō no Shiteki Bunseki* (A historical analysis of the Japanese defense industry) (Tokyo: Ochanomizu Shōbō, 1972), 56.

3 Henry Rosovsky, *Capital Formation in Japan 1868–1940* (New York: Free Press, 1961), 25–26.

4 Kozo Yamamura, "Success Illgotten? The Role of Meiji Militarism in Japan's Technological Progress," *The Journal of Economic History* 37 (1) (March 1977): 113–35.

5 William Lockwood, *The Economic Development of Japan: Growth and Structural Change, 1868–1938* (London: Oxford University Press, 1955), 9.

6 Elizabeth B. Schumpeter, ed., *The Industrialization of Japan and Manchukuo 1938–1940: Population, Raw Materials, and Industry* (New York: Macmillan, 1940), 15.

7 Koyama, 228.

8 Nakajima eventually became Fuji Heavy Industries, Japan's tenth largest defense contractor. Nissan, of course, is one of the world's leading automakers and one of Japan's top fifteen JDA contractors.

[9]It is in this sense that John Dower refers to World War II as "the useful war." See John Dower, "The Useful War," in *Daedalus* 119 (3) (Summer 1990): 49–70.

[10]Laura Hein, *Fueling Growth: The Energy Revolution and Economic Policy in Postwar Japan* (Cambridge: Harvard East Asian Monographs, 1990), 229.

[11]Hideo Otake, "Nihon no 'Gunsan Fukugōtai' to Zaisei Kiki," (Japan's military-industrial complex and the fiscal crisis), pt. 1, *Asahi Jānaru,* 18 July 1980, 12.

[12]*Ekonomisuto,* 11 March 1952; Hideo Otake "Nihon ni Okeru 'Gunsankan Fukugōtai' Keisei no Zasetsu" (The frustrated state of the 'military-industrial-bureaucratic complex' in Japan), in Hideo Otake, ed., *Nihon Seiji no Sōten* (The Japanese political debate) (Tokyo: San Ichi Shōbō, 1984), 21.

[13]Marie Soderberg, *Japan's Military Export Policy* (Stockholm: University of Stockholm, 1987), 51.

[14]Hideo Otake, "Nihon no 'Gunsan Fukugōtai' to Zaisei Kiki" (Japan's military-industrial complex and the fiscal crisis), pt. 3, *Asahi Jānaru,* 1 August 1980, 28.

[15]Quoted in Otake, "Nihon no 'Gunsan Fukugōtai' to Zaisei Kiki," pt. 1, 31.

[16]*Nihon Keizai Shimbun,* 2 August 1953; *Asahi Shimbun,* 18 June 1953.

[17]*JEI Report* #30A, 3 August 1990, 13.

[18]For the ultimate consequences of this and subsequent programs, see US Congress, Office of Technology Assessment, *Arming Our Allies* (Washington, D.C.: US Government Printing Office, 1990). For a blunt assessment of how one nation uses "offset" programs to enhance its commercial competitiveness, see Joo-way Kim, " 'Offset' as an Instrument of National Industrial Policy," S.M. thesis, Sloan School of Management, MIT, June 1991.

[19]This is the description of Senga Tetsuya, former executive director of the Defense Production Committee of Keidanren. He also notes the "kindness and courtesy" extended by US firms eager "to teach" (sell) technology to Japan in the early 1950s, and adds ironically that "it was a bit different than the situation today." See Kondo Kanichi and Osanai Hiroshi, eds., *Sengo Sangyōshi e no Shōgen* (Testimony related to postwar industrial history), vol. 3 (Tokyo: Mainichi Shimbunsha, 1978), 227–8.

[20]James C. Abegglen and George Stalk, Jr., *Kaisha: The Japanese Corporation* (New York: Basic Books, 1985), 126.

[21]Michael Green in "*Kokusanka*: FS-X and Japan's Search for Autonomous Defense Production," MIT Japan Program Working Paper, 90–09, 1990, discusses the difficulties some Japanese politicians had in formally embracing the doctrine of indigenization (*kokusanka*) and even the defense industry itself.

[22]Reinhard Drifte, *Arms Production in Japan: The Military Applications of Civilian Technology* (Boulder, Colo.: Westview Press, 1986), 11, cites without further reference an estimate that Japan received about $10 billion worth of advanced US technology between 1950 and 1983; Thomas R. H. Havens, *Fire across the Sea: The Vietnam War and Japan, 1965–1975* (Princeton: Princeton University Press, 1987) documents the extent to which U.S. military procurement stimulated the Japanese economy during the Vietnam War; and John H. Makin, "American Economic and Military Leadership in the Postwar Period," in J. Makin and D.

Hellman, eds., *Sharing World Leadership? A New Era for America and Japan* (Washington, D.C.: American Enterprise, 1989) estimates that had Japan spent as much of its GNP on defense as the United States, its growth between 1955–1986 would have been reduced by 1 percent annually.

[23]Advertisement by Sekai Electronics in *Aviation Week and Space Technology,* 13 February 1984, and in *Air Force Magazine,* May, July, and September 1987.

[24]Soderberg, 60. Michael Chinworth suggests that formal budgets mask "a massive corporate commitment" to the development of defense technology; see Michael W. Chinworth, "Economic Strategy and U.S.-Defense Collaboration," MIT Japan Program Working Paper, WP 90–07, 1990, 6.

[25]Interview in *Defense News,* 19 February 1990.

[26]Defense Science Board, ed., *Report of the Defense Science Board Task Force on Industry to Industry Armaments Cooperation, Phase II, Japan* (Washington, D.C.: Defense Science Board, 1984).

[27]By contrast, only one of the top ten US defense contractors in the late 1980s was dependent upon defense for less than 10 percent of total sales. Two of the ten, in fact, relied on the military for more than 85 percent of sales. (Unpublished Keidanren memorandum, 30 November 1988).

[28]The Nissan announcement reportedly "sent shock waves to the established defense industry." See "Military Power: Ultimate US-Japan Friction," *JPRS Report,* 2 July 1990, 17.

[29]Ronald Dore, "Goodwill and the Spirit of Market Capitalism," in Ronald Dore, *Taking Japan Seriously* (Stanford: Stanford University Press, 1987), 169–92.

[30]This argument is developed by John Alic, "Military and Civilian Technologies: Synergy or Conflict?", paper prepared for the Workshop on Computation and Information Technologies: Growth, Productivity, and Employment, Jerome Levy Economics Institute, Bard College, 13–17 June 1989.

[31]For a general treatment of the importance of small- and medium-sized firms in the Japanese economy, see David Friedman, *The Misunderstood Miracle* (Ithaca, N.Y.: Cornell University Press, 1988). A detailed study of the relationship of large and small firms in the contemporary Japanese defense industry is in progress by David Friedman and Richard J. Samuels for the National Bureau of Economic Research (forthcoming, 1992).

[32]See Richard J. Samuels and Benjamin C. Whipple, "Defense Production and Industrial Development: The Case of the Japanese Aircraft Industry"; and "Defense Production and Industrial Development: The Case of Japanese Aircraft," in Chalmers Johnson, Laura Tyson, and John Zysman, eds., *Politics and Productivity* (Cambridge: Ballinger, 1989).

[33]Jonah Levy and Richard J. Samuels, "Institutions and Innovation: Research Collaboration as Technology Strategy in Japan," in L. Mytelka, ed., *Strategic Partnerships: States, Firms, and International Competition* (London: Frances Pinter, 1991).

[34]Cited by Green.

[35]These negotiations failed utterly in April 1991.

[36]For examples of these reassessments, see Tsūsanshō, ed., *Nihon no Sentōk* (Japan's choices) (Tokyo: Tsūsanchō, April 1988); and Defense Science Board, ed., *Defense Industrial Cooperation with Pacific Rim Countries* (Washington, D.C.: Office of the Undersecretary of Defense for Acquisitions, 1989). Also see J. Pollack and J. Winnefeld, "U.S. Strategic Alternatives in a Changing Pacific," in a report prepared by RAND for the commander in chief of the US Pacific Command (Santa Monica, Calif.: RAND, June 1990).

[37]In April 1991, two months after hostilities ceased, the Japanese government dispatched minesweepers from the Maritime Self-Defense Forces. This was the first foreign deployment of Japanese troops since World War II and was the object of intense domestic debate.

[38]*Business Week,* 1 April 1990, 28.

[39]This metaphor is often credited to former minister of finance Miyazawi Kiichi. The Pentagon had difficulty acquiring key companies from Japanese electronics firms for military systems deployed in the Gulf War; *San Francisco Chronicle,* 30 April 1991.

[40]*Asaki Jānaru,* 1 July 1988.

[41]*New York Times,* 18 January 1991. In February Fanuc announced it would not buy Moore after all; see *New York Times,* 20 February 1991.

[42]For illustrations, see Soderberg, 42.

[43]See Clyde V. Prestowitz, Jr., *Trading Places* (New York: Basic Books, 1989). For accounts of the dispute see Gregory Noble, "Japan, America, and the FS-X Jet Fighter Planes: Structural Asymmetries in Bilateral Negotiations," paper presented to the annual meeting of the Association of Asian Studies, Chicago, April 1989.

[44]*Wing Newsletter* 22 (20) (24 May 1989).

[45]American Aerospace Industry, "Japan Market Today, Strong Competition from Europe," position paper issued in Tokyo, Japan, February 1991.

Japan in the coming century: Looking East or West?

RONALD DORE

The modernization of Japan's trade policies and social structure, argues Professor Ronald Dore of the London School of Economics, will increase Japan's social instability. The continuation of the outdated Japan-US alliance, he states, only inhibits the growth of the international order; he warns that the day may come when Japan's interests lie with China rather than the US. Dore advocates that Japan adopt a proactive foreign policy, using military force not for reasons of national interest, but only to contribute to the peaceful settlement of international conflicts.

The connection between egalitarianism and industrialization, two of the prominent trends of the twentieth century discussed by Professor Sato, is not easily explained. Tocqueville saw egalitarianism not as a result of industrialization, but as a long-term movement through history that was "a sign of God's mysterious will." There is no need to be quite so agnostic. The economic historian Simon Kuznets argued that over a whole range of countries there was a very common pattern in the relation between income distribution and economic growth. In the early stages of growth, inequality of incomes increased. But then the trend started reversing itself—toward greater *kekka no byodo* (equality of results). Kuznets put the turning point at the stage at which a country's per capita income reaches $500—in, presumably, 1960s dollars. But that was a 1960s theory, and since then much has happened. Rapid development has generated enormous income inequalities in Brazil, but even more rapid and more sustained development has produced quite egalitarian patterns in Korea and Taiwan. Too many historical facts have now accumulated for simple theories to take account of them.

But what seemed to be a general tendency in the most advanced industrial societies—the tendency for income inequalities to diminish, as Kuznets said—may now be reversing itself. One can see reasons why this might be so—in long-term changes in technology accumulation, the shift in the relative importance of material and human capital, and the mechanisms of human capital formation. The increase in income inequality is happening most rapidly in the English-speaking countries where free-market forces are given fullest play, but it seems also to be happening, if more slowly, in countries like Germany and Japan.

In contrast to the increase of social and political problems in the English-speaking societies, particularly the United States, the relative social peace of a more egalitarian Japan has become a not insignificant—and very favorable—part of Japan's image overseas. But there is a question about how long this egalitarianism will last. Intellectual opinion in Japan—all the talk about deregulation, freer markets, ending the "convoy system," etc.—seems to be in favor of a sort of intensification of competition, and a switch to US-style shareholder sovereignty in Japanese corporations. These changes will inevitably increase inequality, unemployment, and probably social instability. Japan may lose its reputation as a relatively benign, peaceful society based on mutual consideration.

There is a question about how long egalitarianism will last in Japan.

That the genie-out-of-the-bottle called nationalism, the other twentieth century trend cited by Sato, is filling our television screens with daily scenes of nationalism-inspired, nationalism-justified horror is undoubtedly true. But the nationalism of ethnic groups that are competing for control of a state apparatus, or trying to free themselves from domination in order to have their own state, is a rather different phenomenon than nationalism in the foreign policies of established nation-states. In the external policies of the major world-player nations, for example, the members of the G-7 or the Security Council, has nationalist self-assertion really come to play a greater determining role, and if so, greater compared to what?

To put the answer in the crudest possible framework, the objectives of foreign policy are broadly: security, economic advantage, and prestige; prestige meaning to give citizens cause to feel national pride. Thucydides called these objectives fear, interest, and honor. A nationalistic foreign policy emphasizes honor more than security or economic advantage. Late-developing countries, those "coming from behind," tend to be more nationalistic, more preoccupied with their "standing in the comity of nations," than are established powers. Compare Japan in the nineteenth century trying to secure revision of the unequal treaties, with contemporary Japan, a good deal more confident of its position in the world.

On the other hand, the Japanese concern compared to the German relative lack of concern with becoming a permanent member of the Security Council shows that there is still a greater tendency for the average Japanese than for the average German voter to see foreign policy issues in terms of "how much does my country count in the world?" Very relevant here are Professor Sato's wise words on the profound trauma the Japanese people suffered from the defeat in World War II.

The Japan-US alliance is clearly on the way to switching from containing Russia to containing China.

In this sense, the most nationalistic of the world powers is probably China, at last confident of its power to master the secrets of modern technology and economic growth, conscious of its huge size, and conscious of the humiliation of having been treated in the century and a half since the Opium Wars as a country of no account.

One more thing needs to be said about nationalism, that *inter*nationalism is not just the opposite of nationalism as just defined, but rather the opposite of what should be called "unilateralism" or national egotism—the aggressive pursuit of national interests with respect to security, economic advantage, or honor. Unilateralism is a policy opposed to cooperation with other nations in the give-and-take search for mutually beneficial compromise and international system-building. In this sense, since the Republicans took over Congress, US policy has swung away from the UN-supportive cooperativism of the early Clinton years. But whether this is merely part of a cyclical trend, a long-term shift consequent on the end of the Cold War and the disappearance of any real challenge to American hegemony, or a projection of the increasingly anarchic individualism of American society, is almost impossible to say. All that can be said with certainty is that phenomena such as the Kurds' struggle for a Kurdistan, Japan or China's concern for their country's prestige in the world power hierarchy, and American unilateralism, are distinct and should not be grouped under the single concept of the "rise of nationalism."

For the more central question of prescriptions for Japan's future, Professor Sato spells out three broad options, namely a minor power, a non-military major power, and an ordinary major power. But is there not also the fourth option of *futsuu yori yoi kuni* (a better-than-ordinary country)? It would be defined as follows: Japan should be (a) proactive in international affairs and (b) willing to use military force in that proactivism, as Professor Sato argues. But in addition, Japan should not use military force like an ordinary power, that is, exclusively or primarily for national interest reasons. Instead, unless under direct attack, Japan should (c) *only* use military force to contribute to the peaceful settlement of international or inter-ethnic conflicts, and to help create and consolidate international institutions.

This fourth option may sound utopian, but actually is less so than the belief of those who think that Japan can somehow keep the high moral ground by making *kokusai kouken* (international contributions) of only money and good advice without the state ever soiling its pacifist reputation by engaging in the use of armed force.

Although many young Japanese are willing to risk their lives for the sake of others, like the volunteers who went to Cambodia, the general tenor of public discussion in Japan does not make the better-than-ordinary country option likely. There is a world of difference between public opinion in Holland, where the Dutch soldiers of the UN Force in Tuzla were widely criticized for not having risked their lives to protect Muslim refugees from the Serbs, and in Japan, where after the death of a Japanese soldier demands for the withdrawal of Japanese troops from Cambodia were strong enough to require an emergency cabinet meeting. But opinions can change. The Dutch have had several centuries to feel themselves at the heart of a Europe that was at the heart of the world. The Japanese still feel themselves to be inhabitants at the periphery.

To counter the trend of nationalism, Professor Sato advocates the maintenance and expansion of existing alliances, NATO in Europe and the Japan-US alliance in the Pacific. Professor Sato speaks of a "security community," but there is all the difference in the world between a genuine "system of collective security" of the kind envisaged on a world scale in Chapter 7 of the UN Charter—a system in which all states agree to join in enforcing agreed rules on any one state that should offend against them—and, on the other hand, a military alliance.

Professor Sato's hope for world stability underwritten by security communities disregards the fundamental point that military alliances are formed against common potential enemies. NATO's creation and the signing of the Japan-US Security Treaty were unthinkable without the threat of Russian power. Many of us hoped that with the collapse of that threat, NATO might evolve into a genuine collective security system within the framework of the Organization for Security and Cooperation in Europe (OSCE, formerly known as CSCE), embracing Russia as well as the countries of Eastern Europe. But this did not happen. It required far too much imagination and far too much sacrifice of existing interests. The maintenance of NATO springs largely from (1) the inertial power of large-budget organizations to secure their own survival; (2) the desire of Britain, France, and Italy to keep Germany from dominating Europe, which they think will be easier if Americans stay; and (3) the desire of European states, including Germany, to keep the US committed to Europe just in case Russian power revives. The last has steadily become the decisive rationale, partly because NATO has foolishly made that rationale manifest in its move to incorporate Poland, Hungary, and the Czech Republic, thus moving the alliance's boundaries right up to the Russian border and leaving the Russians no doubt as to who is the putative enemy. How the maintenance of NATO inhibits the growth of international order was illustrated in the disagreement between NATO, or more correctly the US and Russia, over the command of the peacekeeping mission in Bosnia.

The *dobun doshu* generation of Japanese and Chinese who could swap quotations from the *Analects* has no successor either in Japan or China.

Exactly the same considerations apply to the Japan-US alliance, whose continuance is also a product of inertia. There is a major difference, however. Russia is no longer the alliance's most plausible enemy. The Japan-US alliance is clearly on the way to switching from containing Russia to containing China. One has only to read both American and Japanese commentary on the dangerous signs of Chinese "self-assertiveness." The old joint exercises against an invading "red" army in Hokkaido have given way to exercises involving a "brown" army in Kyushu.

One of the paradoxes is that this situation is happening at a time when the Chinese official position is that the Japan-US alliance neutralizes Japan and removes the danger of Japanese military aggression: at the Osaka APEC meeting the Chinese foreign minister prefaced his tolerant remarks about the alliance by saying "while in principle we think it wrong for countries to keep troops stationed on foreign soil...." It is more likely that the Chinese for the moment are willing to go along with Washington's perception of the situation, if for no other reason than that they do not want to add to the agenda of quarrels with the US.

Even if there is no immediate crisis set off by a Taiwanese declaration of independence, how long are the Chinese going to continue to accept a Pacific dominated by the Seventh Fleet up to the very territorial waters of China? How long are they going to accept the thesis that peace in the East Asian region requires a benevolent American presence? The extent to which Chinese policy is driven by nationalism is perhaps not as much as Japan's was at the time of the unequal treaties in the nineteenth century, but let us assume that it resembles Japan's at the time of the Washington Treaty, when Japan accepted five-five-three as the best deal available at the time. Clearly, Japan at the time could not get a better deal, but that situation would not last forever.

If another Cold War starts, will Japan be happy to be in an alliance whose object is to contain China solely to maintain American global supremacy?

If one projects Chinese growth over fifteen years, or more importantly, projects the growth of Chinese scientific manpower—whatever the post-Deng regime, it is unlikely to be a regime that stints on defense—there is a possibility, even a probability, that China will concentrate enough high-level brains on defense technology to mount a serious threat to US supremacy. For example, for China to design a working ABM system would do just this. There would be all the ingredients for the start of a serious second Cold War.

If another Cold War starts, will Japan be happy to be in an alliance whose object is to contain China solely to maintain American global supremacy? Perhaps the answer is yes. The generation of Matsumura, Takasaki and Saionji, the *dobun doshu* (same culture, same alphabet) generation of Japanese and Chinese who could swap quotations from the *Analects*, the ancient Chinese classic, has no successor either in Japan or China. Certainly, the Japanese media reflects a country in which America's cultural hegemony has firmly entrenched a set of tastes and preferences that, despite all the trade friction and technological rivalries of the last decades, puts Japanese sentiment firmly on the American side in any confrontation with China.

So be it. But try supposing, just occasionally, that the time might come when it looks to the Japanese that the Chinese, and not the Americans, might win.

Economic Myths Explained
Japan's Abiding *Sakoku* Mentality

by Mayumi Itoh

Japan embarked on internationalization *(kokusaika)* as a national objective more than a decade ago. As advertised, this open-door policy *(kaikoku)* was to involve, not only liberalization of trade and the opening of markets to foreign goods, but also reform of immigration practices to open the labor market to foreigners. Tokyo reluctantly enacted *kokusaika* under pressure from foreign governments, especially the United States and European countries, which alleged that Japanese systems were closed, exclusive, and discriminatory against foreign goods and services. Since then, however, Japanese progress has been superficial at best, amounting only to slight relaxations of the impediments against certain foreign imports and the regulations concerning immigration and foreign professional labor. Genuine *kokusaika* will most likely never be achieved without fundamental changes in the Japanese way of thinking.

The pervasive Japanese attitude of exclusiveness stems from two powerful roots: the country's geographic isolation as an island nation and the Tokugawa Shogunate's specific policy of seclusion *(sakoku)* from 1639 to 1868. That combination of natural and voluntary isolation created a uniquely homogeneous culture and parochial mentality that still linger in the habits of the mind that underlie modern Japanese behavior and business practices.[1]

Chalmers Johnson, a specialist in Japanese political economy, calls the psychological barriers to economic internationalism "the cartels of the mind." He argues that such barriers insulate the Japanese from the outside world, preserving their traditional attitudes and ways of thinking. But rather than attributing the mental cartels to Japan's history of seclusion, Johnson maintains that they are the direct result of Japan's restrictive policies, and that the government simply invokes Japan's group-oriented culture to justify them. Johnson argues that these cartels could be changed overnight if the government had any real

[1] See Chie Nakane, *Japanese Society* (Berkeley, Calif.: University of California Press, 1970), pp. 3–8; and Edwin O. Reischauer, *The Japanese Today* (Cambridge, Mass.: Harvard University Press, 1988), pp. 31–36 and 395.

Mayumi Itoh is an assistant professor of political science at the University of Nevada, Las Vegas. She holds a Ph.D. from City University of New York and has published numerous articles on Japan's foreign policy.

interest in internationalization, and that until Japan breaks up these cartels of the mind its process of *kokusaika* is "meaningless."[2]

In truth, that may be a distinction without a difference, since both government policies and business practices derive directly from the *sakoku* mentality. Restrictive government regulations simply codify the preexisting *sakoku* attitude, reinforcing it as a determinant of business practices. Thus, the combination of cultural and man-made mores constitutes a formidable barrier to Japan's internationalization. Because trade liberalization and market opening have been covered extensively, this article focuses on immigration and foreign-labor policies in assessing prospects for Japan's overall *kokusaika*.

Gaijin in Japan

Despite the modern outlook of their society, most Japanese still retain the *sakoku* mentality, and their treatment of foreigners clearly reflects that attitude. The Japanese call all non-Japanese *gaijin,* which literally means "people from outside." While the term itself has no derogatory meaning, it emphasizes the exclusiveness of Japanese attitude and has therefore picked up pejorative connotations that many Westerners resent. The Japanese treat foreign visitors politely, but always as outsiders.[3]

But the picture changes when it comes to *gaijin* who reside permanently in Japan. (As of January 1995, about 1.6 million foreigners, slightly more than one percent of the total population, lived in Japan.[4]) The politeness disappears because the Japanese are not willing to assimilate those they view as outsiders into their society. As a result, *gaijin* residents encounter numerous forms of discrimination. The Japanese treat even the Korean residents of Japan who grew up in Japan and speak fluent Japanese as *gaijin.* A young Korean man recently noted that people cannot tell he is Korean from his appearance or the way he speaks Japanese, but his job applications were rejected because he retains a Korean name.[5] This discrimination extends to leasing homes, where Korean residents often are denied leases, and to marriages, where parents break engagements when they discover that their child's betrothed is a Korean resident. Worse yet, children of Korean residents are common targets of bullying *(ijime)* at school. In a notorious *ijime* incident, a Korean schoolboy in Saitama prefecture, adjacent to Tokyo, committed suicide after persistent bullying by his classmates and a teacher in charge of the class.[6]

The entrenched disaffection for *gaijin* residents extends to the Japanese nationality law, for which Japan adopts the "blood principle" instead of the

[2] Chalmers Johnson, "Artificial Cartels of the Mind Justify Distrust of Japan," *International Herald Tribune,* June 16, 1993.

[3] See Edwin O. Reischauer, *The Japanese Today,* pp. 395–400.

[4] "21 seiki eno joso: rensai 10," *Yomiuri Shimbun,* Jan. 4, 1995.

[5] "Nakuso gaikokujin sabetsu," *Yomiuri Shimbun,* Mar. 1, 1994.

[6] Ibid.

"birthplace principle" in determining Japanese nationality. Originally, the law stipulated that only newborns whose fathers were Japanese could acquire Japanese nationality. But under pressure from foreign male residents who married Japanese women, the Ministry of Justice revised the law in 1989 so that newborns with Japanese fathers or mothers have Japanese nationality. Even with the revision, children born in Japan to resident aliens must undertake naturalization procedures, as if they were immigrating foreigners. In the meantime, they are considered citizens of their parents' native land.

As an exception to the blood principle, the law does allow the birthplace principle for babies born in Japan whose parents are unknown, in order to prevent abandoned newborns from becoming "non-nationalities." With an increase in the number of Southeast Asian women engaging in prostitution in Japan, the number of such abandoned babies has grown. According to 1994 statistics from the Ministry of Justice, 1,500 of the approximately 1.3 million foreigners who registered as residents in Japan did not have a nationality. Among these were 138 infants under age four. By comparison, only 74 such infants were registered in 1992. Furthermore, the ministry estimates the actual number of non-nationality children to be considerably higher because, fearing deportation, foreign women working illegally in Japan do not report their giving birth.[7]

Despite that apparently liberal application of the Japanese nationality law, a 1995 Tokyo High Court ruling exemplifies the continued restrictive attitude. In 1991, a woman, apparently Filipino, left her newborn boy to an American missionary in Komoro. After the Filipino embassy rejected an application for Filipino nationality for the boy, the missionary applied to the Tokyo local government, which registered the boy as a non-nationality foreigner. The clergyman filed suit, alleging that, under the birthplace principle, the boy should have been given Japanese nationality because his mother was unknown. But the court ruled that unless the plaintiff *proved* the boy's mother was unknown, the boy could not obtain Japanese nationality.[8]

Japanese policy toward political refugees provides another example. In 1982, following international pressure and an influx of Indochinese refugees, Japan enacted the seemingly liberal Law Concerning Refugees. Yet, as of May 31, 1995, only 10,015 refugees had emigrated to Japan, 9,807 from Indochina (Cambodia, Laos, and Vietnam) and 208 from other countries.[9] These statistics not only reflect the continuing restrictive immigration policy but also demonstrate that the discriminatory atmosphere created by the *sakoku* mentality discourages extensive immigration. In many instances, even when Indochinese refugees were admitted to Japan, they chose not to stay because of stringent procedures for settlement, and instead immigrated to Canada or the United States.

7 "Kokusaika ni gyakko hanketsu," *Yomiuri Shimbun*, Jan. 27, 1995.

8 Ibid.

9 Jiyu Kokumin sha, ed., *Gendai Yogo no Kiso Chishiki 1992* (Tokyo: Jiyu Kokumin sha, 1992), pp. 330 and 386; and Masahiro Shimizu, letter to author, Aug. 24, 1995.

Unskilled Labor

Though more attention is paid to the *sakoku* mentality in Japan's international business practices, the attitude permeates the Japanese employment system as well. For example, to protect the country's job market, Japanese immigration law bans foreigners from engaging in unskilled labor. However, the internationalization of economic activities has brought about an increase in the number of illegal foreign workers from Third World countries entering Japan with tourist visas. And Japanese businesses, especially middle-sized companies, employ illegal workers because they will perform menial labor for low wages that most Japanese are no longer willing to do. (The Japanese call such undesirable jobs three-K work—*kiken, kitsui,* and *kitanai rodo* [dangerous, hard, and dirty labor].)

With the influx of illegal foreign workers, the Ministry of Justice revised the immigration law in 1989, renamed it the Law Concerning Immigration and Refugees, and tightened regulations on illegal unskilled labor. The revised law punishes those who employ foreigners for illegal labor and those who act as brokers of foreign labor. Nevertheless, the number of illegal foreign workers in Japan rose sharply following the unprecedented boom of the "bubble economy" in the late 1980s.[10] According to Ministry of Justice statistics, the number of illegal foreign workers almost tripled from 1990 to 1993. In July 1990, 106,497 foreigners worked illegally in Japan. By May 1993, the number had risen to 298,646. With the collapse of the bubble economy and Japan's subsequent economic recession, the number of illegal foreign workers declined marginally in 1994. Yet, the Ministry of Justice reported that there were still as many as 294,000 illegal foreign workers in May 1994, most of whom came from Thailand (18.1 percent), South Korea (13.8 percent), China (12.2 percent), or the Philippines (12.2 percent). Among this population, men outnumbered women 70.2 percent to 29.8 percent, with most men working in construction (39.7 percent) and factories (31.6 percent), while women served primarily as bar hostesses (36.5 percent) and factory workers (18.1 percent).[11]

The initial growth in the number of foreign workers was accompanied by increasing social problems involving illegal laborers. The percentage of foreign workers who committed serious crimes rose from 39 percent in 1991 to 53 percent in 1993; the number of drug-related crimes doubled in the same period. In addition, a surge in AIDS cases followed the increase in the number of Southeast Asian prostitutes in Japan. Lastly, many illegal foreign workers are remaining in the country longer (the number who have remained in Japan for more than three years increased from 21 percent in 1990 to 32 percent in 1994), compelling some local governments to adopt welfare measures to improve

[10] The Ministry of Labor, ed., *Rodo Hakusho 1994* (Tokyo: Japan Labor Research Institute, 1994), pp. 51–54.

[11] Ibid.

housing, offer medical and other benefits, and provide education for the workers.[12]

Despite such problems, an increasing number of Japanese favor legalizing foreign labor. Shimada Haruo, a professor at Keio University, argues that foreign workers play important roles in the Japanese economy and society, and that they should be accorded equal rights by the government.[13] In fact, a public opinion poll conducted by the Ministry of Foreign Affairs revealed a surprisingly wide acceptance of foreign workers by the Japanese general public. According to that 1990 poll, 71.4 percent of the respondents favored legalizing the employment of unskilled foreign laborers because foreign workers provided cheap labor and did the three-K work eschewed by the Japanese. However, most respondents (56.5 percent) said such employment should be allowed only with some restrictions. In contrast, only 14.1 percent of respondents favored continuing to exclude foreign workers from unskilled labor, citing such reasons for their opposition as "public order and morality may deteriorate" and "unemployment among Japanese may increase in times of economic slowdown."[14]

Furthermore, a majority of the respondents (55 percent) considered illegal employment to be a necessary evil attributable to "the domestic shortage of labor" and the fact that it was "natural for people from less developed countries to come to Japan in search of higher wages."[15] Many thought the workers would come to Japan regardless of tightened restrictions on immigration, and that, as the most industrialized nation in Asia, Japan had to expect such an influx. Lastly, 41 percent of the respondents favored cracking down on illegal labor only in cases involving organized crime, prostitution, or other serious crimes, while 34 percent favored deporting all violators in strict accordance with the law. Only 11 percent were opposed to any crackdown in business sectors where labor shortages exist.[16] Even though the poll was taken at the height of the economic boom, such public acceptance of foreign workers highlights a discrepancy between public opinion and government practice, which continues to enforce *sakoku* policies toward unskilled labor.

Professional Labor

Japanese labor policies become even more convoluted with regard to professional employment. For example, despite the fact that many local governments repealed the nationality clause for professional employment in the 1980s, in practice these governments still ban foreigners—including Korean residents—from assuming managerial positions in the public sector. The Tokyo

12 "Gaikokujin rodosha," *Yomiuri Shimbun*, Feb. 21, 1995.

13 "'Masatsu' ga kikikan zofuku," *Asahi Shimbun*, June 28, 1995.

14 International Press Division, Ministry of Foreign Affairs, *Survey Reveals Wide Acceptance of Foreign Workers*, July 7, 1991, pp. 1–4.

15 Ibid.

16 Ibid.

metropolitan government recently exercised this policy when it rejected a female Korean health worker's application to take an examination for government managerial posts in March 1994, claiming that managerial employees must be of Japanese nationality. Challenging this unwritten rule, the health worker filed a suit against the government in September 1994, alleging that no law mandates such a policy, and that she was illegally disqualified from taking the examination.[17]

By contrast, strict laws codify the *sakoku* approach within the Japanese legal system. Until 1987, no foreign lawyers could practice in Japan because only Japanese lawyers who had passed the national bar examination could register in the Japan Bar Association. Then, under pressure from the Reagan administration and other foreign governments, the Japanese parliament enacted the Special Measures Law Concerning the Handling of Legal Business by Foreigners. But this law made only superficial changes in the status quo. It licensed foreign lawyers only to offer counsel about the laws of their home countries, while prohibiting them from advising on Japanese laws. (These foreign lawyers are called *gaikokuho jimu bengoshi,* attorneys authorized in Japan to practice the laws of a foreign jurisdiction.[18]) For example, an American lawyer, who was among Japan's *gaikokuho jimu bengoshi* and had worked at a Japanese international business law firm in Tokyo from 1989 to 1995, could only advise on how U.S. laws affected Japanese clients' transactions and their subsidiaries and branch offices in the United States.[19] Indeed, as of August 1995, only 74 foreign lawyers practiced in Japan, 0.5 percent of the total number of lawyers. As a result, the Japanese legal system is faced with increasing demands for reciprocity from law practitioners abroad.[20]

The worst offender in exclusive labor practices is Japan's education system.

Even the Japanese press system suffers from the *sakoku* mentality. News sources are controlled by about four hundred press clubs *(kisha kurabu)* in government agencies, political parties, or big-business groups. As of December 31, 1992, there were 762 foreign journalists *(gaijin kisha)* in Japan—612 men and 150 women.[21] *Gaijin kisha* can get information for articles only from a member of the *kisha kurabu,* and even when *gaijin kisha* are admitted to press conferences or briefings, they cannot ask questions or report on the institutions that provide information. *Kisha kurabu* exert further pressure on journalists (both Japanese and foreign) by monopolizing information sources.[22] In return for information, *kisha* feel obligated to report favorable news about their sources, a practice known as "obliged articles" in Japanese press circles. If journalists

[17] "Zainichi kankokujin hokenfu teiso e," *Yomiuri Shimbun,* Sept. 12, 1994.

[18] See Jiyu Kokumin sha, *Gendai Yogo no Kiso Chishiki 1992,* p. 377; and Johnson, "Artificial Cartels of the Mind."

[19] Nele Freedman, letter to James Lamare, Sept. 15, 1995.

[20] "Gaikoku bengoshi," *Yomiuri Shimbun,* Dec. 9, 1995.

[21] Shimizu, letter to author.

[22] See Johnson, "Artificial Cartels of the Mind."

write negative stories, their access to the sources may cease. Thus, *gaijin kisha* have to follow suit and ingratiate themselves with the Fourth Estate.[23]

Perhaps the worst offender in exclusive professional labor practices is the Japanese education system, which not only perpetuates *sakoku* in its employment policy but breeds the attitude in Japanese students. While the 1982 Law Concerning Employing Foreign Instructors appears to ease restrictions on foreign employment in academic institutions, it fails to overcome the entrenched exclusive mentality. The law stipulates that foreign instructors *(gaikokujin kyoshi)* at Japanese national and public universities must be employed on terms identical to those for Japanese *kyoshi*. However, it leaves the period of service for *gaikokujin kyoshi* to the discretion of each university. Most national institutions have opted for short-term contracts, which average about three years. In 1994, twelve years after the enactment of the law, only four *gaikokujin kyoshi* had received contracts not limited by terms, similar to those held by all Japanese *kyoshi*. Although *gaikokujin kyoshi* now enjoy academic titles and the privilege of attending faculty meetings, they have little clout in academic management because they are dependent on the goodwill of Japanese colleagues for their contract renewals.[24]

As of December 1992, 2,575 *gaikokujin kyoshi*, 2 percent of the total full-time academic staff in Japan, taught at Japanese universities.[25] Yet, the Ministry of Education is trying to fire senior *gaikokujin kyoshi* because they are costly. A memorandum dated December 21, 1992, indicates that the ministry had requested that universities employ younger *gaikokujin kyoshi* in order to cut the budget, and that it considered restricting the number of *gaikokujin kyoshi* to reduce costs further.[26] Ivan Hall, who teaches at Gakushuin University in Tokyo, argues that the Japanese universities' restrictions of *gaikokujin kyoshi* are systemwide and deliberate, and that a genuine attempt to integrate foreign scholars with regular Japanese staff under the 1982 law has failed in the face of the persistent *sakoku* attitude. After Hall and six *gaikokujin kyoshi* met with U.S. ambassador Walter Mondale, the American embassy issued a press release expressing its concerns over the Ministry of Education's protectionism.[27]

The restrictive employment system for instructors also reinforces *sakoku* among Japanese students. Masao Kunihiro, a member of the House of Councillors from the Socialist Party (and recently defeated for a second term), says that, despite foreign pressure for internationalization, the Japanese educational system has failed to bring greater diversity and pluralism to the country because the academic institutions are insulated from the larger society. As such, the system has failed to encourage students "to go beyond the parochial and often

23 Yoshiko Sakurai, "Konnanimo aru Mosukuwa tokuhain no 'tabu,'" *Shokun*, Jan. 1987, pp. 75–76.

24 Ivan Hall, "Academic Apartheid at Japan's National Universities," working paper no. 3, Japan Policy Research Institute [hereafter JPRI], Cardiffa, Calif., Oct. 1994, pp. 4–5.

25 Shimizu, letter to author.

26 Hall, "Academic Apartheid at Japan's National Universities," p. 6.

27 Ivan Hall, "Academic Apartheid Revisited," working paper no. 9, JPRI, Cardiffa, Calif., May 1995, pp. 1–3.

exclusionistic barriers of sovereign nation states in their perception."[28] Instead, Japanese education promotes rote memorization and cut-throat competition for entrance into prestigious schools, which in turn accord graduates access to the governing circles, where they perpetuate the closed system.

Even sports in Japan are not free from *sakoku*. For instance, there are only three foreign professional sumo wrestlers currently active and registered by the Japan Sumo Association. One of them, a Hawaiian, was recently denied the honored title of *yokozuna* he had won in open competition until foreign publicity forced the sumo authorities to relent. Even the Japanese professional baseball association applies a strict quota to *gaijin* players, despite the fact that Japan imported baseball from the United States in 1874. The current agreement limits the number of registered *gaijin* players to three per team, only two of whom can play in any given game.[29]

As well as restricting foreign players—primarily North Americans—from entering the Japanese leagues and improving the quality of play, Japanese baseball policies ensure that those players who are recruited from abroad will face difficulties as minorities on their teams. A discriminatory atmosphere, combined with the language and cultural barriers, prevents foreign players from assimilating with their teammates.[30] As a result, a number of American players have returned from Japan complaining of the mistreatment accorded them as foreigners.

In sum, a widespread *sakoku* mentality afflicts both the public and private sectors in Japan. Immigration restrictions discourage foreigners from assimilating into Japanese society with stringent requirements for Japanese citizenship. Labor *sakoku* bans foreigners from engaging in unskilled labor as well as limits them in professional employment.

The debilitating effects of the *sakoku* mentality on the Japanese decision-making structure, especially the bureaucracy, are compounded by the so-called problem-avoidance principle, which discourages decision makers from changing the status quo. Innovative legislation and policies often fail against this firmly institutionalized cultural structure that sustains Japanese protectionism and resists the changes sought by the United States and European countries. Thus, along with weak government leadership, the *sakoku* mentality constitutes the most formidable impediment to Japan's internationalization.

A Japanese, Not "Asian," Phenomenon

Japan has by no means been the only "closed" economy on the Pacific Rim. Indeed, the other "Asian tigers" have to a great extent looked to Japan as

[28] Masao Kunihiro, "Strengths and Weaknesses of Education in Japan," working paper no. 3, JPRI, Cardiffa, Calif., Oct. 1994, pp. 1–3.

[29] Masahiro Shimizu, letter to author, Sept. 13, 1995.

[30] See Robert Whiting, *You Gotta Have Wa* (New York: Vintage Books, 1990).

their model of the successful state-managed, "export-driven" development economy. Is it unfair, then, to single out Japan for criticism and attribute its exclusionism to strictly national causes? No, it is not. For while Japan has only reluctantly begun moving toward internationalization, its Asian neighbors have begun their own programs of globalization in earnest.

For example, the Republic of China on Taiwan has taken several steps to improve economic relations with its neighbors. First, Taipei adopted a more open policy toward mainland China that expanded cross-Straits exchanges to include cultural, educational, and economic activities. President Lee Teng-hui also launched his "Southward Policy" in 1994, designed to promote economic and trade cooperation with the Association of Southeast Asian Nations and enhance the region's economic integration. In addition, as its "initial action" at the November 1995 Asia-Pacific Economic Cooperation (APEC) forum meeting in Osaka, Taipei promised to reduce tariffs for more than seven hundred items and to deregulate foreign investment, transportation, finance, and import approval.

In contrast, the Japanese government lacks zeal for its own internationalization and is undertaking the program only upon external pressure. While a superficial or quantitative internationalization—as exemplified by the glut of foreign goods in Japanese daily life and the unprecedented number of Japanese tourists (13.6 million in 1994)—has made some progress, a qualitative *kokusaika* has yet to reform the exclusive Japanese mindset. That is so despite the fact that former prime minister Yasuhiro Nakasone declared the creation of an internationalized Japan at the Japanese parliament in 1984.[31]

Although Japan achieved its status as the world's second-largest economy more than a decade ago, it has yet to demonstrate international leadership abilities or earn international respect. For example, at the November APEC meeting in Osaka, Japan staunchly resisted liberalization of agricultural products.[32] And in the November 1995 joint meeting of the representatives of the European Union (EU) Parliament and the Japanese parliament held in Tokyo, the EU side asserted that Japan has made insufficient progress in realizing trade deregulation and playing an active role at the United Nations.[33] Indeed, so resistant are the Japanese to meeting *gaijin* concerns halfway that the Murayama coalition cabinet even refused to pay state compensation to the so-called comfort women who were forced to provide sexual services to Japanese soldiers during the war.

Not surprisingly, a *Yomiuri Shimbun* poll conducted in late 1994 revealed that overseas leaders and intellectuals are pessimistic about Japan's internationalization. The responses from one hundred leading politicians, high-ranking government officials, and literary intellectuals from around the world indicate that they view the present Japan as an "economic animal," "culturally being closed," and "having an identity crisis." The poll also reported a wide gap

31 Seisaku Kagaku Kenkyujo, ed., *Nakasone Yasuhiro Shuyo Enzetsu Shu* (Tokyo: Seisaku Kagaku Kenkyujo, 1984), p. 32.

32 "APEC Osaka kaigi," *Yomiuri Shimbun*, Nov. 15, 1995.

33 "Nihon no kiseikanwa fujubun EU shiteki," *Yomiuri Shimbun*, Nov. 22, 1995.

between hopes for Japan in the twenty-first century and predictions of what the country will actually accomplish. Seventy-eight percent of respondents said they hoped Japan would become an open country in the twenty-first century, whereas only 28 percent thought Japan would reach that goal. Similarly, 77 percent said they hoped Japan would become a democratic country, compared with 53 percent who believed it would happen. Also, 62 percent hoped Japan would become a country that other nations could trust, but only 25 percent thought Japan could accomplish that end.[34]

Conclusion

The tide of Japan's internationalization is irreversible, but the country's progress is sluggish. Though it is in Japan's own interest to achieve *kokusaika* and thereby escape self-imposed isolation from the rest of the world, Japanese culture and history impede changes to *sakoku* policies and practices. So far, external pressure has proved to be the best way to achieve change in Japan, hence the United States should continue to pressure Japan to liberalize its markets and internationalize its society. Such pressure need not be confrontational or adversarial, as it sometimes has been in the past; rather, it can take the form of persuasion or collaboration. The United States should try to convince the Japanese people that *kokusaika* will benefit those who have sacrificed their private interests for the sake of national economic growth in the postwar period. For instance, Japanese consumers and consumer advocacy groups should understand that market liberalization will greatly reduce the costs of goods and services ranging from rice, Japan's number-one staple (Japanese consumers have yet to benefit from the rice liberalization agreement under GATT in 1993), to phone service, which is monopolized by a former public corporation and three new private corporations.

The United States should also collaborate with proponents of *kokusaika* in Japan. For example, it can work with the associations of Korean residents and groups of foreign residents who seek Japanese nationality and equal rights. Washington should also mobilize U.S. professional groups—such as academic institutions, bar associations, the press, and sports organizations—to pressure their Japanese counterparts and Tokyo to adopt more open-door policies for professional labor. In addition, cooperation between Washington and friendly elements of the Japanese press could produce massive publicity campaigns for Japan's labor *kaikoku* and overall *kokusaika*. These persuasive tactics should be carried out not only through U.S.-Japanese bilateral channels but through larger forums with European and Pacific Rim countries, such as the Group of Seven summits and APEC meetings. Lastly, the U.S. government should be patient and seek long-term, sustainable solutions rather than quick and superficial results. It should be recalled here that the United States, too, once clung to

[34] "21 seiki eno joso," *Yomiuri Shimbun*, Jan. 10, 1995.

protectionist policies that specifically discriminated against Asian goods and immigrants: the Arthur administration's Chinese Exclusion Act in 1882; the Coolidge administration's ban on Japanese immigration in 1924; and the Hoover administration's sky-high Smoot-Hawley tariff of 1930, to name just a few. Washington must recognize that it will take a long time for the Japanese to overcome the burdens of our history as well as their own.

By the twenty-first century, however, Japan must become an open society in which foreign residents enjoy the same benefits and entitlements as the Japanese. As Suh Yong-dal, a Korean professor at Momoyama Gakuin University in Tokyo, recently stated, "The litmus test for Japan's internationalization is whether it can create a society in which both the Japanese and foreigners can coexist."[35] For if Japan's government and people do *not* make every effort to pass this test, their country will be surpassed by its own Asian neighbors, whereupon the Japanese will be able to cling to *sakoku* in peace, because the rest of the world will no longer care.

35 "Nihon no gaikokujin mondai' kogi," *Yomiuri Shimbun*, June 22, 1995.

THE KOREAN "COMFORT WOMEN"

Movement for Redress

Chunghee Sarah Soh

On February 6, 1996, the United Nations pronounced its conclusive condemnation of Japan for forcing tens of thousands of women—referred to as "comfort women"—into sexual slavery for Japan's imperial troops during World War Two. In her report to the U.N. Human Rights Commission, Radhika Coomaraswamy, the U.N. special investigator into violence against women, concluded that Japan must admit its legal responsibility, identify and punish those responsible for the sex slavery during the war, compensate the victims, apologize to the survivors in writing, and teach its students this hidden chapter in Japanese history.[1] It is notable that the U.N. recommendations resemble so closely the demands that the Chŏngdaehyŏp (Korean Council for the Women Drafted for Military Sexual Slavery by Japan [KCWS]) has made consistently since its inception in 1990.[2]

The issues involved in the "comfort women" problem, one may suggest, transcend the realm of "militarized prostitution" into that of "sexual slavery" based on gender, class, ethnicity, and the state. Coerced sexual labor, that is, sexual slavery, was inflicted primarily upon lower class young females of colonial Korea by imperial Japan during the Pacific War, but Japanese women and women of other occupied territories such as Taiwan, the Philippines, Indonesia, Burma, and Thailand were also used as "comfort women." There is no way to determine precisely how many women were forced to serve in

Chunghee Sarah Soh is Associate Professor in the Department of Anthropology, San Francisco State University. The author wishes to acknowledge the travel grant from the Northeast Asian Council of the Association for Asian Studies for support of field research in South Korea in January 1995. Earlier versions of this article were presented at the Rocky Mountain/Southwest Regional Japan Seminar, Dallas, Texas, April 1995, and a colloquium sponsored by the Center for Korean Studies, University of California, Berkeley, April 1995. The author thanks an anonymous reader for helpful comments.

1. *San Francisco Chronicle*, February 7, 1996; *Han'guk Ilbo*, February 8, 1996.
2. Chŏngdaehyŏp is a Korean acronym for the Chŏngsindae munje taech'aek hyŏpŭhoe (the KCWS).

this way but estimates range from 70,000 to 200,000, about 80% of whom were Korean.[3]

It is important to note at the outset that the majority of the former Korean "military comfort women" (*chonggun wianbu* in Korean, *jugun ianfu* in Japanese) were systematically and often coercively recruited by the Japanese forces under the banner of Chŏngsindae ("Voluntary" Labor Service Corps). They were not camp-following prostitutes, as the euphemistic phrase "military comfort women" might suggest. In this article, I use the terms "military comfort women" and "comfort women" interchangeably to follow the conventional usage, and the quotation marks surrounding these terms are maintained throughout the text in order to underline the hidden nature of sexual slavery in the euphemistic phrase "comfort women."

The purpose of this article is to deepen understanding of the complex issues involved in resolving the "comfort women" problem by concentrating on the evolution and impact of the Korean "comfort women" movement for redress. The focus is on the Korean case because Korean women constituted the great majority of the violated women and because the efforts of women leaders and former "comfort women" in South Korea were essential in bringing this issue to the attention of the international community.[4] An analytical perspective that considers the intersections of gender, class, ethnicity, sexual culture, and the role of the state will provide the key to understanding not only the phenomenon of the "military comfort women" itself, but also the unfolding of the recent public debate on the issue and the domestic and international processes involved in resolving it.

Chŏngsindae, the "Voluntary" Labor Service Corps

The institution of military "comfort stations," where sexual needs of Japanese soldiers were met under the supervision of the state, was in place by early 1932 at the latest. It existed in Japan and abroad wherever Japanese troops were stationed until the end of the Pacific War in 1945.[5] In view of the fact that prostitution was licensed and actively regulated by the state in imperial Japan, the provision of "comfort women" for the military may be seen as an

3. *Han'guk Ilbo* (Hawaii edition), August 26, 1992.

4. Materials obtained in 1992 from Lee Hyo-chae, co-chair of the KCWS, formed the initial source of data for this work. Additional data were gathered from a survey of the literature and media reports and in interviews conducted during two trips to South Korea in 1995 with former "comfort women" and with leaders of the KCWS seeking reparations on their behalf.

5. Yoshimi Yoshiaki, *Jugun Ianfu Shiryōshu* [Collection of reference materials on military comfort women] (Tokyo: Ōtsuki Shoten, 1992); "Documenting the Truth: The Japanese Government and the 'Comfort Women' Issue," paper presented at the annual meeting of the Association for Asian Studies, Boston, Massachusetts, March 1994.

instance of state control over soldiers' sexual behavior.[6] Since Korea was under Japanese colonial rule from 1910 to 1945, Japan chose to use Korean women as sex laborers while urging Japanese women to marry young and bear many children to fulfill "the national mission of motherhood."[7]

Japan began drafting Korean women in full force from around 1937 when its army invaded China and the soldiers raped and murdered tens of thousands of Chinese women in Nanjing. At that time, the Japanese army had "comfort women" from Japan, who were mainly former professional prostitutes and some of whom had venereal diseases. In order to combat the spread of disease and prevent sexual crimes by Japanese soldiers against the women of occupied territories, the military leadership suggested that the government recruit unmarried young women from colonial Korea (presumed to be virgins and therefore free of sexually transmitted disease) as "comfort women" for the Japanese army. Japan also began an active assimilation program for Koreans in 1937, which included the "Pledge of the Imperial Subjects," hoisting of the Japanese national flag, worship of the emperor, and attendance at Shinto ceremonies. Other policies followed, requiring changing of Korean names into Japanese and creating a new national identity for the colonized Koreans. The government thus established the legal grounds for mobilizing Koreans into its imperialist war and in 1939 began to enforce the all-out systematic mobilization of Koreans of both sexes for the war effort as members of the Chŏngsindae (lit., voluntarily submitting-body). Tokyo sent Korean laborers to Japan, Sakhalin, and many parts of Asia. In fact, the existence of sizable Korean communities in China, the former Soviet Union, and Japan is a vivid legacy of Japanese colonial rule.

As the Sino-Japanese War escalated into the Pacific War in 1941, the drafting of Korean laborers became more organized and compulsory. Almost six million Koreans were drafted as soldiers and/or forced laborers throughout the war, representing approximately 20% of Korea's population. It is important to note that although the drafting of women was made legal by 1942, female recruitment was nominally carried out on the basis of "voluntary" participation. This is why the Japanese government persistently denied until 1993 any coercion in the recruitment of Korean women into the Yŏja Chŏngsindae (Women's Voluntary Labor Service Corps). Although some women in the Chŏngsindae volunteered to work in factories and hospitals, many were recruited with false promises of good compensation for their labor in these facilities and then sent to the military comfort stations. Other women were

---

6. See Sheldon Garon, "The World's Oldest Debate? Prostitution and the State in Imperial Japan, 1900–1945," *American Historical Review*, 98:3 (1993), pp. 710–32.

7. Miho Ogino, "Abortion and Women's Reproductive Rights: The State of Japanese Women, 1945–1991," in *Women of Japan and Korea: Continuity and Change*, Joyce Gelb and Marian Lief Palley, eds. (Philadelphia: Temple University Press, 1994), p. 71.

coerced into joining the Labor Service Corps, and still others were simply abducted. Even school girls between the ages of 12 and 14 from Cholla Province were conscripted as sex slaves.[8]

Thus, the term Chŏngsindae has come to mean "military comfort women" in the minds of the general public in Korea because most of these women were conscripted under the banner of that organization. South Koreans today generally refer to the surviving "comfort women" as *Chŏngsindae halmŏni* (grandmothers), while the official reference term is *Ilbonkun wianbu* (comfort women for the Japanese troops). The activities of the KCWS to date have concentrated on the issues of "military comfort women" to the discontent of those men and women who were conscripted into forced labor at various war-related industries.

Sexual Culture and the Political Economy of Sex

Although factors such as the lack of documentary evidence and the reluctance of surviving "comfort women" to reveal their past may be offered to explain the long silence over the issue of sexual slavery within Korean society, I suggest a major factor at the heart of the matter is the cultural legacy of a patriarchal society, which has maintained double standards for sexual behavior for men and women. In the traditional Korean patriarchy, the sexual culture condoned, if not encouraged sexual freedom for men (infidelity if married), while women's sexuality was rigidly controlled by standards of virginity/chastity. Unmarried women had to maintain their virginity until marriage and widows were expected to be chaste. Regardless of the individual circumstances, women who lost their chastity were considered sullied, made to feel ashamed, and likely to be ostracized even by their own families. (Even a Christian church deemed a Dutch woman unfit to be a nun because she had been forced to serve as a "comfort woman.")

In this cultural context, many women committed suicide after being raped or in order to avoid being raped during the two Japanese invasions of Korea during the Chosŏn Dynasty in the late 16th century. Their deaths were recognized as honorable deeds of virtuous women (*yŏllyŏ*). It is remarkable that after the Japanese retreated and King Sŏnjo conferred awards on outstanding loyal subjects (*ch'ungsin*), filial sons (*hyoja*), and virtuous women (*yŏllyŏ*), the number of women exceeded by nearly five times the combined number of

8. Study by the Korean National History Compilation Committee, reported in *Korea Times* (Los Angeles edition), June 15, 1992.

the two male categories receiving the royal commendation.[9] In recent years, young male criminals in South Korea have taken advantage of this traditional view by raping women in front of members of their families in order to ensure that the robbery would not be reported to police. The media refers to these raping robbers as "family-destroying criminals" (*kajŏng p'agoebŏm*) because of the shattering impact of their behavior on the viability of the family; the raped woman is now sullied in the eyes of her husband, herself, and other members of the family, which may eventually break up under the psychological strain.

In the sexual mores of the Korean patriarchal family, then, it is understandable that the survivors of sexual slavery wished to conceal and forget their tragic past lives as "comfort women," if only to avoid the shame they would bring to their families. Some of these women actually committed suicide, and the aging survivors were resigned to keeping their deep *han* (resentment and anger) to themselves—until 1991 when Kim Hak-sun came forth to testify to her life as a "comfort woman." The majority of Korean "military comfort women" seemed to have come from poor families in rural farming areas and had little formal education; even if they had wanted to redress the injustice done to them, they had little means to right the wrongs they suffered. Customarily, it is women of poor families who are the first to be exploited to satisfy the presumably uncontrollable sexual appetites of men with wealth, weapon, or power. It is no surprise, therefore, that the Japanese imperial forces targeted women of poor, rural families in their "slave hunt" expeditions.[10]

When women activists finally raised the issues of the Chŏngsindae, the initial response of the South Korean government was to ignore them. The ostensible reason for the government's silence was the lack of documentary evidence on which to press charges against Japan, since the Japanese government had destroyed most of the records relating to "comfort women." Besides, the 1965 normalization treaty between South Korea and Japan, which did not include any debate on the issues of the Chŏngsindae, foreclosed the Korean government from making any further claims for reparations for damages incurred during the colonial period. Nonetheless, the way the South Korean government handled the demands of women activists on the issue of "military comfort women" can be understood by considering not only the patriarchal culture context of androcentric sexism but also by traditional elitist attitudes in dealing with social injustice inflicted upon the poor and the

---

9. Interview with Chung Sei-hwa, president of the Korea Women's Development Institute, August 29, 1995; Kim Ok-gil et al., *Han'guk yŏsŏngsa* [History of Korean women] (Seoul: Ewha Womans University, 1972), p. 401.

10. See, for example, Yoshida Seiji, *Watashi no Senso Hanzai: Chosenjin Kyosei Renko* [My war crimes: The forced draft of Koreans] (Tokyo: San'ichi Shobo, 1983).

powerless in Korean society. Opinions expressed by a former Korean ambassador to Japan illustrate the point. He was reported in the media as stating that the investigation of the Chŏngsindae issue was "unimportant" and questioning the veracity of statements by these women from poor families in rural areas. The adverse response was such that he had to visit the KCWS to explain the "misunderstanding" of his statements.[11]

Moreover, economic development policies of the South Korean government since the early 1960s have included the exploitation of young women not only as cheap laborers at manufacturing companies but also as sex workers in international tourism. To help earn foreign currency, the government has condoned, if not openly promoted the commoditization of sex by using young women as *kisaeng* (professional female entertainers) for foreign male visitors. The *kisaeng* party became so popular among male Japanese tourists that a national women's organization in Japan sent a letter of protest to the Korean tourism association in 1973.[12] In addition, the continued presence of U.S. troops in South Korea has unequivocally contributed to the creation and maintenance of the localized sex industry around military bases. Ironically, the media still use the word *wianbu* ("comfort women") to refer to the women who cater to the sexual desires of American troops. The sexual violence against contemporary Korean "comfort women" by American soldiers has been reported in the Korean mass media from time to time,[13] but the unequal terms in the Status of the Forces Agreement (SOFA) and the low social status of the women involved in sex crimes committed by the U.S. military have combined to help the criminals get away unpunished. The exploitation of women's sexuality as a commodity prospers under the political economy of transnational capitalism in contemporary South Korean patriarchy.

The Chŏngsindae Movement

The only war crimes trials against sexual slavery that have been held involved a small number of interned Dutch women in Indonesia in 1948, and those trials ignored the same ordeals suffered by Indonesian women. For more than four decades after the Pacific War, none of the affected nations in

11. *Han'guk Ilbo*, January 12, 1993.

12. See Han'guk Kyŏhoe Yŏsŏng Yŏnhaphoe [Korean church women united], *Kisaeng Kwan'guang* [Tourism] (Seoul: Author, 1983); Matsui Yayori, "Why I Oppose Kisaeng Tours," originally published in Japanese in 1974 and excerpted in *International Feminism: Networking Against Female Sexual Slavery*, K. Barry, C. Bunch, and S. Castley, eds. (New York: International Women's Tribune Center, 1984), pp. 64–72.

13. See Lee Jin-sook, "The Murder of Yoon Geum Yi," *Korea Report*, 1993, pp. 16–17, for a recent and most cruel case involving the killing of a prostitute (Yoon Geum Yi) by an American G.I. (Kenneth Markle). The murder helped trigger the formation of the grass-roots movement, National Campaign for the Eradication of Crimes by U.S. Troops in Korea, in 1993.

Asia officially raised issues concerning the wartime sexual abuse of their women by the Japanese military. The unfolding of the Korean Chŏngsindae movement for redress suggests that feminist political activism has been essential to raising the public consciousness about the problem of "military comfort women." Although books on the Chŏngsindae have been published in Japan since the 1970s,[14] the politicization of the issue by feminists and by Christian women in both South Korea and Japan began in the late 1980s.

Feminist Political Activism for Redress

In April 1988 the Korean Church Women United (Han'guk Kyohoe Yŏsŏng Yŏnhap) sponsored the International Conference on Women and Tourism on the island of Chejudo in South Korea. It was there that Yun Chung-Ok of Ewha Womans University first presented her research on the Chŏngsindae issue, which helped the participants from Korea and Japan see the underlying connection between the issues of the "comfort women" in colonial Korea and the *kisaeng* tourism in contemporary Korea. In January 1989 members of women's organizations staged a demonstration march in Seoul protesting the government's plan to send an emissary to the funeral of Emperor Hirohito. They also drafted a letter mentioning the need to address the Chŏngsindae issue. But, it was in the state visit of President Roh Tae Woo to Japan in May 1990 that feminist activists found a major political occasion in which to raise the issues of the suffering of the Korean people during Japanese colonial rule in general and reparations for "comfort women" in particular.

Just before Roh's visit, South Korean women's organizations issued a list of demands to be made to the Japanese government, one of which was that Japan investigate the Chŏngsindae issue and apologize for its involvement. Notably, during a state banquet for President Roh, the new Emperor Akihito—as a symbol of the Japanese nation—formally expressed his regrets for the sufferings Japanese colonial rule caused the Korean people. However, when Councillor Motooka of the upper house of the Japanese Diet demanded on June 6, 1990, that government investigate the "military comfort women" issue, the government refused, insisting on its official position of regarding the institution of military "comfort stations" as private enterprise.[15] Korean women's organizations then sent an official letter to Prime Minister Kaifu prior to his visit to South Korea in October 1990, demanding an admission, an apology, and compensation by his government for the sexual slavery of Korean women. And in November 1990, various women's organizations

14. For example, Kim Il Myon, *Tenno no Guntai to Chosenjin lanfu* [The emperor's forces and Korean comfort women] (Tokyo: San'ichi Shobo, 1976).

15. Nishino Rumiko, *Jugun lanfu* [Military comfort women] (Tokyo: Akashi Shoten, 1992).

joined together to form the Chŏngdaehyŏp under the leadership of Yun Chung-ok and Lee Hyo-chae.

In August 1991 Kim Hak-sun, a widow in her late sixties, became the first Korean woman to give public testimony to her life as a "comfort woman" for Japanese troops during the Pacific War, and then in December under the sponsorship of the Association of Pacific War Victims and Bereaved Families, a group of Koreans including Kim Hak-sun, filed a lawsuit against the government of Japan for damages incurred during the Pacific War. Other former "comfort women" have initiated separate lawsuits, such as one filed in 1993 by four former members of the Chŏngsindae at the Shimonoseki branch of the Yamaguchi District Court, as they were abducted to Shimonoseki from Korea during the war. They demand an official apology and damages of $2.29 million.[16] Generally, the plaintiffs' demands include formal apology, compensation, construction of a monument, and the correction of Japanese history textbooks to teach the truth about the "comfort women."

A major portion of the credit for raising public consciousness about this issue both domestically and internationally belongs to several Korean and Japanese women, including the co-chairs of the Chŏngdaehyŏp, Yun Chung-ok and Lee Hyo-chae. Lee and Yun were professors at Ewha Womans University where they taught sociology and English literature until their retirements in 1990 and 1991, respectively. Besides their educational and occupational similarities, the two women have much in common in their personal backgrounds. Both are from a Christian family and their fathers were pastors. Neither has ever married.

Yun says that both of her parents came from a family of independence fighters, and that her father, who harbored strong anger over Japanese colonization of Korea, emphasized the importance of women's enlightenment in reclaiming national sovereignty. "Knowledge is power" was the motto with which she was raised. According to Yun, her father was furious when her elder sister chose to marry instead of continuing with higher education to become a professional. She said her father thought that any fool could get married and that his intelligent daughter should work to achieve something more than that.[17] Yun said that she still has the memory of being forcibly fingerprinted at her school in 1943, after which she withdrew from school for fear of being dragged into the Chŏngsindae. When liberation came in 1945, she noted the total lack of mention of the "comfort women" and was perturbed not to find any reference to them in the writings of Korean historians. Around 1980, after reading about "military comfort women" in a book writ-

16. *Korea Times*, January 6, 1993.

17. Interview with Yun Chong-ok, January 7, 1995.

ten by a Japanese about forced laborers during the Pacific War, Yun Chung-ok began her research on the issue.

Also growing up as a daughter of a Christian pastor, Lee was educated in the United States.[18] She earned a master's degree in sociology and went on to become one of the leading sociologists in Korea. Lee also has long been known as an activist scholar; she was fired from her faculty position at Ewha Womans University (but later reinstated) for her active involvement in the democracy movement during the period of political oppression under the Park regime in the 1970s.

Learning of Yun's research on the "comfort women," Lee suggested that Yun present her findings at the International Conference on Women and Tourism, and since the establishment of the Chŏngdaehyŏp in 1990, the two women have worked tirelessly with a small number of researchers (some of them Lee's former students) and dedicated staff members. Yun directs research and follows developments in the compensation dispute with the Japanese government while Lee oversees the task of bringing the matter to the attention of the larger international community. The Korean National Christian Church recognized their efforts by giving both Yun and Lee a Human Rights Award in December 1994. It is noteworthy that Korean leadership in bringing the "comfort women" issue to public attention has come from elderly Christian women who have personally challenged conventional female lifestyles of women and successfully withstood the pressures of the traditional gender-role ideology. The small crammed office of the Chŏngdaehyŏp, which operates on a "shoestring budget" based mostly on private donations, illustrates the financial and sociopolitical difficulties of a social minority involved in contesting patriarchal states with feminist visions for a more just society.

From a Bilateral Compensation Dispute to an International Human Rights Issue

A major issue in the public debate in both South Korea and Japan involving the "military comfort women" has been the official role and responsibility of the government of Japan. The Japanese state did not admit its involvement in the management and supervision of the "comfort stations" until mid-1992, several months after the publication by Professor Yoshimi of his discovery of official documents confirming the state's heavy involvement in the "comfort women" system. Seeing that neither the Korean nor Japanese governments were responding positively to efforts to resolve the problem, Lee Hyo-chae, as a co-chair of the KCWS submitted a petition to the U.N. Human Rights Commission, dated March 4, 1992, requesting that the Commission investi-

18. Interview with Lee Hyo-chae, August 23, 1995.

gate Japanese atrocities committed against Korean women during World War Two, and help pressure the Japanese government to pay reparations to individual women who have filed suit. The UNHRC responded by placing the issue on the official agenda for its August 1992 meeting in Geneva, where delegates from the Chŏngdaehyŏp and one former "military comfort woman" testified. Due in part to the lobbying efforts of feminist and humanitarian activists, the UNHCR's Subcommission for the Prevention of Discrimination and the Protection of Minorities called the Japanese "military comfort women" system "a crime against humanity that violated the human rights of Asian women and the international agreement prohibiting forced labor that Japan signed in 1932."[19]

Even after admitting the state's involvement, however, Tokyo still denied until 1993 that any coercion was exercised by the state in the recruitment of Korean "comfort women" and denied any possibility of material compensation to the survivors by Japan.[20] Generally speaking, the male-dominated elite discourse as represented by the government officials, intellectuals, and opinion leaders of both countries seemed to regard the "comfort women" problem primarily as an economic compensation issue, with scant attention paid to the violations of human rights of these women. The public debate on the issue in Korea and Japan has been discordant and shifting since Kim Haksun's public testimony in 1991. Yun Chung-ok said that even feminist activists in Japan do not agree with the Korean demand to punish those who were responsible for the sexual abuse of "comfort women." At the weekly Wednesday noon demonstration in front of the Japanese embassy in Seoul, which began in January 1992, I observed a small group of elderly former "comfort women," the Chŏngdaehyŏp staff members, and several other supporters shout in unison slogans such as "Apologize!," "Punish!," and "Compensate!" Some former soldiers in Japan rationalized the atrocity as a natural part of warfare, and pointed out that everybody had suffered during the war.[21] Other Japanese charged the Koreans with trying to make money out of the colonial past to which some humiliated Koreans responded by suggesting that the Korean people forgo any demand for material compensation from Japan over the "comfort women" issue and that as fellow citizens, they offer financial support to the survivors.[22] It was an emotional, reactive move to help preserve the self-respect and national pride of Koreans.

A nationwide fund-raising drive thus began in South Korea in December 1992, and by the following June 200 million wŏn (about US$250,000) had

19. Alice Y. Chai, "Asian-Pacific Feminist Coalition Politics: The *Chŏngsindae/Jugunianfu* ('Comfort Women') Movement," *Korean Studies*, no. 17 (1993), pp. 67–91.

20. *Han'guk Ilbo*, July 7, 1992, August 4, 1992.

21. Nishino, *Jugunianfu*.

22. *Han'guk Ilbo*, February 12, 1992; *Chosun Ilbo*, July 5, 8, 1992.

been raised, one-fifth of the original goal according to Yun Chung-ok. Buddhist monks and believers also started raising money in 1992 to help build the House of Sharing (*Nanum-ŭi chip*) for the survivors.[23] In January 1995 seven former "comfort women" were living together in the temporary, rented House of Sharing in Seoul. To the disappointment and concern of the activists and litigants, this eventually became the official position of the new Kim Young Sam administration as well. The president announced in March 1993 that the government would seek no material compensation from Japan for former "military comfort women" but would insist that the government of Japan thoroughly investigate the matter to uncover the truth and make a comprehensive, formal apology. Kim seemed to believe that his new policy would stake out a position of "moral superiority" for South Korea in forging a new relationship with Japan in the future. The legislature swiftly passed a special act to support the former "comfort women," and the government disbursed a sum of five million wŏn (approximately US$6,250) to each survivor in August 1993, and announced it would pay additional monthly support (250,000 wŏn in 1995). Many Koreans seemed to feel that their government has taken care of the problem well. A middle-aged taxi driver in Seoul, for example, told me that Koreans should be more future-oriented rather than digging up the colonial past such as the "comfort women" issue, and that Koreans should expend their energy in catching up with Japan.

Tokyo seemed to regard President Kim's position as a friendly gesture, and by the summer of 1993, following a direct hearing session in Seoul with former "military comfort women," Japan finally recognized coercion in its recruitment of "comfort women" and their transportation to "comfort stations." It also admitted that it had violated international humanitarian laws by persecuting Korean women.[24] In November 1994 the International Commission of Jurists (ICJ) recommended that the Japanese government pay, "as a purely interim measure," US$40,000 to each survivor.[25] Within a week after the ICJ statement a group of 105 lawyers (37 Koreans and 68 Japanese) released a statement that proclaimed the responsibility of the Japanese government to compensate the former "military comfort women" based on inter-

23. Committee for the Construction of the Nanum-ŭi chip, *"Nanum-ŭi chip Charyŏjip* [Collection of reference materials] (Seoul: Author, 1993).

24. Takagi Ken'ichi, "The War Compensation Issue of Japan: Its Development and Assignments," paper presented at the annual meeting of the Association for Asian Studies, Boston, Massachusetts, March 1994.

25. Ustinia Dolgopol and Snehal Paranjape, *Comfort Women: An Unfinished Ordeal* (Geneva, Switzerland: International Commission of Jurists, 1994), p. 105. The ICJ, a nongovernmental organization headquartered in Geneva, is composed of distinguished jurists from around the world who work toward full observance of the provisions in the Universal Declaration of Human Rights.

national laws.[26] The official Japanese response to the mounting pressure from the international community was to deal with the compensation issue at the non-governmental level. By December 1994, Tokyo had drawn up a compensation plan that called for raising non-government funds to pay a lump sum to each survivor. The Chŏngdaehyŏp rejected this proposal, demanding that the *government* of Japan, as perpetrator of the crime, pay the compensation.

In contrast to the adversarial nationalistic undertone in the discussions between the governments, feminist activists and members of nongovernmental organizations in South Korea were able to forge an international coalition with their counterparts in Japan, Taiwan, the Philippines, and Thailand to help reclaim the human rights of former "military comfort women." The Asian Women's Solidarity Forum, for instance, held its third conference in Seoul in 1995, and adopted a resolution denouncing the plan to sidestep responsibility for war crimes by Japan by paying from nongovernmental funds. In response, Japan revised its plan to establish the Asian Women's Fund (Zaidanhojin Josei no tame no Asia Heiwa Kokumin Kikin) to compensate former "comfort women" and be used in connection with issues such as violence against women.[27] Although the fund relies mostly on voluntary donations, the Japanese government also contributes funds to be used for medical and welfare care of former "comfort women" under the revised plan. At the U.N. World Conference on Women in Beijing in September 1995, the Japanese government delegation remained silent over the "comfort women" compensation issue, in contrast to the active participation of Japanese representatives in the International Symposium on Violence Against Women in War and Armed Conflict.[28]

Statements by both Japanese Prime Minister Hashimoto Ryutaro and Japanese government spokesman Kajiyama Siroku in response to the latest U.N. recommendations indicate that the U.N. demands may not change Japan's basic position of disclaiming any legal responsibility for the sexual abuses.[29] After meeting with Hashimoto in May 1996, Miki Mutsuko, the widow of a former prime minister and one of the most prominent proponents of the Asian Women's Fund, resigned from the panel of backers of the Fund, stating that Hashimoto's ideas were too different from hers. It is still not certain whether Prime Minister Hashimoto will honor a pledge by his predecessor, Murayama Tomiichi, to write a letter of apology to each of the former "comfort women."

26. *Han'guk Ilbo*, November 29, 1994.

27. "Today's Japan," TV news show aired on channel 32, San Francisco, June 15, 1995; pamphlet published by Asian Women's Fund, supplied by Glenda Roberts.

28. *Chosun Ilbo*, September 14, 1995.

29. *San Francisco Chronicle*, February 7, 1996; *Han'guk Ilbo*, February 8, 1996.

Conclusion

Professor Yun Chung-ok of the KCWS stated during our interview in 1995 that the achievements of the Chŏngsindae movement have surpassed her wildest dream. Indeed, the Korean "comfort women" movement for redress may be regarded as a notable victory in feminist political activism. Its remarkable success in making the "military comfort women" problem a universal moral issue of women's human rights is owed in part to the dramatic transformations in national and international political structures over the past several years. These transformations include the collapse of the Cold War world order in the international community and the democracy movement of the late 1980s in the Republic of Korea, which resulted in the restoration of civilian government in 1993. For Japan, the issue of "military comfort women" turned into an unexpected political embarrassment, damaging its national "face" in the international community. Tokyo tried to exercise pressure against the U.N. investigations, and officials worked hard—and successfully—to prevent the general assembly meeting of the U.N. Human Rights Commission in Geneva in April 1996 from adopting a resolution on the "comfort women" issue.[30]

The sexual exploitation of women has been a common concomitant to the military activities of many nations and the provision of local women by colonial military services for the sexual needs of soldiers is not unknown. Nonetheless, what is unprecedented about the system of "comfort women" for Japanese troops in the Pacific War is that it was a systematic, long-term institutionalization of female sexual slavery, and that these women were mostly colonial subjects from poor families who were coercively drafted by a state power. This is vastly different from random rape incidents perpetrated by individual soldiers during warfare or from the recent rape case of a school girl by American soldiers in Okinawa. One may also point out here that prostitution, by definition, includes payment for sexual union, and implies a certain degree of choice. It is notable that police ordinances of imperial Japan permitted licensed prostitutes the freedom to cease their trade even if the proprietor did not countersign their applications.[31]

In contrast, slavery carries the notion of the social outcast, a person as property, and compulsory labor. Testimonies of former "comfort women" reveal that most had been forced into compulsory sexual labor, and were under virtual house arrest in army "comfort stations," despised as colonial subjects, and depersonalized as the common property of the soldiers who

30. *Han'guk Ilbo*, December 13, 1992, June 12, 1996.

31. Garon, "World's Oldest Debate," p. 711.

called them their "sanitary public toilets."[32] Many of them received no payment for their sexual labor. Therefore, feminists and human rights activists have argued that the lives of Korean "military comfort women" should be conceived of as *sexual slavery*, enforced under the direction of the Japanese government, not as prostitution. Until 1993 Japan maintained its position that these women engaged in prostitution voluntarily, and in May 1994, Japanese Minister of Justice Nagano Shigeto asserted that the Korean "military comfort women" were "public prostitutes."[33]

To the extent that both prostitution and the Japanese institution of military sexual slavery are rooted in the exploitation of women, one may argue that the distinction between prostitutes and "military comfort women" is problematic. But prostitutes do not normally work under the threat of lethal weapons, while testimonies of former "comfort women" abound with instances of physical threats, and some bear scars and disabilities inflicted upon them by their military masters. One of my informants, who was forcibly drafted at the age of 13, has a deep sword scar in her permanently disabled left arm, the price of her refusal to accommodate the sexual demands of a soldier. She also asserted that she was imprisoned for several months for her act of disobedience. Her experiences underline a fundamental difference between "comfort women" as sexual slaves and prostitutes as sex workers: namely, physical violence and the abject lack of autonomy to which sexual slaves are subjected, in contrast to some sense of self-respect and hope as expressed, for example, by women sex workers for the American military in contemporary Korea.[34] Thus, it was state power that made the difference in the Japanese institution of sexual slavery and helped sustain the long silence over it in both Japan and South Korea.

The compensation dispute over the "comfort women" issue has strained bilateral relations between the two countries. Ethno-nationalistic sentiments have given rise to a renewed sense of historically rooted mutual hostility and contempt. One may ask at this point whether or not the courts in Japan will concur with the international community in regarding the institution of military sexual slavery as a violation of human rights and order the state to compensate the survivors. A recent Japanese Supreme Court ruling on voting

32. Chŏngdaehyŏp and Chŏngsindae Yŏn'guhoe, eds., *Kangje-ro kkullyŏgan chosŏnin kunwi-anpudŭl* [Forcibly drafted Korean military comfort women] (Seoul: Hanul, 1993); Watanabe Kazuko, "Militarism, Colonialism, and the Trafficking of Women: 'Comfort Women' Forced into Sexual Labor for Japanese Soldiers," *Bulletin of Concerned Asian Scholars*, 26:4 (1994), pp. 3–17; Yun Chung-ok," Jungshindae—Korean Military 'Comfort Women'," unpublished ms., n.d.

33. *Han'guk Ilbo*, May 7, 1994.

34. For life stories of female sex workers in the U.S. military bases in Korea, see Sandra Sturdevant and Brenda Stoltzfus, *Let the Good Times Roll: Prostitution and the U.S. Military in Asia* (New York: New Press, 1992).

rights of long-term resident aliens (most of whom are of Korean ancestry) in local elections offers some hopeful grounds for such a possibility. On the other hand, populist sentiment in Japan, characterized by its victimization from the atomic bombs, seems to oppose any conciliatory gesture, even on the 50th anniversary of the end of World War Two. Recent Japanese publications on the war have included novels depicting a fictionalized Japanese victory, and right wing opposition in the Diet against a proposed resolution to apologize for Japan's war crimes resulted in a watered-down version that pleased no one. These activities reveal the depth of ethno-nationalism on the part of some Japanese in leadership positions, and augur ill for a pro-human rights verdict on the pending "comfort women" lawsuits. It will take years before Japanese courts decide on war compensation suits, and Kim Hak-sun, for one, asserted during our interview that Japan has adopted the tactic of waiting until the death of the aged litigants and that Koreans cannot win in a bilateral deal with superpower Japan. She feels the only hope is pressure from the international community and organizations. The movement leaders in South Korea seemed to share this view; they demand that Japan not be allowed a seat on the U.N. Security Council unless it resolves its wartime crimes, including the sexual abuse of "comfort women."

Regardless of the legal decision on the compensation for "comfort women," the widespread exploitation of female sexuality will continue without revolutionary transformations in the masculinist sexual culture, the political economic system of the transnational capitalist sex industry, and the gender gap in wage income resulting in the feminization of poverty. Continuous work in feminist and humanitarian political activism is needed in order to realize more egalitarian and peaceful gender relations in many contemporary patriarchal societies, and global recognition of the concept of women's human rights—however they may be defined in different cultures—will help curb various forms of violence against women.

LAURA E. HEIN*

Free-Floating Anxieties on the Pacific:

Japan and the West Revisited

Although the idea of "national character" has been attacked often, it lives on in the minds of human beings who conduct international relations. The daily newspapers are full of quotes about "ancient Slavic emnity," "we Japanese," or "the American way of life." These generalizations often are drawn along lines of racial identity, national culture, or degree of modernity. Considerable recent scholarship on the formation of these powerful concepts has enriched our understanding of how people both imagine their own national community and contrast it with others. Yet much of this same literature has focused on the way that contemporary individuals often lose sight of that complexity and instead accept narratives of unified unbroken tradition–even patently false tradition.[1] As yet, however, this complex

*Thanks to Ken Alder, Bruce Cumings, Jeffrey Hanes, Tessie P. Liu, Melissa Macauley, James Oakes, Michael S. Sherry, and Louise Young for helpful comments on this article, as well as to audiences at the Midwest Japan Seminar and the Association of Asian Studies.

1. William Roseberry, *Anthropologies and Histories: Essays in Culture, History, and Political Economy* (New Brunswick, 1989), 200–201, 205–7; Jay O'Brian and William Roseberry, "Introduction," *Golden Ages, Dark Ages: Imagining the Past in Anthropology and History* (Berkeley, 1991). See also "Forum on Universalism and Relativism in Asian Studies," *Journal of Asian Studies* 50 (February 1991): 29–34, 67–83. James Clifford, *The Predicament of Culture: Twentieth-Century Ethnography, Literature, and Art* (Cambridge, MA, 1988), emphasized culture over either politics or economic relations and so can be seen as providing theoretical justification for the kind of obfuscation I deal with here. Rosalind O'Hanlon and David Washbrook have made precisely this argument in "After Orientalism: Culture, Criticism, and Politics in the Third World," *Comparative Studies in Society and History* 34 (January 1992): 141–67. Nonetheless, I found Clifford's observations helpful in examining assumptions about "tradition" and "culture." Or as Micaela di Leonardo argues in *Gender at the Crossroads of Knowledge: Feminist Anthropology in the Postmodern Era* (Berkeley, 1991), all societies today are equally part of global modernity. Only their place within that configuration varies, not their age. Also see Tetsuo Najita, "Presidential Address: Personal Reflections on Modernity and Modernization," *Journal of Asian Studies* 52 (November 1993): 845–53. See William W. Kelly, "Finding a Place in Metropolitan Japan: Ideologies, Institutions, and Everyday Life," in *Postwar Japan as History*, ed. Andrew Gordon (Berkeley, 1993), 189–238, for other discussion in the context of Japan studies. Eric Hobsbawm and Terence Ranger, eds., *The Invention of Tradition* (Cambridge, England, 1983); Benedict Anderson, *Imagined Communities: Reflections on the Origins and Spread of Nationalism* (London, 1983); Edward W. Said, *Orientalism* (New York, 1979). Also see Werner Sollors, ed., *The Invention of Ethnicity* (Oxford, 1989); David Theo Goldberg, ed., *Anatomy of Racism* (Minneapolis, 1990); and Harumi Befu, ed., *Cultural Nationalism in East Asia: Representation and Identity*, Research Papers and Policy Studies 39 (Berkeley, 1993).

DIPLOMATIC HISTORY, Vol. 20, No. 3 (Summer 1996). Published by Blackwell Publishers, 238 Main Street, Cambridge MA, 02142, USA, and 108 Cowley Road, Oxford, OX4 1JF, UK.

literature has had little impact on diplomatic history and analyses of contemporary international relations.

Amy Kaplan suggested one promising direction when she called in this very journal for analyses of the ways that American anxieties about their own society have been projected abroad. Thus, for example, American pronouncements about postwar Europe tell us more about the United States in the late 1940s than about Germany.[2] The overpowering sense of anxiety that Kaplan documents is extended in this essay with regard to U.S.-Japanese relations. Indeed, that anxiety is palpable: The tone of discussion in both Japan and the United States over the last decade has consistently anticipated major conflict between the two nations. That sense of an impending clash is much influenced by a basic assumption about the two societies–that Japan and the United States embody two fundamentally different kinds of civilizations.

But it is not enough to examine American night terrors about Japan. International historians must also pay attention to other peoples' rhetoric about the differences between their own society and the United States. Thus, Japanese pronouncements about the world beyond their shores should tell us about culturally specific forms of Japanese divisiveness, contestation, and cultural anxiety rather than simply about either "misperceptions" or "Japanese reality." Thus, the steady stream of pronouncements by Japanese government officials castigating labor strife, uppity women, and racial minorities in the United States could, in Kaplan's approach, be fruitfully analyzed as a map of elite Japanese anxieties about class, gender, and racial conflict *in Japan* projected onto another continent.[3] Moreover, that tangle of anxieties powerfully affects American perceptions of Japan, particularly when it resonates with anxieties about class, gender, and race on this side of the Pacific.

Indeed, Japanese pronouncements are picked up in the United States (although not as often or quickly as American ones are in Japan). The two national discussions thus interact with and build on each other in complex ways. Many of the recent efforts toward "self-reflexivity" in anthropology and other disciplines have emphasized the way in which metropolitan researchers imposed their values on others. Currently, Western scholarship on other parts of the world is under attack for appropriating the voice and authority of local peoples.[4] But in a difference that has everything to do with Japanese power in the world today, that imbalance is far less marked in studies of Japan than in previous decades or than it still is in studies of, say, African societies. In fact, most recent analyses of Japan have both Japanese and Western adherents. The story here is less and less one of the arrogant West

2. Amy Kaplan, "Domesticating Foreign Policy," *Diplomatic History* 18 (Winter 1994): 97–106.

3. See Ellen Hammond and Laura E. Hein, "Multiculturalism in Japanese Perspective," *Journal of American-East Asian Relations* 1 (Summer 1992): 145–69, for a longer discussion.

4. Clifford, *The Predicament of Culture*, 80–91.

imposing its categories on a supine Japan and far more of two sites of activity, both contested, reinforcing each other in intended and unintended ways.

Common basic assumptions about Japan have shifted radically over the last fifty years, however. As discussed in more detail below, after World War II most Japanese and Americans saw Japan as participating in a general pattern of modernity, conceived by nearly all in positive and universalist terms. Few people thought then that the Japanese past held the secrets of Japanese peace and prosperity. In the mid-1970s that assumption began to shift at both the popular and scholarly levels, and fifteen years later, scholars who argued that Japan embodied a unique form of modernity were far more popular in both Japan and the United States than those who continued to see Japan as part of a universal trend.[5] The main way that Japan differs from the West, most argued, is its employment of a variety of means unavailable elsewhere to create social consensus, although the specific mechanism varied with the analyst. Thus, within an astonishingly short time, the relationship between Japanese society and some universal modernity (however imagined) shifted radically. Moreover, the depiction of Japan as incommensurable set a tone of fundamental conflict in Japan's international relations, just as the older modernization theory implied tutelage.

While the sheer silliness of much public discussion on Japanese uniqueness is annoying, more disturbing is the way in which those pronouncements were deployed. Statements about Japanese difference (like Japanese "backwardness" before it) were routinely used to explain Japan's modern economic development, contemporary political practices, and special incompatibility with other nations, particularly the United States. Thus, on both sides of the Pacific, U.S.-Japanese trade tensions were commonly handled as the latest efflorescence of enduring and deep transhistoric differences. Indeed, international trade disputes or problems within strategic alliances were often the proximate reason for theorizing on the subject of timeless Japanese society. Arguments for unusual internal cohesion within Japan always also implied inevitable conflict with other societies. These assumptions never were used to predict easier economic or cultural interaction with North American or European nations (although sometimes they were deployed to predict better relations with Asian countries). The kinds of problems generally invoked to explain international friction elsewhere (or in Japan before 1945)—such as competition for the same resources, tensions within a single international capitalist economy, or friction over immigration—were all too often neglected in explanations of postwar Japan.

---

5. Most senior scholars of Japan began their careers critiquing modernization theory's (and vulgar Marxism's) insensitivity to the nuances of specific cultures and histories. That battle still is being joined today in several forms. Most notable is the political-economy-based critique of neoclassical economic models. See Chalmers Johnson, "Studies of Japanese Political Economy: A Crisis in Theory," in *Japanese Studies in the United States*, part 1: *History and Present Condition* (Tokyo, 1988), 95–113.

At the same time, discussion about the nature of the two societies became a way to create and maintain domestic national myths about each. Most notably, in the United States, discussions about Japan served to explore thoughts that were otherwise taboo in America. Contentious ideas, such as that economic prosperity is incompatible with either democracy or multiculturalism, could be explored in both dystopian and utopian directions. Discussion framed in the free-floating context of "Japan" did not need to confront the extent to which America already failed to live up to its ideal of equal access to life, liberty, and the pursuit of happiness. This submerged debate also helps explain why "Japan is unique and unchanging" rhetoric in the United States was applied indiscriminately to explain not only both economic efficiency and inefficiency but also political unity and infighting. Similarly, America provided precisely the same kind of imaginary landscape for the Japanese. Notably, theories about Japanese difference worked to obscure precisely those historical shifts in Japan that most closely mirrored changes in American society. What if Japan were to welcome immigrants and cultural diversity? All those who wished to imagine could look to the United States for either hopeful or terrifying lessons. At the same time they could reinforce the notion of Japanese homogeneity while eliding the presence of discrimination and dissent in their own society. The pattern interweaving these analytical discrepancies and ideological continuities has structured not only what Americans and Japanese think about each other but also what they think about themselves. I suspect that it is this imaginative function that explains the zombielike perpetuation of so many absurd theories about each nation, theories that haunt attempts at international communication.

JAPAN'S PLACE IN MODERNIZATION THEORY

Both theories that emphasize Japanese particularity and that stress a universal path to social development have had long histories in Japan. Indeed, theories of Japanese national uniqueness centered on the emperor and a mystical racial unity were official dogma until 1945. Nonetheless, the carnage and stupidity revealed by defeat in World War II forced most thoughtful Japanese to revise that position. In the West, the prevalent wartime assumption had been that the Japanese were simply barbarians, whether due to genetic differences, psychological makeup, or some uniquely Japanese socialization. For those who believed that socialization was the key, Japan was usually described as being stuck in the feudal or traditional past—that is, still living the Tokugawa life.[6] In a variant of divergence theory, the assumption was that the rest of the technologically advanced world had achieved civilized status and only Japan could not.

The universalist model that gained the most support before and immedi-

6. Nakamura Masanori, *The Japanese Monarchy, Ambassador Joseph Grew, and the Making of the "Symbol Emperor System," 1931–1991* (New York, 1992); John W. Dower, *War without Mercy: Race and Power in the Pacific War* (New York, 1986).

ately after the war among educated Japanese was Marxism. Marx's emphasis on class conflict as a driving force for historical change provided an attractive theoretical explanation for the enormous dynamism that characterized early-twentieth-century Japanese society. The transitions that Marx and Engels posited from slave to feudal to bourgeois to socialist society not only plausibly matched Japan's past and present but also provided a vision for the future. After the war, Marxism's scientific rationality together with its hopefulness gave the approach even more prestige.

In Japan, as elsewhere, Marxism was challenged in the 1950s and 1960s by another universalist approach, often dubbed modernization theory. Modernization theory, crudely put, posited a universal, quantitatively measurable movement of all societies toward a single ideal form of organization that can be described as "modern." Modernization theorists used a variety of measures of a society's approach to modernity, but most were either economic, mainly aspects of industrialization, or some measure of the trend toward mass society, such as high literacy rates or mass participation in political life. High marks on one of these measures often were assumed to mean progress toward the whole, and one of the great weaknesses of this approach was its insensitivity to the way that, for example, greater industrialization could actually preclude democracy. In general, Weberian rationality was often the working shorthand for modernity in modernization theory as opposed to a somewhat unexamined "traditionality."[7]

Modernization theory was characterized by a teleological assumption that we are all progressing up toward a higher plane known as modernity, and usually by a smug assertion that Britain and the United States were the farthest along that universal road and that Western-educated elites were far ahead of the provincial yokels of their own countries. Almond and Coleman, for example, routinely described the world as including "modern Western" and "transitional non-Western" countries. The theory was explicitly anti-Marxist in its stress on evolutionary change rather than revolutionary breaks. Moreover, as is well known, it was seen by both scholars and American government officials as a blueprint for international development in the service of redrawing alliances against the USSR in the Cold War.[8]

Japan was very quickly incorporated into a starring role in modernization studies because it seemed to offer a rare twentieth-century example of eco-

---

7. Gabriel A. Almond and James J. Coleman, eds., *The Politics of Developing Areas* (Princeton, 1960); W. W. Rostow, *The Stages of Economic Growth: A Non-Communist Manifesto* (Cambridge, England, 1960). Michael Adas has written specifically on the use of technological achievement to define modernity in *Machines as the Measure of Men: Science, Technology, and Ideologies of Western Dominance* (Ithaca, 1989).

8. See Almond and Coleman, *The Politics of Developing Areas*, 11–25. Sasaki Ryūji, *Sekaishi no naka no Asia to Nihon* [Asia and Japan in the context of world history] (Tokyo, 1988), argued that Rostow did create a blueprint for American postwar policy, although Yui Daizaburō assessed his thesis critically in "Sengo nihon shi to sengo sekaishi o dō tsunagu ka?" [How to connect postwar Japanese history to postwar world history?] *Rekishigaku Kenkyū* 604 (March 1990): 21–27.

nomic prosperity under capitalism with political stability and without a class revolution. Japan also provided the ideal case for the liberal argument that neither white skin nor the Protestant ethic was essential to modernization. It was designated very early as the prime example of development along these lines, and as early as 1961, Edwin O. Reischauer described Japan as a "model" for underdeveloped countries that wished to modernize. Frequently, Japan's modernization was framed specifically as a contrast between Japanese success and Chinese failure to negotiate the transition to modernity.[9] That early and abiding interest in Japan means, among other things, that there is a rich legacy of debate about modernization theory in relation to Japan, making studies of Japan useful for a general reevaluation of modernization theory as a theory of international relations and development.

Modernization theory as applied to Japan by Americans was very much part of the politics of its day. It explicitly attacked both Marxist and divergence analyses of Japanese society. Thus, academics turned to topics such as comparative study of political modernization in Japan and Turkey, which searched for standard typologies of modern development. Even the "dark valley" of the 1930s was recast more optimistically as an era with unusually difficult "dilemmas of growth." American policymakers also feared that the popularity of intellectual Marxism in Japan could mean a policy "tilt" toward the Soviet Union and/or the People's Republic of China. John Dower has shown how explicitly the modernization paradigm was incorporated into official American foreign policy as an important ideological weapon in the Cold War.[10] Edwin Reischauer, in his dual role as Harvard academic and ambassador, embodied the effort to reorient Japan at both the theoretical and the policy levels by providing the Japanese with an alternative explanation of twentieth-century change.

Modernization theory had a mixed reaction in Japan. Many postwar Japanese intellectuals resisted modernization theory because of its amoral stance on issues of war and repression. They were most deeply disturbed by its ability to shrug off World War II and the problem of war responsibility altogether–the central intellectual concern of the early postwar years. As elsewhere, Japanese critics also questioned modernization theory's focus on ruling elites and lack of attention to dissent within Japanese society. Equally

---

9. Nakayama Ichirō debate with Edwin Reischauer, "Nihon kindaika no rekishiteki hyōka," *Chūō Kōron* (September 1961): 89. Recently, Japan has been much touted as a model for Eastern European nations, but now it is a model for the transition from a planned to a free-market economy, unlike the older (and continuing) idea of a model of change from "traditional" to "modern" society for the Third World. Paul Cohen, *Discovering History in China* (New York, 1984), 39, 112–25.

10. Robert E. Ward and Dankwart A. Rustow, *Political Modernization in Japan and Turkey* (Princeton, 1964); James Morley, ed., *Dilemmas of Growth in Prewar Japan* (Princeton, 1971). Also see the other five volumes of this Princeton University Press modernization of Japan series, beginning with Marius Jansen, ed., *Changing Japanese Attitudes toward Modernization* (Princeton, 1965); and John W. Dower, ed., *Origins of the Modern Japanese State: Selected Writings of E. H. Norman* (New York, 1975).

disturbing to them, in the modernization paradigm, capitalism reemerged as vindicated in its prewar Japanese manifestation, and thus in essential form. They also were troubled by the unself-conscious celebration of American norms as an essential stepping-stone on the path to modernity.[11]

Nonetheless, even Japanese critics appreciated the way modernization theory rebutted the Allies' wartime propaganda depictions of them as something divergent and incapable of becoming human. In its broadest outlines, convergence theory invited Japanese into the community of nations and the human race. In this sense, modernization theory was simply an elaboration of the occupation assumptions that the United States was in Japan to "teach democracy." And, as MacArthur made painfully clear when he described the Japanese as "like a boy of twelve," the ability to learn democracy was linked to a belief in social and political immaturity. While this characterization was embarrassing, many Japanese shared the assumption that Japanese were politically immature. Such language was common in the writings of prominent Japanese intellectuals of the first postwar decades.[12] Horrified by their own complicity in the wartime system, these thinkers accepted the idea of tutelage. For many, the universalism of modernization theory significantly offset the condescension of its practitioners.

Indeed, many leading Japanese intellectuals took seriously modernization theory. These were usually social scientists who were disciplinarily committed to universalism but dissatisfied with Marxism to some degree. Thus, the critique of Marxist historical models engaged them intellectually and politically. For example, while someone like Nakayama Ichirō, a leading mathematical economist, bridled at the ethnocentrism of Rostow's concept and suggested that each nation's tradition would contribute to modernity in its

---

11. Maruyama Masao and Toyama Shigeki quoted in John Hall, "Changing Conceptions of the Modernization of Japan," in Jansen, ed., *Changing Japanese Attitudes toward Modernization*, 7–42. See also Toyama Shigeki, "The Meiji Restoration and the Present Day," *Bulletin of Concerned Asian Scholars* 2 (October 1969): 10–14; Nakayama Ichirō in debate with Edwin Reischauer, "Nihon kindaika no rekishiteki hyōka," 84–89; and Takeshi Ishida, *Japanese Political Culture: Change and Continuity* (New Brunswick, 1983), ix–xviii.

12. MacArthur quoted in Richard B. Finn, *Winners in Peace: MacArthur, Yoshida, and Postwar Japan* (Berkeley, 1992), 292. This sense of Japanese political immaturity is not entirely gone either inside or outside Japan. An Associated Press article printed in the *Chicago Tribune* of 1 October 1992 flatly stated that the political corruption scandal exploding around Shin Kanemaru, and specifically the deference shown the LDP kingmaker by the Tokyo prosecutor's office, "shows a lack of sophistication in Japan's democracy, which dates from the U.S. occupation after World War II." The article then quotes Kaoru Okano, a professor of politics at Meiji University, that "Japanese democracy can only be said to be in its kindergarten stage." No similar assessment of the maturity of democracy was prompted by the concurrent attempt by the GOP White House to use the justice system here to hide prior acceptance of an Italian bank's routing of loans to Iraq through its Atlanta office. Masao Maruyama, "Author's Introduction," *Thought and Behavior in Modern Japanese Politics* (Oxford, 1963), xii–xiii; Ōkōchi Kazuo, *Sengo Nihon no Rōdō Undō* [The labor movement in postwar Japan] (Tokyo, 1955). See also J. Victor Koschmann, "Intellectuals and Politics," in *Postwar Japan as History*, ed. Andrew Gordon (Berkeley, 1993), 395–423, for a more richly developed history of high intellectual Japanese thought in the postwar period.

own way, he chose to work within the Weberian modernization framework in general. He introduced a 1963 article as "a conscious effort to identify some of the points at which two different kinds of civilization – the industrial and the traditional – come into contact within the Japanese setting. The processes of industrialization have a logic all of their own. It is a logic which will penetrate any traditional society, to the extent that it becomes involved in those processes." While this echoed Marx's assumption that new economic relations will force the creation of a new kind of society, Nakayama nonetheless spent much of his career searching for ways to defuse class conflict rather than assuming its inevitability. Other influential economists, such as labor relations theorist Ōkōchi Kazuo and the most prominent academic specialist on industrial and energy policy, Arisawa Hiromi, shared this universalist approach and also appreciated modernization theory's emphasis on the normality and rationality of Japanese actors.[13]

Finally, as is so often the case in twentieth-century Japanese history, some Japanese writers very early on applied modernization theory with the same self-congratulatory slant that also marred so much American and European thinking on grand issues of civilization and modernity. One example appeared in the 1962 comments of political scientist Seki Yoshihiko, who argued that democracy was possible in Japan because "in her social structure Japan is closer to the West than to other Asian countries. This makes it difficult to impose totalitarianism on Japanese society." Seki had just helped found the Social Democratic party and was by no means at the right-wing fringe of the intellectual spectrum in Japan at the time. Nonetheless, as early as 1962 he had begun to range Japan together with the modern West *against* the rest of the world. Never mind that the concept "totalitarian" was originally developed to explain twentieth-century European societies. Seki's quick appropriation of those political categories to flatter Japan and sever it from the rest of Asia is one reason why it seems inadequate to dismiss modernization theory entirely as a theoretical arm of neocolonialism, although it certainly has been deployed that way. Noted political scientist Masumi Junnosuke, writing with Robert Scalapino, has similarly written of the "universal appeal" of Western values to the educated elites of the Third World.[14] Modernization theory has been too useful to *Japanese* intellectuals for neocolonialism to be the only story. This utility does much to explain modernization theory's vogue in Japan as well as in the United States.

Nonetheless, as time went on, modernization theory lost prestige in

---

13. Laura E. Hein, "In Search of Peace and Democracy: Postwar Japanese Economic Debate in Political Context," *Journal of Asian Studies* 55 (August 1994): 752–78. Jeff Hanes has traced a very similar set of attitudes among architects and city planners in Japan – and a similar trajectory to a sense of difference in later decades. See his "From Megalopolis to Megaroporisu," *Journal of Urban History* 19 (February 1993): 56–94.

14. Seki Yoshihiko, *New Politics* 1 (Winter 1962): 62–64; Junnosuke Masumi and Robert Scalapino, *Parties and Politics in Contemporary Japan* (Berkeley, 1962), vii. See also Laura Hein and Ellen Hammond, "Homing in on Asia" (in author's possession).

Japan as it did elsewhere. Its blatant Eurocentrism in Western practice as well as its indifference to repression and war continued to trouble many Japanese. In the late 1960s, an awareness of ecological damage was added to the earlier social critique. And, like the later Latin American dependency theorists, Japanese scholars found the analyses of relations between countries, especially imperialists and colonies, far too shallow. Modernization theory tended to treat each nation as self-contained, without any consideration of the ways that foreign relations could affect such trends as urbanization, industrialization, and higher literacy rates.

But more was involved than the conceptual shortcomings of modernization theory. The climate in which such scholarship operated had shifted radically by the mid-1970s. It had become harder for scholars anywhere to see the United States as the epitome of rational modernity in the face of the debacle in Vietnam, violent social protest at home, and the decline of American hegemony abroad. Meanwhile, high-speed economic growth had transformed Japan. Little changed in the formal economic and security framework of U.S.-Japanese relations, but scholarly and popular writing about the two nations did shift radically on both sides of the Pacific from the late 1970s.[15]

DIVERGENCE THEORIES

Modernization theory is no longer the main way people on either side of the Pacific explain Japan. That is, *historically*, the debate between Marxists and modernization theorists in both the United States and Japan was resolved by a massive shift in emphasis to the particular and the divergent. By the early 1980s, the dominant paradigm explaining recent Japanese history had become its fundamental difference from the West rather than an updated version of modernization theory.

Much of this scholarship was of extremely high quality and compelling in its particulars. The point here is not to deny the real cultural and social differences between Japan and the United States or research that documents those differences. Rather, it is that more recent work asked different questions than did older work. Instead of researching Japanese history and society for tools to evaluate its degree of modernization according to some externally derived formula, for the last fifteen or twenty years scholars have searched for Japan's distinctive features—particularly those contributing to rapid economic growth and a stable social structure. That shift in the intellectual framework of studies of Japan occurred on both sides of the Pacific.

Since explaining Japan's unusually high rate of economic growth was the problem absorbing most students of postwar Japan at the time, it is not

15. Richard J. Samuels makes a similar point in "Japanese Political Studies and the Myth of the Independent Intellectual," in *The Political Culture of Foreign Area and International Studies: Essays in Honor of Lucian W. Pye*, ed. Richard J. Samuels and Myron Weiner (Washington, 1992), 17–56.

surprising that Japanese work on economic history and the history of technology provided one striking example of this shift. Essays produced thirty years ago were usually case studies or extrapolations of general theories of modernity developed by such scholars as Alfred Chandler, Simon Kuznetz, J. M. Keynes, and Joseph Schumpeter.[16]

In contrast, recent Japanese scholarship on economic history has done two things: pushed the frontiers of modernity farther into the past and emphasized the particularity of Japanese development. In an irony that undergirds one of this article's main themes, Western scholars closely associated with modernization theory actually pioneered the effort to recast the Tokugawa period (1600–1868) as "early modern." For example, John W. Hall's work celebrated such elements of the past as the Tokugawa legal system for its rational, impersonal (within each class at least) protomodernity. Hall's interpretation of Tokugawa Japan – the archetype of repressive feudalism for earlier scholars – as "early modern" later became standard in Japan as well as in the United States and Europe.[17] For example, a 1989 series on the Japanese economy published by Iwanami Press, which brought together most of Japan's distinguished economic historians, strongly emphasized the Tokugawa legacy as the basis of modern economic growth. It is not coincidental that those centuries were ones of minimal interaction with industrialized Europe. In other words, by moving modernity back before the Meiji Restoration, scholars headed much farther toward a description of a nationally specific path to modernity.[18] Interestingly, many of the authors in this series began their careers by attempting to adapt the Kuznetzian formulation of modern economic growth to Japan. Originally well within the modernization paradigm, their more recent work stressed traditional, indigenous, and unreplic-

16. For example, see Kazushi Ohkawa and Henry Rosofsky, "A Century of Japanese Economic Growth," and Yasuzo Horie, "Modern Entrepreneurship in Meiji Japan," both in *The State and Economic Enterprise*, ed. W. W. Lockwood (Princeton, 1965), 47–92, 183–208; Ohkawa Kazushi, *Differential Structure and Agriculture* (Tokyo, 1972); and Tessa Morris-Suzuki, *A History of Japanese Economic Thought* (London, 1989).

17. John Hall, "Rule by Status in Tokugawa Japan," *Journal of Japanese Studies* 1 (Autumn 1974): 39–49; Sidney Crawcour, "The Tokugawa Heritage," in Lockwood, ed., *The State and Economic Enterprise in Japan*, 17–44; R. P. Dore, "The Legacy of Tokugawa Education," in Jansen, ed., *Changing Japanese Attitudes*, 99–132. For older English-language work on prewar society as militarized see most of the memoirs and reports created by occupation officials, including Supreme Commander for the Allied Powers, *Political Reorientation of Japan: September 1945–September 1948*, 2 vols. (Westport, 1970).

18. The Iwanami imprimatur is significant, given that the same publisher brought out the 1932 "kōza," which gave its name to one wing of Marxist thought in Japan. Yasuba Yasukichi and Inoki Takenori, eds., *Nihon Keizai Shi*, vols. 1–8 (Tokyo, 1989). Also see the remarkable review by Kozo Yamamura in *Journal of Japanese Studies* 17 (Winter 1991): 127–42, and ones by Sugihara Kaoru and Makino Fumio in *Japan Forum* 3 (April 1991). Two scholars who have personally traversed this path from research on the Japanese case within universal development to the unique nature of Japanese history are Hayami Yujiro and Yamada Saburo. See Yujiro Hayami and Saburo Yamada, "Agricultural Productivity at the Beginning of Industrialization," in *Agriculture and Economic Growth: Japan's Experience*, ed. Kazushi Ohkawa, Bruce F. Johnston, and Hiromitsu Kaneda (Princeton, 1970); versus Yujiro Hayami and Saburo Yamada, *The Agricultural Development of Japan* (Tokyo, 1991).

able features to explain growth. Here is a case where specific individuals (and their students) have really moved quite far along a single line of argument over the years from a convergence to a divergence model, suggesting that the two paradigms are not exactly opposites. These are all economists who are disciplinarily committed to a universalist paradigm, so it is particularly interesting to see them move toward a Japan-is-unique framing.

Their search for a unique modernity involved other elements as well. Recently published Japanese scholarship stressed, for example, the ways in which economic development in Japan was marked by cooperation rather than competition, attention to quality rather than quantity, and technology geared toward diversity rather than standardization. These analyses were much more nuanced and historically sensitive than were the older ones and are probably better history. Indeed, they paralleled recent work on Europe that has shown how varied economic development was on that continent and even within regions of the archetypal case itself, England.[19] Unless the Japanese studies are integrated with similar analyses of European or American regional and temporal variation, however, they often serve to reinforce the idea that Japan alone deviated from an otherwise standard path of development.

Another trend in Japanese scholarship over the last two decades has emphasized the history of local places and common people. It celebrated a different kind of modernity, based less on rationality and bureaucratic systems than on the emotional closeness of the village community and the common good sense of ordinary people. That work has spanned the political spectrum in Japan. For example, the "people's history" movement of the 1970s turned attention to the local, the particular, and the many variations within Japanese society in part as a way of empowering local activists. It celebrated the community values of peasant villages but was consciously deployed against a monolithic idea of Japanese culture and specifically was anti-elite. Thus, it repudiated prewar dogma, rejecting unified theories of historical development for Japan as a unit as well as for humankind. It also mirrored contemporary trends in American political and academic life toward "small is beautiful" campaigns and social history based on oral interviews, a rarely noted parallel. Like their American counterparts, those efforts often evolved out of the left wing and counterculture. Yet this work, too, when developed within a larger context of assumptions about Japanese "groupishness" versus American individualism, could underline the "Japaneseness" of a local community rather than its

19. Nishikawa Shunsaku and Saito Osamu, "The Economic History of the Restoration Period," and Yoshida Mitsukuni, "The Restoration and the History of Technology," both in *Meiji Ishin: Restoration and Revolution*, ed. Nagai Michio and Miguel Urritia (Tokyo, 1985), 175–91, 192–204; Tessa Morris-Suzuki, "Sericulture and the Origins of Japanese Industrialization," *Technology and Culture* 33 (January 1992): 101–21; Chie Nakane and Shinzaburō Oishi, eds., *Tokugawa Japan: The Social and Economic Antecedents of Modern Japan* (Tokyo, 1990). Charles Sabel and Jonathan Zeitlin, "Historical Alternatives to Mass Production: Politics, Markets and Technology in Nineteenth-Century Industrialization," *Past and Present* 108 (August 1985): 133–76.

smallness, organization along affective ties, complex relation to a metropolitan community, or other qualities that characterized local communities in many parts of the world. Certainly, some Japanese nationalists in public life chose to interpret the "people's history" in this way.[20]

Indeed, a more nationalist thesis, that Japanese society as a whole is fundamentally different from its Western counterpart, was more widely disseminated at scholarly and popular levels in Japan. Several very influential scholars have argued that uniquely Japanese forms of culture and social organization were the foundation for an unparalleled modernity (or even postmodernity). Others based similar claims on racial or linguistic identity. The idea that Japanese really are different was, if anything, a more closely held belief among Japanese than Americans. An entire genre dedicated to this principle, called Nihonjinron studies, stuffed whole bookcases in nearly every Japanese bookstore. Harumi Befu, who has analyzed that literature in detail, pointed out that commonly accepted ideas about racial and linguistic identity (and, less plausibly, physical peculiarities of the Japanese brain and intestines) operated to unify Japanese in much the same way that the national flag, national anthem, and royal family did in other countries but could not in Japan because of the close association of those symbols with defeat in World War II. This difference paradigm, then, curbed the kind of thinking that predominated in Japanese academic circles in 1960.[21]

That more nationalist strain of divergence thought also took hold in the United States and Europe, eclipsing modernization theory. More scholarly

20. J. Victor Koschmann, ed., *Authority and the Individual in Japan* (Tokyo, 1978), esp. Sakuta Keiichi, "The Controversy over Community and Autonomy," 220–49; Irokawa Daikichi, *The Culture of the Meiji Period* (Princeton, 1985); Carol Gluck, "The People in History: Recent Trends in Japanese Historiography," *Journal of Asian Studies* 38 (November 1978): 25–50. Kathleen Neils Conzen presented suggestive parallels from within the American tradition in her analysis of the way that nineteenth-century German Americans saw themselves as different from their neighbors because of their greater love of nature, of high culture, and of the family rather than the lone individual. "Ethnicity as Festive Culture: Nineteenth-Century German America on Parade," in Sollers, ed., *The Invention of Ethnicity*, 44–76. See also Lawrence Olson, *Ambivalent Moderns: Portraits of Japanese Cultural Identity* (Savage, MD, 1992); and for analyses of related intellectual thought H. D. Harootunian, "Visible Discourses/Invisible Ideologies," in *Postmodernism and Japan*, Special Issue of *South Atlantic Quarterly* 87 (Summer 1988): 453–60.

21. Murakami Yasusuke, Kumon Shumpei, and Satō Seizaburō, *Bunmei to shite no ie-shakai* (Tokyo, 1979)–translated in condensed form as Murakami Yasusuke, "Ie Society as a Pattern of Civilization," *Journal of Japanese Studies* 10 (Summer 1984): 281–363–is one influential example. See also Murakami Yasusuke, "Ie Society as a Pattern of Civilization: Response to Criticism," ibid. 11 (Summer 1985): 401–21. Harumi Befu, "Symbols of nationalism and *Nihonjinron*," in *Ideology and Practice in Modern Japan*, ed. Roger Goodman and Kirsten Refsing (London, 1992), 26–46; Harumi Befu, "Nationalism and *Nihonjinron*," in *Cultural Nationalism in East Asia: Representations and Identity*, ed. idem (Berkeley, 1993), 107–35; Harumi Befu, "Internationalization of Japan and *Nihon Bunkaron*," in *The Challenge of Japan's Internationalization: Organization and Culture*, ed. Hiroshi Mannari and Harumi Befu (Tokyo, 1983). See also Peter N. Dale, *The Myth of Japanese Uniqueness* (London, 1986). Right now, this concept is being updated as the Asian model rather than the Japanese model, particularly in Singapore, where the judicial sentence of caning has become a vehicle for the argument that authoritarianism contributes to economic growth and political stability.

formulations focused on Japan's fundamentally different social organization, while more journalistic ones tended to emphasize culture. The difference argument was epitomized by a sociologist, Ezra Vogel, and a political scientist, Chalmers Johnson, who both argued that the major institutions of Japanese society, especially industrial and government-business relations, are fundamentally different from Western ones. Vogel made the competition with the United States explicit in the title of his 1979 book, *Japan as Number One*, while Johnson shifted the entire English-language debate with his 1982 depiction of the twentieth-century Japanese government as a "developmental state," rather than the "market-rational system" that evolved in the United States. He stressed such things as government efforts to cultivate a high savings rate and develop an industrial policy to explain Japan's economic performance and dismissed cultural arguments as irrelevant fictions. Another leading sociologist, R. P. Dore, has published similar arguments. Patterns of social organization that developed in the twentieth century, rather than ancient tradition, formed the basis of their argument for a different kind of modernity. These authors worked hard to distinguish themselves from those, such as James Abbeglen, who argued as early as 1958 that Japanese management had successfully retained Tokugawa-era paternalism and so avoided the labor strife that plagued Western corporations. They have not been very successful, particularly after the distinction was blurred again in more popularized versions in the 1980s.[22]

The main reason why the institution-culture distinction blurred so easily, however, was that the proponents of both arguments shared the same goal. They all went beyond identifying specific practices (whether institutional or cultural) as unique to Japan; they also assigned larger causal meaning for those practices. They not only argued that Japan is more a group society and the United States more an individualistic one but also used that observation as a springboard to *explain* such large phenomena as differences in rates of economic growth and the low and declining crime rate in postwar Japan. Those differences were then used in two ways: to predict international

22. The leading English-language surveys of Japanese political economy in the early 1970s and the 1980s exemplify this shift as well. See Hugh Patrick and Henry Rosofsky, eds., *Asia's New Giant: How the Japanese Economy Works* (Washington, 1976); and the three-volume series *The Political Economy of Japan*, ed. Yasusuke Murakami and Hugh Patrick (Stanford, 1987, 1989, 1992). See also Chalmers Johnson, *MITI and the Japanese Miracle* (Stanford, 1982); and Ezra Vogel, *Japan as Number One* (Cambridge, MA, 1979). One of the reasons Johnson gives for Japan's difference is its late-developer status (after Gerschenkron). Although this is a status that theoretically links Japan to other late developers, it has become a factor that sets Japan apart from all Western countries in most analyses. R. P. Dore, *Taking Japan Seriously: A Confucian Perspective on Leading Economic Issues* (London, 1987). James Abbeglen, *The Japanese Factory* (Glencoe, IL, 1958). See Koji Taira's brilliant critique of Abbeglen, which points out the absurdity of thinking about a highly developed economic system such as postwar Japan in terms of preindustrial values. *Economic Development and Cultural Change* 10 (January 1962): 150–68. James Fallows, *More Like Us* (New York, 1989); idem, "The Japanese are Different," *Atlantic Monthly* 258 (September 1986): 35–41. Karel van Wolferen, *The Enigma of Japanese Power* (New York, 1989).

relations between Japan and the United States (and Europe) and also to establish justifications for certain kinds of behavior in both Japan and the United States. It is this aspect of their work that is both most influential and most troubling.

Inevitably, this assertion of essential difference – whether based in modern social institutions or premodern culture – was meant to have implications for contemporary economic and political relations between Japan and the Western nations whenever it was invoked. The debate was driven by the same concern in Japan, where, probably, the majority of Japanese today believe that a racial sensitivity to nature, combined with a mastery of science, does determine the contemporary yen surplus.[23] The contrast with the West is revealed by the subjects nearly always chosen for study: government-business collaboration; labor-management cooperation; respect for authority, including teachers, police officers, and male househeads; and economic nationalism. Discussions of those Japanese issues instantly became discussions of fundamental and non-negotiable difference – with obvious implications for foreign relations directly. Moreover, these sweeping statements about Japanese society always carried with them some kind of model for appropriate national behavior in the world. Although those models always exaggerated the contrast between Japan and the West, they were sometimes presented as positive and sometimes as negative. For example, Japanese labor relations can be seen as an incredibly repressive system, which destroys individual autonomy, or as essential to capitalist development. It has been presented both ways both at home and abroad.

Similarly, the characterization of bureaucratic rationalization as the key to modernization – a common feature of modernization and the "developmental state" wing of divergence theory – can be dangerous even when it is admiring. Many tomes in both English and Japanese have celebrated the efforts of a small group of elite leaders in creating the postwar Japanese economic "miracle machine." Older works tended to do so within a comparative framework, more recent ones in order to contrast Japan to the West. Most of them wildly overstated elite farsightedness; but, more importantly, they suggested that economic prosperity occurred because Japanese elites were uniquely free to work out problems in a purely technical or even intuitive way without the need to respond to political pressure. By suggesting that the sources of economic growth sprang from the elite's ability to prevent open discussion of important issues, many writers on Japan have gone a long way to discredit democracy. This argument taken to its logical conclusion suggests, conversely, that pluralist civil society is the source of economic decline.[24]

Interestingly, strong empirical evidence that Japanese social consensus,

---

23. Ishihara Shintarō. "Danko 'No' to iu beki jōken" [The circumstances under which Japan must say a firm "no"] *Bungei Shunjū* (August 1991): 132.

24. See Laura Hein, "Growth versus Success: Japan's Economic Policy in Historical Perspective," in *Postwar Japan as History*, ed. Andrew Gordon (Berkeley, 1993), 99–122.

when it appeared, was hard won and needed continual renewing, failed to dent the overall framework of divergence theory. For example, the valiant labors of historians of industrial relations, such as Sumiya Mikio, conclusively demonstrated that Japan's system was in no way traditional and can much more easily be explained in very modernist (and even class-warfare) terms. While the practical, contested, compromised, and often renegotiated nature of industrial relations is now accepted wisdom among labor experts, their work rarely has been incorporated into larger theories. This seems a serious omission, since industrial relations provided an original foundation stone for most divergence theories and a crucial touchstone for evaluations of backwardness within modernization theory.[25]

THE LATE 1980S: FROM JAPAN AS MODEL TO JAPAN AS MENACE

In the last decade, the main trend in Western studies of Japan was a shift from largely positive evaluations within the basic assumption of fundamental difference to largely negative ones. Often those studies built on Japanese analyses—both critical and self-congratulatory. Indeed, recent theories of Japan's difference as articulated outside of Japan have begun to evoke older theories of Japan's backwardness in eerie ways. In the early and mid-1980s, divergence theorists mainly wrote about Japan's efficient manufacturing sector and how difference helped create economic growth. They argued that difference explained efficiency and economic success in some absolute sense. That emphasis shifted in the late 1980s after more work was published on Japan's inefficient sectors, such as farm policy, retail, and finance. Suddenly, difference seemed to explain insularity (inefficiency as a deliberate barrier to foreigners) and irrationality (acceptance of priorities that do not seem cost-effective).

Not coincidentally, the revaluation of Japan's difference as menacing appeared with a fear of economic domination by Japan in the United States, Canada, and Europe. By 1990 the dominant description of Japan was that it played by different rules and was winning a war that began with trade and ended with cultural domination. The image of vast economic strength *incorporated* the critique that not all aspects of Japan are economically rational. This insight (true of all individuals and societies) could be most usefully used to introduce the existence of conflict and political difference within Japan and to note the similarity of those lines of conflict to other societies. Instead, it most commonly was used to incorporate ideas of irrationality into our picture of the unique economic giant. Two journalists, James Fal-

25. Sumiya Mikio, "Development of the Lifelong Employment System," *Developing Economies* 4 (December 1966): 499–515; Solomon B. Levine, *Industrial Relations in Postwar Japan* (Urbana, 1958). For recent work that acknowledges this material but still fails to incorporate it see William Chapman, *Inventing Japan: The Making of a Postwar Civilization* (New York, 1991), esp. 111, 118.

lows, *Atlantic Monthly* editor and author of *More Like Us*, and Karel Van Wolferen, Dutch correspondent in Japan and author of *The Enigma of Japanese Power*, have been most influential in disseminating this view. Those authors argued that not only Japan's social organization but also the entire contemporary culture differs fundamentally from those of the West–in ways that make Japan dangerous to others. Fallows bluntly rejected universalism in explaining his view of the greatest misconception that Americans hold about Japan: "that it is fundamentally like the United States; that it is modern and must be like the United States; and that the more time passes the more like us they will become. That is a deep error in my view." Japan became a juggernaut out of control: Van Wolferen argued (in a Pearl Harbor anniversary piece) that Japanese-U.S. conflict would likely develop out of "Japan's single-minded, politically driven and evidently unstoppable economic expansion. . . . Japan has no center of political accountability." Previously sanguine scholars, too, have been swept up by the new pessimism. For example, by 1987 Chalmers Johnson had recast his economic "miracle" as an economic outcast.[26] This is modernity untempered by a (Western) sense of moderation or balance.

Again, the cultural and social differences were immediately used to predict dire political and economic consequences–that is, fundamental incompatibility. The sense of menacing difference came through most clearly in analyses of Japanese politics, striking both for their lack of empirical support and for the unwillingness of the analysts to consider cross-cultural parallels. Once again, the problem was set up to explain nationwide Japanese divergence (tied to "tradition") from the Western norm. As such, it closely resembled modernization theory in its assignment of all negative features to a non-Western identity, although recent analysts were more pessimistic about Japan's capacity to "grow out of" its differences. In 1960, Robert E. Ward wrote a classic article that reified ideas about traditional and modern within the modernization paradigm. He compared levels of deference to local political bosses in rural and urban Okayama Prefecture as a measure of the penetration of democracy from the city into the countryside. Ward argued that authoritarianism was a rural and democracy an urban phenomenon in a simplistic assumption that rural communities were closer to the past, confusing geography with history.[27]

---

26. Quote is from *Japan Times Weekly*, 3–9 May 1993, 13. Karel van Wolferen, *New York Times*, 2 December 1991, op-ed page. Chalmers Johnson, "How to Think about Economic Competition from Japan," *Journal of Japanese Studies* 13 (Summer 1987): 415–28.

27. Robert E. Ward, "Urban-Rural Differences and the Process of Political Modernization in Japan: A Case Study," *Economic Development and Cultural Change* 9 (October 1960): 135–66. But note the very sophisticated rebuttal of this approach in the same journal: John W. Bennett, "Economic Aspects of a Boss-Henchman System in the Japanese Forestry Industry," ibid. 7 (October 1958): 13–30. For more on history transposed as geography see Kären Wigen, "The Geographic Imagination in Early Modern Japanese History: Retrospect and Prospect," *Journal of Asian Studies* 51 (February 1992): 3–29.

Precisely the same confusion appeared in the newer paradigm, with an added psychological twist. Recent "common wisdom" about Japan is that it is an apolitical society. That lack of interest in politics was attributed to premodern vestiges by academics Richardson and Flanagan, in *Politics in Japan*, and popularized by journalists. William Chapman devoted an entire chapter to the problem of why Japanese see politics as unconnected to themselves or "the game across the street." Similarly, Karel van Wolferen blasted Japan for its avoidance of politics and political process, arguing that, instead, political power is represented in Japan by a "truncated pyramid" with no clear accountability anywhere. Both authors contrasted Japanese apathy to American political activism, despite such statistics as far higher voting rates in Japan. Van Wolferen tied the apathy to both the manipulative structures of contemporary power in Japan (again, bizarrely arguing that such arrangements are unique to Japan) and to the legacy of feudalism, when political dissent was harshly punished. (Dissent was not tolerated in the 1930s either, but the contrast with Europe is harder to sustain for that decade.) He argued that postwar Japan has no "civil society" and is totally "managed" – and that this is what makes it different from the Western countries.[28]

This is yet another argument that has floated free of its original moorings. Van Wolferen's gloomy political analysis of Japan actually echoed (and was partly derived from) older universalist analyses by Japanese scholars, notably Maruyama Masao.[29] Just as John W. Hall's analysis of Tokugawa Japan has become the basis for arguments about a unique path to modernity, this argument has been lifted out of its original framework rather than reworked internally. Maruyama identified twentieth-century Japanese society as insufficiently politicized in early postwar writings. He argued that the tiny space left for civil society in prewar Japan by emperor-state authority not only contributed to World War II but also was an impediment to Japanese modernity (rather than an emblem of it). He criticized Japan as insufficiently modern but not uniquely so; he also cautioned Americans and

28. Chapman, *Inventing Japan*, draws heavily on the work of Bradley M. Richardson and Scott C. Flanagan, *Politics in Japan* (Boston, 1984). Van Wolferen, Enigma of Japanese Power.

29. Masao Maruyama, *Thought and Behavior.* Van Wolferen follows Maruyama's worries and analysis of prewar Japan in this regard but diverges in his claim that diffuse authoritarianism intensified in the postwar period. Many Japanese scholars struggle with the problem of "managed society" in Japan and elsewhere. See Shunsuke Tsurumi, *A Cultural History of Postwar Japan, 1945–1980* (London, 1987); Watanabe Osamu, "*Yutaka na shakai*" *Nihon no Kōzō* [The structure of Japan's "affluent society"] (Tokyo, 1990); and Rokuro Hidaka, *The Price of Affluence: Dilemmas of Contemporary Japan* (Tokyo, 1980). For Masao Maruyama's views see "Fascism – Some Problems: A Consideration of its Political Dynamics" and "Politics and Man in the Contemporary World," both in *Thought and Behavior*, 157–76, 321–48. Many scholars have pointed out the contrast between presurrender and postwar politics but still see Japan as sui generis in today's world. For example, see articles by Masataka Kosaka, "The Showa Era (1926–1989)," Chikashi Moriguchi, "Rice and Melons – Japanese Agriculture in the Showa Era," and Michio Muramatsu, "Bringing Politics back into Japan," all in *Showa: The Japan of Hirohito*, ed. Carol Gluck and Stephen R. Graubard (New York, [1990] 1992), 27–48, 131–40, 141–54, in addition to works cited earlier.

Europeans that McCarthyism and suppression of antinuclear activists were similar barriers to modernity. One possible move for his intellectual heirs would be to discuss the constraints on political debate in Japan in tandem with similar ones elsewhere (a timid press, ubiquitous lobbyists, huge campaign war chests maintained by legislative incumbents, to name three). A few Japanese scholars have done so, but they struggle against the tide. Having embraced the idea of Japanese difference, their colleagues have few resources with which to rebut the idea that Japan's political problems are uniquely dangerous.

This was not the picture that Western social scientists drew of Japan in the early 1960s. In those days, few American scholars agreed with Maruyama. Rather, they found Japan to be a far more politicized place than the United States. David and Evelyn Riesman, visiting Japan in 1961, commented in their diary that "In comparison with the United States, a large number [of Japanese] read the newspapers and follow political events, even when they reject politics – they start reading the papers very young." Robert Jay Lifton, in an argument for Japan's laggard modernity, explained the intensity of student involvement in politics as a peculiarity of Japanese culture and a way of transposing psychology into sociology or searching for "self-expression via the group."[30] He interpreted Japanese politicization as a sign of group immaturity, exactly reversing the current argument, although not the hierarchy of maturity.

Those observers were right about one thing: The sense that people can change their society through political behavior was very widely shared in Japan at that time. That attitude characterized early postwar Japan far more than it does either the United States or Japan today. A trend toward depoliticization and apathy has characterized *both* societies in the last two decades.[31] It is striking that the memory of this sea change in Japan disappeared along with the change itself, again naturalizing Japanese difference and placing it in spatial rather than historical terms. In other words, the only continuity is the assumption that all Japanese share a unique problem, not the problem itself. In both eras, scholars explained away political friction within Japan and at the same time asserted its inevitability between Japan and the United States.

Meanwhile, in Japan, Maruyama's critics also have embraced analyses of

30. David Riesman and Evelyn Thompson Riesman, *Conversations in Japan: Modernization, Politics, and Culture* (New York, 1967), 18. Robert Jay Lifton, "Youth in Postwar Japan," in *The Challenge of Youth*, ed. Erik H. Erikson (New York, 1963), 277 (originally published as *Youth: Change and Challenge*, 1961).

31. Japan's political upheaval in 1993–94 was almost always described in the United States as a story of how the more things change in Japan the more they remain inscrutable. A more comparative approach would have immediately brought to mind Italy. The collapse of the Cold War revealed the way that the international systems (more specifically, CIA money) sustained the two political structures in very similar ways, leading to very similar implosion of the old Right and Left into a politically bankrupt coalition.

Japan as different, rejecting only the idea that Japan is inferior. Their main audience is domestic, although they write for foreign consumption as well. In fact, some of the most active academic advocates for Japan's unique ability to retain a cultural-social essence from prehistoric times to the present also acted as close advisers to the conservative Japanese government through the 1980s and 1990s. Thus, their depoliticized and dehistoricized characterizations of Japanese life were used explicitly to forge a political consensus around specific government policies. Prominent among those policies has been a more forceful stance on international affairs generally, including a more independent military presence.[32]

The main way that these narratives of Japanese difference affected international relations is more subtle, however. They transformed foreign criticism of Japanese government (or officially sanctioned) activity into attacks on the essence of Japanese society itself. Thus, pressure to end whaling, for example, by this alchemy, became an assault on the entire Japanese culinary tradition. Arguments about extinction of marine mammal species often were perceived in Japan as a mere smoke screen for the real battle over the comparative worth of Western and Japanese cultural traditions. This framing created an impossible dilemma for Japanese marine biologists or ecologically minded citizens who could not express concern for the future of whales (or sea turtles or coral reefs) without being tainted by a faint whiff of treason. Similarly, Japan's legal barriers to rice imports were routinely justified on the grounds that rice growing is at the heart of modern Japanese society.[33]

Arguments that posited inexplicable political harmony within Japan and tied it to inevitable friction with the West enjoyed a remarkable vogue in the United States, as well. For example, in his best-selling book, Fallows devoted an entire chapter to the argument that the Japanese have a cultural propensity to favor producers over consumers and derived this pattern from traditional rice-growing culture. According to Fallows, the group-oriented agricultural tradition predisposed all Japanese to accept a skewed tax and subsidy system that favored farmers. It may be irrational, it may be traditional, but, he believed, it is Japanese.[34]

What is most disturbing is the unsubstantiated argument that the societies of two thousand years ago were carried over in some essential form into

---

32. Murakami, Kumon, and Satō, *Bunmei to shite no ie-shakai;* Harootunian, "Visible Discourses/Invisible Ideologies," for the political activism and its implications.

33. From 1994 the Japanese government did loosen its restrictions on rice imports. Probably the emphasis on rice as the cultural well-spring will diminish somewhat as that political battle recedes into the past. But see Emiko Ohnuki-Tierney, *Rice as Self: Japanese Identities through Time* (Princeton, 1993).

34. Fallows, "The Japanese Talent for Order," in *More Like Us.* See also Lester Thurow, *Head to Head: The Coming Economic Battle among Japan, Europe, and America* (New York, 1992), which states in the first chapter that it is wrong to think in terms of a contest among nations and that we all benefit from strong trade partners but is written entirely within the idiom of head-to-head conflict.

the 1990s. Fallows's "eternal" rice paddies were only invoked to make the differences between the American and Japanese systems seem so long-standing as to be unconnected to any specific political and economic problems today. They were not actually relevant to the *political* function of rice subsidies, Fallows's topic. This ahistorical position also forced Fallows to reject what seems on all counts a far more compelling explanation for the phenomenon of high agricultural subsidies–political dogfighting. That is, the subsidies were the product of a scramble by the Liberal Democratic party for a loyal political constituency, concretely manifested in lavish agricultural subsidies and casual tax enforcement for small businesses; these benefits explicitly were not extended to urban wage workers, the core voters of the Socialist party.

Of course, such a politics-based analysis is incompatible with the more fundamental assumptions that culture drives Japanese life and that rice is a unifying force in Japan. First, it reveals that rice subsidies have developed out of postwar politics rather than tradition. Evidence for this assessment comes from the fact that the prewar story is quite different from the contemporary one. The Japanese government responded to the rice riots of 1918 (commonly thought of as a strong statement of consumer demand) by stepping up imports of rice from Korea and Taiwan. As Michael Lewis showed, that move helped depress domestic agricultural wages in Japan and decrease the degree of food independence of the home islands.[35] While Lewis's research showed that prewar consumers preferred domestic rice, he also demonstrated that government policy gave little consideration to their desires. Rice subsidies–a historically specific postwar policy–were misrepresented by Fallows as an aspect of timeless "Japan." Moreover, the postwar settlement (like the prewar one) encompassed and brokered political and economic conflicts among groups of Japanese rather than reflecting a national consensus to protect rice producers.

In fact, Japanese practice is not only logical, it is also familiar. Rice subsidies performed a very similar political function in Japan, as have sugar, tobacco, beet-sugar, and even rice subsidies in the United States. In both nations, economic irrationality is a function of history rather than culture. The political clout of farmers is out of all proportion to their *current* economic contribution in both economies. In a strict market definition, neither place operates completely rationally and so neither has achieved full modernity in the modernization theorists' sense. Both countries not only subsidize farmers for political and social reasons, but they also are sites of very similar anxieties about the rapid disappearance of agriculture and the possible ill effects of rural decline on national community values. Those domestic anxi-

35. Michael Lewis, *Rioters & Citizens: Mass Protest in Imperial Japan* (Berkeley, 1990), esp. 10–15, 31–36, 246. Note also Charles Horioka's work on the extremely low level of savings in most prewar households, in "Consuming and Saving," in Gordon, ed., *Postwar Japan as History*, 259–92.

eties might usefully be compared to the contemporary United States rather than simply exoticized as unique to growers of *Orzya sativa japonica*. Again, the contrast is painted in the wrong dimensions.

In a different kind of example, the free-floating nature of assessments that transpose political conflict into unique cultural propensities are visible when similar phenomena are analyzed in a completely different way elsewhere. Consider the following explanation by an unnamed American diplomat of widespread tax evasion among love-hotel operators in Argentina. "Argentines never have paid taxes in part because the national character is egocentric. They don't look after each other. They think of themselves first." The facts of tax evasion in the cash-rich, secretive love-hotel industry are identical, but it is almost impossible to imagine applying the diplomat's comments to Japan. This dissonance suggests that not only dces the concept of national character still determine foreign policy around the world, but it also acts to blind us to institutional similarities across national boundaries.[36]

Thus, while modernization theory minimized problems within all modern capitalist economies, divergence theory either defined Japan as a society without serious problems or traced the ones it recognized firmly back to Japan's unique social practices. As John Dower pointed out twenty years ago,[37] one of the problems with modernization theory is that it inadequately problematized institutional repression. Earlier and more sanguine Western examples of divergence theory, such as Vogel's *Japan as Number One*, certainly shared that weakness. In contrast, van Wolferen stressed institutional repression as a key characteristic of modern Japan, while Fallows emphasized dangerous irrationality–and both attributed those faults to uniquely long-lived premodern values. In other words, they marked as problems practices that they saw as characteristic of Japan alone, not other modern societies and explicitly not modernity itself.

Japanese have also contributed to the particularist analytical framework in the last decade by creating a similar story of menacing difference about the United States. In an exact inversion of the arguments described above, America's social and economic problems frequently have been described by Japanese as a product of our very different culture and thus not of shared economic or political institutional structures. Specifically, prominent Japanese writers regularly attribute economic decline to racial plurality, excessive individualism, and lack of self-discipline. If multiculturalism, rather than dilemmas internal to capitalism, produced American economic troubles, then Japanese can indeed breathe easier.

Indeed, the issue of race breaks the surface of debate over and over again. It is only just barely submerged below discussion of the homogeneity of Japan and the multiculturalism of America. Emphasis on this point in Japan

---

36. *Chicago Tribune*, 19 October 1992.

37. Dower, ed., *Origins of the Modern Japanese State*, 74.

renders the rest of the world dangerous and unpredictable for Japanese—further patrolling the boundaries of their group identity. High Japanese government officials regularly let slip their assumptions that too many African Americans, Hispanics, and Jews have caused Western cultural and economic decline. This has translated into policy as well: American open immigration laws and West Germany's "guest worker" policy have been explicitly cited as negative examples justifying minuscule quotas for Vietnamese boat people and nearly unscalable barriers to legal immigration from Asia.[38]

Americans, too, seem astonishingly ready to accept the idea that racial homogeneity has contributed to economic growth in postwar Japan. Just as Asian Americans have been presented by social scientists as the "model minority" for African Americans and Hispanics, Japan works as a countermodel for America by associating economic strength with racial homogeneity. Here is one of the precise and most powerful ways in which American anxieties about domestic race relations reappears transposed as international relations. (This slippage between domestic and international concerns also helps explain why Japanese and Americans alike have such difficulty distinguishing between Japanese citizens and Japanese-Americans.) Japan represents the possibility that capitalism and democracy are only weakly and perhaps negatively linked. In this scenario, (American) democracy and racial equality are pitted against (Japanese) wealth as though each flourished best without the presence of the other. Thus, it was entirely in keeping with the core message of Michael Crichton's mega-bestseller *Rising Sun* to cast an African-American man in the lead role of the movie version.[39] We do not have to ask ourselves why our economic system has failed so many Americans if prosperity was a necessary trade-off for political equality of opportunity.

Difference theory has also contributed to the remarkable tenacity of one other problem in both America and Japan. Notably, war imagery will not go away. While belligerence was seen as residual in modernization theory (and thus insufficiently recognized), in divergence theory it was seen as essentially Japanese (or American). Thus, people outside Japan continually blurred the line between the actions of Japanese warriors, both samurai and World War II soldiers, and of businessmen. Journalistic language constantly

38. See Hammond and Hein, "Multiculturalism in Japanese Perspective." As John Russell has shown for African Americans, the specifics of Japanese racism are directly derived from Caucasian beliefs about African Americans and should not be exoticized either. "Race and Reflexivity: The Black Other in Contemporary Japanese Mass Culture," *Cultural Anthropology* 6 (February 1991): 3–25; idem, "Narratives of Denial: Racial Chauvinism and the Black Other in Japan," *Japan Quarterly* 38 (October–December 1991): 416–28.

39. See Stephen Steinberg, *The Ethnic Myth: Race, Ethnicity, and Class in America*, 2d ed. (Boston, 1989), for the model minority. Michael Crichton, *The Rising Sun* (New York, 1992), relied heavily on the work of Chalmers Johnson, James Fallows, and Karel van Wolferen, as is acknowledged in the final pages.

indulged in military metaphor to discuss economic issues. For one of numerous examples, consider the Luckovitch cartoon: "December 7, 1941: Japan bombs Pearl Harbor/December 7, 1991: Japan buys Pearl Harbor." Meanwhile, in Japan the image of the United States as a permanent warmonger is perennially in fashion. Thus, Ishihara Shintarō is seen as bravely asserting Japan's equal rights by many of his compatriots while the Persian Gulf War frequently was treated as only one recent bloodthirsty episode in American history. And the image of a "second coming of the Black Ships" is still regularly invoked by many Japanese to explain U.S.-Japanese relations.[40] Warmongering for both peoples has become a transhistorical characteristic of the other.

PROBLEMS OF ONE TRADITION, ONE WEST, ONE JAPAN

Indeed, there are a number of serious problems raised by a notion of uniquely Japanese modernity despite its popularity on both shores of the Pacific. Interestingly, some of the most important are identical to those inherent in the radically different modernization theory. First, both the modernization and divergence paradigms deployed the same extremely static notion of the "traditional" and idealized one of "modern." Thus, the idea that Japanese tradition can flourish unchanged in the context of twentieth-century life is remarkably persistent. Moreover, both are completely comfortable with the assumption that "traditional" and "modern" elements coexist in a single society without careful reflection on the fact that tradition cannot persist in some sort of primordial form when stripped of its historical context. None of the authors, whether modernization or divergence theorists, can demonstrate – as opposed to assert – that tradition actually explains contemporary behavior. That is, practices that are situated within some corner of Japanese culture are assumed to represent it in its entirety.[41]

Second, both convergence and divergence theory have employed a remarkably uncritical and undifferentiated vision of "the West." In contrast to conceptualizations of Japan, this image has remained unchanged in its broad outlines throughout the postwar era. Not only were Western Europe and the United States treated as a single unit, but the inhabitants of those geographical regions were routinely confused with an idealized society and

40. See George Friedman and Meredith LeBard, *The Coming War with Japan* (New York, 1991), for a recent example of American fears. The enormous popularity of the book in Japanese translation attests to Japanese ones. For the Gulf War see Steven Weisman, "Japanese and Americans Struggling to Overcome Their Mutual Resentment," *New York Times*, 3 December 1991. For use of the 1853 Black Ships incident as a determinant of subsequent U.S.-Japanese relations (described as rape leading to psychological injury) see Kishida Shū in *AERA*, 15 September 1992. For Luckovitch see *Chicago Tribune*, 13 November 1989.

41. For useful discussions of these issues see Cohen, *Discovering History in China*, esp. 58. See James Clifford, *The Predicament of Culture*; Thomas McCarthy, "Doing the Right Thing in Cross-Cultural Representation," *Ethics* 102 (April 1992): 635–49, for this distinction.

culture. Again, the ideal was distinctly Weberian in its focus on rationality and bureaucratic organization. This fictive West was also generally purported to be universalistic in its values and more attentive to the needs of the individual than the group. Historical, geographic, and ideological divisions were subsumed into a shakily constructed, single Western tradition, falsely suggesting that there has been a unified transhistorical debate to which all Western thinkers have contributed. As philosophers such as Alasdair MacIntyre have argued, most of the great debates inside "the West" today (for example, liberty vs. equality) stem from divergent and unresolvable parts of the European intellectual tradition. (MacIntyre actually provides a sadly apt example for this essay's general thesis. Otherwise a discerning scholar, he resorted to astonishing generalization and polarization of East versus West when confronted with Japan.)[42]

Third, a very similar flattening and stereotyping of the internal dynamics of Japanese society took place when analysts remained wedded to the framework of "the West" and "Japan," no matter whether the relationship was seen as one of comparison, catch-up, or contrast. Most notably, dissent and conflict within Japanese society was made invisible. This was particularly true when dissent was phrased as political or economic problems. In the realm of politics, explicitly political activism and "civil society" were presumed aberrations in the Japanese system. In economics, although everyone agreed that Japan had (some kind of) a capitalist economy, questions specific to the workings of that economic system were elided in these formulations just as they were in modernization theory. Postwar Japan has been the site of tremendous debates over fundamental political and economic issues. Those struggles are very hard to recognize within sweeping constructs like "rice civilization versus meat civilization." Issues of gender discrimination were similarly reified despite massive evidence that the current family/household economy pattern is neither traditional nor static.

Fourth, the grand theories – whether comparing or contrasting – made historically specific analyses more difficult. For example, they shut out discussions of Japan's actions in World War II and their legacy. Many Japanese justify Japanese invasions of China, Korea, and Southeast Asia as liberating those territories from Western imperialism. They have been able to elide specific attention to Japanese actions on the Asian continent by emphasizing global East-West conflict. This is a festering subject and very hard to approach knowing that any conclusions will be used to generalize about all Japanese at all times. (I should add, however, that a number of Japanese historians, including Ienaga Saburō, Yoshimi Yoshiaki, and Yoshida Yutaka,

42. Alasdair MacIntyre, *After Virtue: A Study in Moral Theory* (Notre Dame, 1981), esp. 6–11; idem, "Individual and Social Morality in Japan and the United States: Rival Conceptions of the Self," *Philosophy, East and West* 40 (October 1990): 491–97.

have taken on specific questions of Japanese-Asian relations during the twentieth century with impressive intellectual rigor and bravery.)[43]

A final problem with the "unique Japan" approach is that it obscured the many ways in which modern societies are alike everywhere while highlighting only their differences. Certainly, some of the specific institutional forms by which Japanese firms are integrated or police maintain social order are different from those in the United States, but the identification of those differences only provides weak support for the theory that it is those variances that explain specific outcomes. In many other respects, Japanese firms and police officers today operate very much as do their American counterparts. Moreover, emphasis on nationally different institutional structures sometimes obscures the similarity of their grand functions. Frank Upham's work on law ably demonstrates this point. Although he pointed out the specific ways that the legal system operates differently in Japan, he also directed his readers' attention to the fact that, like everywhere else in the rule-bound world, "elites use legal rules and institutions to manage and direct conflict and control change at a social level" in Japan.[44] Just as in the United States, the law is a powerful tool by which economic and political leaders entrenched themselves against other members of their own society. As such, law is always a contested site, revealing the cleavages and inequities of power within societies whether characterized as "groupish" or individualistic.

Strikingly, problems of democracy, capitalism, oppression, and war were elided in the divergence paradigm – precisely the same problems that disappeared from analysis within the quite different framework of modernization theory. This continuity within such resounding difference reveals the extent to which both paradigms have been deployed to justify and create a tradition/history for the status quo at each moment. These ideological continuities suggest how the dominant debate on both sides of the Pacific could travel so rapidly from convergence to divergence theories. The confusion frequently led into arguments that made little sense and ignored most of the facts. No doubt this tendency also helps explain why the divergence arguments, as they painted Japan in more menacing colors, floated full circle and began to sound like modernization theory again.

Despite the shifts from modernization theory to efficient divergence and on to menacing difference, the same problems continued to evade discussion. Japan throughout was defined as different from and sometimes pathological

43. For a recent example, Minister of Justice Shigeto Nagano was forced to step down in May 1994 for publicly stating that Japanese actions in World War II were justified by Western imperialism and that the Nanking massacre was a fabrication. For scholarship see Saburo Ienaga, *The Pacific War: 1931–1945* (New York, 1978); Yoshimi Yoshiaki, "Documenting the Truth: The Japanese Government and the 'Comfort Women' Issue," presented at the Association for Asian Studies conference, Boston, 24 March 1994; Fujiwara Akira, Awaya Kentarō, Yoshida Yutaka, and Yamada Akira, *Tettei kenshō, shōwa tennō "Dokubakuroku"* [The complete and full "monologue" of the Showa Emperor] (Tokyo, 1991).

44. Frank K. Upham, *Law and Social Change in Postwar Japan* (Cambridge, MA, 1987), 1.

to the "normal" working of modern society. The historical transformation from presurrender to contemporary Japan continued to be blurred, just as it was in the modernization paradigm. Equally significant, the extent to which the problems in Japan's political economy resembled those in other industrialized nations disappeared from all these discussions. Analysis of historical trends visible in *both* Japan and the United States are particularly rare. The contemporary problems of growing wealth inequality and political apathy in both societies today, for example, have been recast in a variety of ways, all of which obscured the commonality of the problems.

Many of those changes deserve historical analysis: One obvious candidate is major postwar domestic protest. First, in Japan after World War II and then in the United States after the Vietnam War, both populations became angry at their own governments for having dragged them into a war they could not support and then turned that anger into a more general reevaluation of national priorities. Those moments of "politicalism" in both societies sharply contrast with the contemporary cynicism that has reigned since the Watergate and Lockheed scandals revealed the structural corruption endemic in both nations' capitals. Such an empirically based approach could step away from discussions of tradition or of types of modernity and assume a single, if somewhat jaundiced, overarching contemporary dilemma. Neither of the traditional paradigms of universality or difference really has helped us understand international relations or historical change in a useful and systematic way.

Tension and conflict between the United States and Japan is real, but that fact does not mean the two social systems are incompatible. Conflict is real–but it is as often based on similarity and interaction than it is on difference. It is also located far more squarely within political and economic institutions (rather than social ones) than is generally recognized. Certainly, some institutions of the Japanese economy differ from those in the United States, but these variances could fruitfully be analyzed as contradictions of capitalism, rather than the clash of capitalism with some other system.[45] All too often, trade frictions are assumed to be the result of the differences rather than the similarities of the two systems. Nor is it a case of friction between traditional and modern ideas, as the older paradigm would have it.

Moreover, the current focus on Japan's fundamental difference obscures the growing interpenetration of the American and Japanese economies (and

45. Often Japanese news is presented as unique for no apparent reason, such as the editorial in the *Chicago Tribune*, 2 September 1992, which appeared under the headline "Japan's unique crisis response." The subject was the recently announced antirecession measures by the Japanese government, which mainly consisted of government spending of $87 billion on public projects, such as highways and hospitals. That government measure was based on the absolutely standard Keynesian assumption that government spending can revitalize the private economy. It mirrored actions taken by the U.S. government as recently as 1975. In short, there is nothing in theory, policy, or experience that is unique about the issues discussed in the editorial.

political systems, although at a slower rate). It has become harder and harder to distinguish between Japanese and American products. One American town council faced this problem recently when it patriotically voted to buy John Deere rather than Komatsu equipment but then discovered that the "Japanese" product was made in the United States while the "American" one was not. Similarly, debates rage in rarified policymaking circles over how to define the nationality of a Chrysler car with an engine from Japan. It is also hard to know how to respond to persistent rumors that Honda plans to relocate its corporate headquarters to the United States unless one accepts this interdependence. Not only are Japanese not unique but their economic fortunes are increasingly undifferentiated from ours. Nor is this interdependence likely to disappear.

This observation should not just be left as an ironic twist to the story. The fact that theories of Japan's fundamentally different culture and society have flourished together with these structural changes suggests inattention bordering on a deliberate not knowing–particularly since the most popular theories are built on such flimsy evidence, like the idea that Japanese unanimously and naturally prefer producers to consumers. It is not enough to respond to such developments by calling for more cultural interactions and getting to know each other better. We *are* getting to know each other better, and this idea is still gaining currency. Nearly 11 million Japanese traveled overseas in 1990–the highest number ever–and 3.7 million of them went to the United States. Meanwhile, Americans reciprocated in ever larger numbers.[46] Moreover, the bloody disintegration of Yugoslavia should be reminder enough that cultural familiarity is no guarantee of good neighborliness.

Rather, as inhabitants of the globe in the 1990s, we need to think more explicitly about the ways that we are connected to each other as human beings and citizens of the global village and honestly face the real tensions that this connection–rather than some fundamental difference–creates. It is our interactions within specific international political and economic institutions that need attention, not our failure to communicate through a common set of values. More careful attention to those institutional frameworks perhaps would help both Americans and Japanese exorcise their own domestic anxieties in ways that did not so thoroughly dehumanize each other. Neither Japanese nor Americans can wish their confrontation with the brave new world of modernity–in all its messy historical guises–to the other side of the world.

46. JETRO, *Business Facts & Figures, Nippon '92* (Tokyo, 1992), 158–59, reports that just under 11 million Japanese traveled abroad, of which 3.7 million went to the United States. Idem, *U.S. and Japan in Figures II* (Tokyo 1992), 107, notes that 2.5 million Americans traveled to Japan in 1989.

TAKASHI INOGUCHI

Japan's United Nations peacekeeping and other operations

Japan's participation in peacekeeping operations, broadly defined, began when the Gulf War of 1990-1991[1] ended. Japan sent minesweepers from its Self-Defence Forces to the Gulf as part of a multinational force, led by the United States, whose task it was to punish Iraq, restore Kuwait's territory, and assure peace and innocent passage. The Gulf War was not a United Nations peacekeeping operation. But it is significant that the intervention was conducted in close consultation with the United Nations Security Council. In fact, it was tied much more closely to the United Nations than was the intervention in Korea in the early 1950s when the United States took a far more unilateral initiative once the Security Council had decided that the United Nations should indeed intervene.[2]

Japan participated in the Gulf War without the sanction of the law which was subsequently to guide Japan's participation in all United Nations peacekeeping and other operations.

Senior Vice Rector, United Nations University, Tokyo, and member of the editorial board of *International Journal*.

1 See, for example, Takashi Inoguchi, 'Japan's response to the Gulf crisis, 1990-1991: an analytic overview,' *Journal of Japanese Studies* 17(summer 1991), 257-73; Peter Polomka, 'Japan as peacekeeper: Samurai state or new civilian power?' *Canberra Papers on Strategy and Defense*, no 97(1992); Andrew Bennett, Joseph Lepgold, and Danny Unger, 'Burden-sharing in the Persian Gulf War,' *International Organization* 48(winter 1994), 39-75.

2 Alan James, 'UN peace operations (past, present, and future) and the role of Japan: a British view,' paper presented at the National Institute for Defense Studies, Tokyo, 7-8 November 1994.

Indeed, participation was the trigger for the International Peace Co-operation Law in August 1992 which would legislate Japan's participation in United Nations peacekeeping operations thereafter. Since 1992 there have been a number of such operations: United Nations Angola Verification Mission II (UNAVEM II), United Nations Transitional Authority in Cambodia (UNTAC), United Nations Operation in Mozambique (ONUMOZ), and United Nations Observer Mission in El Salvador (ONUSAL).[3]

As mentioned above, Japan's participation in the Gulf War was not a normal United Nations peacekeeping operation. Although operations in Rwanda-Zaire were normal peacekeeping operations, Japan's participation was as part of the international humanitarian rescue operations conducted under the aegis of the Office of the United Nations High Commissioner for Refugees (UNHCR). In order to see clearly how Japan approaches peacekeeping operations, it is very important first to identify the context in which Japan's participation in United Nations peacekeeping began. This exercise should reveal why Japan has put certain limits on its participation.

In recent years, three major events have come together which have encouraged Japanese participation in United Nations peacekeeping and other operations: (1) post–Cold War uncertainty and probing for new instruments to help bring about order and stability; (2) increasing external demands on Japan to assume global responsibilities commensurate with its prosperity and economic pre-eminence; (3) Japan's confrontation with its debt to history as the fiftieth anniversary of its defeat in World War II drew ever closer.

First, post–Cold War uncertainty means many things to Japan.[4] The most important to my mind is the disappearance

3 Shunji Yanai, 'Law concerning cooperation for United Nations peace-keeping operations and other operations,' *Japanese Annual of International Law*, no 36(1993), 33-75.

4 Takashi Inoguchi, *Japan's Foreign Policy in an Era of Global Change* (London: Pinter 1993).

of the competition between the United States and Russia and its ramifications for security arrangements between the United States and Japan. The Japan-United States Security Treaty is the major instrument under which the United States assures the defence of – and deterrence of aggression against – Japan. Yet some policy-makers and theorists in Japan see the removal of Russia as the main threat to the United States as encouraging the isolationists within the United States to move in the direction of disentangling American security arrangements with Japan. The two major arguments made by those who wish to retain the arrangements are that the Japan-United States Security Treaty is the key to the stability and prosperity of the entire Asia-Pacific region and that it is the 'cap on the bottle' which prevents Japan from re-emerging as a military power.

Japan naturally advances the first argument – as, indeed, does the United States government. But, given the increasingly selective and sometimes prickly conduct of the United States towards the rest of the world, many Japanese leaders are uncertain about how much longer Japan will be able to rely on this agreement. Yet anyone who has the temerity to voice their uncertainty is immediately condemned for encouraging isolationist thinking in the United States.[5]

United Nations peacekeeping is a useful instrument with which to dispel some of this anxiety because it makes an uncertain world a little more certain. As long as United Nations peacekeeping operations are conducted with the approval, encouragement, and sometimes even the participation of the United States, and within the bounds of Japan's constitution – which is widely interpreted as not allowing Japan to use force in the settlement of international disputes – the Japanese government does not have too much to worry about. Needless to say, if American isolationism were to go so far as to deny the utility

5 Inoguchi, *Sekai hendo no mikata* [Global Changes: An Analysis] (Tokyo: Chikuma shobo 1994).

of the United Nations, then this kind of thinking might not help Japan very much.

The worldwide expectations of Japan's ability and willingness to shoulder global responsibilities has risen in parallel with Japan's rise to economic superpower. As long as Japan's huge trade surplus remains, as long as its per-capita gross national product is one of the largest, such expectations are bound to grow. Accordingly, Japan's financial contributions to international institutions such as the United Nations, the World Bank, the International Monetary Fund, and the Asian Development Bank have been steadily increasing. In many cases, Japan's contribution is second only to the United States. In other cases it is on a par with or even exceeds the United States contribution.[6] Japan's official development assistance has also been steadily rising, with similar results.[7] And the recipients of Japanese aid are not only China and Indonesia and other Asian Pacific countries. By 1989 Japan's official development assistance was the largest in every country in South Asia. More importantly, Japan's direct investment in the rest of the world has been accumulating. At the same time, for its own economic and strategic reasons, Japan has been attentive to every corner of the world.

The demands on Japan to play a larger global role did not stop there. They also included some security related roles, as in the Gulf War. Japan vacillated widely between accommodating and rejecting such demands during the Gulf crisis. In the end, the majority view prevailed. That view is reflected in the International Peace Co-operation Law of 1992, which states that, within the bounds of the constitution, Japan should participate in some peacekeeping and other operations under the aegis of the United Nations and in close consultation with the United States. One view, which was presented forcefully during the Gulf crisis, and one which seemed to be preferred by the United

6 Sadako Ogata, 'Shifting power relations in multilateral development banks,' *Journal of International Studies* (Tokyo) no 22(January 1989), 1-25.

7 Ministry of Foreign Affairs, *Japan's ODA: Annual Report 1993* (Tokyo: Association for Promotion of International Cooperation 1994).

States government, favoured the use of Self-Defence Forces for much wider and deeper participation. However, that view subsided once the Gulf War was over.[8]

The fear that Japan might re-emerge as a power to be reckoned with lingers in certain neighbouring countries – the two Koreas, China, and some countries of the Association for South-East Asian Nations (ASEAN), for instance. China does not like the idea of Japan becoming a permanent member of the United Nations Security Council. And the Republic of Korea and the ASEAN countries do not like the idea either if it means that Japan would acquire veto power. The fear also lingers in the United States and in some European countries: for example, the United States postal service had planned a stamp commemorating the dropping of atomic bombs on Japan – at least until the Japanese government protested and the United States Department of State intervened, killing the plan.

There is also a problem with Japan's image over the issue of reparations for 'comfort women,' which has been raised in some Asian countries, in Europe, and in Australia. The Japanese government refuses to pay reparations to individuals. As far as it is concerned, the matter was settled long ago by the peace treaties between Japan and other states; the issue, if it is to be taken up at all, will have to be handled by the private sector.

The issue of nuclear non-proliferation haunted Japan throughout 1994 when North Korea refused to submit its nuclear power stations to the scrutiny of the International Atomic Energy Agency. Fortunately, an agreement was reached between North Korea and the United States in October 1994. The suspicion that not only North Korea but also South Korea and, most importantly, Japan may have nuclear ambitions is widely held by many people in the rest of the world who find it difficult to believe that in the face of a nuclear threat from North Korea either country would not be prepared to strike

8 Ozawa Ichiro, *Nihon kaizo keikaku* [Plan to Reform Japan] (Tokyo: Kodansha 1993).

back. It is well known that Japan has been producing a large amount of plutonium and an advanced rocket.[9]

In order to reduce its debt to history, a number of ideas have been gaining ground. An obvious idea, and one unlikely to meet with much criticism, is to encourage the Japanese to confront their history through a re-examination of that history of war and colonialism, often in joint publications with other Asian historians. Prime Minister Tomiichi Murayama announced in autumn 1994 that the government would establish a library of Asian historical materials so that Japanese and other Asian historians could collaborate on modern Asian history and Japan's role therein.

Secondly, the Japanese government has decided to manufacture fast-breeder reactors in which produced plutonium can be utilized inside the reactors rather than sent out of the country for reprocessing in France and the United Kingdom.

Thirdly, the rest of the world is to be given a good impression of peaceful and self-disciplined Japanese forces participating in United Nations peacekeeping and other operations.

It is very important to recall these three strands when examining Japan's policy toward United Nations peacekeeping operations; singly or in some mixture of any two or all three, they will influence any decision the Japanese government may have to take.

UNITED NATIONS PEACEKEEPING AND OTHER OPERATIONS

Within a very short period after 1990, Japanese peacekeepers found themselves undertaking a variety of tasks in diverse locations. As mentioned above, the Japanese assigned to themselves the role of minesweeping after the Gulf War. Their next assignment was in Cambodia in 1992-3, where the United Nations Transitional Authority for Cambodia was supervising free elec-

9 Takashi Inoguchi, 'Security and political interests: pro- and anti-proliferation in northeast Asia,' in Andrew Mack, ed (Geneva: United Nations Institute for Disarmament Research, forthcoming).

tions. Here Japanese civilians would monitor elections, build roads and other transportation facilities, and render medical and other assistance to Cambodians. In Rwanda, where the Japanese came shortly after the American and French forces withdrew, the task was defined as international peaceful rescue operations under the aegis of the Office of the UNHCR.

The years between 1990 and 1995 have been ones of daunting global change. Most significantly, post–Cold War euphoria has given way to a certain disillusionment in the New World Order and the United Nations. Japanese participation in and perceptions of peacekeeping operations undoubtedly have to be viewed through the prism of global change. Before I try to draw any conclusions, it might be useful to list the operations in which Japan has participated and to summarize their major features.[10]

The assigned task of the United Nations Angola Verification Mission II was to monitor the presidential and parliamentary elections in September 1992. Three civilians, one from the central government, one from a prefectural government, and one from the non-governmental sector, participated for a two-week period.

In Cambodia, UNTAC's assigned tasks included (1) engineering and other logistic support in the form of a 600-man Self-Defence Force battalion of engineers, (2) eight Self-Defence Forces officers as military observers, (3) 75 police officers serving as civilian police, (4) 41 civilians to monitor the election, and (5) co-operation in kind, consisting mainly of medicines and medical equipment, televisions, video cassette recorders and portable generators, AM radio receivers, and cassette players. The Self-Defence Forces engineers and officers served for six months, at which time they were replaced by

10 Yanai, 'Law concerning cooperation'; see also the special volume devoted to Japan's international co-operation in *Toki no Ugoki* [Trends], 15 December 1994. For useful case studies of United Nations peacekeeping and other operations towards conflict resolution, see Kevin Clements and Robin Ward, eds, *Building International Community: Cooperating for Peace: Case Studies* (Sydney: Allen and Unwin 1994.)

another battalion of engineers and eight more officers for another six-month stint. Civilian police participated for nine months.[11] Civilians working on election monitoring were in Cambodia for only two weeks. Forty-one polling station officers were recruited from the non-governmental sector, the prefectural governments, and the central government.

In Mozambique, the operation included (1) transport control, provided by one Self-Defence Force company of 48 men for a period of six months replaced once for another six months, (2) headquarters staff officers in the form of five Self-Defence Forces officers for six months who were replaced by another five for a further six months, and (3) election monitoring by fifteen monitors from the central government, prefectural governments, and non-governmental organizations. The companies consisted of officers and soldiers from the Ground, Maritime, and Air Self-Defence Forces. ONUMOZ's task is to facilitate the peace process on the basis of the 1992 peace accord between the government and rebel forces.

In El Salvador, ONUSAL is responsible for monitoring elections. Fifteen civilians participated for one week in the presidential and parliamentary elections of March and April 1994. An additional fifteen civilians were sent for another week during the second round of the presidential election. The monitors were recruited from the non-governmental sector, the central government, and one prefectural government.

The assigned task of the Office of the United Nations High Commissioner for Refugees in Zaire (UNHCR-Zaire) was to help refugees directly or through non-governmental organizations and by so doing to restore order and stability. UNHCR-Zaire is under its own command and is not part of the United Nations Assistance Mission in Rwanda. The Ground Self-Defence Forces sent an investigative mission of 23 in 1994 while 260 rescue personnel were sent to conduct medical, preventive, and water

11 On 4 May 1993 one police officer was killed and four others were wounded.

supply operations in October 1994. The Air Self-Defence Forces sent 23 investigators in September 1994, while 115 air transport personnel conduct air transport of goods and personnel between Nairobi and Goma. Ten officials from the prime minister's office, the ministry of foreign affairs, and the defence agency have been staying in Goma and Nairobi to facilitate the tasks of the Self-Defence Forces.

It should be clear from this account that Japanese participation in all of these missions was in keeping with the five principles of its peacekeeping law:[12] (1) agreement on a ceasefire shall have been reached among the parties to the conflict; (2) the parties to the conflict, including the territorial state(s), shall have given their consent to the deployment of peacekeeping forces and Japan's participation in such forces; (3) the peacekeeping forces shall maintain strict impartiality, not favouring any party to the conflict; (4) should any of the above requirements cease to be satisfied, the government of Japan may withdraw its contingent; and (5) use of weapons shall be limited to the minimum necessary to protect the life or person of personnel engaged in international peace co-operation assignments.

Thus the peacekeeping operations bill authorizes the government of Japan to carry out the following kinds of assignments:[13]

1 monitoring the observance of cessation of armed conflict or the implementation of relocation, withdrawal, or demobilization of armed forces as agreed upon among the parties to armed conflict;
2 stationing and patrol in buffer zones and other areas demarcated to prevent the occurrence of armed conflict;
3 inspection or identification of the carrying in or out of weapons and/or their parts by vehicles and other means of transportation or travellers on foot;

12 Yanai, 'Law concerning cooperation.'
13 *Ibid.*

4 collection, storage, or disposal of abandoned weapons and their parts;
5 assistance in the designation of ceasefire lines and other assimilated boundaries by the parties to armed conflict;
6 assistance in the exchange of prisoners-of-war among the parties to armed conflict;
7 supervision or management of the fair holding of parliamentary elections, plebiscites and other elections or voting assimilated thereto;
8 advice or guidance on and supervision of police administrative matters;
9 advice or guidance for administrative matters not included in 8 above;
10 medical care, including sanitary measures;
11 search for or rescue of affected people or assistance in their repatriation;
12 distribution of food, clothing, medical supplies, and other daily necessaries to affected people;
13 installation of facilities or equipment to accommodate affected people;
14 measures for the repair or maintenance of facilities or equipment damaged in conflict necessary for the daily life of affected people;
15 measures for the restoration of the natural environment subjected to pollution and other damage by conflict;
16 transportation, storage or reserve, communication, construction, or the installation, inspection, or repair of machines and apparatus not included in 1 through 15 above;
17 tasks other than those mentioned in 1 through 16 above, as prescribed by Cabinet Order.

The guidelines and the law reflect the two major constraints on broadening and deepening Japanese peacekeeping operations – the inward-looking pacifism and the debt to history – when they were drawn up and legislated respectively. Indeed, the requirement that a ceasefire accord exist before Japanese peacekeeping troops are allowed to participate means that Japan can take part only in those United Nations peacekeeping operations that Marrack Goulding, the former United Nations under-secretary-general for political affairs, calls the third category, namely, helping to implement negotiated agreements (Namibia, Cambodia, Angola, Mozambique, El Salvador).[14] Goulding's other categories are not easily acceptable to Japan. They are preventive deployment as in Macedonia; traditional peacekeeping (Near East, Kashmir, Cyprus, Iraq-Kuwait, Croatia); protecting delivery of humanitarian supplies (Bosnia-Herzegovina, Somalia, Rwanda-Zaire); 'painting a country blue' (that is, sending United Nations Blue Helmets to establish order as in Somalia); ceasefire enforcement (possibly in Bosnia-Herzegovina); and peace enforcement (Kuwait).

Even when Japan did participate, it confined itself to certain types of activities or certain types of local situations. The Japanese participation in the Gulf War was confined to minesweeping operations after the war was over. Its operations in Zaire-Rwanda were placed under the aegis of the UNHCR, operating in Zaire and between Kenya (Nairobi) and Zaire (Goma). Yet the generally solid work of the Japanese troops and civilians in many of these operations, in terms of self-discipline, effectiveness, low profile, and generosity, can only enhance Japan's international reputation.

This year marks the fiftieth anniversary of the end of World War II and of the birth of the United Nations system. It is also the year in which the peacekeeping operations bill must be reexamined, according to law. Japan has to face three major foreign policy issues which have a bearing on its participation in United Nations peacekeeping operations.

14 Marrack Goulding, 'Current rapid expansion unsustainable without major changes,' in John Roper, et al, *Keeping the Peace in the Post–Cold War Era: Strengthening Multilateral Peacekeeping* (New York: Trilateral Commission 1993), 91-101.

RAMIFICATIONS FOR FOREIGN POLICY

Japan must decide whether it wants to be a traditional great power or a global civilian power.[15] As its participation in international security exercises increases, its constitution is bound to become a barrier – or at least a nuisance factor – whether the exercises are multilateral military interventions or United Nations peacekeeping operations. The recent Higuchi report on national defence[16] would seem to indicate that Japan is prepared to go ahead with enhancing and enlarging international security efforts, including United Nations peacekeeping operations, without the sanction of an amendment to the constitution. But if Japan opts for vigorous international security efforts, the constitutional issue cannot be avoided. After all, living down the legacy of World War II has been a goal of the Japanese government over the longer term. The issue is whether or not the constitution is a negative legacy. So far the revisionists do not seem to have a majority either in the Diet or amongst the electorate. Recently, when the world's largest newspaper, *Yomiuri shimbun*, presented a draft proposal for a mildly revisionist constitution, the majority of the electorate and the government itself took it calmly, if with little enthusiasm. It would appear that Japan has opted for a role as a self-restrained, modest global civilian power – at least as long as the international environment does not change drastically in terms of United States security predominance and global market access.

Second, Prime Minister Kiichi Miyazawa made explicit in 1992 in the United Nations General Assembly that Japan wanted permanent membership on the Security Council in the near future, possibly as early as 1995. Since then, the Japanese

15 Hanns W. Maull, 'Germany and Japan: the new civilian powers,' *Foreign Affairs* 69(winter 1990-91), 91-106; and 'Germany and Japan: the powers to watch?' paper prepared for the World Congress of the International Political Science Association, 20-25 August 1994, Berlin.

16 Advisory Group on Defence Issues, *The Modality of the Security and Defense Capability of Japan: The Outlook for the 21st Century* (Tokyo: Ministry of Finance 1994). This report is often called the Higuchi report after the official who chaired the advisory group.

government has worked hard towards this goal. It argues that the five permanent members (the United States, Russia, China, France, and Britain) – all states that possess nuclear weapons – cannot guarantee international peace and security in a post–Cold War world in which there is a proliferation of low-intensity conflicts. Furthermore, Japan's financial contribution to the United Nations is ranked second only to that of the United States (representational equality and organizational health; or no taxation without representation). Furthermore, the Security Council has to redefine its tasks to encompass the burgeoning economic, technological, ecological, and social dimensions of security (non-militarization of security and globalization of once low-priority domestic issues).[17]

If Japan is given permanent membership, with or without veto power, it is bound to face a number of occasions on which its position differs significantly from that of the United States – as indeed has often been the case in the General Assembly.[18] In the fifteen years following the expansion of the Security Council in 1956 from 11 to 15 members, Japan was often not even a non-permanent member of the Security Council and did not have to make its position explicit on many issues. Permanent membership might serve to reinforce the already intermittently difficult relationship between Japan and the United States. Mexico refused for a great many years to become a non-permanent member of the Security Council because it did not want to reveal its divergence from the United States on almost every issue before the Security Council. Japan could find itself pushed into more wide-ranging peacekeeping operations. After all, Japan's participation in the aftermath of the Gulf War was a result in part of wide policy divergences from the United States.

Then there is the perennial question of the debt to history, which could flare up in the year of the 50th anniversary of the

17 Foreign Minister Yohei Kono's speech to the United Nations General Assembly, 27 September 1994.

18 See, for example, Kawabe Ichiro, *Jonin rijikoku iri* [Joining the United Nations Security Council's Permanent Membership] (Tokyo: Iwanami shoten 1994).

end of World War II, just as it did in the Gulf crisis. The crux of the matter is that many Japanese have shaped their national identity on the basis of a memory of modern Japanese history in which 'the Japanese have been working hard to occupy an honourable place in the world.' In this scenario, the aberrations of the 1930s and 1940s were brought about by military cliques, the Japanese wars against the West were part of imperialist wars among major powers, and their colonialism and wars against other Asians were very regrettable but partly inevitable in a nation which wanted to avoid playing an inferior and subservient role among imperialist powers.[19] Today, a majority of Japanese are determined not to repeat the mistake of assuming military roles.

As some scholars have pointed out, the Japanese memory of war has something in common with the memories of East and West Germany and of Austria.[20] Although Japan may be slightly less harsh on itself, it shares with West Germany a burden of blame. Like East Germany, Japan also lays blame on war cliques. Communists and some others argue that a sizeable number of people fought such a disastrous course at home, mostly from prisons, to terminate imperialist wars. Like Austria, Japan portrays itself as a victim of war, especially in light of the bombing of Hiroshima and Nagasaki, which is anxious to renounce the apparatus of war in the future. More generally, while the Germans blame themselves but see one chapter of modern German history closing with the Third Reich and a new chapter starting in 1945, the Japanese are less harsh on themselves and see modern Japanese history as a continuum from pre-1945 through post-1945.

19 Takashi Inoguchi, 'Japan and Pacific Asia: reflections on the fiftieth anniversary of the end of World War Two,' *The Japan Foundation Newsletter* 22 (February 1995), 1-5.

20 Robert Aspeslaugh, 'How the GDR, FRG and Japan processed their war history: lessons for education for peace,' in Takayanagi Sakio and Kodama Katsuya, eds, *Japan and Peace* (Tokyo: Mie Academic Press 1994), 126-65; see also Ian Buruma, *Wages of Guilt: Memories of War in Germany and Japan* (New York: Farrar, Straus & Giroux 1994).

But this determination has been made possible by a pacifist constitution and the Japan-United States security treaty, both of which ensure that Japan will be defended by the United States. Without the treaty, Japan's security would be much harder to ensure. Yet a majority of Japanese favours a self-interested, inward-looking pacifism over enhanced security efforts even though the growing demands on Japan to play a larger global role are irresistible – and those demands include security roles. Last, but by no means least, any decisions about enhancing Japan's role are 'increasingly dictated by the self-interested need to sustain international stability and economic prosperity.'[21]

The possibility of enhancement is bound to be met with unease by some of Japan's neighbours, as it was during the debate on whether and how Japan would use its troops during the Gulf War. In the end, there was not much opposition to sending minesweeping troops after the war.[22] Japan's desire to play a greater role in the United Nations, whether through peacekeeping operations or as a permanent member of the Security Council, will be constrained somewhat by the preferences of its neighbours.

FUTURE DIRECTIONS FOR JAPAN'S PEACEKEEPING OPERATIONS

The Japanese experience over the past five years shows that there are a number of possibilities which might be explored in the interests of enhanced and enlarged peacekeeping operations. These fall into three major categories.

Firstly, the mechanisms through which Japan can share training and exercise facilities bilaterally, regionally, and multilaterally should be developed. Given the increasing demand for and the increasingly diverse tasks confronting peacekeepers, training and exercises have become much more important.[23]

21 Inoguchi, *Japan's Foreign Policy*.
22 Inoguchi, 'Japan's response to the Gulf crisis.'
23 Masashi Nishihara, 'Trilateral country roles,' in Roper et al, *Keeping the Peace in the Post–Cold War Era*, 49-66.

During the Gulf crisis, I proposed that the United Nations establish several training centres throughout the world, each with its own specialization, so that the troops equipped with a particular expertise could be easily identified and assembled for specific missions.[24] Both Australia and Canada have already established such centres.

Secondly, one should develop the mechanisms through which the United Nations and its member countries can identify places where preventive missions can be useful in the resolution of conflict and the prevention of disaster. For that purpose the United Nations secretariat, the Security Council, the Economic and Social Council, and other relevant United Nations organizations have to enhance their policy planning ability to come up with intelligent estimates of the demand for and supply of such missions and to increase their ability to carry out their missions in close co-operation with the five permanent members of the Security Council, the traditional peacekeepers, and the two new comers (Japan and Germany).[25] Although the ability of the United Nations and regional institutions should not be overestimated, one should work toward raising their intelligence and performance collaboratively. For instance, the Japanese record of assessing local situations is acclaimed in Mozambique, the Japanese regular air transport between Nairobi (Kenya) and Goma (Zaire) is highly appreciated, and its lightly armed, self-disciplined, military presence in Goma is seen as a positive factor for order and stability there. One would hope these experiences might be more widely shared and utilized.

More indirectly, the Japanese emphasis on infrastructure cannot be overstressed. Good communications and transportation are often keys to preventing conflict and disasters and to restoring order and stability. United Nations peacekeeping operations should place far greater emphasis on the task of building infrastructures. For instance, Japanese minesweeping

24 Inoguchi, 'A job for the men from the UNPKO,' *Far Eastern Economic Review*, 13 December 1990, 24.

25 Nishihara, 'Trilateral country roles.'

was highly appreciated by all the oil-exporting countries in the Gulf. The Japanese engineer battalion in Cambodia was acclaimed for its solid road construction work. For such efforts to be carried out effectively, some United Nations organizations like the United Nations Development Program, the World Health Organization, and the United Nations Environment Program, other international organizations like the World Bank, the International Monetary Fund, and regional development banks, and the aid donors must all be more fully utilized. Japan's emphasis on non-military aspects of security and its demands for a redefinition of the tasks of the Security Council can be pushed along the same line.

This is merely a selective list of possible future directions for Japanese peacekeeping and other operations, including lessons the Japanese have drawn from their experiences over the last five year. They do not indicate future directions which would go far beyond the Japanese constitution and the preferences of the Japanese electorate and the world community.[26] Although much limited, Japanese aspirations and achievements may have some wider significance to United Nations peacekeeping and other operations in general.

Yet possible candidates for Japanese participation in United Nations peacekeeping and other operations keep coming up. Macedonia was raised as a possibility; the Conference (later the Organization) for Security and Co-operation in Europe suggested in autumn 1994 that Japan might consider participation in Nagorno-Kabarakh; and the latest is the possibility of Japanese participation in the Golan Heights. Debates on the pros and cons of participation will likely affect the process of assessing, and possibly revising, the peacekeeping operations bill,

26 See Aurelia George, 'Japan's participation in UN peacekeeping operations: radical departure or predictable response?' *Asian Survey* 33(June 1993), 571-4; Ronald Dore, *Koshiyo to ieru Nihon* [Japan that can say, let us do it this way] (Tokyo: Asahi shimbunsha 1993); Tanaka Hidemasa, Takano Takeshi and Kawabe Ichiro, *Igiari Nihon no Jonin rijikoku iri* [No to Japan's accession to the Security Council's permanent membership] (Tokyo: Daisan shokan 1994).

which comes up for review in 1995. And that process is likely to interact with the Japanese equation in which the constitutional issue, the Security Council's permanent membership issue, and the debt to history issue function as major parameters.

JAPAN'S 1991 MINESWEEPING DECISION

An Organizational Response

Peter J. Woolley

Japan's decision to deploy minesweepers to the Persian Gulf in the spring of 1991 following the War for Kuwait received little attention outside Asia. The *Washington Post* (25 April 1991) reported Japan's announcement of the deployment on page 21; a report of the minesweepers leaving port two days later merited page 11. The *Wall Street Journal* (25 April 1991) ran a brief story on page 10 suggesting Japan's action was a cautious but important step for its government and armed forces. The *New York Times* had little to say at all. Such scant attention has also been the case in academic writing. By contrast, the deployment of those naval forces was a topic of great interest to the United States government before and during the Gulf War, as it was of interest to Chinese, Australian, Indonesian, Korean, Malaysian, and Singaporean officials. Japan's press and public also found the event noteworthy.

Thus, among those who followed the matter at all, the dispatch of the ships fell on a continuum somewhere between unremarkable and an event of signal importance. While a few analysts examined Japan's policy responses to the Gulf War *in toto*, they did not examine Japan's decision to deploy minesweepers in the Persian Gulf as a discrete event. How did Japan's government come to select this specific and peculiar policy option? The answer to this question may not be startling, but because it is not startling it goes against some of the received wisdom on decision-making in Japan. Some analysts described the decision as the product of rational actors who considered specified Japanese national objectives—the Rational Actor Model. Others assessed the decision as the result of bargaining among various polit-

Peter J. Woolley is Associate Professor of Comparative Politics at Fairleigh Dickinson University, Madison, New Jersey. In 1994–95 he was Advanced Research Scholar at the Center for Naval Warfare Studies, U.S. Naval War College.

ical actors—the Governmental Politics Model. But the decision might be best understood as an organizational output born of standard operating procedures and routinized institutional behavior.[1]

Revelation and Reaction

A novel appraisal of Japan's overseas deployment of naval forces, set forth later in this article, stands out best against a background of typical evaluations of Japan's Gulf War policies. Those opinions fell roughly into three categories: (1) *the critics* who wanted more from Japan; (2) *the apologists* and incrementalists who wished to explain Japan's predicament to the critics; and (3) *the alarmists* who found disconcerting the signs of a newly assertive Japanese government.

Dismay, disappointment and criticism. The most common American reaction to Japan's Gulf War policies was disappointment or annoyance. In the view of many commentators, Japan's policy responses were simply too slow—as well as too little. Critics found Tokyo's lethargy intolerable and claimed that it should have responded quickly and positively to a world crisis that required decisive action by the world's most capable and affected powers.[2] The *Washington Post* (17 March 1991) reported that 30% of Americans had "lost respect for Japan because of the Gulf crisis." The dismayed commentators turned easily to detraction. Since they had established that Japan's reaction was slow, the next question was why.

The variety of answers largely centered on the peculiarity of Japan and the Japanese; and Japan's specific behavior in response to the Gulf crisis was put into a general context of its behavior on a range of political issues. For example, a *New York Times* columnist explained that Japan's "dithering passivity on all but trade" is because Japan is "incapable of initiative, in a sense immature."[3] If Japan was slow, critics reasoned, this showed once again that Japan was not a reliable ally of the United States. Or worse, Japan was confessing to the long pressed charge of being a free-rider in international security affairs. The *New Republic*, in the mood for puns, called it "burden shirking," and a leading Japan specialist in the op-ed section of the *Wall*

1. The basis of this analysis thus comes from Graham T. Allison, *Essence of Decision* (Boston: Little, Brown, 1971). Allison's trifurcated framework was applied to the U.S. government but is a useful tool for examining and categorizing the varied analyses of Japan's decision to deploy minesweepers in 1991.

2. For an excellent treatment of American perceptions, see R. Christopher Perry, "American Themes Regarding Japan: The Persian Gulf Case," in Robert J. Puckett, ed., *The United States and Northeast Asia* (Chicago: Nelson-Hall Publishers, 1993), pp. 273–99.

3. Flora Lewis, "The Great Game of Gai-atsu," 1 May 1991, p. A25.

Street Journal, not in the mood for apologies, referred to "bogus constitutional excuses."[4]

By the time Japan decided to send minesweepers to the Gulf in addition to contributing $13 billion dollars to the war effort, the dismayed commentators saw the naval force as a late, feeble gesture made long after all the important decisions and risks had been taken by more courageous, better organized, reliable countries. One academic reviewer characterized it as the "belated dispatch of four small wooden minesweepers two months after the hostilities ended."[5]

Apologists, incrementalists, and optimists. Not everyone was dismayed. Plenty of Japan-watchers attempted to put Japan's various reactions to the Gulf War in a context of Japanese strengths and limitations. Some among them stressed the incremental nature of Japan's changing foreign policy and emphasized what Japan might be able to do in the post-Cold War era. Some stressed that Japan's government had overcome enormous obstacles to change, and almost all pointed to what Japan had actually done rather than what it had not done.

Incrementalists saw in Japan's Gulf War policies evidence that Japan was changing, albeit slowly. They could point out that there was an enormous commitment of money in support of the allied military action against Iraq. There was a robust discussion of the overseas use of Japan's Self-Defense Forces (SDF) and civilian personnel, a debate that in itself was a rather new phenomenon even if it exasperated Japan's critics in the United States and Europe. And finally the entire episode sparked legislation that would smooth the way for Japan's participation in U.N. peacekeeping operations. Debated long and hard in the Diet, the legislation spawned a cottage industry in speculation about Japan's future role as a peacekeeper within or without the United Nations.

Incrementalists saw Japan's role in the Gulf War as altogether encouraging. And indeed, many encouraging signs were available to those who needed a lift of spirit: the government was openly sympathetic to the West's policy and strategy, and it provided many billions of dollars of aid to the United States, furnishing this money even though it was linked to an immediate tax hike. Finally, Japan made good on its promise to participate in U.N. peacekeeping activities, sending SDF personnel to Cambodia and Mozambique and helping with relief activities in Rwanda. The deployment of minesweepers to the Gulf fit nicely into the accumulating evidence that Japan was

4. John B. Judis, "Burden Shirking," 4 March 1991, p. 21; Donald Hellmann, "Japan's Bogus Constitutional Excuses in the Gulf," 6 February 1991, p. A12.

5. David Arase, "New Directions in Japanese Security Policy," *Contemporary Security Policy*, 15:2 (August 1994), p. 46.

taking seriously its new commitment to a cooperative international order. The *Wall Street Journal* (April 25, 1991), for example, called the deployment of the JMSDF ships a "cautious but significant step in [Japan's] effort to define an international role beyond that of banker and trader."

Others were looking not to the future but emphasizing what Japan had actually done in the Gulf crisis and the enormous effort Japan had made to overcome opposition and apathy at home. These apologists were understandably sympathetic to Japan's peculiar difficulties with the question of war. If Japan was slow or hesitant, if Japan lacked confidence or if the government encountered opposition to its support for the Gulf War—all of this was to be expected. Apologists recalled the stubborn pacifist segment of public opinion that, like the Peace Constitution, was the legacy of Japan's bitter war experience in the 1930s and 1940s. They pointed to the difficulty posed by Article Nine of the Constitution, which was so plainly restrictive and could not be twisted much further than it already had been by the establishment of substantial ground, air and naval forces. This group of commentators thought criticism of Japan a bit unreasonable. How could the Western allies think that Japan would suddenly shed its immunities and auto-limitations in order to participate in a war on the opposite side of the globe?

The apologists, if they mentioned the minesweeping expedition at all, pointed out how carefully circumscribed that mission had to be in order to maintain public support for such an unusual use of the SDF. The minesweepers had to be deployed after rather than during the war because it was important not to associate the SDF's actions with the aggressive and forceful actions taken by the United States. The minesweepers had to operate only in international waters, and they were merely clearing obstacles to navigation, a routine function of any respectable coast guard.

Prime Minister Kaifu might be counted first among the apologists. Having suffered the slings and arrows of outraged American journalists and members of Congress, Kaifu felt compelled to emphasize how much Japan had done for the allies. "It just makes me gnash my teeth that the kinds of things we've done have not been properly valued," he said. Kaifu asserted that rather than "too little too late," Japan had done "as much as possible, as quickly as possible."[6] The prime minister could point out that Japan's financial burden for the war ranked behind only that of the United States, Kuwait, and Saudi Arabia. The prime minister could also brag that Japan had quickly frozen Iraqi assets and embargoed Iraqi oil and that Japan's first financial commitment to the U.N. coalition came 10 days ahead of Germany's. Kaifu's final gesture of solidarity with the United States was to sign off on the deployment of

6. "Japan's New Frustration," *Washington Post*, 17 March 1991, p. A21, 26.

JMSDF ships to the Persian Gulf, a gesture that, like Japan's other Gulf War policies, attracted less attention abroad than he wanted and expected.

Alarmists and prophets. In a final category of opinion makers were those who saw Japan's Gulf War policies in general and the deployment of minesweepers in particular as a signal, if not revolutionary event in contemporary Japanese history. For countries uneasy with a rearmed Japan, any military action on Japan's part was unwelcome. China warned all along that Japan should not get ideas about dispatching forces out of its area and was predictably critical when the decision was made. Its official news agency, Xinhua, called the plan "a dangerous first step in sending troops overseas." The Soviet Union's news service TASS said that "Japanese military circles and politicians . . . have decided to use the Gulf crisis to make a breakthrough in economic and military-political terms on the international scene." North Korea also made a predictable fuss, and the Philippine government asked that the Japanese assure Asia "that they will not start building up their military might."[7]

These alarmed parties, joined by others on the Pacific Rim and by Japanese opposition groups, believed that encouraging Japan's military development by, for instance, asking it to send SDF personnel to the Gulf War theater was a foolhardy policy eventually to be regretted by everyone. Perhaps the kindest among them would echo the sentiments of the president of Singapore who once likened the Americans' encouragement of Japanese military development to giving liquored candies to an alcoholic. The prime minister was no kinder. Asked if Japan had not changed since the war, Lee Kuan Yew referred to the well-known French maxim: "the more it has changed, the less it has changed."[8]

E pluribus unum. What all these views had in common when explaining, deploring, or defending Japan's policy responses during the Gulf War is that they all tended to portray Japan as *unique*. The dismayed Japan bashers saw Tokyo's policy responses as peculiarly inadequate as compared to the responses of other (read West European) American allies. Japan, they concluded, is unique in its desire to avoid the costly and difficult responsibilities of a wealthy and powerful nation that has profited from free trade and the U.S. security umbrella. In this view, burden-shirking was simply reflective

7. "Xinhua on Japan's SDF Deployment to Gulf," Foreign Broadcast Information Service, *Daily Report, China* (hereafter FBIS, *DR/CHI*), also Yang Bojiang, "Gulf War Challenges Japan's Foreign Policy," *Beijing Review*, 22–28 April 1991, pp. 9–11; TASS report, "Japanese Intentions in Gulf Worries Neighbors," in FBIS, *Daily Report, Soviet Union*, 24 October 1990, p. 13; "Philippines Demands Rationale," FBIS, *DR/CHI*, 30 April 1991, p. 2.

8. "Lee on Japan's Deployment in Gulf, U.S. Bases," in FBIS, *Daily Report, East Asia* (*DR/EAS*), 8 November 1990, p. 34.

of a flawed culture. And the deployment of those four small wooden minesweepers was a belated, cynical gesture designed to placate critics or to serve some other selfish agenda.[9]

The incrementalists also tended to portray Japan as unique if only because one must emphasize the gradualist nature of policy changes in Japan. Other countries may be capable of making bold departures in policy when the situation warrants but in Japan consensus must emerge (e.g., through *nemawashi* and *ringosho*). This recurring theme is not applied with such regularity to the foreign policy of any other industrialized democracy.

The apologists likewise point to the unique constraints on Japan's foreign policy makers: the peace constitution, a pacifist public, a vociferous opposition that wishes to interpret Article Nine as strictly as possible, and the need to build consensus. These factors prevent Japan (a unique state or *tokushu kokka*) from being like normal states (*zairaigata kokka*). In such a peculiar context, Japan's policy responses, including the deployment of minesweepers, must be seen as an unusual and admirable show of action and solidarity with the United Nations.

Finally, the alarmists, who saw in Japan's policy responses a harbinger of a revolution in Japanese foreign affairs, more than implied that Japan is somehow unique. In their view, postwar reforms had merely whitewashed the old militarism. They watched carefully the decisions made in Tokyo throughout the Gulf War, not least of all the decision to dispatch the SDF. Hence, a Singapore newspaper ran the headline: "Japan Impatient to Make Breakthrough in Military, War Issues."[10]

So while all of these views of Japan may hold kernels of truth, all tend to rely on the notion that only peculiar reasons can explain Japan's behavior. That Japan is unique is a popular theme among Japanese, non-Japanese, and especially Americans. But it is a view equally inviting to skepticism. Japan's decision to send minesweepers might be understood more clearly without recourse to the uniqueness of Japan: the Japanese government sent minesweepers to the Persian Gulf because minesweeping was a routinized

9. In one view "the main reasons [for the deployment of minesweepers] were (1) to provide a symbolic gesture of human support for multinational effort and strengthen U.S.-Japan ties; (2) to break the deadlock within the country on nonfinancial contributions to world problems and serve as a precedent for future SDF dispatch abroad; and (3) to allow Japanese companies to be included in lucrative reconstruction projects in the Gulf Region." Courtney Purrington, "Tokyo's Policy Responses During the Gulf War," *Pacific Affairs*, 65:2 (Summer 1992), p. 171.

10. "Singapore Press Cites Action," in FBIS, *DR/CHI*, 30 April 1991, pp. 2–3. Chinese Premier Li Peng in March 1991 warned the People's Congress that "the Chinese and Japanese people should maintain common alertness against the tendency of a handful of people toward reviving Japanese militarism." "Li Peng Delivers Report at 25 March Session," in ibid., 27 March 1991, pp. 9–36.

task, and among the organizational responses available to Japan this one was well prepared by both the Defense Agency (JDA) and the JMSDF.

The Organizational Response

Many criticisms of Japan's policy responses during the Gulf War implied the rational actor model of governance in which policy is the "purposive acts of a unified national government."[11] Some critics were frustrated because, as they saw it, Japan's responses were not rational for a great power with an interest in protecting oil supplies, maintaining stable prices, and wanting to be a responsible member of the international community. Others saw in those same responses an ultra-rational agenda that merely presented itself in the guise of inaction and hesitancy. The Japan of the Japan bashers is "centrally controlled, completely informed, and value maximizing,"[12] and we might add, this ultra-rational behavior is uniquely Japanese. Or as one Gulf War reviewer put it, "Japan has been portrayed as the home of selective and clever players with ruthless and scornful attitudes."[13]

In an attempt to balance the critics, apologists generally tended toward a more complex and dynamic view of Japan's policy responses as generated by the governmental politics model in which relevant actors behave "according to various conceptions of national, organizational, and personal goals" and where governmental decisions are "a resultant of various bargaining games among players in the national government." Players in this conceptual model make policy "not by a single rational choice but by the pulling and hauling that is politics."[14] Thus, the apologists saw Japan's pluralistic society pulling in different directions: there were the various opposition leaders parties and leaders, the pacifist tendencies of the public, the monetary and fiscal sensibilities of the Ministry of Finance, the hawkish factions of the Liberal Democratic Party, and external pressures from Asian neighbors as well as from the United States.

To earn their living, Japanologists, following the governmental politics model, recounted in great detail the preferences and politics of the relevant players. Opponents of the minesweeping mission included all the opposition parties save the Democratic Socialist Party (DSP) led by Keigo Ouchi. Supporters included: Keidanren Chairman Gaishi Hiraiwa, Chamber-of-Commerce Chairman Rokuro Ishikawa, Japan Employers' Federation President Eiji Suzuki, and leading members of the LDP: Koji Kakisawa, chairman of the LDP's National Defense Commission; Tadashi Kuranari, chair of the Se-

11. Graham C. Allison, *Essence of Decision*, pp. 4–5.

12. Ibid., p. 67.

13. Christopher Perry, "American Themes."

14. Allison, *Essence of Decision*, pp. 6, 144.

curity Research Commission; former Foreign Minister Shintaro Abe; former Prime Minister Nakasone; former Prime Minister Takeshita; faction leader Michio Watanabe; former Deputy Prime Minister Kanemaru; and many other notables. Prime Minister Kaifu was said to be a fence-sitter who required great persuasion before he accepted the views of the hawkish politicians. In this view then, Japan's behavior resulted from the normal pulling and hauling that is (uniquely) Japanese politics.

But the third model of governmental behavior has been left aside by most analysts. The organizational process model would suggest that Japan's government acts as its organizations enact routines. Minesweeping was an organizational routine; other policy responses involving the SDF simply were not available because little or no routinized behavior existed. Such analysis does not lend itself to exciting headlines for opinion pieces, nor would apologists find gratifying the dryness of this model. But it has its place among explanations and may be found satisfying when other models have yielded all the insights they will. Moreover, the organizational process model does not rely on any unique characteristics of Japan but rather on the generalization that governments consist of organizations that produce dry-as-dust outputs. Japan, like any other country, consists of such organizations, and from their repertoire of routines Japan's Gulf War policies were constructed.

In the case at hand, the Defense Agency (JDA) was among the many organizations in Japan that might have responded to the Gulf War. The JDA in turn consisted of the Ground, Air, and Maritime Self-Defense Forces (JGSDF, JASDF, JMSDF). These "existing organizations, each with a *fixed* set of standard operating procedures and programs" largely defined the government's military options. These options had been "determined primarily by routines established," or not established, "in these organizations prior to that instance."[15]

Establishing Routines

The government's routinized policy options in the Gulf crisis were essentially three. The first was the payment of money to the United States and to other "front line countries"; the second was the deployment of minesweepers; a third possibility was the dispatch of civilian or military planes for transporting civilian refugees and for resupply and delivery of humanitarian aid. Two of these options were in fact selected, coordinated, and carried out. The third was partially carried out. In large measure the routines had been established by 1987 or 1988, several years prior to the Gulf War.

15. Ibid., p. 68.

Persian Gulf 1987–91 and checkbook diplomacy. Between January 1987 and July 1988, ten Japanese-owned merchant vessels suffered attacks in the Persian Gulf or in the Strait of Hormuz through which some 55% of Japan's imported oil was shipped. Similarly, oil tankers under many flags were casualties of the prolonged war between Iraq and Iran. The eventual U.S. response to these attacks was to police the international waters of the Gulf; Kuwaiti oil tankers in particular were reflagged as U.S. vessels and given U.S. naval escorts. Several Western European navies joined the effort, as did the Soviet navy.

Washington requested that Japan join the West Europeans in deploying naval vessels for escort duty and minesweeping. Tokyo considered the request seriously but declined. Instead, Prime Minister Nakasone took the only slightly unusual step of helping to finance the allied naval operations by making direct, cash payments to the U.S. government. The event was only slightly unusual because Japan had been using money in various ways for a long time as a substitute for military expenditures.

Payments went out in many forms but chief among them were Overseas Development Assistance (ODA) and both direct and indirect subsidies of U.S. armed forces stationed in Japan. ODA by the late 1980s had not only grown to the point where it exceeded U.S. foreign assistance but was more and more frequently justified in politico-strategical terms. Even Japan's annual defense White Paper explained that ODA was meant to "influence the peace and stability of the international community."[16] Likewise, Japan's subsidy of U.S. forces stationed in its territory steadily grew until it covered about half of the estimated costs of those forces. Thus, offering financial assistance to the U.S. for its 1988 Persian Gulf operations was even then a part of an established routine of subsidizing U.S. armed forces and providing money to help maintain stability in the international system. The only new wrinkle was the direct link of specific U.S. military operations to money that Japan specifically appropriated.

The Persian Gulf crisis in 1990 was on a much larger scale but the routine was similar. Checkbook diplomacy was a well-practiced strategy, one that the Ministry of Finance (MOF), the LDP, and the cabinet understood, and one that had a record of success. The only thing left to haggle over was the precise amount of aid to be offered to the U.S. and others. What was unprecedented in 1990–91 was the size of the military operation in which Japan's chief ally was about to engage and, therefore, the amount of money to be offered. One might speculate that any hesitancy on Japan's part in the winter months of 1990–91 was due to the relative inexperience of the MOF with

16. See, for example, JDA, *Defense of Japan 1990* (trans. by *Japan Times*), p. 81.

such a large-scale and costly venture. But in the end, aid was forthcoming—in amounts larger than ever before and it was appropriated more swiftly.

Minesweeping routines. As the Gulf crisis moved toward a Gulf War there were only two practical military responses to be offered by the relevant organizations of the Japanese government. One of these options was air transport, the other was the deployment of minesweepers. For the JMSDF, and perhaps for all the services taken together, there was probably a no more routinized military operation than the clearing of seaborne mines. Article Nine of the Constitution notwithstanding, the practice of minesweeping went back to the days of surrender and was thus older than the present Constitution. Even as World War Two ended, Japanese minesweepers searched the nation's waters to remove or destroy tens of thousands of mines sowed by both American and Japanese naval forces. And even after the disbanding of the rest of the imperial navy, Japan's minesweepers continued to operate under the rubric of the Maritime Safety Agency. These same vessels were called into service by the U.S. at the start of the Korean War, and without the knowledge of the Japanese public, several dozen of them worked in late 1950 to clear mines in foreign territorial waters—Korean harbors—as the American navy was woefully short of both minesweeping vessels and experienced crews.

In 1987 the situation was not all that different from 1950. The Americans were again short of both minesweepers and crews. In fact, one might say that minesweeping was one organizational response to a crisis the U.S. Navy was not prepared to make. The navy had not needed to clear mines from U.S. waters since 1942, and had not launched a single new minesweeper since 1958. By 1987 the few that it operated were in the naval reserve and in need of some repair if they were to be sent overseas. Testifying before Congress, Secretary of the Navy Garrett explained that the navy "spent more than 25 years not developing or buying new minesweepers or minehunters."[17] The U.S. had tended to rely on NATO allies for minesweeping chores and U.S. naval officers saw mine countermeasures as a career dead end.

By contrast, the JMSDF operated 42 modern mine warfare ships manned by experienced crews. Many officers at command level had served years aboard minesweepers and contributed their experience in mine countermeasures to the construction of new minesweeping ships. Moreover, by 1988 Japan had about five dozen escort vessels equipped with some of the latest weapons technology, including ASROC, CIWS, Harpoon ship-to-ship mis-

17. Navy Sec. H. Lawrence Garrett III, testimony of 21 February 1991 quoted in Tamara Moser Melia, *Damn the Torpedoes: A Short History of U.S. Naval Mine Countermeasures, 1777–1991* (Washington, D.C.: Navy Historical Center, 1991), p. 129; also John F. Tarpey, "A Minestruck Navy Forgets Its History," *Proceedings*, U.S. Naval Institute, vol. 114 (February 1988), pp. 44–47.

siles, and Sparrow antiair missiles. In operational terms, the U.S. request for help from the JMSDF was quite logical. The JDA's Maritime Staff Office (MSO) in 1987 began to calculate what would be required of them were they to deploy minesweepers as far away as the Persian Gulf. This "case study" (what the Americans would call a contingency plan) proved useful not in 1987–88, as the government decided against deploying any SDF personnel abroad, but in 1990–91 when organizational responses to the Gulf crisis were reconsidered.[18]

In addition to the MSO's unofficial plans, a private think tank in Tokyo undertook its own study of the situation. Its membership included a number of elected LDP officials and many retired JSDF admirals and generals but, unlike the MSO, it had no legal restrictions on what it could publicly suggest and discuss. For this Strategy and Research Center, two retired JMSDF admirals went aboard the U.S. naval vessels in the Persian Gulf to observe the allied operation and report back on whether and how JMSDF participation might be feasible in the future. Their report, subsequently circulated in the Diet, the Foreign Ministry, and the Maritime Staff Office,[19] concluded that the JMSDF could successfully undertake an escort or minesweeping mission in the Persian Gulf.

So when the next Gulf crisis broke out just two years later, the scenario was repeated. As early as August 1990, President Bush, in a conversation with Prime Minister Kaifu, reportedly suggested that Japan might contribute minesweepers to the allied buildup.[20] Australia's Prime Minister Robert Hawke in September 1990 said he would "welcome a Japanese decision to send minesweepers to the Gulf or get involved militarily in other ways." And Britain's Foreign Secretary Douglas Hurd, who also visited Tokyo in September, said: "If Japan can manage it within its Constitution, it can contribute armed forces. That is fine. We welcome Japanese minesweepers."[21] These officials were all well aware of this particular organizational response that Japan was capable of making.

Meanwhile, the JMSDF quietly dusted off the studies it had made in 1987–88 and began to update and revise those plans. Public and private debates over how to respond to the Persian Gulf situation began anew, and advocates for the JMSDF could now argue with some conviction not only the legality of an overseas deployment of the SDF but, more importantly, that the

18. Such a study cannot be referred to as a contingency plan because that would imply that formal authority had been imparted to the JDA or MSO and that in some measure the action contained in the plan had been legally sanctioned.

19. Author's interview with Admiral Manabu Yoshida, JMSDF (ret.) and Vice-Admiral Taketo Takata, JMSDF (ret.) who went to the Gulf and wrote the report, 25 July 1991.

20. FBIS, *DR/EAS*, 16 October 1991, p. 1.

21. Ibid., 18 September 1990, p. 74, and 11 September 1990, p. 7.

JMSDF was perfectly capable of performing the mission, that minesweeping was an appropriate response to the crisis, and risks were minimal.

JASDF routines. When the time came to decide whether Japan could make an outward and visible sign of support for its United Nations allies, the cabinet had a second feasible plan for the Defense Agency. The ASDF had offered its organizational response to the Gulf crisis: air transport. The air service had cemented plans to help repatriate refugees from Jordan, Iraq's neighboring country. The plan was convincing enough that in January 1991 the cabinet made legal preparations to allow the JASDF to fly its transport planes overseas.

It appeared as though the JASDF would be the first service to break the barrier to overseas deployment. Pilots were on alert for several weeks in January and February 1991 as the war began in earnest, and U.S. Air Force officers briefed JASDF pilots on air routes to the crisis region, standard procedures, possible dangers, and even desert survival techniques. Pallets with food, spare parts, medicines, and other supplies were set out and ready to be loaded—if orders were issued.[22]

The JASDF plan had a hidden flaw. Its organizational response depended for success upon the cooperation of the country into which its planes would fly for air control, maintenance, and refueling. Jordan, having supported Iraq and with a large and restless population of Palestinians, was not enthusiastic about America's Japanese allies operating in Amman. Further, the airlift of refugees did not require the specialized services of an armed air force, especially one whose C-130 transport planes could each carry only 30 passengers. Large civilian airliners were already ferrying refugees, and as it turned out, plenty of civilian aircraft were available to the International Organization for Migration, which was coordinating the evacuation of refugees. The organizational response of the JASDF was superfluous.

The Final Choice

In the end, orders came only for the JMSDF, a logical outcome. Of the three branches of the SDF, only the Maritime Force had substantial overseas experience as it had been allowed for almost two decades to conduct overseas training missions. Another important difference was that the JMSDF was well ahead of its sister services in planning, experience, and the effort to convince the cabinet that its mission could be completed. The MSDF began its planning—or re-planning—in early September 1990, while the ASDF did not initiate any studies until early November, almost four months after the crisis began. The GSDF began even later and made only minimal progress.

22. Author's interview with JASDF officers and instructors at the Air Staff College and Yokoda Air Base, July 1991.

The cabinet was able to select MSDF plans simply because its members were by then familiar with those plans and confident in the prospect for success.[23]

Thus, it was somewhat misleading when SDF Chief of Staff Makoto Sakuma announced on April 15, 1991, that the government had formally asked the SDF to "consider formation of a minesweeper squadron, equipment needs, and compile specific information on floating mines in the Gulf."[24] Such a squadron had been "considered" quite thoroughly, and the planning was done. Only one week later the government announced its intention to deploy the minesweepers overseas, and within days the vessels left port. The JMSDF plans were ready, the JMSDF was ready, the task was well rehearsed. The organizational output of the JMSDF had, in effect, triumphed over other possibilities.

This turned out to be not the "belated dispatch of four small wooden minesweepers" but rather a well-planned deployment of modern warships with experienced crews. In fact, six ships were deployed in all. The flagship, *Hayase*, was 2,000 tons, and her four minesweeping companions were each about 500 tons and were relatively new ships, commissioned since 1988. One tender also went, the 8,150-ton *JDS Tokiwa.* It is true that four of the ships had wooden hulls; even the most modern minesweepers are constructed of wood in order to minimize the possibility of accidentally detonating magnetic influence mines.

Even the question of whether this particular organizational response was belated is debatable. It may be that Japan's public relations vis-à-vis the U.S. would have been better had the deployment come sooner in the Persian Gulf episode, but it also may be that no response could have satisfied an American public primed to discount all that the Japanese government did. Whichever the case, had Japan's minesweepers been sent much earlier in the crisis they probably would have been of little use to an American ally that for a long time had not valued mine countermeasures in its planning.

In Operation Desert Shield, U.S. navy minesweepers were a low priority, and before February 1991 they were not assigned a support ship that would have allowed them to operate at sea for extended periods. And their assigned port was Abu Dhabi, some 500 miles from the minefields. American minesweepers spent the months leading up to the outbreak of war in training. They were not to see action until well after the air war got under way because General Schwarzkopf did not want the minesweeping operation to touch off

23. This was also the conclusion of several members of Sorifu, the prime minister's research office, interviewed by the author on 24 July 1991. SDF officers in various branches agreed with this assessment, as did Shunji Taoka, a senior staff writer at *Asahi Shimbun*, interviewed on August 9, 1991, who called the decision a "bureaucratic predisposition" and "not a cultural one."

24. "Study of Minesweeping Mission Ordered," FBIS, *DR/EAS*, 16 April 1991, p. 11.

any explosions or confrontations before the deadline of the allied ultimatum had passed.

Moreover, the allied plan of attack on the Iraqi army turned out not to include an amphibious assault on the Kuwaiti coast. Thus, minesweeping before the allied ground attack was little more than an effort to keep up the appearance that an amphibious landing might occur.[25] Had Japan's minesweepers been deployed in a more timely fashion, in September for example, they merely would have kept the allied minesweepers company in Abu Dhabi. Thus, the usefulness of this particular organizational response by the JMSDF would have been rendered minimal by the organizational outputs of the U.S. armed forces, which did not include or require mine countermeasures. But neither was the deployment of the JMSDF minesweepers irrelevant. Anti-shipping mines being the poor man's device, Iraq sowed some 1,200 of them in a huge semicircle 30 to 60 miles from the Kuwaiti coast. By all accounts, the JMSDF performed at the elevated level expected of its long experience and organizational attention.

Conclusion

Some conclusions about Japan's policy responses to the Persian Gulf War can be drawn differently, having looked through the prism of the Organization Process Model. For example, the ever popular question, "why did Japan not do more," can be reasonably answered, at least in part, without reference to public polling results, the peace Constitution, and the rest of the familiar baggage that accompanies discussions of Japanese public policy. Japan's various policy responses to the Gulf War were in large measure what Japanese organizations had been prepared to do before the war. The amount and kind of preparation for these responses was in direct proportion to the kinds of experiences Japan's organizations had been through and what they had learned from them. Rather than concluding that weak and hesitant responses to the Gulf Crisis revealed some deep flaw in Japan's government, one can equally conclude that Japan's organizations had minimal exposure to the type and intensity of international conflict that the 1990–91 Persian Gulf episode turned out to be. Even so, under slightly irregular circumstances, Japan's policy responses were within the predictable range of organizational routines. And finally, from this recent history we may learn what organizational responses Japan is likely to make in the future.

25. Even so, two U.S. warships hit mines. "The mining of two important Navy warships in waters believed to be mine-free once again emphasized the U.S. Navy's recognized failure to sustain adequate combat MCM capability." Melia, *Damn the Torpedoes*, p. 129.

Ezra F. Vogel

PAX NIPPONICA?

Future historians may well mark the mid-1980s as the time when Japan surpassed the United States to become the world's dominant economic power. Japan achieved superior industrial competitiveness several years earlier, but by the mid-1980s its high-technology exports to the United States far exceeded imports, and annual trade surpluses approached $50 billion a year. Meanwhile, America's trade deficits mushroomed to $150 billion a year. By late 1985, Japan's international lending already exceeded $640 billion, about ten percent more than America's, and it is growing rapidly. By 1986 the United States became the world's largest debtor nation and Japan surpassed the United States and Saudi Arabia to become the world's largest creditor.

In the past, the United States has been able to make up for its worldwide merchandise trade gap with trade in services, including interest payments. But as Japanese services expand worldwide and the United States begins paying out more interest than it receives, the United States suffers not only from a merchandise trade gap but a continuing current account trade deficit.

America's GNP may remain larger than Japan's well into the 1990s (depending on exchange rate measurements), but there are many reasons to believe that Japan will extend its lead as the world's dominant economic power in the years ahead.

II

Japan's growing economic power is solidly based in three crucial areas: the "new industrial revolution" in manufacturing technology, the concentration on the service sector, and the expansion of research and development activities.

The Japanese are poised to take the lead in the "new industrial revolution" that is bringing new microelectronic and laser controls to the production process. Electronic controls greatly

---

Ezra F. Vogel is Professor of Sociology and Director of the Program on U.S.-Japan Relations at Harvard University. He is the author of *Japan As Number One* and *Comeback.*

reduce the need for production-line workers and increase the flexibility of manufacturing. Technologies for replacing broken tools and parts automatically, for instance, permit increasing numbers of robots and other tools to operate untended all hours of the day. Companies and countries that install such technologies ahead of others are likely to gain great competitive advantage in reducing costs.

Japan continues to introduce about as many industrial robots as the rest of the world combined, several times the rate of introduction in the United States; its dominance in numerically controlled machine tools is even greater than in robots. Although progress in introducing computer-controlled modules and flexible manufacturing systems is more difficult to measure, Japan continues to extend its substantial lead in these areas. Why is Japan doing so well in applying the new manufacturing technology? Automation requires detailed work by vast numbers of electrical engineers, and Japan turns out more such engineers than any Western country—about 50 percent more each year in absolute numbers than the United States. Furthermore, a far higher proportion of electrical engineering graduates go into manufacturing in Japan than in the United States.

Senior Japanese managers who personally took part in the introduction of basic technological changes that took several generations to install in industries in the West are more knowledgeable than Western managers about how to administer large-scale industrial change. Japanese workers have learned that they do not lose jobs with fundamental technical change, and that firms which introduce new technology quickly are the stronger for it. With lifetime employment, Japanese workers are not frightened by new technology and want innovations that will keep their companies strong in the future. Needless to say, the low cost of Japanese capital and the almost universal training in science and math among Japanese workers reinforce these advantages.

Although the growth in Japanese productivity began to slow down in the 1970s, the introduction of increased automation in the 1980s allowed the pace to pick up, and Japan's rate of productivity increase in manufacturing now far exceeds that of other industrialized countries.

In the mid-1970s, the Japanese began targeting the service sector, along with high technology, as the most promising growth area. They have started concentrating financial resources and talents into services with the same systematic determination that they once applied to manufacturing. Rapid expansion can be seen in areas like fashion, movies, television programming, publishing, consulting, real estate, design, construction, leisure, tourism, advertising, insurance and finance. Domestic companies in these sectors are already sufficiently established that exports are beginning to grow rapidly.

Expansion in the service sector is facilitated by the rapid accumulation of capital and by technological breakthroughs, particularly the new Japanese word processor, which makes possible for the first time the widespread capacity to type in phonetic syllables and achieve outputs of Chinese characters. The unrivaled information networks of the world's six largest general trading companies, all of them Japanese, greatly assist worldwide expansion in the service sector. The continued growth of Japanese manufacturing companies will pull along their affiliates in the service sector because of the tight linkages between Japanese companies. Universal and high-quality training in math and science provide ample skilled manpower for the service sector, and governmental efforts to standardize communication networks will in the future provide a sound basis for the growth of service-sector companies.

Finally, the Japanese are rapidly expanding their research and development efforts to stimulate technical progress with commercial applications. The proportion of GNP devoted to R&D will virtually double this decade, rising from two percent of GNP in 1980 to an expected 3.5 percent by 1990. The United States has stabilized R&D expenses at about 2.7 percent of GNP. However, if military research is excluded, Japan is already devoting about as many man-hours to R&D as the United States and will soon be spending about as much for it. If present trends continue, Japan will take the lead in nonmilitary R&D spending by the early 1990s.

Just as Japan built state-of-the-art industrial plants in the 1960s while America maintained its stock of older facilities, so Japan is now building state-of-the-art R&D facilities while America maintains many older laboratories. Most Japanese research is done in large companies that use the new technology for their own manufacturing. Much of America's R&D, by contrast, is done in small, innovative companies that sell their technology to others, including the Japanese. American R&D is more accessible to Japan than Japanese R&D is to the United States, since much of it is done in open universities as well as these small companies, and since Japanese scientists can easily follow American R&D literature. Japanese government aid to research is significant not so much for its magnitude as for its capacity to ensure that the nation adapts quickly to promising leads and fosters cooperation and specialization among firms to make better use of national resources.

What are the implications of these successes for the global political balance? Will Japan use its economic dominance in world affairs to become a military superpower?

III

After World War II Japanese leaders, convinced that they could not continue to enrich their country through military expansion, began single-mindedly devoting their energies toward economic competitiveness. Like the Venetians and Dutch in their heydays, the Japanese conceived a vision of economic power without military power; their subsequent economic success has not altered this vision. They hope that nuclear weapons have rendered all-out warfare untenable and that, unlike seventeenth-century Holland, they will not suffer for their modest level of military preparedness.

Japanese believe their national welfare has profited by placing priority on economic affairs, and that a greatly expanded military would detract from the willingness of trading partners to welcome their businessmen and their products. They see no need to change their American-imposed "peace" constitution, which prevents them from sending troops or selling arms abroad. Living in the world's most densely industrialized territory, Japanese consider themselves uniquely vulnerable to nuclear attacks and are convinced that possession of nuclear weapons would increase their vulnerability.

Many Americans believe that Japan enjoys a "free ride," taking commercial advantage of opportunities provided by a stable world maintained largely at American expense. Japanese, however, argue that they pay for their own military defense and contribute substantially to America's forces in Japan, thus freeing the United States to concentrate its energies elsewhere. They believe that Americans spend excessively on defense because they exaggerate the Soviet threat and that they are unnecessarily provocative. For all their dislike of the Soviet Union, Japanese believe that if they remain firm in negotiations, avoid provocations and modestly increase military preparations, the risks of conflict can be reduced. They do not believe that the more they arm the safer they are.

Although worried about being drawn into conflicts through excessively intimate ties to a belligerent United States, most Japanese believe it is in their interest to maintain the military alliance with the United States. Many scientists and engineers would prefer an independent science and technology policy and fear the constraints that Americans might impose on defense technology developed jointly, but some are ready to cooperate with the United States in weapons development, especially if it opens doors to new American defense technology.

In any case, Japanese are unlikely to spend as much as two percent of their GNP for defense by the year 2000, but they are prepared to increase their contributions to maintain world security as Americans feel less able to afford the expense. They will, of course, use their contributions to gain leverage to represent their own interests. They are already the world's seventh-largest military power, with highly sophisticated weaponry, and their military power will grow. But at least for this century, Japan will in the military sphere accept a Pax Americana, perhaps eventually growing into a Pax Americana-Nipponica.

IV

As an alternative to military power, internationally minded Japanese have begun to envision their country becoming a world leader by assisting the southern tier of developing countries and championing their cause in international meetings. Japanese economists have argued in influential Japanese journals that Japan should rapidly increase its "contributions to the world public good." Cosmopolitan journalists, aware that the world has criticized the lack of Japanese contributions to Vietnamese refugees, have worked to dramatize the problems of African hunger and Mexican earthquake recovery so as to increase private as well as public Japanese aid. Some ordinary Japanese citizens who lived as youths in China, Korea and Taiwan during the Japanese occupation have worked to establish person-to-person relations with people of these countries. Idealistic young technicians have volunteered for a Japanese version of the Peace Corps. Development planners are guiding the planning and construction of modern facilities in China and Indonesia. Political leaders, aware of international pressures for Japan to uphold its fair share of world burdens, have argued for an expansion of Japan's role in these areas rather than in military affairs. And they realize this can only be achieved with the cooperation of their closest and most important ally, the United States. Japan is now beginning to increase rapidly its aid contributions.

Japan has considerable resources, aside from capital, to play such a role. Japanese bureaucrats bring great skills in careful planning, long-term continuity, integrity and enforcement of high standards of job performance. Japanese trading companies have the capacity to put together international development projects on a commercial basis. Japanese are ready to send corps of specialists abroad to take part in these projects.

Japan has consistently lagged behind other industrialized countries in the proportion of GNP devoted to international aid efforts. Despite the intentions of many idealists, elemental nationalism that has resisted aid-giving abroad, especially outside Asia, has proved to be much more powerful. As individuals, Japanese have unsurpassed capacity for hospitality, but as a nation Japan has tended to pursue its own narrow interests. At least until now, in battles within Japan between nationalists and internationalists, power has tended to gravitate to the former. The highest Japanese leadership regularly makes commitments of aid on the occasion of foreign state visits. Although officially strings are no longer attached, terms are generally not attractive, feasibility studies often lead to delays or postponements, and locals often feel compelled to purchase products from Japanese companies attempting to expand local markets. Some cynics have charged that Japanese foreign aid is given less from genuine human compassion for the needy than from a desire not to appear overly selfish compared to other countries.

Moreover, anti-Japanese sentiments remain strong in Asian countries and are emerging in other developing countries. In part this is the inevitable remnant of World War II and the result of envy. But it is also fueled by the perceived arrogance, exclusiveness and discrimination of Japanese toward others at home and abroad, and by questions about promises made to gain contracts and hidden problems that later emerge to increase costs to the purchaser. Expression of such sentiments is muted by foreign leaders who want Japanese technical and financial assistance, but it is a powerful force that has explosive potential.

At some point, foreign pressure for Japan to assume a larger burden, and growing Japanese sympathy for the plight of the Third World poor, may lead to a further speed-up of aid even beyond the substantial increases already projected. Prime Minister Yasuhiro Nakasone has already outlined a vision of 100,000 foreign students studying in Japan by the year 2000, and comparably bold plans are being enunciated by prominent Japanese to assist foreign nations. Many Japanese educators realize that they must do a great deal more to open their educational and research institutions and technology to foreigners.

Recently, Japan has shown a remarkable ability to forge a consensus on new public issues such as pollution and social welfare, evidence that in Japan a fundamental sea change can occur in a short time. It is therefore possible that, before the end of the century, Japan will undergo a similar sea change in its commitment to international aid programs and its receptivity to foreigners in Japanese society. If so, it is likely to be generated from Japan's own initiatives. Although cosmopolitan Japanese are prepared to cooperate with other donors in foreign aid, many officials and much of the public believe Japan is now strong enough that it does not need to ingratiate itself with the United States by aid-giving in the pursuit of strategic interests defined by U.S. priorities and objectives.

For the foreseeable future Japan is likely to make steady and sizable incremental increases in foreign aid. In a country where consensus is important and must involve many groups, a pattern of consistent incremental increases of aid, like military spending, is easiest to manage. Given rapid Japanese economic growth, these increases in foreign aid may be large enough to make Japan the largest single aid donor by the mid-1990s and to permit a number of significant new initiatives. These will not be large enough in this century to embrace worldwide development efforts in a Pax Nipponica.

V

Until now the Japanese have not had a clear vision of a new world trade order. They have essentially accepted existing international institutions and learned how to promote their national interests within that framework. They are not yet sufficiently comfortable with their newfound economic success to consider reshaping the international trade order.

However, for the first time since 1853, when Admiral Matthew Perry forced the opening of Japan's ports to foreign trade, the Japanese feel strong enough to achieve their long-cherished patriotic dream: to resist—with all due politeness—foreign pressures to accept arrangements that give advantages to other countries. Through long decades of subservience to the United States, the Japanese have learned how to develop and use whatever leverage they have to achieve their goals. They have learned how to delay and postpone while being polite, yielding only when all other choices seem absolutely exhausted. They are prepared to make pragmatic adjustments where necessary, but the prevailing consensus is that they should yield to American pressures on trade as little as possible.

In the Japanese view, America's wants and demands are endless. Any concession leads to endless demands by U.S. congressmen and other groups for more. It follows that the best way to respond to American pressure is to lengthen and complicate the solution of any problem, to find ways to slow down implementation while maintaining an overall friendly climate.

Underlying Japanese attitudes on international trade is the conviction that it is in their interest to produce goods for their own consumption and for export, and to buy as few manufactured foreign goods as possible. Many Japanese now have confidence in Japan's ability to buy needed resources and imports, but policies and attitudes are still conditioned by the desperation they felt in the wake of World War II shortages and the 1973 oil shock. Japanese leaders can conceive of future emergencies caused by difficulty in importing needed resources or loss of competitiveness in international markets to newly industrializing countries. It follows that they must continue their neomercantilist policies of manufacturing as much as possible at home and importing only a minimum of manufactured goods from abroad. Most foreign specialists are convinced that Japanese efforts at "import promotion" do not yet represent a fundamental change in attitude but are more an effort to persuade foreigners that Japanese markets are already open.

Japan's neomercantilist policies after World War II centered on export promotion to acquire needed resources. Knowledgeable Japanese are proud that they developed their own unique strategy, but they bristle at the charge that it was unfair. Why should Europe and the United States presume to set the standards of what is fair and unfair in world markets? In their view

Japan has, by and large, followed international laws and won in international economic competition by producing higher-quality goods at better prices. Other countries have controlled imports in pursuit of national goals—why should Japan be singled out because it has done so more successfully? If anything, Japanese believe they have learned the rules as played by the West, and have beaten the West at its own game.

In the early decades after World War II, Japan became accustomed to protecting infant industries and nursing them to international competitive standards. Only when there was virtually no danger of foreign products competing successfully in their home markets would they slowly and reluctantly reduce formal tariff barriers. They made it virtually impossible until the 1970s for foreigners to own their own subsidiaries in Japan or to have even indirect economic control over firms in Japan. They established vertical linkages between companies that made it very difficult for foreign companies to penetrate Japanese markets even when foreign products had competitive advantages. Japanese officials found ways to slow down the approval process for competitive foreign products. Japanese industrial-sector associations found ways to work with officials in setting standards, allowing fees for pharmaceutical and medical products, restricting procurement of foreign products and delaying the entry of such goods until domestic makers could make competitive products.

Despite *tatemae* (general statements of principle) and the growing conviction of some Japanese leaders that these practices must go, Japanese economic power is sufficiently decentralized that it is largely in the hands of working-level professionals, many of whom still believe that these practices remain in Japan's interest.

Most American trade officials see their responsibility as keeping a "level playing field." But Japanese trade officials are the same ones who are responsible for maintaining the competitive success of Japanese products in their jurisdiction. They therefore fight to protect areas where they are not competitive, e.g., soda ash, timber, agricultural products, telecommunications, medical instruments and pharmaceuticals. The Japanese government enjoys a great continuity of bureaucrats who see their responsibility not as keeping the playing field level but as achieving and maintaining the market superiority of their products and restraining foreign imports while maintaining an appearance of fairness.

Many formal barriers to trade have been removed, and many Japanese genuinely believe that they are as open to competitive foreign trade as other powers. They believe that they have fewer tariffs than most other nations, and that the ones they do have are among the world's lowest. In their view the European Economic Community has more barriers than Japan; even the United States has far more barriers than most Americans know about, including various state regulations that make importing difficult. Many Japanese are convinced that if all tariff and non-tariff barriers in Japan and the United States were lowered, the trade imbalance with the United States would actually increase. They believe that if voluntary restraints on textiles, televisions, cars, semiconductors and other products were lifted, they would have far greater sales to the United States, but that even if all restraints on foreign products were lifted in Japan, few American products would be able to compete successfully in the Japanese market.

The Japanese worry about American protectionism, but they sense that American moods go in cycles, and they therefore adopt strategies to overcome temporary American outbursts. Observing congressional voting proclivities with great care, they are convinced that Congress will have great difficulty uniting to impose any serious protectionist measures that Japanese businessmen cannot get around. They also see strong American pressures against protectionism: the consumer movement; the interest of the American defense establishment in purchasing goods around the world; the desire of American leaders to maintain goodwill, not only with Japan but with the rest of the world; the desire of economists who want to keep world markets open; the concern of certain American businessmen to protect their niche in the Japanese market, however small, or their marketing of Japanese-made products.

To represent their interests within congressional and administration circles in Washington, Japanese hire former high American government officials of both parties as lawyers, consultants and public relations specialists. They send and receive goodwill missions. Prime ministers make speeches urging Japanese to buy foreign goods, which frank Japanese acknowledge may be aimed more at foreign than domestic audiences. Japanese bureaucrats in JETRO (the Japan External Trade Organization) help arrange "import fairs" of boutique goods, food products and other goods that have at best minor significance in the trade balance. New trade packages and concessions are announced, often timed to forestall American actions.

Now that the Japanese have achieved what they consider superior economic performance, ardent nationalists are prepared to explain to foreigners that if they want to succeed in Japan they must work harder, improve their products, their prices, their commitment to the market, their after-sale service. And even government officials who act with diplomatic restraint are now proud that Japan is strong enough to resist endless rounds of pressures.

Lacking a vision for a new world trade regime, Japanese are still uncomfortable thinking of themselves as the dominant economic power, let alone as capable of imposing a Pax Nipponica over world trade. But the combination of their superior competitiveness, their dominance in financial circles as the world's leading creditor, their superior information network, and the dependence of others on Japanese products and technology creates great de facto power. This power will enable Japan to dominate world trade and use its power, as it has in the past, to serve its national interests and enhance the well-being and economic security of its people.

VI

Japanese, by habit and design, are reluctant to call world attention to the full scope of their international economic success. Americans and Europeans understandably find it difficult to acknowledge the extent to which their global economic power has declined at the expense of their competitor in East Asia. The international problems that arise from increasing Japanese economic power have therefore not received the attention they deserve. Let us enumerate some of the problems that the rise of Japan poses for the United States.

Can the United States stem its relative economic decline? A careful analysis of Japan's competitive advantages suggests that the problem is far deeper and requires a far more concerted effort than most Americans realize. Public discussion of these issues has unfortunately been dominated by economists who take far too narrow a view of the problems and think chiefly in terms of exchange rates, interest rates and savings rates. The problems are much larger. Japanese managers have access to lower rates of capital and a less costly, more committed and better trained work force. For example, over 94 percent of Japanese complete high school compared to less than 80 percent in the

United States, and Japanese students have much higher average math and science scores than their American counterparts.

Japanese government and private business collaboration makes it very easy to move flexibly in concentrating national resources on important, commercially relevant research and development. Japanese business makes constant surveys of manpower needs. Cooperation between government and business makes for more rapid adaptation to changing training requirements.

The Japanese government's neomercantilist policies help keep savings rates high, the cost of capital low, the commercialization of new inventions rapid, and trade barriers in line with national strategy. Cooperation between government and business and the relatively low reliance on regulation and unpredictable litigation reduce investment risks. Retraining and incentive programs provide new job opportunities for those displaced by a changing economic structure, thus helping to maintain a social fabric in which the overwhelming majority of people identify with and share national goals.

It is clear that a commitment to focus on these areas is desirable for achieving American foreign policy objectives, as well as for improving American welfare. It is not yet clear that America has the political will to overcome the decades of complacency that stemmed from the unique period following World War II, when, as the only major power not severely damaged, it could succeed economically without special efforts.

Can U.S. and Japanese macroeconomic policies solve the trade imbalance? Western economists hope the trade gap might be substantially narrowed by the appreciation of the yen, but past experience is not encouraging. Since 1971, when the exchange rate was 360 yen to the dollar, every time the yen appreciated significantly, American trade balances maintained a temporary plateau but did not significantly improve. Japanese firms simply restrained price increases to retain their share of the market. Then, as Japanese firms gained further productivity advantages, their market share again increased. Once manufacturing plants and skills moved to Japan and the newly industrialized countries, the depreciation of the dollar did not lead to a substantial return of manufacturing to the United States. Exchange rate adjustment, in short, is an adjustment to superior Japanese improvements in productivity, and does not solve the problem of continuing American economic decline.

Some Western economists note the disparity between Japanese and Western savings rates and believe the problem could be solved if the Japanese would stop sacrificing and spend more. They vastly underestimate Japanese consumption and naïvely hope that more Japanese consumption would increase Japanese imports or at least restrain Japanese exports. But the "sacrifice" of Japanese consumers, except for the problem of housing in metropolitan areas, is a myth. The Japanese have gained far more improvements in living standards in recent years than the citizens of any Western country. Although not yet caught up with the most advanced Western countries in housing space, indoor plumbing and car ownership per capita, Japan's general consumption levels have already surpassed West European levels.

Given its population density and excellent rail transport, the number of automobiles in Japan may already have reached an optimum. In personal electronics and cameras, specialized clothing and many luxury items, Japan has already surpassed the United States in per capita consumption. Japanese spend far more on weddings and other ceremonies and more than twice as much on tourism per capita than Americans. Even in housing, during the 1970s and 1980s the Japanese made about 50 percent more housing starts per capita than Americans. Even affluent Japanese do not wish large entertaining space at home, preferring to use hotels, restaurants and special centers where facilities far surpass those in the West.

In sum, Japanese consumers do not feel they are sacrificing, and if they were to spend still more there is no indication they would buy significantly more foreign products. Nor will the Japanese government greatly stimulate further spending, since Japan has a large budget deficit and Japanese leaders have formed a powerful consensus that long-term national prosperity requires putting a cap on government spending. In short, Japanese trade surpluses with the United States are not likely to be resolved by changes in the exchange rate or by changes in Japanese macroeconomic policy. The reasons for Japanese economic success are much deeper.

Can the United States encourage the Japanese to make it easier for foreign companies to operate in Japan? The pressure on Japanese to open their markets further has had considerable impact since the mid-1960s, but over the last several years the improvement has been modest at best. Part of the problem is that the behavior of sectoral associations and the vertical connections between firms make it difficult for foreign firms to penetrate. The complexity of trade issues leaves great opportunities for loopholes for those who do not consider it in their interest to open the market more thoroughly.

Although specialists disagree on how much difference it would make to the trade balance if Japanese markets were thoroughly open, it is generally agreed that American exports to Japan might initially increase only several billion dollars a year. However, decisions by American firms to locate in Japan, to build up their staff and presence there, would give them a base for further expansion; they would be ready to take advantage of new opportunities that would undoubtedly have a much larger effect in the long run. Furthermore, the opportunity of foreign companies to achieve economies of scale by selling in both the large Japanese and American markets would improve their long-run competitive positions in many products, even if it did not have a large immediate impact. Clearly, American firms should be playing a larger role in the Japanese market.

The export of American manufactured products to Japan has, in fact, increased in recent years. A further opening of the Japanese market would have a very important long-range political significance. When Japan was weak, other countries were willing to tolerate considerable protectionism in the Japanese market. Now that Japan is stronger, political antagonism not only strengthens anti-Japanese feelings but strengthens protectionist pressures in the United States and elsewhere. Given these pressures, which are rooted in real economic adjustment difficulties and compounded by a sense of unfairness on the part of the Japanese, it is unlikely that the White House and the State Department can contain the political pressures for long. Perhaps a greater danger than an American administration implementing or supporting restrictive trade legislation is the danger of emotional outbursts in Congress and elsewhere that would trigger similar emotional reactions in Japan. The challenge for an American administration is to press Japan with sufficient vigor to reduce such outbursts, while containing pressures for more sweeping protectionism.

It is unlikely that Japan will open its markets significantly without American pressure to require it as a condition for continued access to important parts of its own domestic economy. Some thoughtful internationalists in Washington and Tokyo have suggested that it would be useful for Tokyo to undergo a consensus-building process of developing a new open-market strategy, much as it developed a new consensus after the first oil shock of 1973. But given current Japanese attitudes, such a consensus-building process is unlikely to bring about major change unless there is an urgent worry about Washington's capacity to deny significant market access without a substantial expansion of foreign access to Japan's market. The question for Washington is how to stimulate this consensus-building while avoiding the dangers of protectionism. Given all the problems of inspection and regulation, perhaps some arrangements specifying total amounts or market shares in certain key sectors in exchange for comparable shares in the Japanese market are the most promising. Indeed, confronted with possible American legal action in the case of alleged dumping of semiconductors, the Japanese have proposed just such a solution.

How would an economically dominant Japan reorder the international trade regime and how might America best adapt? Given the ability of certain large Japanese companies to invest in excess capacity and engage in forward pricing to increase market share, in strategically important products it will be difficult for medium-sized foreign companies concerned with near-term profits to avoid being wiped out. In critically important areas like steel, ships, cars and semiconductors, therefore, Japanese market advances may be limited only by de facto cartel arrangements that set limits on market share. In effect, this is what the United States has asked Japan to enforce through voluntary restraint agreements in sectors like textiles, television sets, steel and cars. Within Japan, the government and sectoral associations have been able to manage cartel-like arrangements that restrain the largest companies and strengthen the advancing companies so as to maintain competitive pressures and protect the consumer. Being accustomed to such arrangements at home that limit market share and specify specialization and location, Japanese, despite natural desires to expand international market shares wherever possible, would not find it difficult to agree to international cartel-like arrangements in many products.

VII

The issue for the future international trade regime is not likely to be free markets or protectionism, but the nature of a mix that provides some cushioning for a nation's industries and populations against sudden disruption, while encouraging international trade and providing opportunities for developing countries to expand their manufacturing exports. It may well be that the multi-fiber arrangements which set limits on national textile exports, with all their difficulties, provide a more accurate and feasible vision of the shape of international trade than the American vision of an open and level playing field. The question is how to create agreements with sufficient flexibility to allow newly emerging countries to increase their share gradually and to maintain the benefits of competitive market pressures. Given the declining competitiveness of American business and the political pressures from U.S. business, labor and Congress, America may have no choice but to work toward such agreements. It is in this sense—the capacity of Japanese competitiveness to dictate such a solution—that the international trade regime may well be moving toward a Pax Nipponica.

The prospects for the next few years, therefore, are for a pattern of limited and uneven Pax Nipponica, led by a country of modest military strength, of limited ability to attract a foreign following and to give foreign aid, but of great economic leverage. It is surely in the interests of Japan, as well as the United States and Europe, to work toward the expansion of partnerships and multilateral intertwining in the Pacific basin and elsewhere. In the foreseeable future, no matter how extensive this intertwining, the economic leverage of Japan, the world's most competitive economic power and biggest creditor, is likely to grow and to be used in pursuit of neomercantilist objectives.

Collaboration or Conflict? Foreign Aid and U.S.-Japan Relations

Robert M. Orr, Jr.*

THE JANUARY 1989 announcement that Japan's ODA (Official Development Assistance) disbursements would probably supersede U.S. foreign aid totals had been expected for at least two years. Ever since 1985, when Japan's aid doubling plans (begun in 1977) were boosted by the dramatic appreciation of the yen it was inevitable that the day would come when Japanese foreign aid superseded that of U.S. foreign aid, especially as the U.S. aid program was facing severe budget limitations.

Japan has traveled a long road in a short time. Within days of the government's announcement that Japan would be the largest donor, Japanese television was reminding viewers that only twenty-five years ago the Shinkansen (bullet train) had been built just prior to the Tokyo Olympics as a World Bank project. The television programs also mentioned that Japan was the second largest recipient, after India, of World Bank assistance at that time. In fact in 1990 Japan will finally be taken off the World Bank's borrower list by paying back its final installment. In other words in twenty-five years Japan had gone from being one of the largest receivers of foreign aid to becoming the largest donor of foreign aid. This change from recipient to the world's largest donor of foreign aid has also been mirrored in the overall U.S.-Japan relationship. Whereas twenty-five years ago Japan had a net trade deficit with the United States, today it enjoys an approximate $50 billion surplus. In 1964 Japan's Self-Defense forces had a minor regional role in the Pacific but in 1988 Japan's defense budget appeared to be the third largest in the world after that of the U.S. and the Soviet Union.

In part, Japan's rapid development is of course a direct result of America's calculated foreign policy following World War II. One of the underlying tenets of that policy was to create conditions for the promotion of economic development and democracy and by doing so to prevent, or at least minimize, the advance of Soviet-sponsored communism. Now,

* This article was originally presented at the 41st annual meeting of the Association for Asian Studies held March 17-19 1989 in Washington, D.C. The author is grateful for the comments and contributions of fellow panelists, Dennis Yasutomo, Alan Rix, Bruce Koppel and Susan Pharr. Thanks is also due to Temple University Japan and the East-West Center in Honolulu for their support.

however, America has seemingly been unable to come to terms with the fruits of her policy. With this in mind this article will attempt to address the role that foreign aid has come to play between the U.S. and Japan as Tokyo forges ahead in its new role. The aid relationship spans two other major concerns of U.S.-Japan ties, namely defense and trade. Aid has emerged as a trade issue through American concerns about Japanese aid tying (i.e., with commercial strings attached) and "strategic assistance" has been factored into debates over burden sharing and defense.

In this article I will pose three fundamental questions. First, how different is Japan's approach to foreign assistance from that of the United States? Secondly, how has this created bilateral conflict? And third, has there been cooperation in the area and if so, what kind? Finally I will suggest that for purposes of both promoting greater compatibility between the aid programs of the U.S. and Japan and enhancing economic development there needs to be more stress on collaboration in the future.

Differences and Similarities: Two Donors Look At Foreign Aid

The basic differences between how the United States and Japan approach overseas assistance stem from cultural traditions and policy making. Susan Pharr has suggested that "charity" is a foreign concept in Japan and that "Japan's aid approach could be seen as closely paralleling the Republican approach addressing the problems of the poor domestically within the U.S.: involve the private sector, make the recipient of aid self-reliant [as] soon as possible and avoid give-aways." Pharr goes on to relate this to Japan's own consciousness about development during the Meiji and post-World War II periods and discusses its potential lessons for third world nations.[1] In a sense then the Japanese approach to giving aid appears altruistic as well as being carefully planned for it suggests an overall philosophical approach to aid, albeit one that is in conflict with other donors.

Others have also argued that Japan's approach to aid is indeed very consistent. In this view Japanese aid is perceived as an extension of the notion of Japan Inc., so that Japanese aid, in conjunction with investments and trade, is primarily used as a means of promoting Japan's overseas commercial interests.[2] Specifically this view of Japanese aid assumes that often the aid is closely tied to the purchase of Japanese equipment and consulting services by the country to whom the aid is given. Even when the Japanese government attempts to point out its aid initiatives do not have such eco-

[1] Susan J. Pharr, testimony before the U.S. House of Representatives Committee on Foreign Affairs, Subcommittee on Asian and Pacific Affairs, September 28, 1988.

[2] David Arase, "Japanese Bilateral Official Development Assistance" (paper presented at conference organized by the Ph.D. Kenkyukai, International House, Tokyo, Japan, August 26, 1989). While Arase does not argue that Japan's aid is heavily tied, he does see aid, investment and trade policy used by Japan as an effort to build a Tokyo-centered Asian trade bloc.

nomic ties attached, the advocates of the Japan Inc. theory doubt the Japanese government's sincerity and instead see the government's actions as merely camouflage devices to mask their real intentions of using aid to promote Japanese commercial goals.

Such camouflage takes two main forms. One is so-called LDC untied assistance, whereby only Japan and developing countries can compete for a Japan-funded aid project. The critics' rationale here is that the Japanese government, by allowing only Japanese companies and, for example, firms from a recipient such as Bangladesh to compete to build a hydro-electric plant, the winner of the bid is a forgone conclusion: Japan.

The second and most prominent criticism of Japanese aid policy in recent years has to do with Japan's extensive usage of infrastructural assistance, sometimes known as a capital assistance, which is largely funded by loans in yen. It is this approach, critics charge, that guarantees a strong private-sector role in Japan's aid program and ensures that aid is used as a commercial tool.

Although I would suggest that the third category of criticism, concerned with what is called "strategic aid," is of less significance as a source of conflict between the United States and Japan, it is nonetheless a frequent subject of bilateral discussions. "Strategic aid" is assistance earmarked for, to use the Japanese phraseology, "countries bordering areas of conflict" (*funso shuhen koku*). There has been a noticeable increase in this practice over the past ten years. Countries such as Pakistan, Turkey, Egypt, Jamaica, to name a few, have become major recipients of Japanese aid.[3] The United States, with apparent success, still applies pressure on Japan to give more than 70 percent of its aid to Asia. Indeed in 1971, 98 percent of Japanese ODA went to Asian nations. The notion that the Japanese government is involved in "strategic aid" remains unaccepted in Japan, both at the public and official level — the Foreign Ministry denying that any such concept exists. This only adds to the confusion over the real intentions of Japanese aid in countries with which Tokyo otherwise has little contact.

The final school of thought on Japanese foreign aid looks at the kind of bureaucratic politics approach described by Alan Rix wherein conflict over aid policy making is reviewed as being so intense and rivalry among the relevant ministries so acute that it is next to impossible for a single over-arching "philosophy" or for that matter "conspiracy" to emerge.[4] It should be noted that this view applies only to the policy-making level rather than the level of implementation. It is at the latter level that the private sector

[3] See Dennis T. Yasutomo, *The Manner of Giving: Strategic Aid and Japanese Foreign Policy* (Lexington: Lexington Books, 1986).

[4] See Alan Rix, *Japan's Economic Aid* (New York: St. Martin's Press, 1980); also Alan Rix, "Japan's Aid Philosophy," in Susan J. Pharr, ed., *Japan and the United States in the Third World*, forthcoming.

is best able to wield influence. This is in part because of the "request basis" (*yosei shugi*) approach to aid by which recipients put forth requests to the Japanese government for certain kinds of projects. Despite all forms of untying (extending loans without obliging the borrower to purchase goods from those issuing the loan) these requests can and often are manipulated by Japanese consulting and trading companies. Thus, the main effect of untying is to drive up the costs of project bidding for Japanese companies.

My own views on Japanese foreign aid are most closely aligned with Rix. However, there is a major caveat that needs to be added. Foreign pressure has also molded the form which Japanese aid takes, particularly, as mentioned before, as applied by the United States.[5] Japan is highly sensitive to the way in which other nations, but most particularly industrialized states, see her. Seizaburo Sato has noted that one of Japan's greatest foreign policy fears is that of international isolation.[6] Indeed, one of the underlying reasons for expanding aid as dramatically as Japan has seems to be related to this concern. The Foreign Ministry's 1988 aid white paper called *Wagakuni no Seifu Kaihatsu Enjo* [Our Country's Development Assistance] very early on says, with almost Meiji era clarity, that "catch other donors" (meaning the west) was an important impetus for spending more money on foreign aid.[7]

One of the great ironies is that the American foreign aid program once looked very much like Japan's. Throughout the 1960s, American aid planners focused largely on capital-projects-oriented assistance. In 1973, with the passage of the "New Directions" legislation and the annual expansion of the Foreign Assistance Act, via congressional amendments, emphasis was increasingly placed on the needs of the so-called poor majority. This resulted in a shift away from infrastructural aid toward technical assistance. Eventually almost all the members of the Development Assistance Committee came to focus on technical aid through the provision of grants. Thus in many ways, Japan's aid program, with its dual infrastructural and loan aid harkens back to an earlier time in North-South relations.

Another area of difference between the U.S. and Japan is in the area of recipient "graduation" such as when Japan tends to change the mix of assistance, from grants, for example, to concessional and non-concessional loans, depending upon the level of GNP per capita. The fact that middle income countries predominate in Asia explains, in part, why Japan extends mostly OECF (Overseas Economic Cooperation Fund) yen loans to the

---

[5] See chapter 5 in Robert M. Orr, Jr., *The Emergence of Japan's Foreign Aid Power* (New York: Columbia University Press, 1990).

[6] Seizaburo Sato, "The Foundations of Modern Japanese Foreign Policy," in Robert A. Scalapino, ed., *The Foreign Policy of Modern Japan* (Berkeley: University of California Press, 1977), p. 375.

[7] Ministry of Foreign Affairs, *Wagakuni no Seifu Kaihatsu Enjo*, vol. 1 (Tokyo: Ministry of Foreign Affairs, 1988), p. 5 (hereafter cited as *Wagakuni*).

region.[8] Nonetheless this approach ensures that Japan will always have a role in a recipient country's development, even after it has officially "graduated." Under the U.S. Agency for International Development (AID) approach which, again, has mainly focused on "Basic Human Needs," countries that reach a certain stage of development are simply "graduated" (graduated from the ranks of aid recipients). Plus, from FY1989 AID's entire program will be grant funded. There is no "after-presence" like Japan's except through the Trade and Development Program, which does not have anywhere near the funds available that Japanese institutions such as the Export-Import Bank have. Nonetheless AID documents suggest that a reappraisal of U.S. graduation policy may be underway. In the U.S. government document "United States Official Development Assistance: The Program, the Process and Special Issues" 'graduation' is discussed in terms which are strikingly similar to the Japanese description of "graduation." The document states that "we must look increasingly to the industrial sector to provide the stimulus for growth and opportunities for employment." Later in the document it is suggested that Lesser Developed Countries (LDC's) must be moved away from emphasis on primary products and toward manufacturing and exporting finished products.[9] These approaches bear little resemblance to Basic Human Needs.

Since the inception of the Reagan Administration in 1981 there has been greater emphasis placed upon conditionality of assistance or what a former AID administrator described as "being the tough banker." Japan has been much more reluctant to push economic planning reforms on recipient governments on a bilateral basis.

THE ARENA OF CONFLICT

Some of these conflicts in approaches constitute the areas of greatest disagreement between the United States and Japan. However, in order to understand this more clearly, we must ask ourselves whether things are as U.S. critics of Japan's aid program say they are. Is Japanese aid really basically a predatory instrument of commercial policy? Are there changes being undertaken to lessen the capital projects nature of the program? To what extent has Japanese ODA facilitated exports to recipient countries?

Before addressing these issues, an examination as to why the U.S. no longer focuses on capital projects is revealing. AID, rightfully I would argue, raises concerns about the ability of recipients to pay back large scale loans

[8] Ninety-four percent of Japan's aid commitments for Asia in Japan Fiscal Year 1988 were OECF yen loans.

[9] United States Agency for International Development, "United States Official Development Assistance: The Program, the Process and Special Issues," prepared for the Conference on ODA Management and Asia's Economic Development, East-West Center, Honolulu, Hawaii, May 10–13, 1988.

in the event of a global economic downturn which, in particular, affects primary products and commodity prices.[10] In other words loans conceivably create more debt rather than development although the Japanese counterargument is that loans impose fiscal discipline on recipients. But even more interesting is AID's admission that "the increased cost of capital projects and the dwindling U.S. economic assistance levels (in real terms) prevent AID from being heavily involved in capital projects."[11] Thus we are presented with the spectacle of Japan's infrastructurally oriented aid program being criticized half for substantive reasons and, at least by implication, half because the U.S. can no longer afford to fund capital projects.

The volume of aid pumped into the Japanese system far exceeds the administrative capacity to handle it. According to the Japanese Foreign Ministry while ODA budget levels multiplied by more than 5.2 times from 1977 to 1987, staff was increased by a mere 1.5 times.[12] The total number of Japanese aid personnel stationed abroad in 1988 was 357. This contrasts with AID which had 1,275 U.S. personnel abroad plus 1,170 foreign nationals involved in administering the program. In 1987 there were 26 Japanese aid professionals in Indonesia responsible for administering over $700 million in Japanese aid. In FY 1989 AID had 41 Americans plus 69 local employees to implement a program of a little more than $57 million.[13] This indicates the very different natures of the programs (since BHN type assistance is generally more labor intensive) and that compared with the U.S., Japan relies more on the private sector to implement its program. As with other aspects of Japan's economic policy, the dividing line between the private and public sectors is a thin one indeed.

In addition to criticism of Japan's emphasis on infrastructural assistance, the U.S. has also claimed that Japan, while perhaps moving toward generally untied loans in some categories, has nevertheless maintained tying status when offering engineering consultant services. The concern has been that tying these consultancies will guarantee that other aspects of the project will remain tied.

Up until May 1988 all engineering consultancies were LDC untied, which, as mentioned before, was widely viewed as a "smokescreen" device for tied aid. Since that time the government has moved to untie consultancies in stages. For example, by 1990 the engineering specifications part of yen loans to Thailand, Papua New Guinea and the Philippines will be generally untied. This new scheme has resulted in a firestorm of lobbying by Japanese construction and consultant companies which fear steep increases

---

[10] *Ibid.* p. 1.

[11] *Ibid.*

[12] *Wagakuni*, p. 253.

[13] Correspondence with Robert Halligan, director of personnel, United States Agency for International Development.

in the cost of doing business through yen loans. The strong reaction caught the Japanese government by surprise and encouraged decision makers to slow down the process. Thus the untying of consultancies for China and Indonesia, Japan's two largest recipients of yen loans, has been temporarily suspended.

Another American criticism of loans has been the creation of debt. In an effort to remedy this problem, Japan has been increasingly, but slowly, moving toward more program lending. In JFY1987, 27 percent of all yen loans were program. Because of severe debt problems, most countries in Southeast Asia are no longer enthusiastic about yen-denominated project loans from Japan. In 1989 Malaysia refrained from requesting such loans. Only south Asian nations are interested in this form of assistance. In the case of Indonesia, fully 60 percent of the yen loan assistance it currently receives from Japan goes toward servicing its public debt to Japan! Last year Indonesia for the first time requested dollar denominated loans from Japan, which the Ministry of Finance quickly turned-down.[14]

Despite the emphasis on yen loans and infrastructural assistance, there are indications, at least on a *prima facie* basis, of some decline. In a survey taken by the Overseas Construction Association of Japan, a decrease in orders from ODA related construction can be clearly discerned.[15]

TABLE 1

RECEIPTS IN BILLIONS OF YEN

	1983	1984	1985	1986	1987
LOANS	1,008	344	569	415	361
GRANTS	442	461	327	507	391
TOTAL	1,450	805	896	922	752

Although there are obvious fluctuations there does appear to be a downward trend particularly in terms of construction/capital projects that are funded by yen loans. There are three probable reasons for this: (1) the dramatic rise in the yen (*endaka*) since 1985 has made it more costly for Japanese businesses to operate abroad; (2) the general untying program has made the "cost of doing business" somewhat more expensive; and (3) the increasing shift

[14] "Japan Balks at Indonesia Debt Plan," *Asahi Evening News*, 8 June 1988. Indonesian officials also reportedly proposed paying back yen loans at the 1986 dollar exchange rate level if dollar-denominated loans were not possible.

[15] The Overseas Construction Association consists of fifty-six of the largest construction firms in Japan. This survey was taken of its membership. While there are half a million construction companies in Japan it is primarily the members of the Overseas Construction Association which carry out aid projects.

toward program lending. These figures are hardly conclusive because of the fluctuations and extent to which the industry's lobbying effort will be successful. In addition, we must beware as to what constitutes a "Japanese company" in some developing countries. For example, according to one observer in the case of Thailand many local companies are really thinly veiled Japanese firms with token Thai management.[16]

But there may be some light at the end of the proverbial tunnel on this issue. Increasingly, non-Japanese companies are aggressively bidding on Japanese aid projects. In particular, British firms have been very active. In 1987, Japan agreed to allow British Crown agents to implement a major portion of Tokyo's $500 million package in sub-saharan Africa. At the June 1989 Paris summit Japan announced that an additional $600 million grant package would be extended to the region and that the Crown agents would continue in their role as implementors. British consulting firms, in conjunction with the Japanese government, have organized seminars designed to educate prospective bidders about the tender process. There are increasingly successful non-Japanese bidders but one case bears mentioning. In January 1989, the British General Electric Company successfully won a $64.8 million contract to supply signalling equipment to the Thai National Railway which is to be funded by OECF yen loans. In winning the bid for the Japanese aid project British General Electric Company beat out Mitsui.[17] There have been several other examples of British successes in winning bids on Japanese aid projects, such as in Papua New Guinea and China. There are still restrictions on foreign bidders, most notably in the area of development surveys for grant-aid projects. This is partially because there are legally imposed budgetary time restraints on disbursements and the government feels that relying on foreign firms would hinder its ability to conform to the time limits. Also, grants come directly from the General Account Budget (i.e., taxpayers' money) and therefore open bidding is more difficult to justify publicly. The government points out that none of the major western donors untie grants.

Thus most of the untying progress has been in the area of yen loans, particularly relating to procurement. The table on the next page shows just how many accomplishments have been made in this category.

[16] See Prasert Chittiwatanapong, "Japanese Official Development Assistance to Thailand: Impact on the Thai Construction Industry," unpublished manuscript, Faculty of Political Science, Thammasat University, Bangkok, Thailand.

[17] "GEC wins Japan-backed signal deal with Thailand," and "Breaking the Japanese Stranglehold," *Financial Times* (London), 20 January 1989, pp. 1, 6; also "GEC signs record rail contract: Mitsui beaten for OECF Loan," *Nation* (Bangkok), 20 January 1989, p. 13.

TABLE 2

PROCUREMENT SHARE BY NATIONALITIES OF CONTRACTORS (percentage)[18]

	JFY83	JFY84	JFY85	JFY86	JFY87	JFY88
Local Costs	3	2	5	3	6	5
LDCs	26	22	28	32	41	45
Other OECD members	6	7	11	14	12	17
USA	3	3	4	3	4	5
Japan	63	66	52	48	38	27

Of course, these figures say nothing about the all important consulting category, an area in which many Japanese claim that they are weak. But insofar as it relates to untied procurement through yen credits, the table suggests that international bidders, particularly from recipient countries, can and do win supplier contracts, thus debunking a widely accepted myth that Japanese aid projects are largely constructed merely to provide an outlet for Japanese products.

The table also tells us something else. The percentage of American companies winning bids is not only less than global trends indicate but also the *rate* of increase has been slower. One could conclude that this may be a contributing factor to the more vocal American criticism of Japanese aid policy.

To be sure the story is different when we examine the percentage shares in terms of Japan's overall ODA loans (including tied, LDC untied and generally untied). Nonetheless the percentage returning to Japan has dropped significantly. In 1981 71 percent of all ODA loan procurement contracts went to Japanese companies. By 1987 that figure had dropped to 56 percent, which is less than other donors.

If we accept the claim that Japanese aid is used primarily to promote commercial interests then we must assume that those countries which have received the most significant increases in Japanese economic assistance also are importing more goods from Japan. Otherwise, again accepting this view, Japan would not continuously expand aid to those countries.

[18] Data compiled from Japan's Ministry of Foreign Affairs and the OECF.

TABLE 3

SHARE OF MERCHANDISE IMPORTS AND ODA VOLUME FROM JAPAN[19]

	1978		1987	
	Import %	ODA Volume	Import %	ODA Volume
Indonesia	30.1	227.59	33.4	707.31
China	28.5	-	23.3	553.12
Philippines	27.5	66.47	16.6	379.38
Bangladesh	13.1	119.62	14.0	334.20
Thailand	30.7	103.75	26.0	302.62
Malaysia	23.1	48.00	21.7	276.45

These countries are major recipients of Japanese ODA. In two out of the six countries the percentage of imports from Japan dropped while the aid volume dramatically increased in all the countries in the chart. Despite substantial increases in Japanese aid to these countries, the share of imports from Japan either only marginally expanded or, in four out of the six, actually dropped. There are a number of possible reasons for the drop in import percentage, such as a downturn in their economies which could have been reflected in a diminished demand for imports. In reality, however, as is well known, Asia has experienced a booming growth throughout the decade discussed. Only the Philippines experienced negative growth during any part of the decade.[20] China was not even a recipient of Japanese ODA in 1978 and did not feel the brunt of disbursements until 1982. While the absolute volume of imports from Japan may have increased to these aid recipients, the figures suggest that the Japanese aid program has not permitted it to muscle out other trade partners and donors.

In the past the linkage between Japan's commercial interests and aid was rather clear cut. There remain some aspects of Japanese aid policy where there may be a clearer relationship between economic interests and overseas assistance, such as in consulting services. However, I would submit that it is hardly a closed case.[21] These tables show that Japan's aid program is not solely a tool for commercial interests.

---

[19] Import data compiled from the *Asia-Pacific Report: China in the Reform Era* (Honolulu: East-West Center, 1989), p. 120. ODA volume figures for 1987 are from *Japan's Official Development Assistance: Annual Report* (Tokyo: Ministry of Foreign Affairs, 1988). The figures for 1978 were supplied by the Ministry of Foreign Affairs.

[20] Between 1983 and 1985 the Philippines experienced a real per capita GNP decline of -5.7 but have experienced limited growth since then.

[21] See Bruce Koppel and Michael Plummer, "Cooperation or Co-Prosperity? Asian Perspectives on Japan's Ascendancy as an ODA Power," *Asian Survey*, forthcoming. The authors conclude that nations in developing Asia do not necessarily see Japanese foreign aid as a hegemonic tool.

THE ARENA OF COLLABORATION

Despite the very different natures of the two programs and the criticism of Japanese aid efforts emanating from Washington the two sides have often had a collaborative relationship as well.[22] In addition, as I have suggested, U.S. pressure can sometimes play an important role in shaping the kind of foreign aid policy made in Tokyo. Usually this pressure is delivered during the course of bilateral coordination meetings.

The bilateral dialogue over aid at the level of AID administrator talking to the director-general of the Japanese Foreign Ministry's Economic Cooperation Bureau began in 1978. These meetings have been conducted on an almost annual basis since then. These talks have focused on exchanging views on both countries' bilateral aid programs on a regional, sectoral and policy level. In January 1985 at the Reagan-Nakasone summit in Los Angeles it was agreed to pursue bilateral discussions focusing on the strategic aspect of aid. This dialogue is carried out by the Undersecretary of State for Political Affairs and one of Japan's two deputy foreign ministers.

Lower level discussions are conducted with more frequency, usually when aid officials visit each other's capitals. Without doubt the most significant and substantive dialogue at this level was held in May 1988 at the East-West Center in Honolulu. Over a three-day period, focusing on India, Indonesia and the Philippines, AID officials from the rank of assistant administrator on down met with Japanese Foreign Ministry officials from the rank of deputy director general of the Economic Cooperation Bureau as well as with representatives from the OECF and JICA. This meeting produced progress toward joint projects in India and Indonesia, progress which was later followed up in the field.[23]

Nevertheless, *how* coordination is to be carried out has been subject to considerable debate. In the late 1970s and early 1980s jointly financed aid projects were thought to be the main way to carry out cooperation. While several joint projects were inaugurated, because of conflicting budget cycles as well as the very different approaches to foreign aid noted above, they have never really become a cornerstone of cooperation. Moreover, political expectations for the projects tended to outrun the reality of making the cooperation work effectively while remaining true to concrete developmental objectives.

Thus, coordination has tended to sputter. From the American side it seems to take on new life when there is a commitment demonstrated at the

[22] See Robert M. Orr, Jr. "The Aid Factor in U.S.-Japan Relations," *Asian Survey*, vol. 28 (July 1988). Also see Julia Chang Bloch, "The U.S.-Japan Aid Alliance: Prospects for Cooperation in an Era of Conflict," USJP Occasional Paper (Cambridge, Massachusetts: Program U.S.-Japan Relations, Harvard University [1989]).

[23] Michael Richardson, "U.S.-Japan Set Joint Aid Efforts on Southeast Asia," *International Herald Tribune*, 17 May 1989.

political appointee level. When that interest is not apparent it is reflected by a lack of bureaucratic enthusiasm. The Japanese side proposed the initial coordination in 1978. In recent years, as Japan gradually emerged as the world's leading donor, interest in having bilateral talks outside of the DAC framework has expanded. Today Japan conducts aid discussions with Great Britain and Australia as well as with several other DAC nations. Therefore the "urgency" of dealing with the Americans has abated somewhat. Furthermore, Japanese aid planners have tended to be reactive to U.S. suggestions concerning issues of coordination and discussion rather than developing an agenda of their own which they could pursue with the Americans.[24]

One area in which there have been fairly persistent discussions on aid has been concerned with the Philippines' economic recovery plan. Officials from both governments have met repeatedly in Washington, Tokyo and Manila in order to map out coordination of their respective aid efforts. These talks have not been without their disagreements as both parties have pressed to address issues most relevant to their interests.

As Japanese aid levels have grown other parts of the U.S. government have also become interested in Tokyo's ODA. This has largely been associated with the concept of "burden sharing." The Department of Defense recognizes that Japan has virtually reached a limit with regards to increases beyond current levels of defense spending and has therefore come to view aid as a partial means of fulfilling security requirements. This was at least tacitly acknowledged in 1988 when the Department of Defense called on Japan to fulfill its regional role through the extension of more strategic assistance. By openly requesting Tokyo to extend more "strategic assistance," DOD caused considerable distress among Japanese government planners who, as mentioned earlier, do not like to be publicly associated with strategic objectives.

The U.S. Congress has also become more interested in Japanese aid questions. In the fall of 1988 concurrent resolutions were passed in both the House and the Senate urging that further cooperation and coordination between the U.S. and Japanese aid programs be intensified. A sense of the Congress resolution attached to the 1990–91 authorization of appropriations urged Japan to increase aid expenditures to a level roughly commensurate with the combined defense and aid expenditures of NATO nations in GNP terms.[25]

---

[24] See Bloch, "U.S.-Japan Aid Alliance," p. 84. She describes this relationship as the "usual pattern of the U.S. initiating and Japan reacting."

[25] The House passed H.Con.Res. 387 sponsored by Doug Bereuter (R-NE) and the Senate passed S.Con.Res.157 introduced by Bill Bradley (D-NJ). The Defense Department authorization amendment to s.1352 was offered by Sam Nunn (D-GA) and John Warner (R-VA).

The opening up of the Japanese aid program to foreign bidders has also triggered government-to-government cooperation. Following the examples of Britain and Australia, USAID sponsored two seminars in May 1989 for the benefit of American businesses who might be interested in bidding on Japanese aid projects.

Conclusions

It is clear that there are some very profound differences in the ways which Japan and the United States address questions of economic development. The U.S. has leaned toward a charity and/or strategic rationale. While there is a lessening of infrastructural aid extended by Japan, this is still a significant factor and translates into the provision of far more loans than any other donor. Japan's regional focus is Asia while the United States has extended more assistance to strategically important areas which often host American military facilities. This has led to a clash of philosophies between the United States and Japan most evident in American perceptions of Japan using aid as a commercially predatory instrument. While capital-projects-oriented aid lends itself toward major private sector activity, the tables that I have presented in this article suggest that the commercial use of aid by Japan is not a "cut and dried" affair. Non-Japanese involvement in the implementation of Tokyo's foreign assistance is on the rise. Nonetheless, Japan's construction industry is known for its tenacity and the pressure it exerts on the Japanese government to limit bona fide untying will not abate.

But there is another dimension to aid dialogue between the United States and Japan for while such talks might appear sporadic they are bound to take on an increasing importance. I would argue that the best means of making sure that the kind of economic development that takes place genuinely helps those in the developing world who most need aid is to intensify the U.S.-Japan aid dialogue. Japan has been the largest donor in Asia since 1977 and the increasing presence of Japanese aid will gradually expand Japan's economic clout in other fields regardless of whether aid is tied or not. America's aid profile, however, has noticeably diminished and in order to maintain and help shape economic development in Asia, the United States must attach higher priority to aid coordination with Japan at a variety of levels. Consideration should be given to creating a permanent U.S.-Japan aid coordination committee along the lines of the committee which coordinates bilateral security relations. This would ensure that there is a consistent flow of information being exchanged.

Pressure on Japan's aid program has had an effect and it is difficult to conceive of Japan moving toward deemphasizing aid's commercial content without such pressure. The pressure will no doubt be maintained but it also must be tempered by the long term vision in which consultative mechanisms play an increasingly important role.

Temple University, Japan, October 1989

Perennial Anxiety: Japan-U.S. Controversy over Recognition of the PRC, 1952–1958

Sayuri Shimizu
Michigan State University

From the moment of the establishment of the People's Republic of China (PRC) in the fall of 1949, Japan and the United States dueled over policy toward the Communist regime. Following Prime Minister Yoshida Shigeru's reluctant decision to sign a postwar peace treaty with Chiang Kai-shek's Nationalist government in Taiwan, Japan was forced to forgo diplomatic relations with the PRC for two decades until President Richard Nixon's dramatic rapprochement with Beijing finally permitted it to restructure its China policy in 1972. Nonrecognition of the PRC was one of the prices Japan had to pay for its reinstatement, under U.S. tutelage, in the postwar world overshadowed by Soviet-American confrontation and revolutionary nationalism. However, this nominally independent diplomatic choice made at the close of the Occupation period hardly put the matter to rest. Japan's yearning for formal relations with the mainland Chinese regime strained its nascent alliance with the United States. American officials recognized the enormous sway the PRC held over Japanese of all political shades and persuasions. While scorning the Japanese left's cult of the New China, U.S. policymakers chafed at the flirtation that Japanese conservatives carried on with the Chinese Communists. Through the 1950s, either out of historical nostalgia, political expediency, or neocolonialist impulse, growing ranks of conservative politicians, industrialists, and businessmen courted the PRC.[1]

Unlike the leftists, many Japanese conservatives accepted America's PRC nonrecognition policy and consistently disavowed any intent to embrace the PRC as the legitimate Chinese state. Their agenda was, or so they claimed, solely economic, and their interest did not extend beyond doing business with the government that happened to control the mainland Chinese market. They cleverly disguised their crass economic revanchism as high-minded pragmatism, which came to be popularized after 1954 as the doctrine of *seikei bunri*—the separation

The Journal of American–East Asian Relations, Vol. 4, No. 3 (Fall 1995)

1. Masatoshi Sakeda, "Kouwa to kokunai seiji," in Akio Watanabe and Seigen Miyasato, eds., *Sanfranshisuko kōwa* (Tokyo, 1986), 87–112; Furukawa Mantaro, *Sengo Nicchuu kankeishi* (Tokyo, 1981), 2–50.

of politics and economics. As early as 1949, the incipient form of this doctrine was enunciated by Yoshida himself. Setting the tone for conservative opportunism regarding Asian revolutionary nationalism, he argued that China's political coloration had nothing to do with the question of whether his country should trade with it or not; given its geographical proximity and the prewar patterns of trade, the Chinese mainland was Japan's natural commercial outlet, and he cared little whether China was "red or green."[2]

Projected on the struggle for legitimacy between two Chinas, however, postwar Japan's peculiar strain of political ecumenism carried disturbing implications for the United States. Relinquishing any exclusionary Greater East Asia under its military control and astutely forswearing claims to leadership of anti-Western Pan-Asianism, Japan appeared to have meshed its designs for the Chinese mainland neatly with America's strategic objectives for the Far East. Some officials in the Eisenhower administration, including the president, saw positive good in restoring a Sino-Japanese commercial connection. The rehabilitation of this prewar trade link might assist Japan's self-reinvention as an economically content, stabilizing political force in revolution-plagued Asia. Furthermore, Japan's ties with the PRC, if successfully limited to the commercial field, might lessen Beijing's economic and diplomatic dependence on the Soviet Union. The difficulty of sustaining its draconian multilateral embargo program, especially in the absence of voluntary cooperation from the Western industrial allies, also entered into America's cost-benefit calculations. This line of strategic thinking in Washington fathered Washington's own corollary of the *seikei bunri* doctrine, and some American policymakers proposed using Sino-Japanese nonstrategic trade as an instrument of U.S. Far Eastern policy.[3]

America's ambivalence about the Japan-PRC relationship complicated it's effort to persuade this trade-dependent ally that the PRC deserved harsher trade sanctions than China's Communist brothers in Eastern Europe. When the Western allies intensified their campaign to unify programs restricting trade with the European and Asian components of the Communist bloc in the mid-1950s, Japan was eager to spearhead the effort. In addition to frontally challenging the U.S.-instigated international trade embargo, the Japanese eroded the walls of economic containment with a more subtle resistance. Between 1952 and 1958, Japan signed a total of four so-called "private-sector" trade

2. Nancy Bernkopf Tucker, "American Policy Toward Sino-Japanese Trade in the Postwar Years: Politics and Prosperity," *Diplomatic History* 8 (Summer 1984): 193.

3. Gordon H. Chang, *Friends and Enemies: The United States, China, and the Soviet Union, 1948–1972* (Stanford, Calif., 1992), 80–115.

agreements with the PRC. Justified as an effort to regulate and stabilize bilateral commercial relations in the absence of governmental relations, this channel of people's level contact with the Chinese Communist authorities in effect provided both Japanese leftists and opportunistic traders a powerful mechanism for subverting both official Japanese China policy and the U.S. policy behind it. Leftist challengers used this ostensibly economic interaction to fortify bilateral relations, gradually increase the official flavor of the exchange, and lay the groundwork for diplomatic recognition. Some conservatives joined to circumvent the official noncontact policy, which stood in the way of trade, but others were primarily interested in advancing themselves in the internecine war among conservatives.[4]

This gray area in Japan's relationship with the PRC kept the question of Tokyo-Beijing diplomatic relations alive, and the issue periodically flared up—to the annoyance and ultimately the consternation of officials in both Washington and Tokyo. What Japanese and some American policymakers sought to cordon off as a strictly economic question was actually a highly contested locus where economic, social, political, and diplomatic interests contended. This study attempts to demonstrate how private-sector trade initiatives inexorably became a diplomatic powder keg with two volatile constituents: Washington's dilemma over Sino-Japanese relations and Tokyo's ambiguous commitment to America's China policy. These tensions in the trans-Pacific alliance generated multiple loci of power and resistance, which made the early post-Occupation U.S.-Japanese partnership a highly complex relationship, as it remains today.

On 1 June 1952, barely two months after Japan's reinstatement as an independent state, three Japanese citizens signed a private-sector trade agreement in Beijing with the PRC's Committee on the Promotion of International Trade (CCPIT). One signer was an opposition *Ryokufūkai* member of the Diet, Kora Tomi, whose torturous journey to Beijing involved defiance of the Yoshida government's official China policy at multiple levels. In April, she participated in the Moscow International Economic Conference, organized at the initiative of the Communist Camp as part of its coordinated campaign to expand East-West trade. One of the conference's organizers, President Nan Hanchen of the Chinese People's Bank, urged Japan's participation, first in late 1951 and again in February 1952. The Yoshida government responded to this Communist peace offensive by denying passports to prospective travelers to the Soviet capital. Kora thwarted this obstruction by

4. For the role of the China problem in the division among Japanese conservatives see Haruhiro Fukui, *Party in Power* (Canberra, 1970), 227–62.

traveling to Paris, then working her way to the Soviet Union via Copenhagen and Helsinki. She was later joined in Moscow by two other opposition leaders, Miyakoshi Kisuke and Hoashi Kei, who also traveled through Copenhagen. At the invitation of Lei Reimin, vice minister of the Chinese Ministry of Foreign Trade, who had also participated in the Moscow conference, they extended their odyssey to include a visit to the PRC in mid-May. Tokyo officialdom had no way of preventing the three self-appointed private ambassadors, physically out of its reach, from visiting the capital of the China it refused to recognize at America's behest.[5]

But the trip and the Foreign Ministry's failure to make good on its promise to prevent Japanese participation in the Moscow Conference did not concern American officials enough for them to chastise the Yoshida government. Although he realized that the three legislators' glamorizing accounts of the New China might generate some political momentum, Robert Murphy, the first post-Occupation U.S. ambassador to Japan, dismissed the stories that appeared prominently in the Japanese press. The visit by Kora and her fellows to Beijing, however, quickly blossomed into discussions with the CCPIT aimed at defining the terms of trade relations with the Communist state. The resulting agreement, which Kora, Miyakoshi, Hoashi, and Nan signed, provided for barter trade between the two Asian countries in the amount of 60 million pounds sterling each way. Commodities to be traded were divided into three categories. The most controversial class of Japanese exports to the PRC, Category A, comprised strategic goods whose export was clearly prohibited by the international embargo. Prospective Category A exports to Japan by the PRC included those commodities of greatest interest to the Japanese, such as iron ore, coking coal and soy beans.[6]

The report of the agreement prompted the Yoshida government to publicly dismiss the accord as invalid both legally and practically. This time, the American embassy was alarmed, for the list of exchangeable goods and commodities clearly indicated that the PRC was trying to extract embargoed capital goods, transportation equipment, and steel

5. Murphy to Acheson, 31 May 1952, RG 59, SD 493.949/5-3152, National Archives, Washington D.C. (hereafter cited in SD file numbers); letter from Nan Hanchen, 14 Feb. 1952, Nicchu Boeki Sokushin Giin Renmei, ed., *Nicchū kanksei shiryōshū* (hereafter cited as *Shiryoshu*), 134–35; Furukawa, 36–39; Kei Hoashi, *Soren Chugoku Kiko* (Tokyo, 1952), 4–57; Tomi Kora, *Ahinsa wo Ikiru* (Tokyo, 1983), 140–46; Murphy to Acheson, 27 May 1952, SD 493.9431/5-2752.

6. Fukukawa, 40–42; Murphy to Acheson, 27 May 1952, SD 493.9431/-5-2752; Kennan to Acheson, 31 May 1952, SD 493.9431/5-3152; Hoashi, 323–24; Gaimusho Ajia Kyoku Chugokuka, ed., *Nicchū kankei kihon shiryōshū, 1949–1969* (hereafter cited as *Kihon shiryōshū*) (Tokyo, 1970), 43–44.

products from Japan by preying on the country's need for certain industrial raw materials and foodstuffs. To dispel U.S. concern, the Japanese Foreign Ministry enumerated practical problems left unresolved by the agreement. Aside from the inherent limits of barter trade, which requires the balancing of exports and imports, the agreement was in fact nothing more than a written statement of intent to trade. In the absence of a bilateral payments agreement, open-account trading between the two nations was next to impossible, and cash payment in dollars or pounds sterling was equally unfeasible because of both nations' meager foreign reserves. Finally, the PRC's fierce economic nationalism would not permit the export of goods desired by Japan except in exchange for proscribed strategic goods.[7]

Murphy, however, correctly identified the agreement's real significance as symbolic. Three Japanese public figures, although acting in their private capacity, entered into a compact, although nonbinding, with a representative of the Communist Chinese authorities. Their status as legislators unmistakably gave the document an aura of quasi-official government action, and accorded an element of legitimacy to exporting strategic goods to a Communist government still actively engaged in the Korean War. America's anti-PRC policy and the Japanese government's commitment to remain within its parameters would be correspondingly delegitimized in the court of Japanese public opinion. Ambassador Murphy saw great subversive potential in this semi-governmental overture cloaked as the action of private citizens.[8]

If the first unofficial Sino-Japanese trade agreement was little more than symbolism, the next agreement, reached in October 1953, conspicuously enhanced the subversive quality of Sino-Japanese "non-governmental" commercial exchange. Again, an unmandated exchange led to the second trade accord, which took place against a backdrop of markedly greater flexibility in the PRC's foreign policy posture toward Japan. Setting the basic tone of China's unfolding peace offensive, Premier Zhou Enlai presented the Communist leadership's corollary of the *seikei bunri* doctrine to Ohyama Ikuo, a leading leftist Japanese intellectual and one of the most vocal critics of Yoshida's foreign policy. In a private audience in September 1953, Zhou stressed his country's resolve to dethrone the Nationalists as the internationally recognized government of China. The chief obstacle to reciprocal recognition by the PRC and Japan remained, as far as Beijing was con-

7. Kora signed the agreement in her capacity as the Japanese representative to the Moscow International Economic Conference, Hoashi as representative of the Sino-Japanese Trade Promotion Association, and Miyakoshi as director of the Dietmen's League for the Promotion of Sino-Japanese Trade. Murphy to Acheson, 31 May 1952, SD 493.949/5-3152.

8. Ibid.; Kerr to State Department, 4 June 1952, SD 493.9431/6-452.

cerned, the Yoshida government's refusal to renounce diplomatic relations with Taiwan. However, the absence of formal relations between the two governments should not keep the peoples of both countries from reinforcing their friendship through cultural and economic exchange. Zhou proposed an active exchange of people's representatives between the two countries to foster cooperation in functional areas.[9]

Zhou distinguished the people of Japan from the government in power, and did not make a Japanese break with Taiwan the absolute prerequisite for cooperation in nonpolitical matters. He thus offered new terms for a bilateral relationship that were decidedly more conciliatory and pragmatic than Beijing's earlier blanket condemnation of Japan for accepting the halfway peace settlement crafted in San Francisco. This emerging Chinese variant of the *seikei bunri* doctrine indicated the PRC's receptiveness to the more organized trade initiatives launched by Japanese in the late Yoshida period. In January 1953, Hiratsuka Tsunejiro, director of the Dietmen's League for the Promotion of Sino-Japanese Trade, a nonpartisan parliamentary group established in 1949, approached Nan Hanchen about arranging a meeting in the PRC to promote trade. Carefully couched in the language of private economic diplomacy, Hiratsuka's letter to that leading Chinese trade official bore an unquestionably political subtext. Identifying his group as a nonpartisan association of Diet members at the service of the Japanese people's aspiration to foster trade with China, Hiratsuka evaded the question of whether or not he was speaking for the Japanese government. He also limited the scope of his proposition to trade, but his position gave his approach a subtle yet distinct political flavor.[10]

Delivered by a group of private citizens visiting Beijing to discuss the repatriation of Japanese nationals left in the Chinese mainland after World War II, Hiratsuka's missive carried a potent message of defiance of and nonconformity with the Yoshida government's official China policy. Initially the Foreign Ministry refused to issue a passport to a leading member of the repatriation negotiating team, Kora, on the grounds that she had violated the nation's passport law when she made her historic visit to Beijing via Moscow. Following a public outcry, the ministry was forced to reverse its position, indicating the degree to which Tokyo was losing control of nongovernmental outreach to the PRC.[11] Once the letter was delivered, Nan responded by raising

9. Talks between Zhou and Ohyama, 28 Sept. 1953, *Kihon shiryōshū*, 50–52.

10. Hiratsuka to Nan, 25 Jan. 1953, *Shiryōshū*, 144–45; statement by Nan, 5 Mar. 1953, ibid., 145.

11. Furukawa, 54–62.

the political content of the exchange and extending an official CCPIT invitation to the Dietmen's League, calling the league the political representative of the Japanese people. Nan's offer to receive the parliamentary group in the absence of diplomatic relations indicated how astutely the PRC leadership exploited Japan's obvious trade hunger to blend economics and politics while accepting Japan's *seikei bunri* doctrine. Furthermore, Nan checkmated the Japanese parliamentarians by urging them to host a Chinese trade delegation in Japan in the spirit of reciprocity.[12]

These exchanges alarmed the American embassy, which correctly realized that the Chinese were trying to reopen the question of diplomatic relations with the aid of some Japanese public-sector elements claiming to act as private citizens. In the face of intensive lobbying by the Dietmen's League and government agencies bent on promoting Sino-Japanese trade, such as the Ministry of International Trade and Industry (MITI), the Foreign Ministry promised embassy officials that it would not permit the legislative group to bring PRC officials into Japan under the pretext of trade promotion. In mid-September, Foreign Minister Okazaki Katsuo told the Dietmen's League that such a mission from Communist China would under no circumstances be admitted into Japan. Nan lambasted Okazaki and his ministry's rejection of the Chinese proposal as indicative of the Yoshida government's hostile attitude toward the government and people of China. But neither the Chinese nor the Dietmen's League was about to allow this setback to stall a burgeoning working relationship between PRC authorities and various Japanese nongovernmental organizations. As a compromise, they agreed that only a Japanese delegation would make a visit, but that the Dietmen's League would publicly declare its commitment to seek a change in the government's policy of refusing to admit PRC trade representatives into Japan. Japan's twenty-five-member trade mission, comprising thirteen members of the Diet and twelve industrialists, headed for Beijing in late September.[13]

As the legislative body became more systematically involved in nongovernmental contact with the pariah state, the China trade question came to be irreversibly enmeshed with political mobilization in Japan against Prime Minister Yoshida. Ikeda Masanosuke, who headed Japan's first trade mission to the PRC, epitomized this political fusion. A point man for the renegade anti-Yoshida faction of the Liberal Party, the standing director of the Dietmen's League fastened on the China problem as a weapon with which to assail the prime minister

12. Exchange of telegrams, Hiratsuka and Nan, 20, 22, and 25 Sept. 1953, *Shiryōshū*, 147–49.

13. Ibid.; Masanosuke Ikeda, *Nazo no kuni: Chūkyo tairiku no jittai* (Tokyo, 1969), 334–36.

and the postwar settlement he personified. In the immediate wake of the Korean armistice, Ikeda cosponsored a Diet resolution urging the government to promote Sino-Japanese trade more aggressively. This illustrated how anti-Yoshida forces, both within and outside of the conservative camp, linked their partisan agendas to the unfolding new phase in international politics. Ikeda's public statement, issued before heading for the PRC, resonated with China's people's diplomacy in a rather contrived way. The objectives of this mission, he declared, were to deepen friendship between the peoples of China and Japan and to expand bilateral trade on the basis of equality and reciprocity. But by emphasizing the historic significance of the group's excursion as "the first official visit to Communist China by elected representatives of the Japanese people," this anti-Yoshida, anti-Communist politician further clothed the overture to the PRC with an aura of legitimacy and official government participation.[14]

His Chinese hosts aggressively seized the opportunity offered by Japanese domestic politics. Upon the Japanese delegation's arrival, Nan proposed that negotiations commence to update the bilateral trade agreement. Although unprepared, the Japanese delegation accepted the sudden invitation. A month-long negotiation in Beijing, again outside the reach of Tokyo officials, led to the second Sino-Japanese private-sector barter trade agreement in late October. Signed by the CCPIT and the Dietmen's League, the distinctly official tone of the trade accord could not be entirely obscured by the qualifying "private-sector" in its title. At the initialing ceremony, Nan again distinguished between the people and the government of Japan and called the Japanese people a victim of Washington's tyranny and the Yoshida government's sycophantic diplomacy. This theme was amplified in Vice Premier Guo Moruo's remarks to the visiting delegation. Guo held firm to the PRC's position that the severance of diplomatic relations with the Nationalists must precede establishment of relations between Japan and the PRC. But in the absence of this fundamental requirement for national reconciliation the peoples of both countries should engage in constructive economic and cultural cooperation. A cooperative framework in the technical areas would provide the foundation for eventual political reconciliation.[15]

The conciliatory tone of the Chinese leadership's exhortation actually stood in contrast to the rockiness of the negotiations, which became seriously deadlocked over several points. As in the previous agreement, the Chinese successfully placed items of interest to Japan

14. Furukawa, 54–56; Berger to State Department, 5 Jan. 1954, SD 493.9431/1-554.

15. Second Private-Sector Trade Agreement, 29 Oct. 1953, *Kihon shiryōshū*, 57–59; statement by Kuo, 28 Oct. 1953, ibid., 52–57.

in Category A of the commodity exchange list to match embargoed strategic goods to be shipped by the Japanese. Both sides bargained even harder over a clause in the accompanying memorandum which stated that each agreed, as a future goal, to station a permanent trade representative's office in the other's country. The inclusion of this proposition was testimony to just how forcefully the PRC leadership pursued the objective of landing its officials on Japanese soil. The establishment of a permanent PRC trade office in Japan carried diplomatic implications far beyond trade promotion. The presence of a permanent administrative office in Japan would imply de facto recognition of the Chinese Communist state. News of this semi-diplomatic concession by the parliamentary mission prompted the American embassy in Tokyo to convey its concern to the Foreign Ministry.[16]

Publicly dismissing the agreement as nonbinding and irrelevant, the Foreign Ministry explained to the embassy that the trade pact was a private arrangement, with no bearing whatsoever on the Japanese government's official position on Chinese representation. American and Japanese officials agreed that the accord would accomplish little in terms of expanding Sino-Japanese trade. The noncongruity of interests between the two parties, which was made obvious by the unrealistic commodity exchange list, convinced them that as long as the multilateral trade embargo remained in place and the PRC's economic nationalism remained strong, the second agreement would again fail to yield results remotely approximating its ambitious target of 60 million pounds sterling each way. But they were distressed to see that Japan's private ambassadors had given in to Chinese pressure and pledged their support for the controversial permanent trade mission clause without consulting with the Japanese government. But the embassy promptly received reassurance from none other than the head of the Ikeda mission himself. Claiming to speak for other conservatives who advocated trading with the Chinese Communists, Ikeda readily admitted that he expected the unofficial accord to accomplish little in stimulating bilateral trade because of the Soviet-bloc orientation of the PRC's foreign trade and general difficulties in trading with that country. But by permitting free expansion of what was an inherently unpromising trade relationship, and by magnanimously receiving Beijing's trade officials, argued Ikeda, the conservatives in Japan and the U.S. government could appropriate the left's principal agenda and undermine its strength.[17]

16. Harrington to Dulles, 3 Nov. 1953, 493.9431/11-355; *Mainichi shimbun*, 31 Oct. 1953; *Asahi shimbun*, 30 Oct. 1953; Kerr to State Department, 9 Nov. 1953, SD 493.9431/11-953; memorandum of Ikeda-Lutkins conversation, 13 Nov. 1953, SD 493.9431/1-554.

17. Memorandum of Ikeda-Martin conversation, 1 Nov. 1953, SD 493.9431/1-554.

Thus conservative critics of the Yoshida government's China policy trivialized the entire question of Japan's postwar settlement with China by reducing the issue to a partisan political ploy. But conservative support entrenched the advocacy of freer commercial interaction with the PRC in the political mainstream in post-Occupation Japan. After Yoshida's expulsion from power in late 1954, conservative support for the admission of Chinese trade officials gathered further momentum. In March 1955, after more than a year of lobbying government agencies, the Dietmen's League finally succeeded in hosting a thirty-five-member delegation of Communist Chinese officials. The ostensible purpose was to negotiate a new trade accord and to afford the Chinese a chance to visit industrial facilities in Japan, all for the sake of promoting Japanese exports to what appeared to be a growing continental market of 600 million Chinese. But all parties, including American officials who nervously watched the Foreign Ministry slowly succumb to pressure from the Diet and MITI, clearly understood that the PRC's real motive was political: It sought to push the Japanese government a step closer to de facto recognition when de jure recognition appeared yet unattainable.[18]

That a trade mission from China at long last materialized revealed the potency and nature of its supporters in Japan. One of the official hosts, the Dietmen's League, had about half the legislative branch as members. The Japan Association for the Promotion of International Trade (JAPIT), established in September 1954 by more than forty leading industrial leaders, had also lobbied vigorously on behalf of the Chinese trade mission. The engagement of this respectable industrial association in the campaign to host Communist Chinese trade officials, coupled with the coming into power of Prime Minister Hatoyama Ichiro who was avowedly committed to defining Japanese foreign policy priorities independently of Washington, indicated how mainstream the quest for a closer relationship with Beijing had become. The leader of the Dietmen's League, Ikeda, was the prime minister's protégé; and JAPIT's founding members included major industrialists such as Murata Shozo, former chairman of Osaka Merchant Marine Company, and two members of the Hatoyama cabinet, Takasaki Tatsunosuke, who headed the Economic Deliberation Agency, and Ishibashi Tanzan, MITI's new helmsman.[19] It became increasingly difficult for the Japanese government, if it indeed so desired, to dismiss calls for reconciliation with the PRC as radical political demands.

Symbolizing the nonideological fusion between conservative business interest and the radical political agenda of seeking a rapproche-

18. Kerr to State Department, 22 Mar. 1955, SD 493.9441/3-2255.

19. Murata Shozo, "Shū Onrai to Atte," *Sekai*, 20 Apr. 1955; Furukawa, 112–14; Drumright to Dulles, 9 Feb. 1955, SD 493.9441/2-955; Kerr to State Department, 22 Mar. 1955, translation of Murata's report on trip to China, 1 Feb. 1955, SD 493.9441/3-2255.

ment with Beijing, JAPIT Chairman Murata engineered an event which threatened to destabilize the triangular relations between Japan, the United States and the PRC. In January 1955, he visited Beijing on behalf of the newly established trade association. Without clearance by the Foreign Ministry, the self-appointed Japanese business envoy proposed to Lei that a new round of Sino-Japanese trade talks should take place in Tokyo, reciprocal commodity exhibitions should be held and efforts should continue to station permanent trade representatives' offices in the other's capital. Upon returning from Beijing, Murata personally lobbied Hatoyama to permit entry of a PRC trade mission which, in Murata's words, would be composed of important Chinese officials. The prospect of the Hatoyama government blessing a visit by PRC officials alarmed the highest level of the State Department, including Secretary of State John Foster Dulles, and when Washington joined the fray, the trade mission question was suddenly taken out of the narrow realm of entry and transit control for foreign trade promoters. The issue now became decidedly a three-way diplomatic combat.[20]

Dulles called the Foreign Ministry to account: How could the newly formed Hatoyama government embark on such a risky venture over an issue so central to the American-Japanese cooperative framework? As the ministry explained, the Hatoyama cabinet, a tenuous coalition of anti-Yoshida forces, was deeply divided over the issue. Ishibashi and Takasaki, both founding members of JAPIT, pushed hard for a forthright government endorsement of the visit; Foreign Minister Shigemitsu Mamoru refused to step out of line with U.S. policy; and Hatoyama found himself caught in between. The polarized cabinet worked out a fragile "understanding" that a PRC trade delegation would be permitted to enter Japan, but that the government would remain completely uninvolved in the undertaking.[21]

But the agreement did not keep Ishibashi from overseeing the drafting of a new trade agreement, and the Foreign Ministry intimated to American officials that the new head of MITI was pressuring industrial circles to accept the terms for industrial raw material imports demanded by the PRC.[22] Ishibashi was not the only public official who meddled in what the Hatoyama cabinet had agreed to portray as a private negotiation between Japanese business representatives and

20. Murata-Lei conversations, 11 and 17 Jan. 1955, Kerr to State Department, 22 Mar. 1955, SD 493.9441/3-2255; Murata Shōzō, *Nicchū kakehashi no ichikiroku* (Tokyo, 1972), passim; Murata's report on trip to China, 1 Feb. 1955, SD 493.9441/3-2255; Allison to Dulles, 29 Jan. 1955, SD 493.9431/1-2855.

21. Kerr to State Department, 22 Mar. 1955, SD 493.9441/3-2255; Allison to Dulles, 29 Jan. 1955, SD 493.9431/1-2855.

22. Memorandum of Okamatsu-Waring conversation, n.d., Kerr to State Department, 22 Mar. 1955, SD 493.9441/3-2255.

Chinese trade ambassadors. As soon as the Hatoyama government decided to permit Sino-Japanese trade talks to take place in Tokyo, Dulles urged the Foreign Ministry to intervene and eliminate pro-Communist elements from the Japanese team, so that the recognition question would not be interposed into the trade talks. The embassy also sought cooperation from MITI's working-level officials to contain Ishibashi's maneuvering and ensure that the terms and conditions of the third agreement would not be so unfavorable to Japanese traders as to make Japan vulnerable to pressure to defy the multilateral strategic embargo.[23]

America's intervention did not stop there. Watching prefectural and municipal governments and businesses and factories stampede for an opportunity to host the group, Ambassador John Allison warned the State Department that the situation threatened to get out of hand. Fearing the accelerating degree of government involvement in the only nominally "private-sector" trade promotion endeavor, Dulles urged the Foreign Ministry to restrict the Chinese mission's inland travels. On 15 March, as requested, the Foreign Ministry ordered Murata and Ikeda to limit the itinerary to the Tokyo and Osaka areas. Its bargaining chip was a threat to withhold entry documents. Meanwhile, reports of Washington's disapproval rapidly dampened the enthusiasm of Japanese businessmen. Firms holding contracts with the U.S. armed forces and others with stakes in exports to the United States reversed themselves and declined to receive the Chinese delegation. Much to the delight of the American ambassador, big business associations, such as the Japan Chamber of Commerce and the Federation of Economic Organizations (Keidanren), also dissociated themselves from the event.[24]

But the battle was not yet over. A week before the arrival of the Chinese delegation, the PRC succeeded in getting the Foreign Ministry to agree to use the title "the People's Republic of China" on the certificates of entry and travel permits in exchange for restrictions on travels in Japan. The Foreign Ministry assured the embassy, as it declared in its press release, that the use of this name in no way constituted a change in Japan's official policy of nonrecognition of the PRC.[25] The Chinese trade delegation arrived in Tokyo on 29 March against the backdrop of this diplomatic victory for Beijing. The five weeks of negotiations culminated in the third Sino-Japanese private-sector trade agreement, signed on 4 May by Murata, Ikeda, and Lei, who did so as

23. Kerr to State Department, 15 Mar. 1955, SD 493.944/3-1555.

24. Ibid.; Allison to Dulles, 17 Mar. 1955, SD 493.9441/3-1755.

25. Allison to Dulles, 23 Mar. 1955, SD 493.9441/3-2355; Kerr to State Department, 4 Apr. 1955, SD 493.9441/4-455; Drumright to Dulles, 23 Mar. 1955, SD 493.9441/3-2355.

the representative of the People's Republic of China Trade Mission to Japan. When Allison obtained an advance draft of the agreement from the Foreign Ministry, he took comfort in the fact that the trade accord, which included only embargoed goods in the most critical Category A, was impossible to implement fully. But the ambassador was disturbed by some of the agreement's ground-breaking provisions. While Article 2 stipulated that barter trade was to be the basic format of trade, Article 5 stated that future transactions would be financed through the open account system to be regulated by a payments agreement between the Bank of Japan and the People's Bank of China. Such an agreement between the two central banks represented another building block of a de facto governmental relationship. Article 8 delineated procedures for joint arbitration of contractual disputes, and Article 9 called for the reciprocal sponsorship of trade fairs.[26]

By far the most controversial component of the agreement was Article 10, which called for the reciprocal stationing of permanent trade representatives. This proposal was conceived in Murata's preliminary agreement with Lei in Beijing, and despite its interference in the Tokyo round of negotiations, the Foreign Ministry could not secure the elimination of this problematic clause from the final text. Furthermore, the ministry could not prevent Japanese citizens acting in their private capacity from agreeing that such permanent trade offices should be accorded privileges comparable to diplomatic immunity. The signatories also agreed to guarantee the safety of each other's nationals engaged in work associated with joint arbitration and trade fairs, and to obtain their respective governments' commitments to do the same. These provisions would have the Japanese government meeting obligations that, while ostensibly related only to trade, were full of diplomatic implications. By systematically insisting on reciprocity in bilateral commercial relations, the Chinese in effect demanded reciprocity in political privileges as well. In this adroit exercise, the Chinese forcefully intermingled the economics and politics of Sino-Japanese trade.[27]

These controversial provisions again split the Hatoyama government. Hatoyama initially inclined toward endorsing the agreement, but Shigemitsu convinced the prime minister that such action would inflict irreparable damage on Tokyo's relations with Washington. The PRC delegation was enraged, but it grudgingly consented to a compromise solution suggested by its Japanese hosts: A letter from Murata and Ikeda addressed to Lei would be affixed to the main text of the accord; the letter would verify that when "representatives of the

26. Allison to Dulles, 17 Mar. 1955, SD 493.9441/3-1755; Allison to Dulles, 4 May 1955, SD 493.9441/5-455; Third Sino-Japanese Trade Agreement, *Kihon shiryōshū*, 83–97.

27. Allison to Dulles, 5 May 1955, SD 493.9441/5-555.

Dietmen's League for the Promotion of Sino-Japanese Trade met with Prime Minister Hatoyama on 27 April 1955, the prime minister expressed his intent to give the accord his support and cooperation." Hatoyama's statement of "support and cooperation" as an expression of the Japanese government's official position was questionable at best. It had been obtained by Ikeda in an informal and nonprofessional setting. Ikeda was subsequently reprimanded by Chief Cabinet Secretary Nemoto Ryutaro for quoting Hatoyama without formal cabinet-level approval. Once cast in a quasi-official light, however, the prime minister's casual utterance took on a political life of its own. In a skillful move to extract maximum diplomatic gain out of the disorganization and confusion in the Japanese official circles, Lei gleefully stated at the signing ceremony on 3 May that the Japanese prime minister's endorsement had given him reason to believe that the new trade accord, unlike its forerunners, would yield satisfactory results.[28]

The unwitting government quasi-endorsement of the third trade agreement triggered a tempest in Tokyo officialdom. Vice ministers of various government ministries called Nemoto on the carpet. The Japanese government could not make such a commitment without preconsultation with the United States, they angrily protested, and in view of the Formosa crisis which began in September 1954, a relaxation of the China trade controls was impossible. After a contentious postmortem, the Hatoyama cabinet managed to agree on a party line: The prime minister was only expressing his general approval of civilian trade between Japan and China; his approbation did not apply to specific provisions of the trade agreement. The Foreign Ministry vehemently advocated this line at the American embassy's urging. Nonetheless, on 16 May, Hatoyama told the Diet that while he could not give the PRC full diplomatic treatment, he "might consider" exchange of consular representatives if the question of recognition was not involved. Shigemitsu also intimated to the Diet that some concessions to the Chinese would be forthcoming.[29]

The State Department bristled at the renewed prospect that the Japanese government might extend de facto recognition to the PRC by opening a permanent trade office. The embassy immediately requested that the Foreign Ministry clarify the offending remarks. Admitting embarrassment over the lack of policy coordination, the ministry conceded that an exchange of "private commercial representatives" without diplomatic status was being considered. Such representatives

28. Ibid.; Furukawa, 118–21.

29. Allison to Dulles, 12 May 1955, SD 493.9441/5-1255; Hoover to embassy in Tokyo, 13 May 1955, SD 493.9441/5-1355; Allison to Dulles, 16 May 1955, SD 493.9441/5-1655.

would be entitled to facilities ordinarily accorded to private commercial representatives, including use of a commercial telegraph system. The ministry said it had no choice because under present legislation, the government could not restrict private communications and private commercial activities. These claims of powerlessness and respect for private economic imperatives would become the ministry's standard excuse as the proposal to open a permanent PRC trade office in Tokyo periodically resurfaced and strained the Washington-Tokyo relationship between 1955 and 1957.[30]

In one such instance, in May 1956, the Hatoyama government announced that it had in principle agreed to an exchange of "private-level but permanent" trade missions with the PRC. The decision jolted American officials, particularly because Shigemitsu and his ministry had responded so well to Washington's wish, not so subtly expressed in late 1955, to limit the number of Japanese visitors to the Chinese mainland through passport control. Pressured by the Dietmen's League and MITI, the Foreign Ministry agreed to explore ways to exchange trade officials without implying de facto recognition, a proposition which to the Americans, sought to achieve the impossible. In justifying this decision to the American embassy, the Foreign Ministry said Shigemitsu and his staff had to bolster their political fortunes to avoid completely losing credibility in Japanese domestic politics. The conclusion of a provisional fisheries agreement with the Soviet Union by one of Shigemitsu's cabinet rivals, Agriculture and Fisheries Minister Kono Ichiro, and the looming prospect of a rapprochement with Moscow, were widely compared to the foreign minister's failure to gain UN membership for his country in December 1955. The Japanese public now looked to relations with the PRC as the next logical step in fulfilling the Hatoyama cabinet's promise of an independent foreign policy. In this domestic political landscape, Shigemitsu and his ministry could ill afford to appear to the public to be perpetual nay-sayers. They had to make at least some gesture of trying to encourage arguably harmless commercial intercourse with the Communist bloc.[31]

Dulles believed that the ministry was practicing its usual art of feigned weakness and trying to enlarge its autonomy in China policy by exploiting a gray area in the definition of Japan's international obligations. But since the existing multilateral East-West trade control agreement did not specifically prohibit the stationing of a foreign trade mission, the secretary had to conclude that the United States could

30. Allison to Dulles, 17 May 1955, SD 493.9441/5-1755; Dillon to Dulles, 6 Dec. 1955, SD 693.94/12-655; Dulles to Dillon, 9 Dec. 1955, SD 693.94/12-655.

31. Hemmendinger to Robertson and Sebald, 1 Oct. 1956, SD 693.94/1-156; Waring to State Department, 18 June 1956, SD 493.9441/6-1856.

not legally force Tokyo to abandon this idea. Moreover, fully aware of Japan's sensitivity to any U.S. move which might be construed as restricting its sovereignty, Dulles resigned himself to instructing Allison to convey Washington's disapproval at the "level of friendly advice." In a subsequent, friendly discussion, Allison warned Shigemitsu that anti-PRC forces in Congress might sabotage the Eisenhower administration's Japan policy. In a similar exchange, Assistant Secretary of State Walter Robertson repeated this warning to Japanese Ambassador Iguchi Sadao. At risk would be Asian economic development aid and the Mutual Defense Program for Japan. Top American and Japanese foreign policymakers agreed that a permanent PRC trade office, even without diplomatic status, would facilitate Communist Chinese espionage activities and create a "false" impression that Japan was drifting toward greater political accommodation with Beijing.[32]

By the spring of 1957, these stopgap American efforts to stifle the courtship between Japan and the PRC were clearly inadequate. In April, the Japanese trade interest group opened a new round of talks with CCPIT to discuss, among other things, a fourth private-sector trade agreement. However, the three sponsoring organizations, the Dietmen's League, JAPIT, and the Japan-China Export-Import Association (JCEIA), which had been established in December 1955 under heavy MITI influence, suspended negotiations in May to await the outcome of negotiations in Paris among the Coordinating Committee's member nations on China trade controls.[33]

From the outset of the preliminary phase of negotiations, held in Beijing, the stationing of permanent trade missions represented a serious bottleneck. Initially the dispute revolved around the Japanese government's fingerprinting requirement. All private visitors who intended to stay in the country for a period exceeding sixty days were fingerprinted. Chinese trade authorities revolted against this Japanese policy on moral as well as political grounds. Lei argued that the measure originated in the Japanese government's attempt to block opium and other contraband smuggling and that Tokyo's refusal to waive this requirement was profoundly offensive to the Chinese people and their lawful representatives. The Japanese Socialist Party (JSP) added another dimension to the debate when it focused on the fingerprint-

32. Dulles to embassy in Tokyo, 23 May 1956, SD 493.9441/5-2356; memorandum of Shima-Parsons conversation, 25 May 1956, SD 493.9441/5-2556; Hemmendinger to Robertson and Sebald, 1 Oct. 1956, SD 693.94/1-156.

33. Thibodeaux to State Department, 11 July 1957, SD 493.9441/7-1157; Thibodeaux to State Department, 30 July 1957, SD 493.949/7-3057.

ing question in its renewed campaign to push the Japanese government toward de facto recognition of the Beijing regime.[34]

The leader of the Japanese government at that time was Kishi Nobusuke, and he added his antirevolutionary policy to the tapestry of international politics in Asia. During a whirlwind tour of Asia in May and June, Kishi enraged the PRC leadership with his anti-Communist grandstanding, complete with an ostentatious endorsement in Taipei of a Nationalist reconquest of the Chinese mainland. At the same time, the Foreign Ministry initially underestimated Beijing's militancy on the issue of fingerprinting and trivialized the entire debate, reducing it to petty international politicking. The ministry persuaded Americans that the Japanese government could call the PRC's bluff: Beijing was merely using the dispute to aid the JSP and fray the Liberal Democratic Party's (LDP) relations with its important business supporters. The Chinese were also hard put to make good on their promise of the lucrative China market, particularly in the aftermath of major steps taken by Western industrial countries in June to decontrol China trade.[35]

Further making a mockery of the *seikei bunri* doctrine, the Japanese government tried to shape the negotiations, which resumed in Beijing in late August, directly. Kishi and Foreign Minister Fujiyama Aiichiro personally pressured Ikeda and members of the government-influenced JCIEA to prevent the issue of recognition of the PRC from tainting the private-sector trade talks. True to his reputation as a supreme opportunist, Ikeda proved to be a cooperative partner in the Kishi government's dubious attempt to depoliticize the Sino-Japanese private-sector trade negotiations through greater government involvement. To ingratiate himself with Kishi and his retinue in the LDP's ever-shifting factional alignment, Ikeda now wanted to distance himself from Socialist members of the Dietmen's League. Before leaving for preliminary discussions in Beijing, Ikeda promised both Japanese and American officials that, as a devoted anti-Communist, he would do his very best to prevent Beijing from exploiting the trade talks to gain even another inch toward recognition and bolster the leftists in Japan. The Foreign Ministry, for its part, reassured Americans that this time around, the Japanese government could force the PRC into

34. Ibid.; Thibodeaux to State Department, 12 Nov. 1957, SD 493.949/11-1257; Lei Renmin, "The Key to the Development of Sino-Japanese Trade" (in Chinese), 3 Sept. 1955, in *Jih-pen wen-t'i wenchien huipien* (*Jih-pen wen-t'i*), 2:171–74; Commentary, "Trade and Fingerprinting," *Renmin ribao* (People's daily), 7 Aug. 1957, in ibid., 182–84.

35. *Asahi shimbun*, 4 June 1957; Zhou's talks with Japanese Radio and Television Corps, 25 July 1957, *Kihon shiryōshū*, 118–20; MacArthur to Dulles, 3 Aug. 1957, SD 493.9441/8-357.

submission. Given the PRC's growing difficulties trading with the Soviet bloc, the nation needed to shift its trade to the Western world. Japan could now afford to be tough on all points, including the fingerprinting issue.[36]

Ikeda's preliminary talks in Beijing quickly proved that the Chinese did not intend to compromise on the status of the trade mission. Faced with the PRC's resolve, the Foreign Ministry's diplomatic muscle quickly began to unflex. On 30 August, Fujiyama began to argue to the new U.S. ambassador, Douglas MacArthur, Jr., that accepting a PRC trade office in Tokyo might not be a bad idea: It would help the government to stop left-wingers from acting as an intermediary between small businesses and PRC trade authorities. By stationing trained personnel, including government officials in Beijing, Tokyo could directly supervise and regulate trade office activities and administer Sino-Japanese trade without formal diplomatic recognition. Fujiyama made the same proposal to Dulles when he visited Washington in late September. The foreign minister's convoluted argument that direct government participation was needed to keep politics and economics separate failed to convince the secretary. Dulles warned Fujiyama of "bad political consequences" if the Japanese government opened a permanent trade organ in Beijing. He did not see how Tokyo could escape the issues of formal recognition and full diplomatic relations once it started to descend the slippery slope of dealing directly with PRC authorities.[37]

By this time, however, the Ikeda mission was already in Beijing with four specific government "instructions." Unlike the agreement signed five years ago, this round of Sino-Japanese trade talks could not be called "unofficial" or "private-sector" by any reasonable speaker. The Japanese delegation arrived at the negotiating table with government instructions in its pocket. Their guidelines indicated that the Kishi government was prepared to make significant political concessions in order not to be held responsible for the breakdown of the negotiations. The Ikeda mission had been told that the Kishi government was open to permitting up to five Chinese trade officials to enter Japan without fingerprinting. The government was also prepared to offer "every convenience" short of formal diplomatic immunity, such as exemption from such normal government requirements as the payment of customs duties and business and income taxes. The Foreign

36. Chumming to Dulles, 6 Aug. 1957, SD 693.94/8-657; Thibodeaux to State Department, 30 July 1957, SD 493.949/7-3057; MacArthur to Dulles, 19 Aug. 1957, SD 493.9441/8-1957.

37. MacArthur to Dulles, 2 Sept. 1957, SD 493.9441/9-257; Thibodeaux to State Department, 21 Nov. 1957, SD 493.949/22-2157; memorandum of Dulles-Fujiyama conversations, 2 and 3 Sept. 1957, State Department Lot Files, Bureau of Far Eastern Asian Affairs, 55D480, RG 59, NA.

Ministry only retroactively informed the American embassy that the Kishi government had authorized the Japanese negotiating team to make these concessions to save the agreement. It justified this fait accompli by citing the aggressive promotion by West Europeans of trade with China. The PRC would soon embark upon a new five-year plan and Japanese industries, especially the steel and electrical equipment sectors, must firmly establish footholds in China. This could be accomplished with the help of a "nongovernmental" trade accord, and it must come into place before Europeans preempted the market, argued the ministry. No longer was any mention made of Japan's sellers market.[38]

The Chinese, however, refused to accept the concessions. They demanded that thirty officials receive fingerprinting exemption and that the Japanese government guarantee the physical safety of the mission's personnel and facilities. Unable to break the impasse, the Ikeda mission returned to Tokyo on 1 November for "consultation with the government."[39] American officials were chagrined that despite Tokyo's direct intervention, or perhaps because of it, the trade talks with the Chinese had turned into a full-blown diplomatic wrangle. Tokyo officialdom and the Japanese business community were gripped by fear of European competition in China, MacArthur warned Dulles; driven by this anxiety, the Japanese government might even grant the PRC de facto recognition at the risk of seriously alienating the United States.[40] The question for the Kishi government boiled down to this: How far was it willing to exceed the parameters of U.S. Far Eastern policy for what it understood to be a probably overrated and assuredly unpredictable market? This issue, threatening to destabilize the delicate equilibrium of the Japanese government's China policy since Yoshida's time, exposed the tensions within the political coalition which had pushed Tokyo to wage a continual, subtle revolt against the dominant U.S. policy.

Ikeda's effort during preliminary talks to persuade Nan to accept some face-saving compromise over fingerprinting split the Dietmen's League. This division exposed the fundamental ideological disunity of the group, whose only common denominator over the past eight years had been expanding trade with the Chinese.[41] After the Ikeda

38. Drumright to Dulles, 20 Sept. 1957, SD 493.9441/9-2057; MacArthur to Dulles, 21 Sept. 1957, SD 493.9441/9-2157; Thibodeaux to State Department, 27 Nov. 1957, SD 493.9441/11-2757.

39. Thibodeaux to State Department, 24 Sept. 1957, SD 493.9441/9-2457; Joint statement concerning the suspension of negotiations, 1 Nov. 1957, *Shiryōshū*, 168–69; MacArthur to Dulles, 1 Nov. 1957, SD 493.9441/11-157.

40. MacArthur to Dulles, 30 Oct. 1957, SD 493.9441/10-3057.

41. Memorandum of Ikeda-MacArthur conversation, 2 Aug. 1957, Thibodeaux to State Department, 14 Aug. 1957, SD 493.9441/8-1457; Ikeda to Nan, 9 Aug. 1957, Nan and Lei to Ikeda, 12 Aug. 1957, *Shiryōshū*, 167–68.

mission returned to Tokyo in November, the PRC's demand for de facto recognition as a price of the new trade pact deepened the schisms among the three sponsoring organizations. In late November, they held a rally to urge the government to take all necessary steps to bring the agreement to conclusion by the end of 1957. Displaying the parliamentary group's split along LDP-JSP lines, LDP members, including Ikeda, conspicuously absented themselves from the rally. Given the increasingly partisan undertone of the national debate, the Kishi government initially sought to escape the dilemma by revising the Alien Registration Law; it sought to extend the length of residency exempt from fingerprinting from sixty days to a year. In stormy Diet debates in early 1958, the JSP effectively attacked the Kishi government for its continued application of the requirement to Chinese trade officials resident beyond the one-year grace period. The Kishi government countered this charge by resorting to an extralegal administrative measure. In mid-February, the Justice Ministry announced that it would exempt individual Chinese trade representatives from the fingerprinting requirement as an "exception," to be granted at the minister's administrative discretion.[42]

America's reaction to this announcement was quick. Despite MacArthur's personal protest, however, Kishi was ready to give the PRC trade office such quasi-diplomatic treatment in order to break the logjam in Sino-Japanese trade negotiations. In the early months of 1958 a recession lingered, elections were scheduled for the spring, and the Japanese were frustrated by the protectionism they encountered in U.S. markets. Kishi was not about to be held responsible for torpedoing China trade by taking an inflexible stand on the Chinese trade mission. Kishi and his party had another compelling reason to make political concessions to the PRC. Japan's growing heavy industrial sectors, the LDP's big-business stronghold, were now at the forefront of the private-sector campaign. They were clamoring for government assistance in tapping what was touted as a growing Chinese market for industrial equipment under the PRC's Second Five-year Plan. Illustrative of this shift in the composition of the China trade interest group, major steel firms—Yawata, Fuji, Nippon Kokan, and Kawasaki Steel—dispatched top executives to Beijing in February to assess the PRC's market potential and to seek contracts for large-scale procurement of iron ore and coking coal. In the ongoing consolidation of the closely contested two-party system, the LDP faced an overriding im-

42. MacArthur to Dulles, 2 Nov. 1957, SD 493.9441/11-2157; Thibodeaux to State Department, 27 Nov. 1957, SD 493.9441/11-2757; statement by Dietmen's League, 23 Dec. 1957, *Shiryōshū*, 169; *Jih-pen wen-t'i*, 2:184; *Asahi shimbun*, 13 and 14 Feb. 1958.

perative to follow the cues of this particular component of Japan's "grassroots" outreach to the PRC.[43]

The weight of big business opinion was not the only constraint on the Kishi government. When the Ikeda mission returned from Beijing in November for consultation, the Kishi government learned that the delegation had fatally overstepped its instructions. In the draft agreement and the accompanying memorandum signed by the Ikeda mission, the Japanese negotiators agreed that, with the consent of the host governments, the proposed trade missions should be given "the right to fly the national flag" on their premises.[44] Even more than Kishi and his party, the Foreign Ministry was petrified by Ikeda's blunder. Denied direct access to negotiations between a group of Japanese politicians and businessmen and their unmistakably governmental Chinese counterparts, the ministry had lost control over the quasi-diplomatic proceedings which carried profound implications for the nation's foreign policy. In the aftershock of the revelation, the ministry could only hope to redeem itself before outraged American officials by blaming it on Ikeda's inept "people's diplomacy." Concerned government ministries had recommended to Kishi that he refuse to take official cognizance of the draft trade agreement and the attached memorandum while secretly providing privileges cited in the documents except for the right to fly the national flag and direct settlement of legal disputes. The latter privilege would imply exemption from Japanese legal jurisdiction.[45]

The commitment made by the trade mission was not only a reflection on the Foreign Ministry's weak command of its jurisdiction and a victory for the Socialists on the ideologically diverse negotiating team. It was the result of Ikeda's personal diplomacy, which reflected what he understood to be the smoke-filled-room quality of the ruling party's decision-making structure. He returned from Beijing in November expecting the leaders of the LDP to extend at least tacit approval for the draft agreement, perhaps in the manner of Hatoyama's verbal pledge of "support and cooperation" for the third trade accord. His souvenir from Beijing, however, was too hot a political potato for the LDP. More important, over the two years since its establishment, the party had become a much more institutionalized entity than the nebula of conservative forces in which Ikeda was used to operating. The day before his mission was to return to Beijing to resume negotiations in

43. MacArthur to Dulles, 13 Feb. 1958, SD 493.9441/2-1358; MacArthur to Dulles, 14 Feb. 1958, SD 493.9441/2-1458.

44. MacArthur to Dulles, 21 Nov. 1957, SD 493.9441/11-2157; MacArthur to Dulles, 21 Feb. 1958, SD 493.9441/2-2158; Furukawa, 146.

45 MacArthur to Dulles, 21 Feb. 1958, SD 493.9441/2-2158.

late February, Ikeda received a notice from the LDP Executive Council: The party's Foreign Policy Research Council, after careful consultation with legal experts in the Foreign and Justice Ministries, had concluded that the LDP could not endorse the draft agreement without revoking his mission's commitment on all points that made the draft agreement acceptable to the Chinese. Any reference to the consent of the Japanese government was to be expunged from the "private" trade agreement; the PRC trade office would not be granted the right to fly its national flag; trade mission members would not be exempt from the jurisdiction of Japanese courts; and finally, the mission should be limited to the minimum number of persons necessary for the performance of its duties.[46]

Upon resumption of the discussions in Beijing in March, Lei refused to give up the clause relating to the national flag, claiming that Zhou's directive would not permit it. He went before the Chinese and foreign press corps in Beijing and defined the question as "a test of the good faith of the official Japanese trade delegation." As Lei pointed out, the Japanese side, in the joint statement signed by the Ikeda mission on 1 November, explicitly accepted the draft agreement and, as an integral accompaniment, the memorandum. Confronted by acute Chinese criticism, the Ikeda delegation again exceeded its government's instructions and signed an almost unmodified fourth agreement on 5 March. The only saving grace was a mutual "understanding" that members of the trade missions were expected to respect laws, customs and practices of their host country in accordance of the spirit of the Bandung Conference. The PRC's trade office was expected to number about twenty, and both sides agreed that the question of national flags was "not an appropriate subject of discussion since diplomatic recognition and raising the national flag had no relationship at a time when neither country recognizes the other."[47]

This lame face-saving effort illustrated the curious coexistence in the Japanese approach of political astuteness regarding U.S. hegemony and legal obtuseness in dealing with the Chinese. Since 1952, the Japanese had used private Sino-Japanese trade initiatives to resist the government's official China policy. They had repeatedly exploited the ambiguity of the negotiators' status and thereby manipulated the legal and political implications of the trade agreements. Within the con-

46. Ibid.; LDP's Four Principles Concerning the Memorandum on the Sino-Japanese Trade Agreement, 22 Feb. 1958, *Shiryōshū*, 170; Clark to State Department, 26 Feb. 1958, SD 493.9441/2-2658; Parsons to Robertson, 6 Mar. 1958, SD 493.9441/3-658.

47. *Renmin ribao*, 4 Mar. 1958; Gene Hsiao, *The Foreign Trade of China: Policy, Law and Practice* (Berkeley, Calif., 1977), 44; MacArthur to Dulles, 7 Mar. 1958, SD 493.9441/3-758; "Understanding on the Fourth Sino-Japanese Trade Agreement and Its Attached Memorandum," 5 Mar. 1958, *Shiryōshū*, 178–79.

fines of U.S. Far Eastern policy, this political acumen allowed these dissenters, and Japan as a nation, to establish a remarkably high degree of autonomy. But in exercising this art of resistance and subversion, the Japanese gradually lost control of a similar game concurrently played by Japan and China. By the time the fourth agreement forced the Kishi government to confront again the fundamental question of Japan's postwar China policy, the country's self-styled private ambassadors were clearly being outperformed by their Chinese counterparts. Deliberately placing themselves outside the direct control and supervision of the state, and shepherded by an old-style politician like Ikeda, who thrived on the unstructured personal politics of bygone days, the Japanese agents of people's economic diplomacy were ill-equipped to wheel and deal with officials of a government whose every move was purposely directed toward one supreme prize: diplomatic recognition.

Kishi promised MacArthur that his government would not let Ikeda's unauthorized concessions push it into recognizing the PRC. This assurance provided little solace to American officials, who believed that, regardless of Kishi's intent, if the Chinese Communist flag were hoisted above a trade mission in Tokyo, it would be widely construed as de facto recognition of the Communist regime, and de jure recognition might become a realistic prospect.[48] But by far the strongest reaction came from Taipei, which had repeatedly issued mild warnings to the Kishi government both directly and through the United States since the inception of negotiations for the fourth Sino-Japanese trade agreement. Upon conclusion of the trade pact, the Republic of China (ROC) began bombarding Japanese and American officials in Tokyo, Taipei, and Washington with threats of dire consequences. Chiang Kai-shek told the United States that he could tolerate most provisions of the agreement, offensive as they were to him, because he recognized Japan's dependence on foreign trade, and his government valued growing economic and political ties with Japan. But if the Kishi government permitted the PRC flag to fly, the Generalissimo would haul down his own flag in Tokyo and sever relations with Japan. To register its protest, the ROC suspended its ongoing trade talks with Japan in Taipei, froze all private business transactions on 14 March, and five days later suspended all procurement from Japan.[49]

48. MacArthur to Dulles, 7 Mar. 1958, SD 493.9441/3-758; MacArthur to Dulles, 12 Mar. 1958, Herter to embassy in Tokyo, 12 Mar. 1958, memorandum of Ogawa-Clough conversation, 12 Mar. 1958, SD 493.9441/3-1258.

49. MacArthur to Dulles, 5 Sept. 1958, SD 493.9441/9-558; Drumright to Dulles, 12 Mar. 1958, SD 493.9441/3-1258; Drumright to Dulles, 13 Mar. 1958, SD 493.9441/3-1358; Drumright to Dulles, 16 Mar. 1958, SD 493.9441/3-1658.

The intense reaction from Taipei added a new dimension to the full-blown diplomatic feud. Dulles employed every possible line of friendly persuasion to convince the irate ROC leader that breaking off diplomatic relations with Japan was not in the best interest of his country. The diplomatic void created would quickly be filled by the PRC, the secretary pointed out, and the Chinese Communists would soon thereafter fly their flag all over Japan with impunity. If Japan, a linchpin of the anti-PRC alliance system in Asia, recognized the PRC by default, "it would only hurt the ROC's own international position."[50] Meanwhile, the Japanese government stood powerless, immobilized by the consequences of Sino-Japanese people's diplomacy and caught between the dueling Chinas. By late March, Dulles suspected that the Kishi government was about to succumb to preelection pressures and officially endorse the fourth trade agreement with the flag clause intact, even at the risk of rupturing the relationship with Taipei. As much as the idea of a Socialist ascendancy in Japan was unpalatable to American policymakers, they feared that if the Japanese government was hounded down this road to de facto recognition, Washington's commitment to enforcing its PRC nonrecognition policy might be called into question worldwide. Upon Dulles's instruction, MacArthur warned Fujiyama: It was time for the Japanese government to stop evading the issue by claiming that Sino-Japanese trade was a matter of private sector agreement; acts of the Chinese communist regime were inevitably official and political. Taizo Ishizaka, the president of Keidanren, and several LDP Dietmembers also received MacArthur's admonition.[51]

In his desperate attempt to stem Japan's drift toward the PRC, Dulles argued that the Japanese must wake up from the lingering prewar dream of economic empire on the Chinese continent and accept the postwar reality. The political and economic partnership with the ROC was much more important, and if the flag dispute resulted in a cutoff of trade by Taipei, Japan would suffer a "loss of substantial present trade in exchange [for] only hoped for future trade. The economic cost of the ROC's shifting [its] trade pattern [is] also considerable" and "the free world['s] best interest [will be] served by the continuation of the economic alliance."[52]

50. Herter to embassies in Taipei and Tokyo, 14 Mar. 1958, SD 493.9441/3-1458; Drumright to Dulles, 16 Mar. 1958, SD 493.9441/3-1658; Drumright to Dulles, 17 Mar. 1958, SD 493.9441/3-1758; MacArthur to Dulles, 18 Mar. 1958, SD 493.9441/3-1858; Dulles to embassies in Taipei and Tokyo, 20 Mar. 1958, SD 493.9441/3-2058.

51. Dulles to embassy in Tokyo, 20 Mar. 1958, SD 493.9441/3-2058; MacArthur to Dulles, 25 Mar. 1958, SD 493.9441/3-2558; Dulles to embassy in Tokyo, 27 Mar. 1958, SD 493.9441/3-2758.

52. Dulles to embassies to Tokyo and Taipei, 27 Mar. 1958, SD 493.9441/3-2758.

At America's peremptory request, in a letter hand delivered to Chiang by Ambassador Horinouchi Kensuke on 31 March, Kishi pledged that his government's policy of nonrecognition of the PRC was immutable. But as to blocking the flying of the Communist Chinese flag over the prospective trade mission, the prime minister could only promise his "utmost effort" to find an administrative solution. Chiang demanded an unequivocal written commitment from Kishi that once the elections were over, the Japanese government would prohibit the public display of the Communist Chinese flag through statutory regulations or local municipal ordinances. In a further intervention in the diplomatic crisis which risked rupturing America's anti-PRC alliance system in Asia, Dulles threw his weight behind the beleaguered Japanese prime minister: Kishi had gone as far as he could in giving assurance on the flag issue without jeopardizing himself, his party and his government, the secretary told Taipei.[53]

On 9 April, Taipei accepted, as an alternative to Kishi's written commitment, Horinouchi's memorandum stating that "after the elections and prior to the establishment of the Communist Chinese trade mission in Tokyo, the Japanese government will make necessary and sufficient efforts by appropriate means in order that the flag will not be raised over the said trade mission or residence of mission members." This piece of a secret document saved the three anti-PRC governments from losing an alliance none could afford to let go. Following this solution, the Kishi government informed the three organizations which signed the fourth Sino-Japanese trade agreement that it would not acknowledge the PRC's right to fly its flag. Kishi also told the Diet that his government would not apply Article 92 of the Criminal Code, which provided for the protection of national flags, to the PRC flag.[54]

The PRC's angry reaction to the Kishi government's decision put the finishing touches on the acrimonious diplomatic imbroglio spawned by Japan's private trade initiatives. Accusing the Kishi government of trying to resurrect a scheme for a Greater East Asian Co-Prosperity Sphere by riding the crest of U.S. power, Chinese trade authorities rejected the fourth trade agreement, relieving the Kishi

53. Dulles to embassies in Tokyo and Taipei, 3 Mar. 1958, SD 493.9441/3-2858; MacArthur to Dulles, 1958, SD 493.9441/3-3158; Drumright to Dulles, 1 Apr. 1958, SD 493.9441/4-158; Drumright to Dulles, 3 Apr. 1958, SD 493.9441/4-358; MacArthur to Dulles, 4 Apr. 1958, SD 493.9441/4-58; Dulles to embassies in Taipei and Tokyo, 4 Apr. 1958, SD 493.9441/4-458; Drumright to Dulles, 7 Apr. 1958, SD 493.9441/4-758.

54. MacArthur to Dulles, 10 Apr. 1958, SD 493.9441/4-1058; Kishi's reply to request concerning Fourth Sino-Japanese Trade Agreement, 9 Apr. 1958, statement by Aichi, 9 Apr. 1958, statement by George Yeh, 9 Apr. 1958, *Shiryōshū*, 180–81; MacArthur to Dulles, 10 Apr. 1958, SD 493.9441/4-1058; Drumright to Dulles, 10 Apr. 1958, SD 493.9441/4-958.

government of its dilemma. The Nagasaki flag incident of 2 May, in which two Japanese extremists hauled down the PRC flag at a Chinese postage stamp and paper craft exhibit, only accelerated the coming of the inevitable. The culprits were arrested but not prosecuted for destruction of the flag. In retaliation, the PRC suspended all economic and cultural exchanges with Japan as of 11 May. Vice Premier Chen Yi's vitriolic commentary, issued two days earlier, in effect announced the end of the PRC's espousal of the *seikei bunri* doctrine, which had informed Beijing's extensive people's diplomacy with all who claimed to be private citizens, not official representatives of the Japanese government. Chen inveighed against Kishi and his followers for using Sino-Japanese trade as a means to their ultimate ends of "currying favor with the U.S." and conspiring with "Chiang and his clique" against China. Marking the end of the honeymoon period in the PRC-Japanese relationship, Chen declared that New China could live without trading with Japan; to think otherwise was the "hallucination of an idiot." Under an increasingly bellicose foreign policy and the centripetal drive of the Great Leap Forward, the PRC would indeed live without Japanese trade for some time to come, until Beijing's deteriorating relations with Moscow and internal economic dislocations forced it to seek out the old commercial suitor earnestly waiting just across the sea.[55]

The period between 1952 and 1958 was a time for slow reawakening for both the PRC and Japan. The Chinese leadership gradually came to realize that it could not use promises of trade to coax Japan into breaking off from its American benefactor. Beijing's subsequent insistence on diplomatic settlement as the nonnegotiable precondition for reopening trade relations fortuitously relieved the United States from dealing with the ambivalence in its own policy and the dilemma which Japan's tenacious pursuit of this particular trade partner posed. But Japan bore the most lasting imprint of the collapse of Sino-Japanese economic diplomacy in 1958. Presented with an opportunity to redefine his country's postwar China policy, Kishi reaffirmed in no uncertain terms the choice Yoshida had made with great reluctance at the end of the Occupation period: China, as defined by the Japanese government, was Chiang's China, not the Communist government in control of the Chinese mainland; and Japan, choosing as a truly sovereign state, would continue to execute its antirevolutionary covenant with the United States.

55. MacArthur to Dulles, 14 Apr. 1958, SD 493.9441/4-1458, Nan to Ikeda, 14 Apr. 1958, *Shiryōshū*, 181–85; MacArthur to Dulles, 6 May 1958, SD 693.94/5-658; Pilcher to Dulles, 10 May 1958, SD 693.94/5-1058; statement by Chen, 9 May 1958, *Shiryōshū*, 185–87.

The U.S.-Japanese Alliance at Risk

by G. Cameron Hurst III

Foreign policy, as expected, was not much of a campaign issue in 1996. Bob Dole criticized the administration's foreign policy as "incoherent and vacillating," and the Clinton camp parried that criticism by emphasizing the candidates' common ground on major foreign policy issues. Still, there was the president, on the eve of the first debate, earnestly refereeing negotiations between Prime Minister Benjamin Netanyahu and President Yasir Arafat at the White House. It mattered little that no agreement was reached; the point for Bill Clinton was to look presidential.

But crisis diplomacy and photo opportunities do not add up to a foreign policy, and that has nowhere been demonstrated more tellingly since the end of the cold war than in regard to the U.S.-Japanese alliance. Both the Bush and Clinton administrations termed it the most important bilateral relationship in the world. Why then has Japan been virtually absent from the media and public dialogue of late, and has seemingly failed to register on the administration's radar screen as well?

The media inattention is more understandable. Absent a major outbreak of violence, momentous political change, or serious economic issues, the media allocate little coverage to foreign affairs at all. But there is no excuse for the U.S. government, regardless of its party affiliation or domestic and foreign priorities, to neglect Japan even for a moment. Japan is among America's most important allies, enjoys the world's largest budget surplus, and is poised to exert greater influence internationally. But in place of earnest dialogue and efforts to adjust U.S.-Japanese relations in search of a stronger partnership, there have been acrimonious debates over trade, complicated by the criminal actions of some U.S. servicemen in Japan, leading only to rising anti-Americanism on the part of many Japanese, especially Okinawans. If the Clinton administration does no better than that in its second term, the United States may have no "partnership" to save four years from now.

G. Cameron Hurst III is a professor of Japanese and Korean studies and the director of the Center for East Asian Studies at the University of Pennsylvania. He is also a senior fellow at the Foreign Policy Research Institute.

The Evolution of the Alliance

The bilateral relationship anchored by the U.S.-Japanese security treaty is a legacy of the cold war, and its current problems stem from that fact. The emergence of communist regimes in China and North Korea in the late 1940s caused the United States to reverse its policy of demilitarizing and reforming Japan in favor of rebuilding this former enemy into a bulwark and junior partner in the struggle to contain communism in Asia. The trade and security issues that perplex the United States today are legacies of that anxious era.

First, the "Peace Constitution" that MacArthur forced on the Japanese took root more deeply in the populace than even Americans had anticipated. As early as 1950, following North Korea's invasion of South Korea, the United States pressured Japan to rearm. But Prime Minister Yoshida Shigeru extracted maximum benefits before Japan would join America's anti-communist camp, made only minimal concessions towards rearmament, and instead allowed the United States to establish military bases throughout the archipelago.

Secondly, in its haste to revitalize Japan, the United States left its prewar bureaucracy intact, abandoned industrial deconcentration (the anti-*zaibatsu* campaign), purged leftists and opposed vigorous labor unions, and allowed conservative Japanese to focus single-mindedly on economic reconstruction. America aided Japan's techno-nationalism still more by opening its own markets to Japanese exports and facilitating technology transfer. Economic and security interdependence grew apace, and Americans gave little thought to the possibility that the pupils might someday overtake their mentors.

The alliance worked well. Japan flourished as a "bastion of democracy," and its reconstruction was so successful that by the 1980s the two nations had, in Clyde Prestowitz's memorable phrase, "traded places." Japan replaced America as the world's leading creditor, and America became the world's largest debtor. To be sure, Japan did (under American pressure) steadily increase spending on its Self-Defense Forces to the point where Japan has the third-largest defense budget in the world today. And yet Tokyo still contributes little to the security of the East Asian region, much less the global community, having only in 1992 grudgingly passed legislation allowing the dispatch of small forces to supervise Cambodian elections. Indeed, as of the mid-1990s, while America has become self-absorbed with domestic issues, Japan has made only tentative moves towards a more independent diplomatic stance and still relies heavily on the "free security" provided by the United States. More than one cynic has noted that "the cold war is over, and Japan won."

Where the Alliance Stands Today

By most counts, the U.S.-Japanese relationship is an enormous success. More than 40,000 Japanese students annually study at American colleges and universities. Sister cities welcome delegations of farmers and Boy Scouts. Congressmen and Diet members routinely participate in exchanges, as do scientists and Rotarians. Cooperative relationships between U.S. and Japanese industrial firms increase daily. Sushi is as popular in Los Angeles as Big Macs are in Kyoto. Japanese teenagers adore American rap music, and American kids practice karate.

But beneath the veneer of interdependence lies an ugly reality. America once was deeply respected in Japan, and Americans were considered paragons of virtue. But today America is reviled in Japan. Author Ishihara Shintaro, who regards Americans as full of "hubris and self-righteousness," may be an extreme example.[1] But other critics routinely describe Americans as "lazy," "undereducated," and "arrogant." Many Japanese consider America a declining power: crime-ridden, drug-addicted, profligate—and eager to blame Japan for its economic problems rather than face up to its own decay.

America, in turn, has its Japan-bashers, who point to huge trade surpluses as evidence that the Japanese do not "play by the rules" and complain about the "free ride" Japan enjoys in defense. And what is most damaging of all, political leaders in Washington and, to a lesser extent, Tokyo have done little to correct the misperceptions that underlie the acrimony on both sides of the Pacific. No wonder the alliance is in trouble.

Since the opening of the Congress elected in 1994, there has been a distinct sense of drift in U.S.-Japanese relations. Zealous Republican freshmen, eager to enact the "Contract with America," only magnified the trend begun by Clinton in turning American political dialogue inward. With Washington's focus on budget deficits, taxation, welfare, health care, and social security, foreign policy remained on the back burner except during periodic crises in Bosnia or the Middle East. Meanwhile, Japan has been both cautiously searching for a more independent diplomatic stance, yet unsure of America's commitment to East Asian security. Like China and many other nations, Japan has felt neglected, and with reason.

That is not to suggest that the reservoir of goodwill between the two nations is empty. Except for a few stumbling blocks, such as the fiasco over the Smithsonian exhibit on the *Enola Gay*, even the fiftieth anniversary of World War II proved an occasion for healing and celebration of friendship between former enemies. But consider the opposite lessons the two nations learned from that war. Americans remember Pearl Harbor and recall the necessity of global preparedness. Japanese remember Hiroshima and still shrink from engagement abroad.

Now that the cold war is over and a millennium inspires new thinking, voices are heard to proclaim that the security treaty has outlived its usefulness. After all, for one-third of its modern history, Japan has been protected by the alliance. Is not Japan fully able to step forward as a "normal country" once again? Such critics regard maintenance of American bases as outmoded in the absence of the Soviet threat. Indeed, a recent poll showed that Japanese split

1 Ishihara Shintaro and Mahathir Mohamad, *The Voice of Asia: Two Leaders Discuss the Coming Century* (Tokyo: Kodansha International Ltd., 1995), p. 60.

evenly on whether U.S. forces should be withdrawn from their country and that more than 80 percent of Japanese business leaders support reducing U.S. forces on Okinawa. Moreover, all-too-common instances of rape, robbery, and even murder committed by American servicemen in Japan and Korea undermine respect for the United States. Would the United States not be better off, the critics argue, to withdraw U.S. forces to Hawaii, or to bases in the continental United States that might otherwise have to shut down?

Critics of persistent American trade deficits with Japan also demand change. They urge "managed trade" in the form of numerical quotas in manufactured goods and favor imposing sanctions under the "Super 301" provision. Managed trade has in fact been pursued in some areas by the Clinton administration but has not been especially successful. It prompts the Japanese to accuse the United States of bullying and poor business practices, and to threaten to bring the whole matter to the World Trade Organization (WTO). Other, less-frenetic observers of U.S.-Japanese relations take a long-term macroeconomic view of the trade issue and prefer urging negotiations to numerical quotas and sanctions. They also support the security treaty and the maintenance of a strong American military presence in Northeast Asia.

There is much that is persuasive in both sets of critiques. The task is to identify the good points in each and discard the bad. But reason alone, or American national interest alone, is not enough. Japanese politics and feelings must be included in the mix to achieve any progress and to reverse the erosion in the alliance. That is why, as tempting as it is to cut the Gordian knot by imposing sanctions and managed trade, bringing the troops home and telling the Japanese to see to their own defense, the chances are that such precipitous "solutions" would do more harm than good.

Steps for the Future

Former U.S. ambassador to Japan Michael Armacost has asked whether the United States and Japan will be friends or rivals.[2] The two nations will probably be both, and that is the crux of the problem.

Despite the Structural Impediments Initiative (SII) conceived to make Japan more like America, the two nations remain very different types of capitalist democracies. The structural differences in the two political economies derive from divergent historical experiences and are resistant to facile modification in the short run. The United States and Japan will continue to be economic rivals, not only in terms of bilateral trade flows, but as competitors for a major stake in Asia's rapidly expanding economies. They both must strive to make that rivalry as friendly as possible, but areas of intense competition will remain for the foreseeable future. How can Americans ensure that their competition with

[2] See Michael H. Armacost, *Friends or Rivals? The Insider's Account of U.S.-Japan Relations* (N.Y.: Columbia University Press, 1996).

Japan will not turn hostile? How can they cooperate with a manifest competitor? Only by maintaining the alliance the two nations have built up during a half century and redoubling the effort to shore it up.

Diplomatic and security arrangements. The original premise of the security treaty has indeed disappeared. But America and Japan still have an enormous stake in maintaining peace in Northeast Asia. Until inter-Korean relations are resolved and China's future is clearer, an American military presence in Japan—and Korea—remains the best guarantee of peace in the region. Nevertheless, the presence of American troops in Japan is a constant source of bitterness and friction; hence they should be radically redeployed on the basis of a realistic analysis of how many troops and what specific mix of air, ground, and naval forces are needed. There is nothing magic about the numbers currently in place. Given the enormous defense outlays in Korea and Japan, U.S. forces could and should be scaled back so as to mollify those Japanese who want foreign troops out of their country, yet reassure the Japanese as to America's commitment to their defense.

Secondly, the process of selecting, training, and monitoring troops stationed in Japan—and elsewhere overseas—must be improved. Nothing tarnishes Japanese images of the United States more than criminal acts by members of U.S. armed forces. Violent criminal behavior has reached crisis proportions in American cities, but there is no excuse for exporting it. Halting crime among troops abroad must be a top priority for the Defense Department.

Increased Japanese participation in regional and global defense initiatives also must be encouraged. The Japanese taboo against committing troops to international peacekeeping has been broken, and Japan has begun to undertake a greater global role. Residual Asian fears of a "revival of Japanese militarism" are declining. Internally, there is still concern about creeping "militarism," although pacifism has proven more a matter of pragmatism than principle. But attitudes have changed. Long-term, frank discussions between American and Japanese civilian and military leaders for an expanded Japanese role are essential.

Hence, cooperative efforts will be most effective in solving regional problems. The two scenarios for conflict in Asia involve political reintegration: North and South Korea, and China and Taiwan. Japanese diplomatic and economic assistance in both cases is essential. Encouraging multilateral discussion of regional security arrangements may serve to foster support for increased Japanese participation but ought not to preclude close security consultation among the United States, Japan, and South Korea. And while there is no Asian analogue to NATO, the Asia Pacific Economic Cooperation (APEC) forum ought to be nurtured until it can function as a vehicle for collective security discussions.

Trade issues. Washington must continue to employ patient, persistent negotiations on specific trade issues, and earnest efforts to make Japan's trade rules more transparent. Japan's economic nationalism was born in reaction to American commercial demands almost a century and a half ago, in the wake of Commodore Matthew Perry's fleet. The Japanese are exceedingly proud of their economic success: they have pursued trade as national security and created a mercantilistic state that out-trades all others. Americans never sought to balance trade flows when they enjoyed a surplus and cannot expect the Japanese to yield their hard-won surpluses easily.

Still, American pressure remains crucial in reducing Japan's trade barriers. Japan is coming out of a prolonged recession and, like the United States, is experiencing a hollowing out of its economy. Macroeconomic changes are under way, and the deficit is coming down. (The Ministry of Foreign Affairs was quick to issue a report to all Japan studies programs showing that the deficit through June 1996 was down 34 percent compared with the same period last year.[3]) Japan even sounds like the United States when it, for instance, threatens to take Indonesia to the WTO for trying to cut Japan's share of its automobile market. Some Japanese politicians, even some bureaucrats, believe that Japan's markets must be liberalized and consumers given an opportunity to enjoy more reasonable prices. Measured pressure from abroad can help those Japanese reformers, but only if it is constant and quiet, not shrill and unpredictable.

Numerical quotas and Super 301 sanctions should be used, if at all, only rarely. That does not mean that the United States should accede to Japan's position in trade negotiations. While some Japanese mechanisms for discouraging imports are being dismantled, their market remains far less open than the American market, and Washington should never cease trying to pry it open. But let no one forget that, open market or not, there is no way to force the Japanese to purchase products whose quality and prices do not measure up.

Where possible, the United States should rely on multilateral pressures, not because of some inherent multilateral bias, but because most other nations have similar problems with Japan and can enhance American leverage. Thus, the United States should rely on the WTO where its rules are applicable, or consider other forums, including APEC, when other nations have similar complaints to lodge against Japan. Bilateral negotiations must, of course, continue, but multinational pressure may be required to make the Japanese see "reason."

In addition, and perhaps above all, Washington needs to substitute action for words when it comes to putting the American house in order:

First, both parties should strictly adhere to their bipartisan determination to balance the budget. Nothing makes America more competitive than sound fiscal policy. That was one of Japan's strongest recommendations during the SII talks, and it ought to be taken to heart.

Secondly, Americans must increase their personal savings. A major difference in the two economies is that America has maximized consumption while Japan has stressed production and savings. In the SII talks, the Americans suggested the Japanese save less and spend more, while the Japanese advised Americans to save more and consume less. Tax incentives to stimulate further savings, freeing up more funding for reinvestment, should be high on the Clinton administration's list of priorities.

[3] Ministry of Foreign Affairs, *Recent Trends in Japan-U.S. Trade: Free Market Forces Yield Balance of Trade Improvements* (Tokyo: Ministry of Foreign Affairs, Sept. 1996), p. 3.

Thirdly, American business must continue to improve its competitiveness. While Japan's firms have experienced difficulties during the recent recession, U.S. firms have become more competitive. But complacency is hardly warranted. Restructuring ("downsizing") has also caused serious labor dislocations and inordinately increased executive compensation. Research and development need both more corporate and more government attention, as well as a long-term perspective, with quality always the highest priority.

Fourthly, the idea of "industrial policy" should not be dismissed out of hand. East Asia offers abundant examples of successful industrial policy based to some degree on the Japanese model of cooperation between government and business in newly emerging industries and markets. For however persuasive free-market economics may be in theory, in reality government actions at home and abroad create the environment in which all economic activity occurs. At present, the United States too often leaves it to foreign governments to shape that environment.

Lastly, the pro-education rhetoric of both parties must be translated into action. The future of the American economy depends on drastic reforms to improve the educational system. That is a national priority demanding national attention, which is why the Department of Education must be revitalized, not dismantled.

The political arena. In his administration's second term, Clinton must take a deeper personal interest in Japanese relations. Clear and forceful presidential leadership makes cabinet officials aware of his priorities, encourages steady media attention (rather than sporadic, crisis-focused coverage), and informs both Americans and Japanese of his engagement. A "Ron and Yasu" relationship with Prime Minister Ryutaro Hashimoto is not required, but it is necessary to arrange regular reciprocal visits, involve him increasingly in multilateral forums, and restore trust and cooperation between Tokyo and Washington. There must be more to the relationship than harping on trade deficits.

The secretary of state also must devote more attention to Japan. Americans have become far too accustomed to crisis diplomacy, and secretaries too eager to emulate Henry Kissinger's shuttle diplomacy and make themselves principal arbiters of regional conflicts. America may no longer be the world's policeman, but it has become the world's referee. Crisis diplomacy may please the media, but it comes at the cost of neglecting America's most important alliance—just ask Kissinger about his "year of Europe" and, for that matter, Japan.

This deeper and ongoing engagement with Japan requires that a senior figure in the administration be appointed to coordinate Asia policy, and that far more personnel with expertise in Japanese language, area studies, and economics be appointed to the Departments of State, Commerce, and Defense; the National Security Council staff; and the United States Trade Representative's Office.

Washington must also come to terms with the shifts occurring in Japanese politics. The old dominance of the Liberal Democratic Party has been shattered, the conservatives are split, and coalition cabinets may govern in Tokyo for a long time to come. Recent prime ministers have not enjoyed the political clout that some predecessors have, and the bureaucracy remains firmly engaged. That is all the more reason why Japanese relations will require more, not less, attention, patience, and hard work.

Conclusion

For the next several decades, Asia will remain the most dynamic economic and political region. Four of the world's top ten economies—Japan, Korea, China, and Indonesia—will be Asian, and democratic development will proceed apace. There are great economic stakes there for the United States if it remains engaged and develops wise policies with individual nations and within APEC. The most important ingredient of all is the bilateral relationship with Japan. Current trade and security concerns need to be addressed more seriously at the outset of Clinton's presidential term, and not pushed to the back burner as soon as a crisis erupts somewhere else. For if the United States does not freely offer Japan its attention, the Japanese, sooner or later, will get the attention of Americans in ways they are bound not to like.

Ezra F. Vogel

Japanese-American Relations After the Cold War

OF ALL THE COLD WAR ALLIANCES that must now be refashioned to accord with new realities, none is more critical for world order than the one between the United States and Japan, and none is more burdened with complex psychological baggage.

Ambassador Mansfield's favorite expression, "The US-Japanese relationship is the most important bilateral relationship in the world, bar none," is even more true today than when he first uttered it in the late 1970s. America can no longer dominate world affairs as it did in the early decades after World War II when its economy towered over all others. The world economy is far more intertwined than ever before, and the influence of America and Japan, the world's two largest economies, is felt everywhere. The resolution of major global issues requires Japanese as well as American contributions, and this necessitates that the two powers achieve a high level of mutual understanding.

At the grass roots, Americans and Japanese are working together in all major economic and political spheres, their activities and interests thoroughly intertwined. But new doubts about the relationship, set off by the recent spurt in Japan's economic power and by the end of the Cold War, have touched off deep-seated emotional reactions in both countries. Gone is the automatic readiness to unite against communist power and ideology. Gone is America's overweaning confidence and unquestioning generosity; gone also is Japan's deep feeling of dependence and humility. The uncertainty in

Ezra F. Vogel is Henry Ford II Professor of the Social Sciences, Harvard University.

Washington and in Tokyo about the nature of the relationship in the new era has led to drift and frustration at the top that is beginning to take its toll at lower levels as well.

Any meaningful new vision for Japanese-American relations must confront the legacy of the Cold War that began during the Allied Occupation of Japan, from 1945–1952, when Japanese-American ties became deeper than ever before.[1] During the Occupation, Japan's institutions were changed far more than were Germany's. As Yoichi Funabashi says, "the Americans, as good winners, were generous; the Japanese, as good losers, studied hard."[2] American technology and ways of thinking were introduced in every sector of business and private life and, with adaptations, became part of Japan. Television came to Japan during the Occupation, with considerable American programming, enabling Japanese to know American life at a depth inaccessible to previous generations. Japanese were thus Americanized as they were modernized, but Japanese heritage and pride were powerful and survived Americanization, albeit altered in the process. New hybrid institutions and culture took on enormous vigor.

When the Allied Occupation ended in 1952, the Cold War was at its zenith, the Korean War was still unresolved, and the Sino-Soviet relationship was growing stronger. Japan depended on America for its security from nearby menacing communist powers. The Japanese economy was still weak, highly dependent on American technology and markets. Therefore in 1952, the institutions and practices imposed during the Occupation were automatically allowed to continue because Japan did not have the leeway to openly evaluate the alliance.[3]

The Japanese-American alliance thus never made a clean break with its origins in the American dominated occupation. Even in 1960 when Japan had the choice of whether to renew the Japan-United States Security Treaty, the top political leaders rammed through its continuation despite widespread opposition, without a full public debate or analysis. The constitution, imposed by directives from General MacArthur's staff, has never been thoroughly reexamined. The grand reckoning to put aside the postwar era by openly evaluating developments since 1945, which Nakasone called for during his prime ministership in the mid-1980s, had still not taken place when the Cold War ended.

Since 1961, beginning with a speech by Ambassador Reischauer, the United States has referred to the US-Japanese relationship as a "partnership,"[4] but it started as an unequal partnership, and the effect of these origins have not been completely erased either in the United States or in Japan. American feelings of superiority stemming from their roles as conqueror and teacher and their sense of moral righteousness for putting down the aggressor have not disappeared.

Nor have Japanese fully expunged what many felt as the humiliation and legacy of defeat. American troops, part of the Allied Occupation of Japan, have remained on American bases in Japan since 1952 and their image as occupying forces has not fully dissipated. To Japanese the failure of Russia to return the "four northern islands" and the request of Asian nations that Japan apologize for activities of World War II are further reminders that the slate of World War II has not been wiped clean.

To Japanese the fact that they follow the lead of the United States in foreign policy is part of the legacy of defeat in World War II. Of course, Japanese leaders adapted their policies to further their economic interests, but in their view the US-Japanese alliance means that they have not completely had an independent foreign policy. Since World War II Japanese capacity to collect and analyze information relevant to security is still not on a scale to compare with America's. Within Japan's Foreign Ministry, the highest elite track careers have been in the North American Bureau.[5] On all major foreign policy issues, one of the first questions was, "What is the American position?" Most Japanese opinion leaders acknowledge that the alliance with America was in their interest, but the issue was never squarely examined. Only now with the end of the Cold War does Japan have the opportunity to evaluate dispassionately the legacy that became their own without full public debate.

The opportunity for Japan to now examine dispassionately its national interest coincides with the spectacular rise of Japan as a great financial as well as industrial power, with Japan's replacement of the United States as the world's largest creditor. This economic success allows patriotic Japanese who had resented their dependency on America to break the psychological shackles of dependency and to declare that America, with its drugs, crime, poor education, loss of industrial capacity, and inability to control its debts and trade balances, is a nation in decline. Proud Japanese who felt humiliated because of Japan's defeat and economic weakness, can now in effect declare an end to the humiliation.[6]

Americans have been proud of their generosity in providing Japan with security, technology, and markets. Many Americans now feel, however, that the Japanese took advantage of this generosity by pursuing their own narrow interests and that even when the Japanese became rich, they did not assume their fair share of the burdens of maintaining peace. Many Americans could accept Japanese economic victories if they believed that they were won fairly. But in the view of many Americans, Japan unfairly protected its markets from foreign goods, copied American technology, and engaged in predatory practices to destroy American industry.[7] Many Americans responded to Japan's economic successes and new pride not with respect and approval but with moral condemnation for winning victory on playing fields that were not level.

With the collapse of the Soviet Union and the reduction in the external threat, Japan's examination of the Japanese-American relationship became more open. This, together with the drift in the relationship at the top levels allowed the expression of powerful emotions that had long been partially suppressed. The resulting tensions, while not as severe as the 1960 anti-Security Treaty Riots, reached a new height during the Persian Gulf Crisis of 1990–1991 and after President Bush's visit to Japan in January 1992. It is useful to examine these two incidents to illustrate the problems of the relationship after the collapse of the communist threat and the transformation of Japan into an economic superpower.

THE GULF CRISIS

On the eve of the Gulf crisis, Japanese opinion leaders had already begun to reach a consensus that Japan should assume a larger world political role, commensurate with its status as an economic power. Japanese leaders, like those of other countries, believed that after the Cold War, military matters would become less important. It was only natural that as economic matters became more important, Japan, as an economic superpower, would see its global political role expand. When in 1986 and 1987 the yen virtually doubled in value against the dollar and Japanese purchasing power overseas rose accordingly,

Japanese began to talk about noblesse oblige. It followed that Japan should do more to share global burdens.

In the Gulf crisis, Japan found that on issues that could be handled within the Foreign Ministry, experts could respond quickly. Within hours of the invasion of Kuwait, Japanese Foreign Ministry officials, aware of the seriousness of a territorial invasion as a challenge to world order and of America's determination to respond accordingly, were able to move quickly to block Iraq's assets.

But on issues requiring a broader political consensus, Japan became almost immobilized. Japanese political leaders over many decades had placed great value on preserving a consensus-supporting policy. From the time of the invasion of China in 1937 until 1945, Japan's military overwhelmed all civilian institutions; they were in a position to make quick decisions. In postwar democratic Japan, officials were not able to make major decisions so quickly, especially after the public reaction to political leaders ramming through the continuation of the Japan-United States Security Treaty in 1961.

When the Gulf crisis erupted, Japan had not yet reached a consensus about whether there were any circumstances that would justify sending troops abroad. The difficulty of achieving a consensus was compounded by Japan's institutional structures and the political position of Prime Minister Kaifu. The prime minister's office did not have an independent policy-oriented staff comparable to the American president's White House and National Security staff. In the mid-1980s Prime Minister Nakasone, concerned about developing a more centralized capacity to respond quickly to international issues, had begun to develop such a staff but it was still relatively weak. The prime minister in Japan is therefore much more dependent on the bureaucracy than the American president. At the time of the Iraqi invasion, Kaifu was new to his post and in an unusually weak position for a prime minister. Kaifu had not even been in the group of politicians groomed as a possible candidate for prime minister. Under ordinary circumstances, as a member of a very small faction with little leadership experience and political support, Kaifu would not have been considered for the post. But when Prime Minister Takeshita was suddenly removed from office because he was implicated in the Recruit Scandal, the Liberal Democratic Party (LDP), facing a crucial national election, wanted a candidate with the cleanest possible record. Kaifu was selected to pull the party through the election.

The question of sending troops abroad was one of the most sensitive issues on which to obtain national consensus, and it became more sensitive because of American pressure, and also because some Japanese officials saw the Gulf War as a special opportunity. Many did not want to risk the lives of Japanese in this crisis, but the American Embassy in Tokyo warned Japanese political leaders that foreign opinion would be highly critical if Japan was not prepared to risk its citizens' lives, along with those from the United States and leading European countries.

Those Japanese leaders who were convinced that to be a great power Japan had to reinterpret or revise the constitutional prohibition against war making saw the Gulf conflict as a great opportunity. They hoped to use international pressure to overcome the nation's aversion to sending troops abroad. Many Japanese political leaders and bureaucrats, having honed their skill in using American pressure to achieve their own goals in Japanese domestic politics, made it seem as if America was pushing for troops, that America's requests could only be met by sending troops. This maneuver provoked a vehement response from opposition leaders and intellectuals, who felt their chief mission was to prevent the return of Japanese militarism and authoritarianism. Ordinary families who did not care to risk the lives of their sons became equally aroused. The strength of the opposition both surprised and immobilized the political leaders who wished to send troops to the Gulf.

Japanese leaders, weakened by the outpouring of opposition, behaved cautiously. Prime Minister Kaifu announced that Japan would not risk Japanese lives in the Gulf War. When Japanese funds were first appropriated for Gulf activities, Finance Minister Hashimoto announced that Japan would contribute only $1 billion to the effort; that was said to be the limit. After American officials persisted in urging Japanese leaders to send some personnel to the Middle East, Japan announced, long after hundreds of thousands of Americans were in the Gulf, that it would send 100 medical people; in fact, Japan was able to recruit only 20. The medical recruits, arriving in the Middle East without proper preparation and planning, had difficulty finding a useful role and soon returned to Japan. Japan considered sending airplanes and ships, but the unions objected and

Japan Airlines, recently privitized, explained that it was no longer at the beck of a government order and had no planes available.

By the time the American forces began to attack Iraq, Japanese leaders had begun to realize the potential dangers of Western criticism for an unwillingness to share the burdens of preserving international order. Unable to win public support to send personnel, Japanese leaders in the end voted for additional funds.

American officials were in fact also split on what Japan's best contribution to the Gulf War should be. Some, concerned about the dangers of Japanese remilitarization, worried about the complexities of managing forces from so many countries, and were happy to see Japan send money rather than people. Others felt that the American public would never tolerate seeing American troops risk their lives, serving in effect as mercenaries, while Japan simply paid the bill.

In fact, the Japanese had many doubts about America's actions in the Gulf crisis. Some knowledgeable Japanese felt that the United States had made a grave mistake in supplying Hussein with weapons. Japan, they noted, did not sell weapons abroad; without American weapons, Hussein would never have been able to invade Kuwait. Many Japanese, having long feared being drawn into international wars because of trigger-happy Americans, felt that Americans had not fully exhausted the possibilities of nonmilitary sanctions.

Some Japanese wondered whether America had the public support and determination to complete the task of destroying Hussein; they feared he might remain a political force after the war. But Japanese intelligence in the Middle East could not compare with that of the United States, and the Japanese were reluctant to set off a strong American reaction by publicly criticizing American policy, especially when Americans were so determined. The criticisms of American policy were quietly discussed in Japan but not publicly expressed to Americans. Many Japanese leaders were genuinely frustrated that they were unable to be more articulate in explaining their views.

At the critical moment when the Western powers began to plot their strategy in response to the invasion of Kuwait, the center of the planning effort was the UN Security Council. Many in Japan, long upset that smaller powers were permanent members of the Security Council, and that Japan with the second largest financial contributions to the United Nations was not, saw Japan as outside the circle of intimate discussions. The Gulf crisis fueled these deeper resentments about being excluded from permanent membership in the Security Council.

It is perhaps not surprising that most Japanese did not feel a strong emotional identification with American and European efforts in the Gulf. The Japanese public, far more concerned about Japanese lives than the lives of others, were initially riveted to the issue of Japanese hostages. When American bombs began to fall in Iraq, Japanese newspapers recalled how Americans had bombed them during World War II; many Japanese identified more with those on the receiving than the delivering end. Because Iraq was a major oil producer, and because several other Middle East oil producers sympathized with Iraq, Japan was leery about alienating those oil producers.

Toward the end of the crisis, Japanese officials, increasingly worried about foreign reaction, made huge additional payments, totaling $13 billion, providing more than any other country apart from Saudi Arabia. The Japanese were disappointed that America and its European allies expressed almost no public appreciation for this huge financial contribution, which required significant Japanese sacrifices. Japan was condemned by Westerners, especially by Americans, for being so slow in responding to an international emergency and contributing so little to an international order from which they derived such great benefits. Annoyed at those self-righteous Americans who acted as if they enjoyed a monopoly on virtuous behavior, many Japanese recoiled at American criticism, and began to talk more openly within Japan of *kenbei,* their dislike of Americans.

At the same time, many Japanese, surprised at the quickness of the American response to Iraq's invasion of Kuwait, were impressed by the success of American technology, diplomacy, and skillful execution of the war. Awed by American might and vigor, some Japanese expressed the fear that Americans, without a Soviet enemy, would begin to cast their eyes on Japan.

Almost no Japanese felt pride in Japan's indecisive response to the Gulf crisis. Many who watched international television news programs and noted the forces that were dispatched from so many nations felt embarrassed that Japan contributed so little. By the end of the conflict a majority of Japanese felt that America's response to the crisis had been basically correct. The crisis served to strengthen those forces in Japan seeking to develop better mechanisms for making rapid decisions during international crises. It led Japan to send mine sweepers to the Middle East after the war and, by June 1992, to agree to create a peacekeeping organization (PKO) of Japanese servicemen who could be sent abroad under UN command. Because sending troops abroad for the first time since World War II was such a major policy change, the PKO bill was a carefully crafted compromise. Troops from Japan were to be sent only under international auspices and used only for peacekeeping activities. Japanese diplomats carefully prepared other Asian governments for this decision, assuring them that it did not mean a return to militarism.

PRESIDENT BUSH'S VISIT TO JAPAN, JANUARY 1992

President Bush, originally scheduled to visit Japan in November 1991, postponed his trip when a Republican candidate in Pennsylvania, Dick Thornberg, suffered a surprising defeat. The postponement, interpreted in Japan as an embarrassment to Miyazawa, the newly elected prime minister, was thought to be a sign that American leaders were placing Bush's domestic political concerns above the country's relations with Japan. Before the visit, the President announced that the purpose of the trip was "Jobs, jobs, jobs." Accompanied by auto-executives, the visit seemed to place narrow commercial interests above broad national interest. In Japan, the President visited the newly opened Toys Я Us, the first large-scale American retailing establishment in the country. State Department and other officials concerned with East Asia had advised against the President's postponing the trip. They were critical of his decision to stress jobs and to bring along auto-executives. Domestic political considerations won out.

From the Japanese perspective, Bush's policy of enlisting the help of auto-executives seemed ridiculous. Even Americans, showing preference for Japanese-made autos to American-made autos precisely because American cars had a reputation of being of lower quality than their Japanese counterparts, had registered their opinions in the salesrooms of the country. Japanese consumers were not greatly interested in buying American cars. American auto-executives, concerned more about restricting the flow of Japanese cars into the American market than with opening the Japanese market to American autos, had a different agenda than officials in the

Bush administration, concerned mostly about keeping Japan's markets open.

Important discussions between Bush and Miyazawa on a broad range of issues in the post-Cold War era were drowned out by the American media's preoccupation with the auto-executives. To the media, Japanese officials very cleverly focused all the discussion on whether a few additional thousand American cars might be sold in Japan. When the American media focused also on the high salaries of the American auto-executives, dwelling on the poor quality of American cars, the efforts of the American car manufacturers to press their arguments backfired.

The tensions between Japan and the United States reached a peak not during the visit itself but after Bush returned to the United States. President Bush's talk of "Jobs, jobs, jobs" touched off American fury about the inability of American firms to penetrate the Japanese market. While American complaints about Japan's trade practices were not new, automobile sales in both Japan and the United States were very tight; the administration's handling of the president's visit gave new respectability to raw American emotion.[8] A torrent of complaints by American auto-executives, trade unions, laid-off American autoworkers, and their political spokesmen followed.

Japanese auto-executives, concerned about this growing friction, decided to raise prices of many models in the American market, accepting a temporary minor decline in sales to give American automakers a breathing space in generating profits. Public discussions of automobile issues gradually abated, drowned out by the presidential election campaigns.

AN INTERPRETATION OF THE CONFLICTS

The Japanese, analyzing conflicts between the great powers, are drawn to Western explanations about hegemonic stability and hegemonic decline.[9] According to this view, in the late nineteenth and early twentieth centuries, stability was provided by the British; in the decades after World War II, by the Americans. The instabilities that led to World War I and World War II stemmed largely from the decline of British hegemony. The relative decline of American power, and the loosening of the alliances around the world, are thought to be leading to an uneasy period of readjustment. The question asked by

Japanese analysts is whether there will be a new period of cooperation, *pax consortis,* or independence and stronger rivalries.[10]

In the 1990s, the Japanese will certainly develop a greater capacity for independent analysis of their national interest; inevitably, they will find areas where they define their interests differently than Americans. In this period, while old relationships are loosening and new independence is tested, emotions, previously held in check, will come to the surface. The Japanese will continue to wonder how long Americans will have the financial resources and the political will to ensure their security, keep world markets open, and remain generous in sharing science and technology.

The emotionalism of the American response to Japan reflects growing doubts about the ability of US corporations to compete against Japanese firms, to provide employment, to offer a promising economic future for the next generation of Americans. The most intense doubts within the United States are felt in industries and localities under most immediate threat from Japanese competition—automobiles, semiconductors, and electronics.

The new emotionalism had its birth in the special era in the late 1980s when the yen almost doubled in value against the dollar, the Japanese government made cheap money available, and purchases of American companies and property skyrocketed. Many Americans, feeling that ownership was slipping from their hands, feared that America was losing control over its fate. This new fear was reflected in Pat Choate's *Agents of Influence* and Michael Crichton's *The Rising Sun,* each contributing to the new mood.[11] The harsh criticism of Japan stemmed also from the belief that Japan was gaining because of unfair competition, stealing American technology, dumping and maintaining closed networks that effectively shut out American competitors. The idea that Japan had a different culture and a different system was not new; Japanese intellectuals and American specialists on Japan had long argued this. A more intense version of the argument, now called "revisionism," took on a new life when American company executives, workers, and their political representatives argued that they suffered from this different system, which they called unfair.[12]

The emotionalism on the Japanese side stemmed not from fear of economic competition but from the belief that they were not being treated with proper respect. The drive to be accepted, to be treated with honor, has been a powerful motive in Japan since the latter part of the nineteenth century.[13] Many Japanese felt very acutely that they were not accepted as full members of all the informal groups of Western nations that discussed issues like Iraq. In their view, without being fully consulted, they were expected to pay the bill. As cosmopolitan Japanese explained to Americans, that was "Taxation without representation."

Many Japanese did not believe that American laws or perspectives had any superior moral authority. Now that Japan was stronger economically and the Cold War was over, why did Americans continue to lecture them about human rights, the environment, or how to run their domestic economy? After all, America had its own problems with many of its ill-treated minorities. The country wasted energy and spewed out more carbon dioxide and other waste per capita than almost any other. It had badly mismanaged its economy; crime, drugs, educational dropouts, narrow selfishness, and inadequate civic responsibility seemed rampant.

If self-doubts by Americans about their capacity to handle economic issues fueled their anti-Japanese mood, self-doubts by Japanese of their capacity to play a constructive leadership role in the world made them sensitive to foreign criticism of Japan's handling of international affairs. Japan remained dependent on America not only for markets but for resolving many of the more pressing international issues. While some accepted this,[14] others sought passionately to gain and assert their independence both in high technology and in international politics.

TENSIONS IN PERSPECTIVE

And yet, even at the peak of the tensions, public opinion polls showed that most Japanese retained favorable impressions of Americans and most Americans had favorable impressions of Japanese.[15] Americans did not stop buying Japanese products or selling real estate and companies to Japan. For all those whose complaints attracted attention, far more were going about their business working together.

Analogies, sometimes voiced in both countries, between the circumstances of the moment and those in the 1930s were misleading at best. In the 1930s the Japanese military was in the ascendancy, with vast forces overseas. In the 1990s Japan's military remains discredited and discouraged; its budget, now about 1 percent of GNP, is not growing; it is expected that the size of the self-defense forces, 234,000 in 1991, will decline further. In 1991 the Ground Self-Defense Force, wishing to recruit 28,000 people, and offering great incentives for technical training, managed to recruit only 18,000. Before the end of World War II, military occupation of other countries yielded very positive results, gaining access to vital resources, winning strategic geopolitical positions and valuable markets.[16] After World War II it is difficult to find instances where military occupation of other countries has led to comparable benefits. New technology has rendered geopolitical considerations almost meaningless. In the post-colonial era with the growth of democracy and mass media, public opinion in countries with resources is easily mobilized and the possibility of gaining access to raw materials and markets through military occupation seems at best remote. What Japan achieved through military occupation in the 1930s, it now seeks to accomplish by using cash and economic leverage.

In the 1930s the Japanese military was in a position to maintain tight control over the flow of information to the Japanese public; in the 1990s with the spread of consumer electronics, telecommunication equipment, and international satellites, tight censorship over news is impossible. The level of Japanese economic activity, linked to and dependent on foreign trade and investment, is today on a scale unimaginable in the 1930s.

Despite the high level of tension in the relationship between 1990 and 1992, at the grass roots in both countries, relations are closer; activities continue to become more intertwined. In 1984, 12,000 Japanese were studying in the United States; in 1992, 40,000 were doing so. In the late 1980s the increase in Japanese language study in the United States was greater than for any other single foreign language; the number of Americans studying or working in Japan, while still far smaller than the number of Japanese in America, was growing rapidly.[17] All prefectures in Japan pointed with pride to the Americans working on their staffs. Most major Japanese companies began to take foreign interns in the 1980s; in the 1990s, they expected to continue to expand that number, to enhance the responsibilities assigned them within the company.

Joint ventures and alliances between Japanese and American firms continue to expand. American exports to Japan, while still far behind

Japanese exports to the United States, have risen substantially in recent years. Although some Japanese in the United States reported anxiety about the public's reaction to Japan after the Bush visit, the mood has since quieted down. Most young Americans in Japan, who have learned the Japanese language and work in Japanese companies, report that despite certain problems they have excellent relations with many of their Japanese colleagues.

The term "internationalization" remains positive in Japan. Although the stress is more on the Japanese becoming internationalized than in opening Japan to foreigners, the trend toward internationalization is unmistakable. Japanese take great pride in those international officials of Japanese origin like Sadako Ogata, UN High Commissioner for Refugees, and Yasushi Akashi, UN Committee on Trade and Development (UNCTAD) Representative in Kampuchea, who have come to the fore; they are especially anxious to assist them in their international efforts. The Japan Overseas Cooperation Volunteers under Japan International Cooperation Agency (JICA) has almost as many youth per capita overseas as its counterpart, the American Peace Corps.[18]

COMMON INTERESTS BEYOND THE COLD WAR

The common interests that bind Japan and the United States beyond the Cold War stem from their positions of having the world's largest economies and of leading overseas trading nations. Many Japanese, despite considerable nostalgia for a homogeneous society and a desire to avoid foreign entanglements, are too successful around the world to stray very far from the path of further internationalization. While many would prefer not to have foreign laborers live in their neighborhoods, with unemployment running about 2 percent and Japanese workers reluctant to accept work that is "*kiken, kitanai, and kitsui*" (dangerous, dirty, and difficult), the number of foreign laborers is rapidly increasing. Some estimate that the number of illegal foreign workers has already passed one million.

Like Americans after World War I, some Japanese are attracted to isolationism, but the number of Japanese living abroad and the number being trained to go abroad continue to grow. Although many Japanese companies find work with foreign firms frustrating, they are rapidly increasing their alliances with them. Many are planning to expand their sales around the world; their success in global markets cannot be separated from the success of the countries to which they sell. The basic interests of the great trading nations around the world are to maintain the stability of the world economic and trading system, and to increase the flow of goods.[19] These, more than nostalgia for a splendid isolationism or frustration with other partners, determine Japanese behavior.

Although the United States is in relative decline, American corporations retain a substantial overseas investment, in Asia and elsewhere, and they, too, benefit from the global flow of goods and services. Although America's political will to sacrifice for the rest of the world may continue to diminish, the country's international economic interests are not likely to fall in the foreseeable future; neither will America's desire to maintain those interests.

While many individual American companies compete directly with individual Japanese companies, the interests of multinational companies increasingly depart from national interests. Japanese multinationals do tend to be more closely linked to national purpose than the multinationals of other countries. Still, regardless of the country of origin, as multinationals expand and mature, they are prone to grant greater autonomy in decision making to their representatives abroad; executives in charge of local operations around the world begin to have interests divergent from those of home headquarters. Most Japanese companies entered the world markets more recently than multinationals of other countries; though the process of localization may be slower, the direction is unmistakable.

It remains true that the Japanese government works with Japanese corporations to devise an overall strategy for the success of the economy. And Japanese still assume that if Japan makes an item, Japanese consumers should buy it rather than the foreign product. Yet, it is also true that the Japanese government and the business community see it in their overall interest to have thriving economies around the world. While determined to protect their interests, they have shown themselves ready to compromise when other countries or companies are determined to look after their respective interests. The new slogan for the 1990s for Keidanren, the leading business association, is "*kyoosei,*" mutual vitality; they see their interest in preserving the vitality of business around the world, in accommodating to reduce tensions. Japan and the United States, with their common interest in a stable and successful world economic trading system, are increasingly defining their interests in these terms, working together to maintain them.[20]

Although Japan has not yet taken the lead in these efforts, it has worked closely for years with American diplomats to resolve disputes in various parts of the world. The desire to take a leadership role was already evident in the early 1960s when Japan sought to resolve conflicts between Indonesia and Malaysia, and it is now growing rapidly. In 1992, for example, Yasushi Akashi serves as UNCTAD representative in Kampuchea where he is playing an active role in resolving that country's difficulties.

The unresolved question is how Japan can realize its role of preserving world security without dispatching its forces abroad. In Asia, it has already shown a readiness to work with the Association of Southeast Asian Nations (ASEAN) countries to discuss issues of common security and to contribute to that process. So, also, Japanese politicians and defense strategists are continuing to work closely with the United States, convinced that it is in Japan's interest for American forces to remain in Asia.[21]

American military planners, for their part, recognize that the cost of maintaining the American Seventh Fleet in Asia and of continuing to deploy some ground and air forces there is in fact manageable. With new technology able to cover long-range distances, it is less important to maintain large numbers of bases. Access to temporary bases in an emergency situation can provide the capabilities previously enjoyed with permanent bases. Planners have negotiated the right to use certain access points at far lower costs than maintaining existing bases. Since the Japanese now pay about 75 percent of the cost of keeping American troops in Japan apart from their salaries,[22] it costs Americans less to maintain troops in Japan than in the United States. In Asia, where Japanese security issues are most critical, the cost to the United States of maintaining forces is minimal in the context of America's total defense expenditures. Cooperation, involving US and Japanese forces, especially naval forces, is excellent.

It is not in the interest of Japan to promote regional trading blocs that exclude the United States, or are at the expense of the international trading system. In the 1930s when Japan was a regional economic power, not a global economic power, its economic interests were overwhelmingly concentrated in Taiwan, Korea, China, and

Indonesia. Today, when Japan has become a global economic power, it has far greater investment in North America and Europe than in Asia.

To see the world as emerging into three trading blocs is to misperceive the basic reality. It is true that the reduction in barriers to trade, financial flows, and travel within Europe, North America, and Asia have proceeded faster than for the world at large. It is also true that in recent years trade within each of these areas has grown more rapidly than trade between the areas. Still, trade has grown and continues to grow between the three regions; officials representing the European Community and those involved in expanding the North America Trading Agreement have made clear their intentions not to increase barriers to the outside world. Japanese trade with and investment in the European Community have been expanding rapidly; these trends are expected to continue.

Japanese officials have made it clear that they do not intend to convert parts of Asia into a closed trading bloc.[23] As the world's most competitive trading nation, they realize that if they sought to close certain Asian spheres, this would only strengthen protectionist sentiment both in Europe and in North America. That is not in their interest. It is instructive, in this connection, to observe Japan's response to Malaysian Prime Minister Mahathir's call in 1991 for an Asian trade bloc that would exclude the United States. Japanese officials, while not discouraging the idea entirely, hoping to keep up the pressure on Europe and North America not to become more protectionist, said nothing that would suggest any wish to adopt so radical a policy.

Japanese citizen movements and public discussions of environmental issues have grown rapidly. Former Prime Minister Takeshita, leader of the largest political faction, has been particularly strong in emphasizing the importance of environmental issues.[24] Still, the Japanese do not see the issues precisely as Americans do. While the United States may play a larger role in advocating a reduction in fishing, the elimination of whaling, the preservation of rare species, and a slowing down of the felling of virgin forests, Japan is more concerned with controlling emissions, energy conservation, and recycling. The United States and Japan already engage in cooperative projects for environmental control, and these efforts are likely to be expanded in the future.

In the 1980s both the Japanese government and many private associations greatly expanded their efforts to promote Third World development. Again, the Japanese approach is not precisely the same as the American, but their basic interest in providing humanitarian aid, promoting development, maintaining a stable international financial system, and reducing armed conflicts broadly overlap. Although Japan has traditionally focused its aid on Asia, in recent years it has greatly expanded its programs to include poorer nations. Its aid to Africa exceeds that given by the United States and some $800 million is to go to India, though Japan's interests in trade and investment in these poorer areas remain very minimal.[25]

Japanese companies see little short-range business opportunities either in Eastern Europe or Russia. Reluctant to give large-scale aid to Russia until the northern territory issue of the "four islands" is resolved, they were greatly annoyed with the Bush Administration for announcing the East European aid plan before Japan had made a final decision. Still, Japan has been an active participant in the programs the advanced nations have developed to give aid to Eastern Europe and Russia.

In short, American and Japanese interests are basically in concert: to maintain an open trading system, avoid regional conflicts, keep down regional protectionism, defend the global environment, advance scientific discovery, and aid less developed countries. The Japanese public is increasingly supportive of Japan's playing a role in all these areas and in working with the other advanced nations of the world to achieve these purposes.

SUGGESTIONS FOR A POST-COLD WAR AMERICAN APPROACH TO JAPAN

Common Vision of Global Interests, Shared Goals

With the end of the Cold War, there is a need for a new vision to give a positive overall direction to the US-Japanese relationship. To gain broad public support from the many groups in both societies affected by that relationship, private as well as public sector leaders should share in its conception. It ought to be articulated and presented by the top leaders of both societies. The vision ought to set out common interests and common tasks for dealing with basic global issues.

Among the common tasks, maintaining an international economic order with global trade, controlling pollution, providing comprehensive security,[26] assisting underprivileged peoples and nations, and advancing the frontiers in medicine and natural science, must figure. While there are already common American-Japanese efforts in all these areas, they must be expanded and integrated.

Among the leaders in both countries who need to be involved in formulating the vision are: heads of the major political parties, officials from the key branches of government, and leaders in the private sector representing major business, worker, and public interest groups. The process of creating such a vision, with broad-based inputs from both societies, might require one or more years and can help deepen the links between Japanese and American groups that will later be involved in implementing the agreements. The vision ought to be specific enough to establish new common programs. Inputs from other countries should be welcome and the programs should, where possible, include participants from other countries.

Deeper Commitment to the Pacific Region

There is a need for a more specific and detailed vision for the development of the Pacific area, where the interests of Japan and the United States overlap, for cooperative efforts there lag behind those between Europe and North America. Again, inputs must come from all countries in the region, and should address such issues as: the potential for development in the area, the infrastructure needed in telecommunication and transportation, and common security needs.

It is not easy to define the geographical boundaries of the Pacific region. Some common efforts in Asia will include very broad areas, as far east as the North and South American countries bordering on the Pacific, as far west as India and Pakistan.[27] Perhaps the most critical area, however, for additional organizational inputs in the near future is the region where the linkages of international commerce are already great: the countries of East and Southeast Asia, Australia, New Zealand, and North America. This area, already served by APEC (Asian Pacific Economic Council) and PECC (Pacific Economic Cooperation Council), can be the one that provides a framework for greatly expanded activities.

Although the region is growing more rapidly than any other in the world, the United States in recent years has lagged far behind Japan, not only in new investment, but in sponsoring and participating in conferences to discuss major political, economic, cultural, and social issues.[28] Japan is now endeavoring to bring China, North Korea, and Vietnam into the international economic community and to increase mutual trust to head off an arms race in which these countries purchase arms from many parts of the world. It is important that the United States continue to manage our concern with human rights and with the identification of servicemen missing from action in the Vietnam War in such a way that it does not isolate these countries. Isolation could well lead them to a rapid arms build up. The United States needs to make a much greater commitment to the region, both in the private and the public sectors.

Promotion of American Interests in Trade and Investment

There is a need to continue to work on the problem of trade and investment imbalances between Japan and the United States.[29] While Japan has made considerable progress in opening its market since the mid-1960s, foreign companies from all countries still complain that the Japanese market is more difficult to penetrate than that of any other advanced nation. Because the Japanese have had difficulty in securing internal consensus to purchase foreign manufactured goods and to encourage foreign investment, American pressure, long exerted, needs to be continued. That pressure, however, must be applied with a long-term strategy in mind, by well-informed officials who employ a minimum of inflammatory rhetoric.

Since certain American policies make it difficult for foreign goods to enter the United States, American officials would do well to present their views in something other than an idiom that expresses moral self-righteousness. For some American free market economists, businessmen, and politicians, the belief in "free trade" and the denunciation of "managed trade" takes on an almost religious fervor. Yet, America also engages in a considerable amount of managed trade. Japan's "voluntary restraint" of exports to the United States in such goods as textiles, television sets, steel, automobiles, and machine tools, is a form of managed trade, that derives from American pressure.

Close linkages between Japanese firms—*keiretsu,* bank groups, manufacturing company-supplier links, private railways, department store complexes, and wholesale-retail networks—have been very successful. It is naive to imagine that the Japanese will abandon these linkages and government economic guidance for a system that is less competitive.[30] The United States no longer has the leverage to dictate to an economy that is so successful. It does, however, have the world's largest domestic market; there is no reason why access to that market cannot be used as a lever for expanding opportunities in the Japanese market.

Although it is important to continue to press Japan on certain trade and investment issues, the best approach is the Australian model. In 1989, Ross Garnaut, an economist and former Australian ambassador to China, published a report for the Australian Prime Minister and Minister of Foreign Affairs and Trade, advising Australia on how it might respond to the economic challenge from Northeast Asia. The report, *Australia and the Northeast Asian Ascendancy,* argued that since the Northeast Asian markets were the most dynamic in the world, that it was in Australia's interest to do everything it could to participate in those economies. Specifically, Australia was urged to develop more specialists in the requisite languages, to learn more about the markets, and to take part in a greater number of joint ventures and collaborative projects. The government was asked to play a facilitative role in all these efforts.[31] There are great opportunities in Japan for America's firms, with competitive products, who learn the subtleties of the language, understand the society and market. The failure of American firms to hire and train specialists prepared to deal with the markets of East Asia is today a more serious problem than any created by trade barriers.

Response to Competitive Challenges

There is a need to strengthen America's competitive capacity. Nothing that America will do to redefine its interests with Japan in the post-Cold War world is as important as dealing with its own domestic problems. It is now widely accepted that there is a need to balance the federal budget; to increase investment in plant, equipment, and infrastructure; to raise the standards of education, training, and commitment in the work force. Strengthening the American economy and its work force would do a great deal to improve the country's relationship with Japan.

Westerners knowledgeable about Japanese politics recognize, however, that this will not be enough. There is a great need to revise

American thinking on crucial matters. The notion that questions of economic competition can be safely left to companies, and that the government has no role at all is both naive and deceptive. The US government has already been deeply involved in the American economy, protecting steel companies by granting quotas without requiring them to reinvest in modernization of plant and equipment; deregulating the savings and loan industry and then bailing failures out at a tremendous cost to the country; choosing not to support American companies working together to form consortia to promote high-definition television or memory chips; promoting defense industries while refusing to play a role in helping former defense contractors to make the transition to civilian industries. The need is for a more rational policy that will allow companies to perform better in meeting their global competition.[32]

The American government lacks a strong track record in its ability to make decisions about business issues. American business would never tolerate the detailed micromanagement of industrial policy that is prevalent in Japan. But in at least three fundamental areas the American approach can be revised. First, it is in the country's interest, given its high-priced labor force, to maintain strong high-tech industries; this requires incentives for investment, support of cooperative projects where private capital is inadequate, and assistance in helping companies to define their needs so as to create demand-driven new technology. Second, there is a need to adapt financial regulations and financial markets to make it easier for firms to think in long-term categories to develop long-range strategies. Third, the kinds of mergers and acquisitions that have so distracted business leaders need to be more tightly controlled. They have caused such frequent changes of management and direction that America's leading business historian, Alfred Chandler, has observed that they have destroyed the organizational capacity of American firms to compete.

Those who have watched East Asian developments over recent decades recognize that the competitive challenge for the United States is far more serious than most Americans realize and that the country's long-range future depends on dealing with certain fundamental underlying issues.[33] In the 1980s as many American firms became aware of their competitive problems with Japan, they began to work hard to increase the quality of their goods, to improve the efficiency of their operations. But there is only so much that an individual firm can do unless there is a broader commitment by the government to create the kind of environment that will allow firms to concentrate on the long run with a well-trained work force in a stable society. The proportion of America's economic activity now affected by international trade continues to grow so rapidly that it is not possible to isolate the country from certain basic trends. There is no possibility of building a wall to contain the advances in Asia. The competitive challenges should be used to broaden support in American society for dealing with its own problems and for taking an active part in profiting from the vitality of Asia.

ENDNOTES

[1]For an account of the beginning of the Cold War with special reference to Asia, see Yonosuke Nagai and Akira Iriye, eds., *The Origins of the Cold War in Asia* (Tokyo: University of Tokyo Press, 1977).

[2]Yoichi Funabashi, "Japan and America: Global Partners," *Foreign Policy* (Spring 1992): 24–39. For a general account of his views about the post-Cold War era, see Yoichi Funabashi, *Reisengo* (After the Cold War) (Tokyo: Iwanami Shinsho, 1991).

[3]To be sure, Japan derived great benefit from the alliance, even from ARTICLE 9 in which Japan renounced war as the sovereign right of the nation, as Prime Minister Yoshida and his successors realized. For a recent account of this aspect of the legacy see Kenneth B. Pyle, *The Japanese Question: Power and Purpose in a New Era* (Washington, D.C.: American Enterprise Institute Press, 1992) and J. W. Dower, *Empire and Aftermath: Yoshida Shigeru and the Japanese Experience 1878–1954* (Cambridge: Harvard University Press, 1979).

[4]Akira Iriye, "U.S.-Japan Relations Since 1950," in *A Retrospective of Eighty Years of the U.S.-Japan Relationship* (Washington, D.C.: Reischauer Center for East Asian Studies, SAIS, 1985), and Akira Iriye, *Across the Pacific: An Inner History of American-East Asian Relations* (New York: Harcourt, Brace & World, 1967).

[5]For a very nuanced account by three of Japan's most thoughtful ambassadors see Hiroshi Kitamura, Ryohei Murata, and Hisahiko Okazaki, *Between Friends,* translated by Daniel R. Zoll (New York: Weatherhill, 1985).

[6]The best known example is the book by Shintaro Ishihara and Akio Morita, *"No" to Ieru Nippon* (The Japan that Can Say No). The original Japanese version is Shintaro Ishihara and Akio Morita, *"No" to Ieru Nippon* (Tokyo: Kobunsha, 1989). The English version is Shintaro Ishihara, *The Japan that Can Say No,* translated by Frank Baldwin (New York: Simon & Schuster, 1991). These sentiments have been further expanded in Shintaro Ishihara, Shoichi Watanabe, and Waku Ogawa, *Soredemo "No" to Ieru Nihon* (Nevertheless, Japan Can Say "No") (Tokyo: Kobunsha, 1990), and Shintaro Ishihara and Jun Eto, *Danko*

"No" to Ieru Nihon (The Japan That Can Say a Resolute "No") (Tokyo: Kobunsha, 1991).

[7]According to a major 1989 *Times-Mirror*/Gallup Poll, 63 percent of all Americans and 77 percent of the normally sympathetic "Enterprise Republicans" viewed Japan as unfair. Steven R. Saunders, "Japan Seen in U.S. as Unfair, Threat to Economy: Poll," *Japan Times,* 10 March 1989.

[8]For a highly nuanced view of the US-Japanese trade problems, see Guren S. Fukushima, *Nichibei Keizai Masatsu no Seijigaku* (The Political Science of Japanese-American Economic Friction) (Tokyo: Asahi Shinbun, 1992).

[9]See Robert O. Keohane, *After Hegemony: Cooperation and Discord in the World Political Economy* (Princeton: Princeton University Press, 1984), and Robert Gilpin, *The Political Economy of International Relations* (Princeton: Princeton University Press, 1987). For a Japanese interpretation see Naohiro Amaya, *"Saka no Ue no Kumo" to "Saka no Shita no Numa"* (Above the Clouds and Below the Swamp) (Tokyo: Tsuushoo Sangyoo Choosaka, 1985).

[10]Kuniko Inoguchi, *Posuto Haken Sisutemu to Nihon no Sentaku* (The Emerging Post-Hegemonic System: Choices for Japan) (Tokyo: Chikuma Shobo, 1987). See also, Takashi Inoguchi, *Japan's International Relations* (Boulder: Westview Press, 1991).

[11]Pat Choate, *Agents of Influence* (New York: Alfred A. Knopf, 1990) and Michael Crichton, *Rising Sun* (New York: Alfred A. Knopf, 1992).

[12]Chalmers Johnson is commonly cited as the father of revisionism. See Chalmers Johnson, *MITI and the Japanese Miracle—The Growth of Industrial Policy 1925–1975* (Stanford: Stanford University Press, 1982). Other interpretations of MITI's role can be found in James C. Abegglen and George Stalk, Jr., *Kaisha: The Japanese Corporation* (New York: Basic Books, 1985); Daniel I. Okimoto, *Between MITI and the Market: Japanese Industrial Policy for High Technology* (Stanford: Stanford University Press, 1989); and Ezra F. Vogel, *Japan As Number One* (Cambridge: Harvard University Press, 1979). See also the classic statement of MITI policy, "Organization for Economic Co-operation and Development," *The Industrial Policy of Japan* (Paris: OECD, 1972).

[13]Iriye, *Across the Pacific.*

[14]Koutaro Tawara, *'No.2' ga Nihon no Shikata da!* (Japan's Way is Number Two!) (Kyoto: PHP, 1990) and Atsushi Kuse, *Suupaa Nambaa tsuu: Nihon* (Super Number Two: Japan) (Tokyo: Shodensha, 1990).

[15]See the collection of various 1990 polls in "How the Japanese See Themselves. . . and Us," *The American Enterprise* 1 (November/December 1990).

[16]For a comparison of European and Japanese colonial systems, see Lewis H. Gann, "Western and Japanese Colonialism: Some Preliminary Comparisons," in Ramon H. Myers and Mark R. Peattie, eds., *The Japanese Colonial Empire, 1895–1945* (Princeton: Princeton University Press, 1984).

[17]The Japanese have set the ambitious goal of 100,000 for foreign student enrollment in their universities by the year 2000. Recent numbers have grown dramatically within the past few years, but in 1991 only 1,500 of the total 35,000 foreign students were American (90 percent are Asian). US educators hope to

increase this figure to 5,000 Americans in Japanese universities by the year 2000. However, 40,000 Japanese attend American universities. Institute for the Study of Diplomacy, *Japan's Future Global Role* (Washington, D.C.: Georgetown University, June 1992).

[18]In 1989 there were 1,849 Japan Overseas Cooperation Volunteers in thirty-eight countries. Agreements are now in force to provide volunteers to over fifty countries. Association for the Promotion of International Cooperation, *A Guide to Japan's Aid* (Tokyo: APIC, 1990), 53.

[19]One very important original broad-gauged analysis of the post-Cold War era traces the growth of advanced democratic communities between which war has now become unthinkable. See Nakasone, Yasuhiro, Yasusuke Murakami, Seizaburo Sato, and Susumu Nishibe, *Kyoodoo Kenkyuu "Reisen Igo"* (Joint Research, "After the Cold War") (Tokyo: Bungei Shunjuu, 1992), 139–48.

[20]See a discussion of such interdependence in monetary policies in Paul Volcker and Toyo Gyohten, *Changing Fortunes: the World's Money and the Threat to American Leadership* (New York: Times Books, 1992).

[21]For a discussion of Asian views of the Japanese and American military roles see "ASEAN and the Asia-Pacific Region: Prospects for Security Cooperation in the 1990s," Conference, 5–7 June 1991, sponsored by the Philippine Department of Foreign Affairs. For popular accounts of the issue see Damon Darlin, "South Korea, Fearing Japan's Military, Wants U.S. to Remain as Peacekeeper," *Wall Street Journal,* 20 November 1991, and Mikio Sumiya, "Arms Spending Revives Fears of Japanese Militarism," *Sekai,* translated by Asia Foundation's Translation Service Center, 18 May 1987.

[22]Norman D. Levin, "Prospects for U.S.-Japan Security Cooperation: the Mutual Security Treaty and Beyond," from the conference on "Japan's Future Global Role," sponsored by Georgetown University and Japan Economic Institute, 11–14 March 1992, Washington, D.C.

[23]See Prime Minister Ohira's vision for the Pacific Basin in "Atarashi Michi: Kantaiheiyoo Rentai Koosoo" (A New Path: The Concept of the Pacific Basin Community), in Yuichiro Nagatomi, *Kindai o Koete: Ko Ohira Soori no Kisareta Mono* (Beyond Modernity: The Legacy of the late Prime Minister Ohira), vol. 2 (Tokyo: Ookura Zaimu Kyookai, 1983), 54–134.

[24]Takeshita has recently fully embraced green politics. In April 1992, for example, he hosted a meeting of world leaders to help lay the foundation for the June Earth Summit in Brazil in which he took a major role.

[25]For an analysis of Japan's foreign aid, see Association for Promotion of International Cooperation, *A Guide to Japan's Aid* (Tokyo: APIC, 1990); Alan Rix, *Japan's Aid Program: A New Global Agenda* (Canberra: Australian International Development Assistance Bureau Issue no. 12, 1990); Shafiqul Islam, ed., *Yen For Development: Japanese Foreign Aid and the Politics of Burden-Sharing* (New York: Council on Foreign Relations, 1991); and Robert M. Orr, Jr., *The Emergence of Japan's Foreign Aid Power* (New York: Columbia University Press, 1990).

[26]For suggestions on security issues, see Francis J. McNeil, *Reassessing the U.S.-Japanese Security Relationship in the Post-Cold War Context* (Washington, D.C.: Commission on US-Japan Relations for the Twenty-First Century, 1991).

[27]For one thoughtful overview of the Pacific see, Gerald Segal, *Rethinking the Pacific* (Oxford: Clarendon, 1990).

[28]For a fuller discussion of Japan's efforts in the Pacific Rim, see Masahide Shibusawa, *Japan and the Asian Pacific Region* (New York: St. Martin's Press, 1984), and Sueo Sekiguchi, ed., *ASEAN-Japan Relations: Investment* (Singapore: Institute of Southeast Asian Studies, 1983). In a poll of Asian executives, about three-fourths expect that during the next decade Japan will strengthen its role but about one-half expect a substantial withdrawal of US forces, *Keidanren Review* (April 1992).

[29]Dennis J. Encarnation has shown that investment as well as trade has become a critical issue and that ownership did matter. Dennis J. Encarnation, *Rivals Beyond Trade: America Versus Japan in Global Competition* (Ithaca: Cornell University Press, 1992). See also Norman J. Glickman and Douglas P. Woodward, *The New Competitors: How Foreign Investors are Changing the U.S. Economy* (New York: Basic Books, 1989). For accounts of trade issues, see Clyde V. Prestowitz, Jr., *Trading Places: How We Allowed Japan to Take the Lead* (New York: Basic Books, 1988); and Clyde V. Prestowitz, Jr., Ronald A. Morse, and Alan Tonelson, *Powernomics: Economics and Strategy After the Cold War* (Washington, D.C.: Madison Books, 1991).

[30]For an interesting account of Japanese success in devising a system to manage economic issues, see Eisuke Sakakibara, *Shihonshugi o Koeta: Nihongata Shijo Keizai Taisei no Seiritsu to Tenkai* (Beyond Capitalism: The Establishment and Development of a Japanese-style System of Market Economy) (Tokyo: Tooyoo Keizai Shinhoosha, 1990).

[31]Ross Garnaut, *Australia and the Northeast Asian Ascendancy* (Canberra: Australian Government Publishing Service, 1989). For discussions of this report which became the main stream of Australian thinking about how to approach Japan, see J. L. Richardson, *Northeast Asian Challenge: Debating the Garnaut Report* (Canberra: Australian National University, 1991); and "Australia and Northeast Asia: The Garnaut Report," *Australian Journal of International Affairs* (April 1990): 1–51.

[32]For a discussion of the new challenges and discontinuities of American economic and social policies see Robert B. Reich, *The Next American Frontier* (New York: Times Books, 1983); Robert B. Reich and John D. Donahue, *New Deals* (New York: Times Books, 1985); Robert B. Reich, *The Work of Nations: Preparing Ourselves for 21st Century Capitalism* (New York: Alfred A. Knopf, 1991); Lester Thurow, *Head to Head: The Coming Economic Battle Among Japan, Europe, and America* (New York: William Morrow and Co., 1992); and Ezra F. Vogel, *Comeback* (New York: Simon and Schuster, 1985). James P. Womack, Daniel T. Jones, and Daniel Ross, *The Machine that Changed the World* (New York: Rawson Associates, 1990).

[33]One thoughtful essay on this issue is David Halberstam, *The Next Century* (New York: William Morrow and Company, 1991).

WHITHER JAPAN-U.S. RELATIONS?

Elections held in the United States and Japan last fall kept both countries' top leaders in office. U.S. President Bill Clinton began his second term in January, after being reelected in last November's poll. In Japan's October general election, the Liberal Democratic Party, headed by Prime Minister Hashimoto Ryūtarō, substantially bolstered its strength in the Diet, and while failing to capture an outright majority, managed to retain its place at the helm by soliciting the cooperation of the Social Democratic Party and New Party Sakigake (Harbinger), its former coalition partners. Hidden behind this continuity in leadership, however, are dramatic changes in the Japan-U.S. relationship.

When Clinton first took office four years ago, Japan was regarded as a prime focus of U.S. foreign policy. The new administration seemed determined to extract major economic and military concessions from Tokyo, demanding that Japan open its markets and contribute more to defense. This was in large measure a reflection of the national mood. After the 1985 Plaza accord, which sent the yen skyrocketing, Japan had seemed poised to overtake the United States economically, if indeed it had not already. The Japanese, riding the crest of their speculative "bubble economy," were apt to look down on the United States, while Americans, increasingly convinced of a "Japanese threat," were caught up in the new national pastime of Japan bashing. This sort of tension continued through the 1980s and persisted to a considerable degree even after Japan's "bubble" burst. The wariness with which Americans viewed Japan right up until about four years ago unquestionably helped shape Clinton's foreign policy in those early months.

Four years later, it is almost as if Japan had ceased to exist in the eyes of the Clinton administration. During the November election, the Clinton campaign scarcely breathed a word about Japan, and the new cabinet is conspicuously lacking in Japan expertise. Why have things come to this pass? The fundamental reason is that Japan still has not dealt with the aftermath of the bubble economy, lagging behind all the other industrial nations in dealing with the residue of bad debts in its financial sector. As a result, the country's predicted economic recovery has failed to materialize, and by the beginning of 1997, plunging stocks and a slipping yen had observers questioning the economy's future and investors running scared.

As Japan drifts out of focus, China has begun to loom ever larger. Americans are watching the Chinese with intense interest—all the more so because Hong Kong is scheduled to revert to China on July 1 this year. Politically, the focus is on if and when the country will move toward democracy; economically, it is on the possibilities of a market of 1.25 billion consumers; and militarily, it is on China's increasing defense spending and hegemonistic behavior. Unfortunately, however, there have been no formal consultations between Washington and Tokyo on the subject of policy cooperation vis-à-vis China. Moreover, given the current chill in Japan-China relations, Tokyo is scarcely in a position to mediate between Washington and Beijing. To establish a productive three-way relationship with China and the United States, Japan must first strengthen its own ties with China.

The focus of Washington's short-term East Asia policy may be shifting from Tokyo to Beijing, but that does not mean China is poised to take Japan's place. Unlike China, Japan is a valued ally that shares with the United States such fundamental values as freedom and democracy. In economic terms as well, the bilateral relationship between the United States and Japan—the world's two largest economies—is second to none in importance. This means that not only does each country have an obligation toward the other, but both countries have a joint obligation toward the entire world.

In the arena of trade relations, the most important challenges facing us are coordination of macroeconomic policy and structural reform. For example, if the yen continues to drop against the dollar, concerted intervention within the Group of Seven framework will be of critical importance. The Hashimoto cabinet has made administrative reform its top priority, but it must not relax its efforts to achieve structural economic reforms, particularly in the form of deregulation. These much-needed changes will not only help revitalize the moribund Japanese economy but also give a boost to ties with the United States. Where sector-specific trade issues are concerned, meanwhile, it is desirable to refer conflicts to such international organs as the World Trade Organization and avoid turning them into political footballs.

In the realm of security, a "redefinition" of the bilateral security arrangements is already in progress at the working level. The problems surrounding the U.S. military bases in Okinawa have become such a hot political issue in Japan that the fate of the Hashimoto administration may conceivably rest on their resolution. The Americans have shown themselves willing to yield on such key points as the return of the land currently occupied by the Marine Corps Air Station at Futenma, but Japan needs to do its part as well. Specifically, if we are to reap the benefits of bilateral cooperation in the area of defense, Tokyo must adopt a more positive stand on the nation's right to engage in collective self-defense and create a cooperative framework worthy of a country of Japan's stature.

At a summit meeting in July 1993, President Clinton and then Prime Minister Miyazawa Kiichi launched the Japan-U.S. Common Agenda for Cooperation in Global Perspective, a program of bilateral cooperation on problems with worldwide ramifications. Specifically, the Common Agenda calls for Japan and the United States to forge a partnership for tackling such diverse global issues as the environment, technology, population, and the spread of AIDS. Since 1993, the program has been expanded to address even more areas of concern and has made remarkable inroads. Such success stories in the saga of Japan-U.S. relations deserve far more attention than they receive. (Masuzoe Yōichi, political scientist)

Partners for the Coming Century

KOMORI YOSHIHISA

EZRA VOGEL

SAITŌ KUNIHIKO

SAITŌ KUNIHIKO With the start of [U.S. President Bill] Clinton's second term, some observers are predicting that Washington will be stepping up the economic pressure on Tokyo. But I don't think we need to anticipate a return to the stance we saw early in his first term, when the new administration hit Japan with strong demands and insisted on visible results.

If relations between Japan and the United States deteriorate in the new term, the most likely cause will be friction relating to the bilateral security arrangements. I'm afraid that if Japan in some way fails to perform its duties as an American ally, the whole basis of the bilateral relationship could be in jeopardy.

If there were a crisis situation and Japan failed to do everything in its power to perform its duty under the treaty, within the limits of the Constitution and our current interpretation thereof—for example, if it hesitated to provide what the United States expected in the way of logistic support not involving the use of force—the reaction would be, "How can you call yourselves our allies?" At a time like that, bilateral relations would be in real danger. I have a feeling, though, that in such a situation Japan would rise to the occasion.

EZRA VOGEL I see two possible threats to Japan-U.S. relations. One, as Ambassador Saitō suggested, is the danger that Japan might fail to provide adequate support or refuse to send personnel during a crisis. If the Japanese refused to send their own people to a trouble spot when American soldiers were risking their lives there, I think the United States would react sharply. As Americans see it, the Japanese don't have to bear arms, but they need to dispatch personnel—medical, logistic, or whatever—to the trouble spot. This would be particularly true if the crisis were in Asia.

One other thing worries me. I think that Sino-American relations will improve somewhat over the coming year. There might be bilateral summit meetings, for example. Americans sometimes go to extremes. When [President Richard] Nixon visited Beijing in 1972, Americans went overboard about making friends with China. I can imagine a scenario in which Vice-President [Al] Gore goes to Beijing, [President] Jiang Zemin visits the United States, and Clinton reciprocates with a trip to China. Then, if the government in Beijing loosened up a little bit, Americans would get all excited, saying, China is getting better now, it's going to become a democracy just like us, it's going to have a free economy. Meanwhile, the Chinese might also start saying, Let's be friends again, as we were during World War II.

The reality, though, is that while Japan is an American ally, China can't be one—at least, not for the next ten years or so. While Japan is a free country and a democracy, China is unlikely to become one before the middle of the twenty-first century. So, practically speaking, Sino-American relations can't improve by that much, but there's a possibility that the idea will attract a lot of excitement.

My fear is that in that sort of atmosphere, relations between Japan and the United States could become somewhat shaky, and we could see some unfavorable political reactions taking place.

KOMORI YOSHIHISA In many ways, one can understand Americans' sense of affinity with China, but fundamentally speaking, China isn't a democracy and Japan is. What's important in this regard is not simply Japan's position as an ally of the United States but also the basic shared values that form the foundation of our security alliance: democracy, freedom, and a market economy. It's something one hears a great deal in the United States, but unfortunately, it's not emphasized in Japan. For example, when trouble occurred in Okinawa, the Japanese were quick to point up all the problems created by the U.S. military bases there. It would have been nice if at least one of our political leaders had spoken up for the fundamental importance of the bilateral alliance and the shared values that sustain it. But no one said a word about that. I find that very troubling.

Also, let me say a word about the question of how Japan would respond from a defense standpoint in an emergency. If you trace the problem to its origins, you realize that it's the result of the structural lopsidedness, or one-sidedness, that's been the most glaring characteristic of the bilateral defense relationship since its inception. Americans and Japanese view security in a fundamentally different light. It's a historical irony that the security arrangements have become the centerpiece of the bilateral relationship despite this gap. During the cold war, the relationship functioned admirably despite such differences, but that's no guarantee that it will hereafter. For example, even when it comes to logistic support in a crisis situation, under the Cabinet Legislation Bureau's current interpretation of the Constitution, not only is Japan prohibited from sending ships into a battle zone in conjunction with the use of force, it's also prevented from transporting weapons or ammunition to a region where American forces are currently engaged in combat—though apparently food and water are all right. Are ordinary Americans going to understand such an anomalous situation? It's not a normal alliance, that much is certain. For Japan's part, we need to consider what to do about these basic structural problems. We depend on U.S. military force and assume the Americans will come to our rescue in a pinch at the same time that we preach the renunciation of all military force and vow to "export our war-renouncing Constitution to the rest of the world." We can't get away with that anymore.

SAITŌ I agree with you. But it seems to me that the mood is changing in Japan, and people have begun to recognize the necessity of seriously considering and discussing issues of security and defense. There's been quite a bit of open debate on the subject. I'd say the shift began around the time of the war in the Persian Gulf. This is one positive thing that came out of all that. As debate on these issues unfolds, things will change, and the Japanese won't be able to regard security issues solely from their own standpoint, as they have until now.

VOGEL But unless Japan's politicians do a better job of explaining their position publicly, there's a danger that Americans could react emotionally. Where China is concerned, for example, there would be no problem if Washington followed a purely rational approach to policy making. But Americans are an emotional people, and when they react strongly to something, it has an impact on policy. I worry a little about that.

SAITŌ It's true that Americans sometimes lurch en masse in one direction. And I get the feeling that in their hearts, America and China really respect one another. But I don't think there's any need for the Japanese to worry that the United States will abandon Japan in favor of China. China's political and economic systems differ fundamentally, after all, and no one can say when or if they will change. Then there's the matter of Taiwan. When you take Congress into account, the possibility of the United States wholeheartedly embracing China seems very slim. Even if it did, though, that would be no reason for Japan to panic. Friendly relations between China and the United States are good for the stability of Asia. Japan's basic approach should be to continue to tread the path of democracy, freedom, and a market economy, while deregulating so as to make ours an even more open society. If we proceed in that direction, I'm certain that the United States won't decide it doesn't need us anymore.

VOGEL Ultimately it won't, of course, but there could be some rough patches along the way. If relations with China improve, Americans are apt to get into a mood of dumping criticism on Japan. This sort of emotional vacillation could cause problems.

KOMORI YOSHIHISA
Born in 1941. Graduated from Keiō University, where he majored in economics. Has been a reporter for the daily *Mainichi Shimbun*. Is now editor-at-large at the *Sankei Shimbun*'s Washington bureau. Author of *Nichi-Bei ihen* (Japan-U.S. Relations Gone Awry) and other works.

EZRA VOGEL
Received his Ph.D. in sociology from Harvard University. His teaching career at Harvard has been combined with senior administrative responsibilities and work for the U.S. government. Author of numerous works, including *Japan as Number One: Lessons for America*.

SAITŌ KUNIHIKO
Born in 1935. Graduated from the University of Tokyo's Faculty of Law. Joined the Ministry of Foreign Affairs in 1958 and served as vice-minister for Foreign Affairs. Is now ambassador to the United States.

CONSTITUTIONAL LIMITS

KOMORI Getting back to the basic problems in the security setup, I would suggest that in order for the Japan-U.S. Security Treaty to function effectively, Japan needs to revise its interpretation of the Constitution at least to acknowledge the right to engage in collective self-defense. People in Japan talk about the right of collective self-defense as if by acknowledging it Japan would automatically be forced to send combat units and enter into every military conflict in which the United States is involved. That's not true. It should be understood in terms of expanding our options. In any given situation, Japan could also make the political judgment that it should do nothing. But when we start out from the interpretation that we can't transport any weapons or munitions or whatever, no matter what the situation, and that we can't engage in any activity, even outside the battle zone, that might be seen as integrated with some U.S. military action, the lopsided nature of the relationship becomes all too obvious; it's just not reasonable from the standpoint of a long-term alliance. When I make assertions of this sort in Japan, I'm invariably told that my views are nationalistic and will lead Japan down the road to militarism, but that's way off the mark. I'm not advocating amending the Constitution or sending combat troops. I'm simply saying that we have to give ourselves the latitude to supply logistic support in a crisis situation, something expected of any ally. Still, it's not clear just what the Americans really want of Japan in this area.

VOGEL From Washington's standpoint, it would be a tremendous help if the right to collective self-defense were explicitly acknowledged as falling within the limits of the Constitution. The problem would be how to explain that to China. Lately the Chinese have been making noises to the effect that the Japan-U.S. Security Treaty is undesirable and a source of concern to them. For the sake of transparency as well, all three countries, China, Japan, and the United States, need to talk freely. Otherwise, China is apt to misunderstand the situation. Tokyo has to explain to Beijing how it interprets the right of collective self-defense, how far it would go. Actually, China has been a bit worrisome itself of late, building all those new weapons and battleships, but as long as the Chinese adhere to the path of peace, they have no reason to be alarmed.

SAITŌ My view is that even under the current interpretation forbidding Japan to engage in collective self-defense, there's a great deal we can do. Where logistic support is concerned, I think there has to be further study on the question of whether it's really impermissible for Japan to transport weapons and munitions. There are an awful lot of things we really should be able to do under a basic interpretation of the Constitution. My feeling is that we need to examine those areas and discuss them with the United States. Meanwhile, the official Guidelines for Japan-U.S. Defense Cooperation are already being reconsidered.

KOMORI In the final analysis, the whole purpose of an alliance is collective self-defense. Of course, we couldn't have a situation in which Japan and the United States, a military superpower, were fighting all sorts of battles together in remote areas of the world. But in principle, at least, the members of an alliance are supposed to assist one another. And yet Japan has made one-sidedness the underlying principle of its alliance with the United States. The question is whether it can maintain the alliance on the basis of such assumptions into the next century.

VOGEL I'm concerned about that as well. After the incident in which a Japanese girl was raped by U.S. servicemen in Okinawa in September 1995, I spoke with a lot of Japanese politicians, and they all acknowledged the necessity for the Japan-U.S. Security Treaty and collective self-defense. On the American side, though, there could be problems. The White House, the State Department, and the Pentagon handled the redefinition of the security relationship quite skillfully, but I don't think they've adequately explained the situation to Congress. Sooner or later, our politicians are going to start asking why the United States has to spend so much on Japan. Then, if it becomes apparent that Japan is only willing to commit itself so far in regard to collective self-defense, there's every possibility of a powerful reaction on the American side.

SAITŌ This falls outside the realm of bilateral relations per se, but I think that by fulfilling its international responsibilities, Japan can create the conditions for stronger ties with the United States. Japan has benefited more from these past fifty years of peace than any other nation in the world. It just can't continue simply to reap the benefits while leaving the preservation of that peace to others.

Fortunately, though, this perception is taking hold in Japan. Over the last four years Japan has been able to participate in U.N. peace-keeping operations. Of course, any time Japan is obliged to take some action with military overtones, we have to watch the reaction of our Asian neighbors very carefully. Still, there's no reason to expect anything but a positive outcome from our participation in PKO. Japan's first real peace-keeping mission was in Cambodia, and the success of that undertaking had tremendous ramifications. Henceforth, I think Japan needs to dramatically expand its peace-keeping efforts. If our country begins to fulfill its responsibilities in this respect, it will go a long way toward enhancing its importance in America's eyes.

VOGEL That's one key to improving understanding between Japan and the United States. At the same time, I think Japan needs to clarify the principles guiding its political and diplomatic actions and play a more positive international role. Japan is, after all, the only country ever to experience a nuclear attack. And it's also the only major power to renounce the possession of nuclear weapons. Japan provides more monetary aid than any other country, but it needs to be more clear about the principles and objectives that guide its foreign aid program. Japan's role in the international community should be to clearly set forth its peaceful principles and make it clear that it intends to make a contribution, including collective self-defense, on the basis of those principles, not use them to evade its responsibilities.

KOMORI That's a big problem when it comes to Japan's international contribution. There are dirty and dangerous jobs, too, and someone has to do them. If one country announces from the outset, "We're not going to do *that*," then it becomes very difficult to act in concert with others.

There's no question that Japan wants to contribute all it can to world peace. It's also perfectly clear that it wants to avoid any military entanglement whatever. Certainly no one in Japan today harbors ambitions of expanding the country's territory by attacking its neighbors. Quite to the contrary: We don't even take action when other countries trespass on the Senkaku Islands, which are an integral part of Japanese territory. If the Japanese were suddenly to disembark on the disputed islets of Takeshima [which the Koreans call Tokdo], the South Korean army would probably start shooting. There would be a big uproar if Japanese went to the Northern Territories without permission from the Russians. Yet we're always being vilified by China and South Korea for our so-called militarist tendencies. They're bound to say that no matter what we do.

If Japan were to adopt a policy that allowed it to exercise its right of collective self-defense and Beijing reacted negatively, I would hope the United States would do its best to placate the Chinese by explaining that we haven't the slightest desire to invade any other country.

SAITŌ China expressed all kinds of misgivings in response to the April 1996 Japan-U.S. Joint Declaration on Security, but both Tokyo and Washington have taken every opportunity to reassure Beijing that the bilateral alliance is not directed against any third country. Unfortunately, though, the memory of events that occurred fifty years ago is still deeply etched in the minds of the Chinese, South Koreans, and North Koreans. A century may not be enough to erase the memories of countries that were victimized by the war. Of course, we have to conduct our foreign policy levelheadedly, calculating our long-term interests, not acting on the basis of sentimental considerations. But we need to be fully aware of their viewpoint as well.

Also, it shouldn't be assumed that Japan hasn't made any international contribution until now. Its financial contribution has been sizable, and the economic cooperation it has provided in the form of official development assistance, a major focus of Tokyo's foreign policy, has contributed a great deal to global peace and stability in an indirect way. But the crux is that not enough of our contribution has been of the sort that involves direct human effort. A country this powerful really needs to contribute the sweat of its own people.

VOGEL To some extent, China fears Japan's technological and organizational abilities from the standpoint of the long-term situation in Asia, recalling the experience of World War II. But these worries are rather overblown, and they're also fanned by the patriotic current in domestic Chinese politics. And to some degree I think the Chinese are deliberately voicing these fears in order to manipulate international opinion. But then in Japan you have these Diet politicians who every so often come up with some inflammatory statement. I think it's a good idea for Japan to propose joint studies relating to World War II in which scholars from China, Japan, and other countries could address the subject objectively.

KOMORI You're absolutely right. But I have to tell you, Chinese elementary school textbooks contain some astonishing statements. For example, on the subject of the Korean War, they say that the U.S. imperialist forces attacked, crossed over the thirty-eighth parallel, and even bombed Chinese cities. So, of course, China's so-called volunteer forces were obliged to fight back, and China won. I find myself wondering what right a country like that has to criticize Japan's textbooks. So, while I realize that joint studies are necessary and meaningful, I think the results are fairly predictable.

THE COMMON AGENDA

SAITŌ Japan and the United States are currently cooperating on a set of global initiatives known as the Common Agenda [for Cooperation in Global Perspective]. The way I see it, this is a matter of two great industrial powers trying to do their duty vis-à-vis the future of humanity. This project was launched in 1993 as part of the Japan-U.S. Framework for a New Economic Partnership, and it's achieved a tremendous amount in very concrete terms. Our countries have been cooperating and spending large amounts of money to address a wide range of problems, including overpopulation, the environment, AIDS, and children's health, but unfortunately this has gotten very little attention in the media. I think this kind of cooperation is making a very positive difference in bilateral relations. This points up the fact that in addition to Japan-U.S. relations and bilateral cooperation in the narrow sense, we need to keep in mind our shared responsibility for the future of the entire earth.

VOGEL We have an excellent opportunity right now. If Prime Minister Hashimoto [Ryūtarō] and President Clinton can build a strong relationship, they'll be able to lay stress on the Common Agenda during their summit meetings, as in the days of "Ron and Yasu" [President Ronald Reagan and Prime Minister Nakasone Yasuhiro]. And if they bring it up enough at press conferences, eventually the newspapers will write it up.

The fact is that Japan and the United States are involved in extraordinarily beneficial cooperative undertakings all over the world, but people in neither country are really aware of it. One way to see to it that it's better understood is for both Hashimoto and Clinton to stay in power and build a close relationship with one another. I have the feeling that opportunity is about to present itself.

Translated from "21 seiki no mottomo taisetsu na pātonā to shite," in Gaikō Forum, *January 1997, pp. 34–45; abridged by about one-third. (Courtesy of Toshi Shuppan, Publishers)*

The Japan-U.S. Security Arrangements in a New Era

TANAKA HITOSHI

Maybe it is not proper for a bureaucrat to air his personal opinions in public. Perhaps bureaucrats should state their own views regarding policies only in internal discussions within the ministry, and public pronouncements should be limited to the official stance that the government has decided to adopt. Incidentally, in Britain, where the roles of politicians and bureaucrats are very clearly separated, bureaucrats are not permitted under any circumstances to publish views under their own name in newspapers or magazines. The opinion of a ministry can only be given in the name of its minister.

Why, then, do I now present my personal views regarding the Japan-U.S. security relationship, for which I am officially responsible? There are two main reasons. The first is that Japan's security policy, and in particular the Japan-U.S. security relationship, is at a crucial turning point. The provision of security is the most important function for a country to perform. In order to ensure that this crucial job is done properly, it is best to have a domestic consensus reached through ample discussion. As someone who directly participated in the talks concerning the Japan-U.S. Joint Declaration on Security issued in April 1996 and the problem of the U.S. military bases in Okinawa, I believe that explaining the essential issues that Japan and U.S. policy makers have been tackling will contribute to the security debate in Japan, which is so truly essential. Second, I feel that it has become necessary for me as a bureaucrat to explain the fundamental thinking behind the policies we have hammered out. At this point just explaining the policies themselves is insufficient.

While participating in extremely frequent talks with U.S. security policy officials over the past several months, I have been constantly thinking about the questions of how to build a bilateral security system appropriate for a new era and how both Japan and the United States can obtain the domestic support essential for this new system. Above all else it is necessary for us to abandon our ideas of security based on cold-war thinking. In the cold-war period, facing the enormous military threat of the Soviet Union, Japan had to rely completely on the United States to guarantee its security. No realistic alternative was available. But now several years have passed since the end of the cold war, and it has become more difficult to give a lucid explanation of the raison d'être of the existing Japan-U.S. security system. Indeed, I believe that it is now essential to modify this system in line with the changes in the security environment.

THE NEW REALITIES

It is unreasonable to expect the Japan-U.S. security arrangements to be everlasting and immutable even in the face of changes in international relations and the domestic environment. Just as there has been constant discussion of the proper shape of Europe's security system in the wake of the cold war and the advance of integration within the European Union, so the Japan-U.S. security arrangements must constantly be developed in response to changes in international and domestic conditions.

What are the international and domestic changes that may alter the shape of the Japan-U.S. security arrangements? First of all there is a change in the perception of threat. For a while after the end of the cold war some people in Japan argued that because the cold-war structure had not been very evident in the Asia-Pacific region, the end of the confrontation brought almost no change to the threat here. Certainly the kind of tangible easing that took place in Europe with the collapse of the Warsaw Pact and the democratization of Eastern Europe did not occur in Asia. Russia continued to concentrate military forces, including nuclear weaponry, in the Far East, and there is still no World War II peace treaty between Tokyo and Moscow. There has been no change in the latent instability on the Korean Peninsula. And there has been no change in the great anxiety among surrounding countries about China's nuclear arsenal, its military modernization, its claim to the Spratly Islands, and the tension between it and Taiwan.

Despite the absence of tangible changes in the Asia-Pacific region, however, it is wrong to conclude that the structure of danger to Japan's security has not changed at all. The biggest changes brought about by the end of the cold war have been the eradication of the Soviet military threat, which could have led to a large-scale war, and the eclipse of the conflict-deterrent power exerted by the East-West balance. The East-West cold war was "cold" in the sense that it did not involve belligerency. Tremendous military capabilities were required to maintain deterrence; at the same time, however, the cold-war setup fulfilled a

TANAKA HITOSHI

Born in 1947. Graduated from Kyoto University's Faculty of Law. Received his master's degree from Oxford University. Joined the Ministry of Foreign Affairs in 1969; is now deputy director general of the North American Affairs Bureau.

peace-keeping role in preventing the outbreak of "hot" wars. Of course, the question of which will prove more peaceful, the cold-war era or the post-cold-war era, must be left for future historians to weigh, but still it is a fact that in the post-cold-war period we have been unable to prevent some violent conflicts, such as the Iraqi invasion of Kuwait and the civil war in the former Yugoslavia. Even in the Asia-Pacific region, the security problem is undergoing a structural change. The threat of a global war has almost completely ceased to exist, and this is a positive factor for the security of all countries. But at the same time the seeds of local conflicts, which previously had been held in check out of fear that they could trigger a global war, continue to exist. Indeed, there seems to be an increasing danger of these local conflicts' bubbling to the surface. Such conflicts might be local, but for those involved and their neighbors they are quite large enough. One should perhaps say that the true basic issues affecting Japan's security have emerged into view.

The second factor that could bring about a change in the security setup is the change in the domestic situation in Japan. Back in the days when the Japan Socialist Party (now renamed Social Democratic Party), as the largest opposition party, adamantly rejected the Japan-U.S. security arrangements, debate about security issues in the National Diet tended to be extremely confrontational, and there was little room for constructive exchanges. But now as a result of the Socialists' participation in the government and the transformation of their policy stance, the situation is different. A debate without any taboos is now possible in Japan. On the issue of security, it is desirable for the main political parties to be in broad agreement. Many people believe that the base for such a consensus is now taking shape in Japan.

At the same time, the question of how the relationship between U.S. military bases, which are concentrated overwhelmingly in Okinawa, and the local communities around those bases should change in a new security environment has become an important issue in domestic politics. Although I believe that, in terms of political currents in Japan, support for the Japan-U.S. security arrangements is stronger now than it was in the cold-war period, there is less stability than before in terms of the supply of Japanese land for U.S. military bases, which is one of the foundations of the bilateral security setup. Seventy-five percent of the U.S. military bases in Japan are concentrated in a single prefecture accounting for a mere 0.6% of Japan's total area. No one can deny that this situation lacks balance.

CLOSER JAPAN-U.S. CONSULTATIONS

Faced with what appear to be fundamental changes in the situation, what thoughts have been passing through the minds of the Japanese and U.S. security officials as they have been proceeding with their work? Both sides are focused on a common goal, namely, an earnest desire to build the most appropriate security arrangements for Japan and the United States for the twenty-first century. Whenever we met to work on drafting the joint security declaration or to discuss the reduction of U.S. military bases in Okinawa, we always encouraged each other with affirmations that our work was historic and that the cost of failure would be very high indeed. Below I describe my own views concerning the desirable shape of the Japan-U.S. security arrangements for the years ahead in keeping with the joint declaration issued last April.

Some observers complained that the declaration expanded the scope of the Japan-U.S. security treaty, but this is not true. The declaration confirmed Japan's fundamental defense policy of relying on a combination of its own defense capabilities and the Japan-U.S. security arrangements, but it also noted that the two countries, each with its own security policies for the post-cold-war era, would cooperate as allies in the solution of regional issues and global problems on the basis of these security policies. In this case, security policy is a broader concept than defense policy. The Japan-U.S. Security Treaty is a legal framework stipulating a set of rights and duties for the two parties; it is not something whose scope can be broadened through a joint declaration. Considering their respective security policies, I think that it is extremely appropriate for Japan and the United States, as allies, to engage in the exchange of information and to make joint or parallel efforts toward improving the security environment for the stability of the Asia-Pacific region. For example, even confidence-building measures with surrounding countries are something that Japan should undertake in cooperation with the United States rather than on its own. And naturally, Japan's actions must be within the scope permitted by its Constitution.

In the past the central issue for Japan-U.S. discussions was the question of how much of a burden Japan should accept to ensure the U.S. commitment to Japan's defense under the bilateral security treaty. This was a facet of the tendency to see the treaty as one-sided because it imposed no obligation for Japan to defend the United States. Talks thus focused on the strengthening of Japan's defense self-help efforts and host-nation support. Within Japan, meanwhile, there was strong criticism of any moves to promote bilateral discussion of U.S. military strategies or of the functions of U.S. military bases. People argued that such talks could cause Japan to become entangled in an American war or be turned into a pawn of U.S. regional strategy. Influenced by the international and domestic changes in the security environment that I described above, however, the situation is now quite different.

First of all, as a result of Japan's own burden-sharing efforts and America's reappraisal of the Japan-U.S. security arrangements in the post-cold-war era, the recognition that the United States has a crucial interest in the Asia-Pacific region and that the forward deployment of the U.S. military in Japan is extremely advantageous to U.S. security has become more deeply entrenched in the United States. There is thus less need for us Japanese to view the Japan-U.S. Security Treaty as one-sided.

Second, the perception of threat has changed. In the cold-war era security issues were defined in terms of the East-West conflict, centered on the two superpowers of the United States and the Soviet Union. But now they are defined in terms of the special features of the Asia-Pacific region, and particularly the Far East. That is to say, the central security issue now concerns the regional situation, in which Japan cannot help but be directly involved as an actor.

Third, it is no longer possible to discuss the realignment, consolidation, and reduction of U.S. military bases without examining U.S. military strategy and base functions. Japan-U.S. security discussions thus need to focus on four issues: efforts to improve the regional security environment; defense cooperation based on a clear sharing of roles between Japan and the United States in times of emergency; a constant reevaluation of the Japan-U.S. military and defense arrangements, including the level of the U.S. military's forward deployment; and the consolidation and reduction of U.S. military bases in line with this reevaluation, together with consideration of the proper forms of cooperation between these bases and their communities.

DISCUSSING THIS ISSUE IN AN ABSTRACT MANNER, IN TERMS OF THE RIGHTS AND WRONGS OF EXERCISING THE RIGHT OF COLLECTIVE SELF-DEFENSE, IS NOT CONSTRUCTIVE AT ALL.

ESTABLISHING ADEQUATE DOMESTIC ARRANGEMENTS

At present Japan and the United States are engaged in a review of the Guidelines for Japan-U.S. Defense Cooperation, which were drawn up in 1978. These guidelines outline the basic thinking of the two countries regarding three subjects: the establishment of a setup to prevent any invasion of Japan, the response in the case of an armed attack on Japan, and bilateral cooperation in cases where the situation in the Far East outside of Japan has a major impact on Japan's security. Joint research and other related work have been carried out in each area. Since the guidelines were formulated at the time of the cold war, they focus on bilateral cooperation in the hypothetical case of Japan's being invaded within the context of the U.S.-Soviet superpower confrontation. They must now be made to reflect the new security environment of the post-cold-war era. In particular, as I noted above, the chances that the regional situation could exert a direct impact on Japan's security have actually become greater.

Security is a prime area where preparedness is of the essence, and we must therefore check to be sure that our preparations are adequate. If the United States, on the basis of the Japan-U.S. Security Treaty and its agreements with other related countries, moved into action to cope with an emergency situation in the region that had a major bearing on Japan's own security, it is inconceivable that Japan could just stand by with folded arms. Discussing this issue in an abstract manner, in terms of the rights and wrongs of exercising the right of collective self-defense, is not constructive at all.

The work on reviewing the guidelines has involved looking separately at the various phases of a crisis situation—precrisis, outbreak of crisis, fighting, conclusion of crisis—coming up with specific elements of defense cooperation, and considering how cooperation should be carried out. I believe that this kind of defense cooperation should be comprehensive, consisting not only of items relating to the rights and duties stipulated in the Japan-U.S. Security Treaty itself, such as the U.S. obligation to defend Japan and Japan's obligation to supply land for U.S. military bases, but also items that are not duties under the security treaty but are reasonable forms of cooperation between allies. For example, the transportation of people

Japanese and American uniformed personnel enhance their readiness for potential crisis situations through joint exercises.

fleeing from the environs of a crisis that has broken out in the vicinity of Japan and the accommodation of refugees are not directly related to the rights and duties stipulated in the security treaty, but I believe that they are areas in which allies naturally should cooperate. Moreover, confidence-building measures with surrounding countries to improve the security environment and diplomatic measures to prevent the outbreak of crises should be understood as aspects of defense cooperation in the broad sense, and Japan and the United States should conduct studies in these fields.

In tandem with the Japan-U.S. consultations, I earnestly hope that more thorough consideration will be given to the necessary arrangements on the domestic level. For example, private-sector aircraft could hardly be expected to fulfill the role of transporting evacuees in a crisis situation. It is one thing if we declare it acceptable to abandon any noncombatants, including Japanese, who get caught in such circumstances, but if that is not our view, then surely we must consider the possibility of deploying appropriately equipped transport planes and ships of the Self-Defense Forces. In order to make this possible, legislation is required. Also, to enable the SDF to provide direct assistance to the U.S. military in a crisis by supplying fuel and medical treatment, we need to sort out our thinking on the relationship between such assistance and the issue of collective self-defense, enact the appropriate legislation, and make an agreement with the United States. It is also necessary for Japan to implement domestic measures to allow the U.S. military to make priority use of private-sector facilities in emergencies. It is totally inappropriate to argue that steps like these could be taken if and when a crisis actually occurred or that the government could handle such a situation by taking supralegal measures.

The Japanese government interprets the Constitution as prohibiting Japan from exercising the right of collective self-defense, but the problem lies in defining specifically what actions fall under the exercise of this right. In other words, where exactly is the line to be drawn? Under the bilateral security treaty, Japan supplies land for U.S. military bases to ensure international peace and security in the Far East, which is considered to be very closely connected with Japan's own security. Also, Japan provided an enormous amount of money at the time of the war in the Persian Gulf. But these actions are not interpreted as coming under the exercise of collective self-defense. Looked at from the U.S. side, the Japan-U.S. security arrangements are premised on the exercise of collective self-defense. That is to say, the United States would consider an attack against Japan as an attack against itself and would exercise the right of self-defense. Japan, however, does not have a duty to defend the United States outside of Japanese territory, and the Japanese Constitution does not permit the exercise of force by the SDF outside of Japan except within the scope of what can be interpreted as individual self-defense.

The problem here lies in defining exactly what actions would be considered an exercise of force. Would it be considered an exercise of force if the SDF gave information that it possessed to the U.S. military, or supplied fuel, or gave treatment to wounded American troops at SDF hospitals?

Perhaps an even more important point is that Japan, when providing support to the U.S. military, must make an independent judgment on the situation. If the U.S. military were to move into action for the sake of Japan's safety or of security in the Far East, Japan would have to judge for itself whether the action was right or not. And if the decision was that the action was right, Japan would then have to carry out what it considered to be the most appropriate role.

THE OKINAWAN PROBLEM AS A LONG-TERM ISSUE

The Special Action Committee on Okinawa, which began its work in November 1995 and issued its final report a year later, achieved many notable results. Among them were agreements to return more than 20% of the land used by U.S. military bases in Okinawa, including Futenma Air Station, which had turned into the most symbolic issue; to implement noise reduction initiatives; to adjust operational procedures; and to implement measures concerning markings on U.S. official military vehicles. During the period of the committee's work, those responsible in both governments, including the two countries' top leaders, feared strongly that unless a clear direction were shown on the issue of U.S. military bases in Okinawa, the bilateral security arrangements themselves could be rocked from their foundations. This concern certainly provided a driving force for action. But achieving progress was easier said than done. The difficulties may be summed up as follows:

First, taking the need for security as given, from the standpoint of the U.S. military stationed in Okinawa the

KYODO

Senior officials of the two countries express their approval of a report from the bilateral Special Action Committee on Okinawa.

existing level of base functions there was the absolute minimum necessary. There was little room to reduce the acreage of base land or the functions of the bases. Futenma Air Station would be a central base for the U.S. Marines in an emergency and had an important role in the transportation of troops, especially helicopter units, to the front line, as well as in repair work and training. Accordingly, looking at the situation only from the point of view of the U.S. military stationed in Okinawa, which had been given certain roles to play under a carefully designed strategic framework, the return of Futenma posed difficulties.

Second, the return of a facility that was highly problematic in terms of the burden imposed on the local community was bound to lead to strong opposition from those living near proposed sites for relocation of its functions.

Third, landowners who have become dependent on income from leasing land to the U.S. military would hardly be pleased by the sudden return of the land, unless some sort of plan for its conversion to profitable civilian use had been worked out.

These hurdles had to be overcome. For this purpose, the two sides decided to follow certain basic principles. First, they agreed that the deliberations on consolidating and reducing bases would be undertaken as a joint project within the bilateral security framework. Inasmuch as the functions of the U.S. military have a bearing on Japan's own security, it would make no sense for Japan to issue a unilateral demand to the U.S. military to reduce its bases. The two sides must jointly discuss and reach conclusions on such issues as the security functions of the bases, the situation in local communities, and the possibility of moving to alternative bases.

Second, in view of the local situation, there were cases in which the return of land and the dispersal of military functions were very urgent. From this perspective, with firm instructions from Prime Minister Hashimoto Ryūtarō, the Japanese and U.S. sides agreed on the complete return of Futenma Air Station's land and the dispersal of its functions. With regard to some other items, such as the live-fire training over Highway 104, it was agreed that the situation called for removal from Okinawa to the mainland.

Third, it was agreed that problems following the return of facilities and relating to the local burdens imposed by the moving of facilities were matters for the Japanese government to handle in close cooperation with Okinawa Prefecture. At the same time, it was agreed that the Japanese government must earnestly tackle the issue of Okinawa's economic development.

Last September, after a local referendum in Okinawa Prefecture on the bases, the prime minister held talks with Governor Ōta Masahide and paid a visit to the prefecture. In addition, cabinet-level councils were set up to conduct intensive deliberations on policy toward Okinawa and the handling of the bases there. I believe that this sort of concentrated attention, taking the present security environment as a premise and focusing on the accomplishment of specific steps within a limited period of time, is very helpful. But at the same time I believe that the problem of the bases in Okinawa should be seen as a long-term issue, and it should be the object of ongoing reexamination to take into account such factors as any essential changes in the security environment of the region surrounding Japan, any revision of the forward deployment of U.S. troops in the Asia-Pacific region, and progress in the development of Japan-U.S. defense cooperation.

For example, if the system of bilateral defense cooperation is enhanced in the manner that I described above, and Japan establishes a system for conducting logistical support and providing fuel and other supplies in an emergency, this could replace some of the emergency functions that U.S. bases are currently expected to perform. This would make possible greater reduction of the facilities that the U.S. military needs to maintain in Japan during peacetime. Close security ties between Japan and the United States, including efforts to improve the security environment in the region, can promote the cause of scaling down the bases here.

SECURITY IN THE ASIA-PACIFIC

Putting Japan-U.S. security relations on an even more stable footing must be done in such a way as to give a feeling of assurance to other countries in the Asia-Pacific region. Discussions about Japan-U.S. defense cooperation must not fan a sense of wariness about Japan in China and certainly must not be allowed to serve as an excuse for spoiling Japan-China relations. The primary objective of the Japan-U.S. security arrangements is to contribute to the stability and further prosperity of the Asia-Pacific region. From this perspective, building an active security dialogue with neighboring countries is going to become increasingly important from now on.

Of course, regional security issues in Asia cannot be

THE PRIMARY OBJECTIVE OF THE JAPAN-U.S. SECURITY ARRANGEMENTS IS TO CONTRIBUTE TO THE STABILITY AND FURTHER PROSPERITY OF THE ASIA-PACIFIC REGION.

handled analogously to those in Europe. The North Atlantic Treaty Organization, which is an organ of collective defense, and the Japan-U.S. security arrangements, which are bilateral, are quite different. In the Asia-Pacific region, where countries are at different stages of development and have different systems of government, it would not be realistic to aim to establish an organization of collective defense like NATO, in which the members consider an attack against one country in the organization to be an attack against themselves. Bilateral alliances, including the Japan-U.S. security setup, will continue to play an important role in this region. But just as NATO has established a forum for dialogue with countries outside the region, so perhaps it will become necessary for Tokyo and Washington to create forums for dialogue with other countries about Japan-U.S. defense cooperation.

It is to be hoped that all the countries of the region will be able to enjoy security with a sense of mutual trust. To achieve this end, persistent efforts will be necessary. We must strive to foster confidence in the broad sense with regionwide dialogue in places like the ASEAN Regional Forum set up by the Association of Southeast Asian Nations. Furthermore, I think that the proposal for four-way talks on the problem of the Korean Peninsula, the mechanism of discussions among the countries concerned through the Korean Peninsula Energy Development Organization (KEDO) to prevent North Korea's development of nuclear weapons and supply that country with heavy oil and light-water reactors, and the joint public-private dialogue process among Japan, the United States, South Korea, China, Russia, and North Korea (although the latter has not participated yet) are all efforts in the right direction. From now on it would be desirable for the national governments concerned to establish forums for security dialogue concerning issues at the subregional (for example, Northeast Asian) level. I think that this is a matter that should be actively tackled.

CONCLUSION

By working to develop Japan-U.S. security ties, I believe that we can create a more mutual and more reliable set of security arrangements. But in the absence of further basic improvements in the security environment and the establishment by Japan of a system of defense cooperation with the United States based on a clear definition of their respective roles, it would be highly problematic in terms of Japan's own security to suggest that the U.S. Marines in Okinawa are unnecessary or that they be stationed there only in an emergency.

The main problem is that a withdrawal without a logical basis would lead to a decline in deterrent power. The U.S. Marines in Okinawa are inseparable from the Seventh Fleet. If the Marines were sent back to the United States, there would be a major decline in the U.S. rapid deployment capability. Furthermore, the idea that they could come back in times of emergency, even if possible in theory, would run up against many difficulties in practice.

First of all, readiness for an actual military operation must be increased by gaining familiarity with the local topography and base facilities through training. The United States would not be able to carry out its duty of defending Japan if it had to suddenly dispatch troops from back home. And in view of U.S. public opinion, one wonders whether Washington would really decide to go ahead with the dispatch of troops, which would impose heavy costs on the Americans. Withdrawal of the Marines could thus cast doubt on the U.S. commitment to Japan's defense; this would lead to a marked decline in the deterrent power of the bilateral security setup and thus harm the cause of peace in the region.

Second, unlike the present situation, in which a certain level of military force is kept in Okinawa all the time in readiness for an emergency, an arrangement for stationing troops there only in an emergency would involve the large-scale mobilization of troops at a time of tension, which might well have the effect of further increasing the tension.

While the Japan-U.S. security arrangements are subject to change, we should be absolutely clear on the fact that they are not to be allowed to fall below par, because the responsibility of protecting the lives and assets of the nation's people must be carried out with utmost thoroughness. At the same time, we certainly must not forget that peace in the Asia-Pacific region in the twenty-first century requires three factors—solid Japan-U.S. security relations, the U.S. presence, and China's constructive involvement in the international community—and that we have established ties of alliance with the United States because of our common commitment to democratic values.

Translated from "Shin jidai no Nichi-Bei anpo taisei o kangaeru," in Chūō Kōron, *December 1996, pp. 112–20. (Courtesy of Chūō Kōron Sha)*

Economic Relations: What Lies Ahead?

KONDŌ TAKESHI, NOGAMI YOSHIJI, TAKENAKA HEIZŌ

MODERATOR It's not easy to determine the state of the Japanese economy. The growth rate is under 2 percent, and yet the trade surplus with the United States is shrinking. Can we expect this state of affairs to continue?

NOGAMI YOSHIJI I don't think we can expect smooth sailing at the yen's currently weak exchange rate. The U.S. economy is healthy for now, and automobile sales are strong, but if Americans stop feeling confident enough to buy new cars to replace their existing ones, a feeling of tension is likely to arise in the U.S. auto market. Another cause for concern is that America's automakers may complain bitterly about an exchange rate of some 115 yen to the dollar, since the strong dollar hurts their exports to Japan. A certain degree of weakening of the yen may be advantageous in terms of promoting a recovery in the Japanese economy, but we need to be careful about the impact on external economic relations.

If we focus on the need for a domestic recovery, the weak yen doesn't seem that bad, even if there is the issue of upward pressure on import prices. But those of us who are concerned with external friction have a different perspective. The biggest reason Japan-U.S. economic relations were relatively free of trouble during the latter half of President [Bill] Clinton's first term was that the White House didn't come out and declare the relationship bad. But we can't be certain that such negative pronouncements will be completely absent during the second term. The question will be the American economy: In order for the Clinton administration to say that the Japan-U.S. economic relationship is doing all right, the proper macroeconomic conditions will have to be in place.

MODERATOR The potential problem trigger is probably the issue of confidence in the U.S. economy and in the dollar. If that crumbles, all bets will be off. But leaving that issue aside, we in the media are concerned about the yen-dollar rate because we've seen the White House giving very high marks to the bilateral economic relationship for the past couple of years, and we wonder if a further weakening of the yen—beyond the 120-to-the-dollar mark, say—might not provoke a change in this positive assessment.

TAKENAKA HEIZŌ People have been talking about the danger of asset inflation in the United States in connection with the rise of the stock market, but I don't think the threat is that serious. If you look at real estate prices, for example, you find that, unlike in Japan, the market has depth and is basically settled. With asset markets of this sort, the Americans aren't likely to get the speculative bubbles that we had in Japan. As for stocks, there may be some question as to how well their prices reflect real values, but you're not going to see a crash like that in Mexico.

On the other hand, the so-called asset effect is about twice as large in the United States as in Japan, and in that respect the impact of high asset prices on the real economy might be larger than expected.

So far we've been considering macroeconomic factors, but when we look at the U.S. market, one important point to note is the contradiction between the macro and micro levels. A major reason for the American economic renaissance is the big surge that came from shifting to a set of policies oriented to individual responsibility under the market mechanism. The level of social security was lowered, as were effective wage levels, causing unemployment to drop—just the opposite of what happened in Europe. But this was accompanied by distortions in income distribution and sacrifices at the microeconomic level. Economic viability recovered, but social viability came into question. If social problems come to the fore, fiscal measures will have to be taken. And if this then causes the budget deficit to expand, macroeconomic viability will crumble. This is the internal contradiction in the current set of policies.

This brings us to the issue of external economic policy, which involves Japan. In order to get by the domestic contradiction, the United States will have to rely on external demand. Through the 1960s or so, the U.S. economy was self-sufficient, with little dependence on exports. But recently the export-dependence ratio has topped 10 percent, turning the United States into a true trading nation for the first time in its history. Of course it's not possible for external demand to power a huge economy like America's, but exports do form part of the political equation. And here the issue becomes not the size of Japan's trade surplus but the level of its imports. The fall of the yen is a cause for concern in this respect.

JAPAN ON THE DEFENSIVE

MODERATOR If the downward pressure on the yen doesn't let up and the rate of contraction of the current account surplus declines, is there a chance we'll see the Clinton administration once again making an issue of Japan-U.S. economic relations?

KONDŌ TAKESHI
Born in 1941. Graduated from Waseda University, where he majored in political economics. Joined Itōchū Corp. in 1964; is now a member of the board of directors and general manager of the Office of Political and Economic Research. Author of *Beikoku no tsūshō senryaku* (The United States' Trade Strategy) and other works.

NOGAMI YOSHIJI
Born in 1942. Graduated from the University of Tokyo, where he majored in American studies. Joined the Ministry of Foreign Affairs in 1966; is now director general of the Economic Affairs Bureau.

TAKENAKA HEIZŌ
Born in 1951. Received his doctorate in economics from Osaka University. Has been an associate professor at Osaka University and a visiting associate professor at Harvard University. Is now a professor at Keiō University. Author of *Nichi-Bei masatsu no keizaigaku* (The Economics of Japan-U.S. Friction) and other works.

TAKENAKA Unfortunately I think there is. Basically the fact that the United States has turned into a trading nation is a new factor. We can't tell what the next specific problem area will be, but if we look back over our past experience with trade friction, we find a history of things turning into issues even though they shouldn't have. Foreign policy reflects domestic affairs, and so I think it's important to keep this sort of background in mind.

NOGAMI Right now the American economy is in extremely good shape, in contrast to the bleak economic conditions in Japan and Europe, and there's no inflationary pressure at all. Still, given its internal contradictions, the United States wants to see the Japanese and European economies recover and serve as sources of strong demand for its own exports. Europe is currently putting up a united front; its countries are less concerned about enduring a certain degree of economic sluggishness than about achieving the convergence goals of EMU, the economic and monetary union program that's a major item on its political agenda. Meanwhile, Japan is hardly in a position to respond favorably to calls for it to increase its import demand. The authorities have lowered interest rates as far as they'll go, and they have no more tools left for economic stimulus.

What I think the Americans will target next is the regulations governing the Japanese market. Naturally deregulation itself will not produce a major increase in Japanese demand for American goods, but since Washington can't attack Tokyo in the fiscal or monetary policy sectors, it's liable to start talking about issues in the economic system.

MODERATOR So do you expect the second-term Clinton administration to take an approach like that of the former Structural Impediments Initiative?

NOGAMI I would expect to see two approaches. One will involve calling for moves to allow market forces to operate more efficiently and thereby bring latent demand to the surface. The other will be to argue that Japan must open up sectors where the United States enjoys a global lead, such as telecommunications, aviation, and freight. The Japanese will find themselves on the defensive where the Americans are strongest—though there's no telling in advance just where the attack will come.

MODERATOR The photographic film issue has now been taken to the World Trade Organization, but isn't there a chance that we'll see a rerun of the auto industry dispute or other specific issues like the ones that were brought up in the "framework for trade" talks starting in 1993?

KONDŌ TAKESHI Sector-specific issues aren't likely to go away. They may increase or decrease in number, and they may get politicized in some cases and not in others, but they certainly won't totally disappear. Actually it would be wrong to think that an ideal relationship would mean the absence of such issues. It seems to me that their occurrence is proportional to the closeness of the economic relationship. When two sides are competing on an equal footing, these problems are bound to come up.

Where caution is required is in the role played by the governments and politicians on both sides. They need to handle matters in a way that avoids adversely affecting the overall Japan-U.S. economic relationship or inflaming public opinion. If this sort of political mechanism can be made to work, then I think we can pronounce our bilateral economic ties mature.

If the occurrence of sector-specific issues isn't a fundamental problem in Japan-U.S. economic relations, then what is? I would cite two items. One is the question of whether there is a mismatch in macroeconomic policy. And if there is, do the two countries have the political will to fix it? Furthermore, do they have the power to implement policies that can promote greater harmony? The problem is the outlook with respect to these questions.

Second is the issue of the Japanese and American economic systems. It's only natural for them to be different. The important point is what causes them to differ and whether a course has been set that will make the necessary corrections. Here again it's a question of whether the political will exists and whether the power to implement that will is present.

In fact, all the economic problems between Japan and the United States arise from the mismatches in the two countries' macroeconomic policies and economic systems. So these have to be fixed. But it was only with the end of the cold war that the political will to do so emerged. Until then, they had been hidden under the cold-war structure. Even when there was bilateral friction, the approach was to let off pressure through sector-specific issues. But with the end of the cold war, that stopped working.

Keeping an alliance going in peacetime is an extremely difficult undertaking, and there aren't many historical examples of its being done successfully. In this case, since both nations are democracies, moves to deal with structural problems must be undertaken in order to maintain public support for the alliance. The current situation vis-à-vis structural issues is extremely unsatisfactory. To be sure, the Japanese economy has undergone dramatic structural adjustments over the past decade, and it has been established that the necessary political will is there. The same goes for the United States. But in Japan the adjustments haven't been spontaneous; unfortunately, they've been forced on the country by exogenous factors, particularly the exchange rate. So they haven't been carried out in a way that's necessarily favorable for the Japanese economy's future prospects.

In the United States, meanwhile, the adjustment process also remains unfinished. A number of conditions are required in order for it to approach completion. The biggest is global economic growth. And Japan is the country with the greatest capacity to contribute to such growth. This is obvious from the saving-investment balance. Few if any countries can match the scale of Japan's savings surplus. But when it comes to expanding domestic demand, we always end up relying on public works, mismatching intentions and means. I believe that rectifying this is an issue of great significance for the Japanese and American economies.

NEW TYPES OF FRICTION

MODERATOR How do you rate Prime Minister Hashimoto [Ryūtarō]'s second cabinet in terms of political will and implementation power?

TAKENAKA The gap between what the Americans expect of Japan and what Japan has actually been accomplishing has been creating dissatisfaction and friction. Mr. Kondō was quite right about the fact that friction will not go away, and where there's friction, there's bound to be heat. I think we should see this as evidence of the intensity of the bilateral relationship. But it is possible that the logic of the friction will change.

For example, the film dispute has presented us with a different type of friction from before. What the Americans have demanded is retroactive "innovators' profits." This applies to supercomputers also. It's a new form of logic that's not found anywhere in the existing global framework. Japan and the United States are at the frontier, so to speak, in terms of the type of friction between them. That's one point.

Another point is that the Americans are also changing their negotiating tools. In the past they relied on simple threats of exclusion from the U.S. market, the biggest market in the world, if we didn't do what they wanted. But now Japan's trade with Asia is growing much faster than its trade with the United States, so over the long run the impact of this threat will decline.

The Clinton administration will probably shift to an approach of proposing new rules under the WTO or APEC [the Asia-Pacific Economic Cooperation forum]. The idea will be to create a legalistic framework of a sort that's not much favored by Asians. The question will be whether the Hashimoto administration will be able to deal with this approach. In the general election last month [October 1996], all the parties were calling for reform. The difference was that the opposition New Frontier Party [Shinshintō] and Democratic Party of Japan were promising to carry it out in a sweeping fashion, transforming society, while Hashimoto's Liberal Democratic Party was proposing a more gradual approach of responding to changing circumstances. What I think we face now in terms of the Americans' view of Japan is not so much a perception gap as an expectation gap.

I believe there's probably also a difference in how Japanese and Americans evaluate the progress of the structural adjustment process. If you just look at Japan, you see considerable change. But change is relative, and the rest of the world has probably changed more. In the twenty years since the 1970s, the population of the world market has grown from 2.7 billion to 5.4 billion. Two decades ago Japan was a newly industrialized country in a 2.7-billion-person market. But now it's among the leaders in a market of 5.4 billion people. This is such a major transformation that a bit of change within Japan is quite insufficient to match it.

Still, the voters have chosen a more gradual, reactive approach, which will mean a rough start, I believe, for the new Hashimoto cabinet. For fiscal policy, I think the only approach possible is for the administration to try to win confidence through a series of new initiatives, such as drawing up a long-term plan for government finance. The prime minister himself seems quite determined to carry out reforms, so I hope we'll see him and his executive staff display leadership in policy formation.

MODERATOR Mr. Nogami, even if Washington doesn't abandon bilateral negotiations, do you expect to see it placing more emphasis on use of frameworks like the WTO and APEC?

NOGAMI During Clinton's first term, it doesn't seem to me that his administration developed policies creatively or came up with concepts in the context of a broad framework. It was a reactive stance.

Where we see some signs of change is in the deregulation of telecommunications and the revitalization of the U.S. economy through the thorough application of market principles. But in the process of cutting the federal budget deficit, the United States has reduced the level of its external commitments. The economy has been growing, but on the level of policy making, the administration has used up its energy dealing with specific narrow issues; it hasn't been able to come up with comprehensive new ideas covering broad areas. Washington seems to want to create a framework of international rules to govern investment, but the rules it appears to have in mind may be too strict for the developing countries to go along with.

One card that the United States has in its hand when dealing with the rest of the world is its own market and its corporations with highly advanced technology. Another card is its commitment to international political security.

The cold-war structure has disappeared, but in Europe they are talking about expanding the North Atlantic Treaty Organization, and Japan continues to stress the importance of its security treaty with the United States. For other Asian countries also, America's strong suit is in international political affairs. The Clinton administration was somewhat weak in this area during its first term; I wonder how effectively it will be able to play its diplomatic cards during the term to come.

BEYOND BILATERAL ISSUES

MODERATOR In closing I'd like to ask your suggestions and views of the prospects for settling the problems in Japan-U.S. relations and for discussions between the two countries that go beyond bilateral issues to the area of international frameworks.

KONDŌ The Japan-U.S. relationship, both economic and political, has two aspects: First is the bilateral dialogue through which each tries to improve the other from its own viewpoint. Second is the global Japan-U.S. relationship, in which the two countries discuss ways of improving the international environment for both of themselves and act to achieve the improvements they desire. These aspects aren't divorced from each other, of course. They have to be dealt with in tandem. The basic framework has been taking shape, and as I see it, the task in the period ahead will be to flesh out the contents and complete the structure.

In order to accomplish this, though, there are two important points that have to be addressed. One is the structural adjustment of the Japanese economy. And since we don't have a political system capable of implementing the proper economic policies, we need to carry out political reform simultaneously with economic reform.

The other point is the angry reaction of China in immediate response to the regionalization of the Japan-U.S. security relationship. The Chinese weren't upset by the regionalization of U.S. military power. This isn't anything new, and the Chinese themselves accept the United States' role as a balancing agent in the region. What provoked their anger was their perception that Japan was globalizing its military power projection potential. Why do they accept American power but not Japanese? It's a question of the difference between the two countries' acceptability and credibility in the international community. In order to take initiatives to improve the global situation, Japan needs to establish a level of international trust at least close to that which the United States has. This is a pressing requirement.

In specific terms, this means achieving acceptability in East Asia. For this reason I believe that we must deal urgently with the issue of history. The Europeans spent decades coming up with a common history of their continent, which is now being taught in schools. Japan should place high priority on working together with countries like South Korea and China to compile a common history of East Asia. This is something that won't happen unless Japan takes the initiative, and it's a condition we must meet so as to become an accepted member of the international community and play a constructive global role.

TAKENAKA In order for Japan to participate in the framework-building process, it's important for it to have influence as an accepted partner. But when our country raises the banner of free trade in forums like the WTO, people complain about all the regulations hindering free trade in Japan's own domestic market. Dealing with this state of affairs is a prerequisite to wielding acceptable influence. And in order to carry out the necessary economic reforms, we must reform our political system.

Another issue is social reform in the broad sense of the term. Recently it was reported in the papers that a third Japanese person was starting to work in the WTO secretariat. The number of Japanese employees in such international organizations is altogether too small. Americans play a very prominent role, and their presence has resulted in the emergence of a "Washington consensus" in favor of the doctrine of free trade and sound money, as taught in economics courses in the United States. Also, when China wanted to implement a Western-style accounting system, it turned to American CPAs [certified public accountants].

Japan needs to develop its professional power. We have no international lawyers to speak of, for example. Ameliorating this situation will require broad social reforms, including changes in education and also in our systems of professional qualification. This is a task that has to be undertaken in units of ten or twenty years. But I do think the time has come for us to add this to the reform agenda.

NOGAMI First of all we need to build our economic self-confidence. Whenever the Japanese economy gets a bit shaky, we tend to overreact, as with the current talk of "Japan passing," the idea that the rest of the world is passing us by without a glance. But if you view Japan from Southeast Asia, our economy appears tremendous. We should keep this in mind. Instead of getting all caught up in negotiations with the United States over every little problem, we ought to be conducting a dialogue that takes a broader view of the global economic scene.

Another point is that global economic affairs in the period ahead are going to be intimately linked to political affairs, as we can see well from the example of China. The existing set of arrangements doesn't allow for in-depth discussions that take these links into account. We need to quickly settle our petty bilateral troubles and clearly recognize what our ultimate priorities are. The greatest task facing us now is for both Japan and the United States to develop their capacity to discuss the future management of the world economy.

Translated from "Nichi-Bei kankei no kagi o nigiru kōzō chōsei mondai," in Gaikō Forum, *January 1997, pp. 86-99; shortened to about half. The original article was based on a round-table discussion conducted on November 7, 1996, moderated by Komago Shigeru, Deputy Economic News Editor,* Nihon Keizai Shimbun. *(Courtesy of Toshi Shuppan, Publishers)*

FORESIGHT NEEDED IN JAPAN-U.S. TIES

OKAZAKI HISAHIKO

The worst kinds of diplomatists are missionaries, fanatics and lawyers.

Sir Harold Nicolson (1886–1968)
British diplomat and author

When the Clinton administration was launched in 1993, the United States was in the midst of a Japan-bashing mood. This mood was not created by the new Democratic administration—it was a legacy of the two previous administrations.

Before former U.S. President George Bush assumed office, the Reagan administration seized upon Japan's poorly exploited geopolitical potential and financial resources to establish a military balance of power in the Far East with Japan and the United States on one side and the Soviet Union on the other.

Japan, criticized until that point as a cold-war "free rider," had arrived, albeit belatedly, ready to serve on the last front of that conflict—which eventually ended with the Soviet Union giving up its arms race with the United States. It was the "Ron-Yasu" age—the high point of post–World War II Japan-U.S. relations, forged by former U.S. President Ronald Reagan and then Prime Minister Nakasone Yasuhiro.

When the Bush administration was sworn in, cold-war warriors like Reagan, George Shultz, Caspar Weinberger, Gaston Sigur, and Richard Armitage left the scene. The arms race with the Soviet Union left the United States burdened with twin budget and trade deficits, and dissatisfaction with Japan among U.S. economists and business leaders, restrained from criticizing this country during the cold war, burst forth. Japan's bubble economy was at its zenith. In the eyes of Americans, Japan was an eight-foot giant. The elated Japanese became arrogant, infuriating Americans even more by criticizing their work ethics. Japan bashing in the United States reached a post–World War II high.

Japan's bubble economy had already burst by the time U.S. President Bill Clinton took office, but the country still looked six feet tall to Americans. The immediate task for the new U.S. administration was to eliminate the twin deficits, particularly the trade deficit with Japan. In the United States, new administrations always hammer out fresh policies in an attempt to distinguish themselves from their predecessors. The Clinton administration was no exception. It set numerical targets in its trade disputes with Japan. Because the concept of numerical targets was unpopular, the administration later adopted a different term for it, but the purpose has always been the same. The demands for numerical trade targets quickly chilled the friendly mood between Japan and the United States.

The "Structural Impediments Initiative," which preceded the numerical-targets approach, was aimed at forcing Japan to liberalize its economy. While liberalization was opposed by certain industry sectors and the Diet members and bureaucrats who represented their interests, it was supported by the majority of the Japanese business community and most economists. But the concept of numerical targets is anathema to economists. Moreover, to attain the targets, the United States had to promote exports from certain of its corporations; such moves were opposed by rival Japanese companies and raised doubts in Japan about the U.S. government's ethical standards. As a result, the United States alienated its constituency in this country, and bilateral relations chilled almost to the freezing point.

A sense of crisis gripped national security officials. Security experts in both countries recognized the Japan-U.S. alliance as vital to peace and stability in Asia. They feared the alliance might be impaired. The so-called Nye Report of February 1995 was written in this climate of concern. Differing from many of the Pentagon's post-cold-war reports, the Nye Report declared the United States had no intention of further reducing its military presence in Asia. This statement allayed fears among some Asian countries that at some point U.S. troops would be withdrawn. The report also said economic friction between Japan and the United States should not be allowed to undermine their alliance. This passage became particularly important when Japan-U.S. economic negotiations finally broke down. Its impact was so great that some Americans lamented the fact that the United States had abandoned the greatest weapon it possessed in dealing with Japan.

Japan-U.S. relations began to improve. The economic negotiations were settled at the end of June 1995 and the strong yen gradually declined in a corrective depreciation. Japan is now in the depths of a recession. To the United States, this country now appears only five feet tall. Japanese macroeconomic figures have begun to show clear signs of improvement, reflecting economic trends that have nothing to do with the trade negotiations conducted over the numerical target issue.

Washington's policy of attaching the highest importance to the Japan-U.S. alliance, as set forth in the Nye Report, was unchanged by the fallout over the rape of an Okinawa girl by three U.S. servicemen last year. During the summit between Prime Minister Hashimoto Ryūtarō and Clinton in April 1996, the two countries agreed to reduce and consolidate the U.S. military bases in Okinawa without impairing their functions. The two men also agreed that their countries should cooperate closely in the event of an emergency in the Far East. This was a pivotal event in the post–World War II history of Japan-U.S. relations, and will be counted among the Clinton administration's historic accomplishments in years to come.

So what should be done in the future? There is now a broad consensus within the governments of both countries, among security experts, and between Democrats and Republicans in the United States that the Japan-U.S. alliance should be maintained. The goals for which both countries should strive have become clear, although further effort is required to overcome the many difficulties that stand in the way of achieving them.

The most immediate goal is to settle the Okinawa problem

in a way that will not hurt the operation of the U.S. military bases there. The long-range goal is to make the Japan-U.S. alliance more effective in the event of an emergency, to which end Japan must settle the issue of the right of collective self-defense. The domestic problems that stand in the way of achieving both of these goals must be settled by the Japanese government without bothering the United States.

The United States should adhere to its policy of maintaining its military presence in Asia. This is the linchpin of peace and stability in the region, and is important as a message to China and the Southeast Asian countries—not necessarily to the people of Japan. Some people have hinted at the possibility of the United States' withdrawing its Marines from Asia. The condition for such a pullout, however, is generally assumed to be either a final solution to the situation on the Korean Peninsula, or a Japanese assertion of the right to collective self-defense, in which case its Self-Defense Forces would take over the Marines' role. Such circumstances, however, would make the reexamination of U.S. policy necessary in everyone's eyes. Discussing such a possibility now is not only meaningless but potentially harmful to Asian security, as it could create the impression that the United States is looking to withdraw its troops from the region.

With respect to security, what remains to be done should be carried out mostly by Japan on its own initiative. On the economic front, by contrast, certain issues require serious attention from the United States, though there are also some issues, long overdue for resolution, that Japan must settle by itself—particularly deregulation. What I want to say here concerns the way economic negotiations are conducted. The United States should learn a lesson from the economic friction that threatened to undermine Japan-U.S. relations during the second and third years of the Clinton administration. Bilateral negotiations are, after all, an act of diplomacy. A good diplomat is one who is thoroughly versed in another country's political situation, economy, society, culture, and history, while understanding perfectly his or her home country's domestic needs.

Bilateral negotiations should succeed if negotiators on both sides are experts, as called for above, or listen to the opinion of such experts. The greatest sin a regional expert can commit is to look at an issue not with an objective, impartial attitude but with prejudice, or to limit his or her view to those things that are convenient to see.

This is a difference between diplomats and lawyers. It is not in a lawyer's best interest to look at all things objectively. Lawyers are required to select the facts that are convenient to their case and disregard those that are disadvantageous, even if they are clearly true. Moreover, lawyers need not concern themselves with long-standing friendly relations or establishing a relationship based on trust with the other party. In conducting their "bilateral negotiations," they need not consider the overall "national strategy." They do not even care if the negotiations bog down. Their main concern is not to maintain friendly "bilateral relations," but to assert their own point of view without yielding any ground.

A more basic problem in Japan-U.S. relations is that Japanese negotiators, whether they are officials of the Ministry of International Trade and Industry or the Ministry of Agriculture, Forestry, and Fisheries, are empowered to formulate their own domestic policies and make concessions, while the Office of the U.S. Trade Representative has no such power or capability. The U.S. trade negotiators can only relay Japanese requests to the departments concerned.

Japan-U.S. negotiations, therefore, are marked by a lack of long-range strategy on both sides, and do not sufficiently promote cooperative relations. There is little room for concessions on the U.S. side. The "negotiations" are really just unilateral demands from the United States for concessions from Japan. This is where cultural differences between Japan and the United States come into play. What is par for the course to the Americans, who live in a litigious society, is considered a breach of trust or an abandonment of friendly relations by the Japanese, for whom trust is supremely important.

The most desirable course of action would be for Japan and the United States to conduct their economic negotiations with long-range interests in view and with mutual understanding based on objective judgment, as are ordinary diplomatic negotiations. The United States should at least consult regional experts in the U.S. government who know Japan well before conducting economic negotiations. Japan, well aware of the importance of bilateral relations and the fact it still has much room for deregulation, will always respond to reasonable demands.

If the U.S. government feels its domestic situation does not permit a change in the way it conducts negotiations, Japan must switch to the U.S. method, acting as if negotiating with the United States is not an act of diplomacy, but a courtroom confrontation. In that case, negotiators would have to separate economic affairs from other issues in order not to damage relations. To this end, both countries should handle economic issues in a businesslike manner without taking them to the highest political level—that of the Japanese prime minister and the U.S. president.

The task of handing down decisions should be entrusted to a neutral arbitrating body, as it is in relations between the United States and Canada or Israel, or to the World Trade Organization. A lawyer acting as judge is unthinkable in a society governed by the rule of law. (Okazaki Hisahiko, a former career diplomat, is now a senior advisor at Hakuhodo Inc.)

Reprinted from "Insights into the World: Foresight Needed in Japan-U.S. Ties," in The Daily Yomiuri, *November 25, 1996; slightly edited. Published in Japanese as "Chikyū o yomu: Nichi-Bei no kongo, chōki rieki nentō ni," in* Yomiuri Shimbun, *November 25, 1996. (Courtesy of the Yomiuri Shimbun)*

JAPAN AND THE SPRATLYS DISPUTE

Aspirations and Limitations

Lam Peng Er

The dispute over jurisdiction of the Spratly Islands in the South China Sea has the potential to draw in major powers who are non-claimant states. At issue is the prospect of contention among parties to the dispute posing a threat to maritime communications. Should such a prospect arise, it would pose a serious threat to the interests of Japan. This article assesses the nature of these interests and identifies the constraints on their active pursuit.

Half a century after the end of the Pacific War, Tokyo seeks a political status commensurate with its economic standing; it is no longer satisfied to be merely a prime contributor to the United Nations and foreign aid programs. A desire to play a more active political role developed after the Gulf War in the wake of domestic and international criticism that Japan engaged primarily in checkbook diplomacy. Since the end of the Cold War and the demise of the Soviet Union, some analysts have suggested that if the United States were to reduce significantly its commitment to East Asia, a power vacuum would emerge in the region, which includes the South China Sea. China and Japan are the prime candidates to fill that vacuum. But even if the U.S. remains engaged and the U.S.-Japan alliance is maintained, Japan may still be expected to seek a larger role in regional affairs, one almost certainly extending to the South China Sea.

Much has been written on the Spratlys dispute but such studies have focused on the claimant states, which is understandable because crisis management and conflict resolution in the South China Sea require the participation and consent of these states. Obviously, China receives most attention be-

Lam Peng Er is Lecturer in the Department of Political Science, National University of Singapore. The author would like to thank the Japan Institute of International Affairs for organizational and financial assistance; and Michael Leifer, Okabe Tatsumi, Tomoda Seki, Soeya Yoshihide, Shee Poon Kim, Lee Lai To, S. Javed Maswood, Hari Singh, and N. Ganesan for their comments on earlier drafts of this article.

cause it is by far the most powerful claimant and also has a record of employing force to pursue its various territorial claims. As the sole superpower and the key potential balancer in the South China Sea, the U.S. has also not been ignored. However, a detailed study of Japan and the Spratlys dispute has not yet been undertaken, a gap in the literature that is surprising because Japan is a major power in the Asia-Pacific region whose vital sea lanes of communication (SLOCs) might be threatened should armed conflict break out and escalate in the Spratlys area. Moreover, it is not in Japan's interest for any potentially unfriendly power to dominate the South China Sea. Although Japan is not a claimant state and does not support the territorial claims of any particular country, it is not indifferent to the dispute.[1] A study of Japan's interests and attitude toward the Spratlys dispute is also important because the issue may be seen as a litmus test of Japanese foreign policy in the post-Cold War era. Japan aspires to play a leadership role in world affairs, but if it is unwilling or unable to deal actively with the potentially most destabilizing issue in its own backyard, Tokyo will find it difficult to claim the mantle of regional let alone global leadership.

This article addresses the following questions: what are Japan's historical, strategic, political, and economic interests in the Spratlys? Does Japan have a policy toward and role in the South China Sea conflict? What domestic and international impediments are likely to be faced by Japan should it try to play a political role in the Spratlys dispute? And what conclusions can we draw about Japan's foreign policy in the post-Cold War era after examining the Spratlys case?

Japan's main interests in the Spratlys dispute are the enhancement of its security and status, two goals that can be mutually reinforcing. To have a bigger voice in regional and international security issues would confer status and prestige on Japan. Besides a concern for the safety of its oil tankers in the South China Sea and the belief that regional instability is not in its national interest, Japan is closely watching China's assertiveness in the Spratlys because it has implications for the Senkaku Islands (Dioyutai), which are claimed by both Japan and China. The Spratlys dispute is also a litmus test of China's peaceful intent and good neighborliness, as well as of the viability of embryonic regional multilateral organizations to manage conflict in the post-Cold War era. The immediate cause of Japan's greater interest and involvement in the issue was the revelation of China's disputed occupation of

1. Soeya Yoshihide writes: "The South China Sea conflict is one of the few cases where Japan's national and security interests are evidently at stake in the post-Cold War era." Yoshihide Soeya, "The South China Sea Conflict: Implication for Regional Security and Japan's Response," paper prepared for the international conference on Security Implications and Conflict in the South China Sea: Perspectives from the Asia-Pacific, Institute for Strategic Studies and Pacific Forum, CSIS, November 1995, Manila.

Mischief Reef in the Spratlys in February 1995. However, the impulse to adopt a more active foreign policy posture on regional issues, including that of the Spratlys, came in the aftermath of the Gulf War. As a country seeking great power status, Japan hopes to be consulted and engaged in regional strategic issues. Besides its security interests in the Spratlys, Tokyo is using the dispute as an opportunity to play a larger regional role and acquire international recognition and prestige as a great power.

To deal with the Spratlys issue, Japan has adopted two approaches: multilaterally through the ASEAN Regional Forum (ARF) and bilaterally via direct talks with China. At present, Japan cannot play a unilateral strategic role in Southeast Asia because of its militaristic past and its alliance with the United States. The ARF provides it with access to a multilateral forum through which to be involved in regional affairs. The Spratlys dispute, however, is a double-edged sword for both the ARF and Japan. On the one hand, it provides an important justification for the existence of the forum in the post-Cold War era; a viable ARF may help defuse regional conflict and also allow Japan to fulfill its desire to participate in regional affairs. On the other hand, if the ARF cannot prevent the outbreak of a serious conflict in the South China Sea, the organization will forfeit its credibility and Japan will lose a channel through which to play a regional role. Despite former Prime Minister Murayama Tomiichi's diplomatic efforts to raise the Spratlys issue with top Chinese leaders, Japanese attempts to do so have been rebuffed by China. Beijing believes that any settlement of the dispute should not involve Japan, a non-claimant state. Moreover, China is sensitive to any Japanese attempts to play a larger political role in the region. This case study highlights the limits to Japan's quest for regional security and status.

Japan's Interests in the South China Sea

A Japanese mining company began exploring the then uninhabited Spratlys for mineral resources between 1918 and 1921 before temporarily occupying a few of the islets and excavating guano for fertilizer.[2] In February 1939 Japanese troops occupied Hainan Island and then the Paracel Islands in the South China Sea, and the following month, Japan annexed the Spratlys. Mastery of the South China Sea was critical to its dream of carving out an Asian empire; Japan also built a submarine base on Itu Abu (Taiping Dao), the largest island

2. See Hiramatsu Shigeo, "Chugoku kaigun no minami shinakai shinshutsu" [Chinese naval advance in the South China Sea], *Kokubo* [The national defence], 40:12, December 1991, p. 10; and Takeshita Hidekuni, "Minami shinakai funso no keii to ryoyuken mondai" [The details of the South China Sea conflict and the question of territorial rights], *Ajia Torendo* [Asian trends], 3:59, 1992, p. 64.

in the Spratlys, during the Pacific War. Japan's defeat in the war and the 1952 San Francisco Treaty forced the country to surrender all of its rights to the Spratlys. However the treaty did not specify which country should inherit sovereignty over the archipelago. Tokyo's historical control of the Spratlys still casts a shadow on its present interests in the dispute. Some Japanese who do not support their country's involvement have referred to the San Francisco Treaty and claimed that Japan is obliged by international law not to be involved directly in the Spratlys. Moreover, they have argued that any attempt to play an active political role in the Spratlys issue may arouse regional suspicions that Japan harbors ulterior motives and is trying to resurrect its old imperial claims to the archipelago.[3]

If an armed conflict in the Spratly area were to break out, it might disrupt freedom of navigation or even endanger the safety of merchant ships and oil tankers. Around 70% of Japan's oil imports pass through the South China Sea, and while Japan-bound vessels conceivably could avoid conflict in the Spratlys by sailing around the Indonesian islands and into the Pacific, such an alternative would be costlier and more time consuming.[4] It is not impossible that a prolonged, intermittent conflict might disrupt Japan's critical oil routes and send shock waves through its stock market, dampen producer and consumer sentiment, and plunge its economy into a recession. Even if a localized conflict does not cut the SLOCs, there is still the possibility that a potentially unfriendly power may incrementally and cumulatively extend its control and dominate the South China Sea. Such an outcome obviously would not be in the interest of Japan.

The geographical proximity of Southeast Asia ensures Tokyo's continuing interest in the area. Although Japan has globally diversified its sources of energy, trade, and investment, it sees Southeast Asia as an important market and production center, and the region is also its largest foreign aid recipient.

3. In a roundtable discussion in June 1995 with a group of retired Japanese generals and admirals from the Defence Research Center, the author observed that most of them favored a non-military role for Japan in the Spratlys, or even complete non-involvement; as one general put it: "sawaranu kami ni tatarinashi" [no touch, no divine retribution, or no touch, no trouble]. Tomoda Seki writes: "Japan, who had occupied both Paracel and Spratly islands before World War Two and abandoned all its territorial claims and rights on the islands in the Peace Treaty signed in San Francisco, have *a priori* refrained from any act susceptible of inviting suspicion from abroad of its redemptionist ambition there." See, "Factors of Tension in Southeast Asia: How to Deal with Potential Tension in South China Sea and Cambodia," in *Asia-Pacific and Vietnam Relations*, Institute for International Relations, papers from the second workshop, Hanoi, September 1994, p. 25.

4. Interview with a Japanese Foreign Ministry official from the Regional Policy Division, Asian Affairs Bureau, assigned to watch over the Spratlys dispute, 23 June 1995.

The Spratlys, Senkaku, and the "China Question"

Tokyo sees the Spratlys issue in the wider context of a more assertive and powerful China. Increasingly, no regional issues such as stability in the Korean Peninsula, Chinese nuclear tests, tension in the Taiwan Strait, the viability of a Southeast Asia Nuclear Weapons-Free Zone, and the efficacy of multilateral organizations to manage problems including conflict in the South China Sea can be addressed without China's co-operation. In the past few years, Japanese opinion shapers from various political parties, the Foreign Ministry, the Defence Agency, security think tanks, academia, journals, and the mass media have been considering whether China will act aggressively and unilaterally toward its neighbors once it becomes an economic powerhouse.[5] They ponder this question even though China today gives top priority to its domestic economic development and has a low per capita GNP of only US$435.

Sino-Japanese relations have become prickly. Uncharacteristically, Tokyo slashed its grant aid to China in the face of Beijing's refusal to end its nuclear tests in 1995, and Japan also raised the issue of human rights and the Senkaku and Spratly islands with China that year.[6] To Tokyo, the South China Sea dispute is an additional indicator for gauging the intent and direction of Chinese foreign policy. To Beijing, Tokyo's new assertiveness in these issues is an unwelcome intrusion into its sovereignty. This perception of "interference" reinforces deeply felt Chinese suspicions that its eastern neighbor covets great power status and has not truly repented its militaristic past.[7] Thus,

---

5. The head of the Defence Agency has expressed concern that China is modernizing its nuclear and naval capability. Moreover, he perceives the Chinese navy as "expanding the scope of its activities" especially in the Spratly Islands (*Sankei Shinbun*, 14 September 1995). The director of the First Research Department, National Institute for Defence Studies, writes: "Despite the fact that China and Japan have a close relationship, it remains essentially fragile. . . . Japan is becoming apprehensive about China's military build-up, particularly the naval modernization, its continued supply of missiles to areas of potential conflict, and its testing of nuclear weapons . . . . The evolution of the Chinese navy from a defensive coastal force into an offensive blue-water fleet would be destabilizing because it would change the balance of power in the Asia-Pacific region. This will happen if the Chinese economy continues to expand rapidly." (Masashi Nishihara, "Japan Has Cause to Worry About Chinese Ambition," *International Herald Tribune*, 12 July 1994). Also, the lead articles on the "China naval threat" in *Gunji Kenkyu* (Japan military review), 30:10 (October 1995); and Kojima Tomoyuki, "Chugoku shudo no ajia chitsujo o nerau" [Aiming for a Chinese-led Asian order], *Toa* [East Asia], no. 327 (September 1994).

6. Foreign Minister Kono Yohei expressed these concerns in his meetings with the Chinese prime minister and foreign minister (*Yomiuri Shinbun*, 20 December 1995).

7. For example, Liu Jiangyong, "Distorting History Will Misguide Japan: To Mark the 50th Anniversary of the Victory over Japanese Aggression," *Contemporary International Relations*, 5:9 (September 1995).

any future escalation in the Spratlys conflict may further complicate Sino-Japanese relations. Chinese advances into the South China Sea would alarm certain Japanese elites and raise the specter of a "China threat," while Japanese attempts to urge China to exercise restraint in that area might antagonize and convince many Chinese elites that Japan is attempting to act as a great power again.

China's future direction is an enigma. On the one hand, the country provides a huge and promising market for Japanese goods, services, and investments; on the other, if China's remarkable economic growth is sustained in the post-Deng era, it may have the means to become a regional hegemon. However, as the Chinese economy attains greater maturity in the first quarter of the 21st century, its spectacular growth rate may ease considerably. Moreover, the emergence of a more complex, internationalized economy and a new urban middle class that is less easily controlled by a single communist party-state may, in the long run, contribute to the evolution of less authoritarian and more transparent political institutions. If such a China emerges, alarmist speculation about Beijing as an opaque regional bully may well be proven wrong. But the possibility that China may turn out otherwise is worrisome to Japan.

Further complicating Sino-Japanese relations and Japanese interest in the South China Sea conflict is the linkage between the Spratly and Senkaku islands. When China seized the Paracels from South Vietnam in 1974 and a few islands in the Spratlys from unified Vietnam in 1988, Tokyo did not react with undue consternation. It did not appear to perceive the Spratlys dispute as intertwined with either the Senkaku dispute or Chinese "expansionism" in the region. Moreover, it viewed China's seizure of the islands from Vietnam as an extension of the Beijing-Hanoi conflict against the backdrop of the Cold War. Aligned with the U.S., China, and ASEAN, Japan was opposed to the Soviet-Vietnamese alliance and Hanoi's occupation of Cambodia. Thus, Tokyo was not alarmed by the Chinese-Vietnamese clash in the South China Sea in 1988.

When China promulgated its Territorial Waters Law in February 1992 that incorporated the Spratlys, Senkaku, and other disputed islands, Japan protested against the inclusion of Senkaku. By passing the legislation, China implicitly reserves the right to use force if necessary to defend areas deemed to be Chinese territory, and Japan is closely watching the approaches China is using to support its territorial claims to the islands. When China wanted Japan's participation in a united front against the Soviet Union, paramount leader Deng Xiaoping adopted the flexible approach of deferring the Senkaku dispute to the "next generation." With the demise of the Soviet Union and the promulgation of the Territorial Waters Law, the Senkaku situation has changed. Even though Japan has an alliance with the U.S. and is a bigger power than Vietnam and despite Japanese annoyance and protests, China has proceeded with its oceanographic survey in the Senkaku waters. Beijing has also intensified its exploration for oil and other minerals in the waters adjacent to the island. To some Japanese analysts, Chinese actions in the Spratlys and Senkaku vicinity reflect the emergence of China as a more assertive power with a thirst for oil.[8]

Tokyo faces a dilemma in the Spratlys dispute. If it does nothing and a conflict were to break out, its sea lanes and interests in regional stability might be jeopardized. If it supports the shelving of the sovereignty issue and *joint* economic and scientific development of the adjacent waters as a solution to the Spratlys dispute, the countries that have overlapping claims with Japan can apply the same formula to Japanese-controlled or claimed territories. If Japan is consistent in supporting this formula, China can demand that the same approach be applied to Senkaku, South Korea to Liancourt Rocks, and Japan to the four northern islands (the southern Kuriles). Despite this potential linkage, Tokyo appears willing to assist in "joint development" because it would enhance its prestige as a regional player and help to defuse regional tension.

The ARF and Japan's Search for Security and Status

Aspiring for status in the international system, Japan has taken a number of unprecedented actions in recent years. It organized the 1990 Tokyo Conference to resolve the Cambodian civil war; dispatched troops for United Nations peacekeeping in Cambodia, Mozambique, Zaire, and the Golan Heights; emphasized human rights and democratization as preconditions to Japanese foreign aid; lobbied for a permanent seat on the U.N. Security Council; and suggested setting up a multilateral organization to discuss security issues pertaining to the Asia-Pacific region. To Tokyo, the ASEAN Regional Forum is an arena where multilateral consultation and confidence-building can take place to address regional issues, including the Spratlys dispute. Tokyo has taken credit for initiating the formation of the ARF, as Foreign Minister Nakayama Taro suggested publicly in July 1991 that the ASEAN-PMC (Post-Ministerial Conference) should provide the framework for discussing

8. For example, articles by Hiramatsu Shigeo, "Chugoku kaigun no minami shinakai shinshutsu: Chugoku no ryokaiho to senkakushoto mondai" [China's territorial waters law and the Senkaku islands issue], *Kokubo* 41:9, 1992; "Nansashoto o meguru chuetsu funso to chugokukaigun" [The Sino-Vietnamese conflict over the Spratlys islands and the Chinese navy] in Mio Tadashi, *Posto reisen no indoshina* [Indochina in the post-cold war era] (Tokyo: Nihon kokusai mondai kenkyujo, 1993); and "Nansashoto no jikko shihai ni noridashita chugoku" [China embarking to seize effective control of the Spratlys islands], *Sekai Shuho* [World report], 7 March 1995.

security issues in the region. For Tokyo, the ARF provides an insurance policy in addition to that of the U.S.-Japan alliance with which to face the uncertain security environment of the post-Cold War era; it is also a potential platform on which Japan may play a bigger strategic and political role in the region.

Indeed, the Spratlys dispute serves as a test of whether or not Japan's recent emphasis on multilateral forums to promote regional stability is viable. In the post-Cold War era, the cornerstone of Japanese foreign policy remains the U.S.-Japan alliance, and multilateral forums in the Asia-Pacific region are deemed a supplement to and not a substitute for the alliance. Japan's support for multilateralism stems from the need for additional mechanisms to keep its U.S. ally involved in the region; a regionally acceptable vehicle with which Japan can assume a more active role without resorting to a controversial unilateralism, and a way to keep China engaged in consultation and co-operation with its neighbors. Multilateral forums are expected to enhance confidence-building measures, boost transparency by publishing defense white papers and joining the U.N. arms register, and engage in preventive diplomacy to defuse tensions. Besides the ARF, Tokyo has identified the Workshops on the South China Sea Conflict hosted annually by Indonesia as a multilateral approach to address regional sources of instability, especially the South China Sea conflict.[9] There is the danger, however, that if multilateral organizations merely remain talking-shops that are unable to contain a serious flare-up, these nascent organizations may be discredited. Such an outcome would undermine Japan's security policy of relying on multilateral organizations to supplement the U.S. alliance as well as its pursuit of regional leadership.

Japanese Economic Interests

Although Japan is primarily concerned about the Spratly dispute's implication for its security and status, it is not devoid of economic interest in the South China Sea. Some Japanese trading companies and oil corporations have already sought agreements with Vietnam to exploit the fishing and natural resources in certain areas of the sea, and Mitsubishi Oil Company has discovered a large gas field located about 120 km from Vietnam's southern coast. Extracting oil and gas from the South China Sea, if commercially viable, would be very attractive to Japan because it could further diversify its suppliers and permit access to energy sources from an area much closer to home than the Middle East.

9. Yanai Shunji, "Reisengo no wagakuni no anzen hosho seisaku" [Japan's security policy in the post-cold war era], *Gaiko Forumu* [Diplomacy forum], no. 82 (July 1995), p. 48. Yanai is chief, Comprehensive Policy Division, Ministry of Foreign Affairs.

However, if significant energy resources were discovered in that area, the Spratlys dispute would become even more volatile. Great powers who are non-claimant states, including the U.S. and Russia, would probably be interested in any bonanza and question the attempts of other powers seeking to control oil production in the South China Sea. Tokyo's interest in the area would concomitantly increase with the intensity of great power rivalry. However, Japanese businessmen are likely to rush in despite economic and political risks; Tokyo would probably rationalize its economic activities as being distinct from the question of sovereignty and adopt the well-worn formula of separating economics from politics.

Japan's Role in the Spratlys Dispute

Japan's role in the Spratlys, meant to enhance the nation's quest for status and security, is inhibited by the burden of history. As a result of its militaristic past, defeat in the Pacific War, and legacy of democratization by the U.S. occupation, Japan has a pacifist Constitution and dovish public opinion that constrain the country from being involved in any military conflict abroad. Moreover, the ruling coalition is unlikely to change the official interpretation that Article 9 of the Constitution permits Japan to defend itself but not to dispatch its troops abroad, even for United Nations peace *enforcement* operations, or engage in collective security to resolve international disputes. Even though it jettisoned its pacifist doctrine to join the ruling coalition, the Social Democratic Party (SDP) is temperamentally against committing Japan to any foreign policy venture with any hint of military entanglement. It cannot adopt the politically sensitive military option of resisting an interdiction of the sea lanes in the South China Sea. Although the ruling LDP and the opposition Shinshinto are led by forceful and nationalistic leaders who advocate a bigger political role for Japan, they continue to face the constraints of the pacifist constitution, dovish public opinion, coalition politics, party factionalism, and a cultural norm that inhibits top leaders from acting decisively and unilaterally.

The passage of half of a century since the end of the Pacific War has not significantly eroded the suspicions of China, the two Koreas, and to a lesser extent, the Southeast Asian countries that Japan has not sincerely repented of its imperial past and will repeat its mistakes. The unprecedented post-World War Two dispatch of Japanese peacekeeping troops to Cambodia in 1993, even under the aegis of the United Nations for non-combat activities, initially aroused considerable disquiet in Japan and among its neighbors. While some ASEAN countries are supportive of an American presence in the South China Sea to balance the Chinese, they do not welcome direct Japanese participation in the regional military balance.

In February 1995 Foreign Minister Kono Yohei, during a Diet interpellation about Japan's official position on the Spratlys dispute, pointed out the importance of the South China Sea to Japan as the link between the Indian Ocean and Northeast Asia. While urging dialogue and self-restraint on the claimant states to resolve the dispute, Kono did not propose any concrete role for Japan.[10] Kono was asked whether Japan would slash its foreign aid if China were to advance farther into the South China Sea. Not wishing to offend Beijing, Kono declined to address the question as speculative and hypothetical. When asked whether Japan would exercise leadership and place the Spratlys issue on the agenda for discussion at the Osaka APEC meeting in November 1995, Kono replied that Japan would not do so. This did not indicate the country's indifference to the dispute but that Tokyo felt it was more appropriate to discuss the problem at the ARF, the Workshops on the South China Sea Dispute, and directly with the Chinese rather than at an economic forum.

Japan indirectly plays a critical role in maintaining the balance of power in the Asia-Pacific region through the U.S.-Japan Alliance. Only the U.S. has sufficient weight to balance the Chinese in the South China Sea but the Americans are unlikely to play that role without the logistics and financial assistance that Japan provides. Because Japan has committed itself to the defense of its sea lanes only up to 1,000 nautical miles from its capital, any disruption to its shipping in the South China Sea would be beyond the strategic mission of the Japanese navy.[11] Tokyo would then have to rely on Washington to maintain the safety of navigation in the Spratlys vicinity. In any hypothetical conflict that interferes with international shipping in the South China Sea, Tokyo can still play an indirect role by doing its part to protect its sea lanes up to 1,000 miles and freeing the U.S. 7th Fleet to show the flag in more distant waters.

Some Japanese analysts have proposed a more direct strategic role for Japan in the South China Sea. One group of academics has suggested that Japan and the ASEAN countries co-operate in joint maritime policing activities, while another analyst has advocated a deterrent role for the Japanese

10. Yosan iinkai dai ni bunkakai giroku [Diet's second budget subcommittee proceedings], 21 February 1995.

11. Ha Hong Hai writes: "In case an emergency situation involving armed conflicts occurred there [South China Sea], it would pose to Japan difficult problems concerning sea-lanes protection. Most of the disputed sea areas, however, lie beyond the 1,000 nautical mile limit set by Japan for the purpose of naval and air operations to protect the SLOCs. Any military option by a party concerned would be far more serious for Japan than any regional disputes in the recent past." Ha Hong Hai, "Major Powers' Attitudes Toward Spratly Disputes and Their Implications for the Solution," paper delivered at ASEAN-ISIS Conference, Hanoi, October 1995, p. 5.

navy against China were it to advance its interests further.[12] But these proposals are quite fanciful and are not politically acceptable to Japanese public opinion nor to Japan's neighbors. The Japanese navy currently cannot adopt any autonomous role because its force structure dovetails into U.S. naval strategy and missions. On its own, it lacks aircraft carriers, independent air cover, target acquisition, and sufficient anti-submarine capabilities to play an autonomous strategic role in East Asia.[13]

Quest for an Active Diplomatic Role

The catalyst in Japan's desire to play an active political role in defusing the Spratlys dispute was the Mischief Reef incident, although the impulse to adopt an active foreign policy arose in the aftermath of the Gulf War. Even though Japan had aspired to play a global political role commensurate with its economic status even before the Gulf War, its foreign policy toward "high politics" (strategic, military, and political issues) was best characterized as reactive, passive, and economistic. Its foreign policy initiatives were concentrated on financial and economic issues such as financing for the U.N., Japan's ODA, and World Bank and Asian Development Bank activities. The Gulf War was a turning point; despite its hefty contribution of US$13 billion, Japan was roundly criticized and humiliated for practicing only checkbook diplomacy. A lack of national consensus and weak political leadership about an appropriate non-monetary contribution to the U.N.-endorsed, U.S-led multinational force against the Iraqi invasion of Kuwait resulted in paralysis of Japan's decision-making process. Thus, Tokyo's interest in the Spratlys dispute is, in part, an offshoot of its desire to play a more active political role in world affairs.

The press reported that the Philippines discussed the Mischief Reef Incident with Japan at a vice-ministerial meeting in late February 1995 and requested Tokyo to "persuade" Beijing to act with restraint. Subsequently, a Japanese deputy vice-foreign minister asked China to resolve the problem peacefully at a bilateral vice-ministerial meeting held in Beijing on March 2.[14] Even though Beijing does not welcome third-party involvement in the Spratlys, Tokyo was prepared to act as a bridge between Manila and Beijing, demonstrating Japan's willingness to deal directly with a serious security

12. *Sekai* [World], December 1994, p. 39; Koichi Sato, "The Japan Card," *Far Eastern Economic Review*, 13 April 1995. See also Sato Koichi, "Tonan ajia no anzen hosho to nihon no koken" [The security of Southeast Asia and Japan's contribution], *Gaiko Jiho* [Revue diplomatique], no. 1318 (May 1995), pp. 80–83.

13. Interview with Kimura Kazuo, senior research fellow, National Institute for Defence Studies, JDA, 20 June 1995.

14. *Sankei Shinbun*, 8 March 1995.

problem and in so doing enhance its prestige as a great power involved in defusing regional conflict.

The press also reported in March that Prime Minister Murayama intended to discuss the Spratlys issue with Chinese Prime Minister Li Peng at the U.N. Social Development Summit in Copenhagen, the first time the press mentioned the Japanese prime minister taking a direct interest in the dispute. That discussion did not take place,[15] but in April Murayama met Qiao Shi, chairman of China's National People's Congress, in Tokyo and expressed Japan's concern about a peaceful resolution of the conflict.[16] When Murayama met Li Peng in Beijing in May, he again placed the Spratlys issue on the agenda for discussion. Foreign Minister Kono reiterated Tokyo's desire for the safety of navigation and a peaceful resolution of the Spratlys dispute at the ARF meeting in Brunei in August 1995, where Japan was nominated as co-chair of the intersession group on confidence-building measures. Kono also took the opportunity to offer Tokyo as a venue for the intersession group to begin its work, which may be interpreted as an initiative to gain international recognition of Japan's major power status. Nevertheless, if China refuses to discuss the dispute within the framework of the ARF, Japan has little leverage to change its mind.[17]

Despite Japan's interest in participating in the annual Indonesian-initiated Workshops on the South China Sea Conflict, it has not been invited to attend these quasi-governmental meetings. It appears odd that land-locked Laos is a participant while maritime Japan is not. Certain ASEAN countries support

15. According to the *Sankei Shinbun* (8, 15 March 1995), there were two schools of thought within the Foreign Ministry about the appropriateness of raising the issue in Copenhagen. One opinion stated that Murayama should express Japan's concerns about the Spratlys to China. Another said that the planned meeting of only 20 minutes between the two PMs was too short and could not accommodate a discussion on the Spratlys; Japan should instead discuss the issue of suspected North Korean nuclear development.

16. *Japan Times*, 12 April 1995.

17. Beijing made the following statement at the first ARF meeting in 1994: "The Chinese side has taken note of the suggestion by some countries that the question of South China Sea be included in the agenda of the forum its senior officials meeting. The position of the Chinese Government on this question is well-known as consistent. The Nansha Islands (Spratlys) have since ancient times been a Chinese territory, and China has indisputable sovereignty over the islands and its adjacent waters. Some countries do not agree with us on this question. These differences can be settled through bilateral negotiations. If they cannot be resolved for the timebeing, the parties concerned may shelve the dispute while going for joint development. The Chinese government is always opposed to internationalizing the question of the Nansha Islands. Consequently, we do not believe that the Forum or its senior officials should discuss this question." (Press release, 4 April 1994). However, at the ARF meeting in Brunei in August 1995, China agreed to limited multilateral discussion of the Spratlys between itself and ASEAN members only.

Japan's participation but China has opposed it,[18] preferring that the disputes be addressed bilaterally and that certain non-claimant states (especially big powers like Japan) should not be involved in the issue (although it does not oppose the presence of Laos). By dealing separately with individual and weaker ASEAN claimant states, this "one-giant, one-pygmy" formula is obviously an advantage to China. Some ASEAN countries believe that the participation of non-claimant states like Japan would balance China and perhaps dissuade it from acting unilaterally. In the 1993 Workshop, some delegates suggested that non-claimant states should be allowed to participate in areas that do not impinge on the sovereignty issue. Thus, a non-claimant state like Japan, if invited, could assist with various financial and technical assistance, including oceanographic surveys of the archipelago, marine biology, weather, and tides. Among the claimant and non-claimant states that are interested in the Spratlys, Japan probably has the best financial, skilled scientific, and human resources to assist in joint research and development of the South China Sea. Moreover, because of its long-standing exploration and activities in the Spratlys between 1918 and 1945, it is likely to have accumulated valuable information and knowledge that will be helpful for such activity. Thus far, Japan has yet to receive an official invitation to join the annual workshops in Indonesia.

When given an opportunity to be involved in regional discussions about the South China Sea conflict, Japan has seized it. In November 1995, the Philippines's Institute for Strategic and Development Studies and the U.S. Pacific Forum/CSIS (Center for Strategic and International Studies) organized a Workshop on the South China Sea Conflict in Manila that was opened by President Fidel Ramos and attended by government officials, members of thinktanks, and academics from the Asia-Pacific region.[19] Japan sent a delegation but China was conspicuously absent, probably because it could not agree to the participation of non-claimant states, especially Japan and the United States, in a conference that was co-sponsored by the Americans. Its boycott also meant that nothing related to the Spratlys could be resolved. Indonesian Ambassador Hashim Djalal, who has been responsible for the Indonesian-led workshops, intimated at Manila that Tokyo had floated a trial balloon to the Indonesians by offering to cover the cost of hosting the workshops, paid for so far by the Canadian International Development Agency, on

18. See Sato Koichi, "Minami shina kai o meguru kokusai kankei: Taito suru chugoku kyoi ron to ASEAN" [International relations concerning the South China Sea], *Kokusai Mondai* [International issues], October 1993, pp. 41, 45–48. Even though participation in the Workshops is not on a governmental basis but in principle "track two," China has rejected any Japanese participation.

19. For the view of an organizer of the Manila Conference, see Ralph A. Cossa, "A Ripple Effect in the South China Sea," *Japan Times*, 7 December 1995.

the condition that the workshops be held in Tokyo.[20] The Indonesians declined on the grounds that the Chinese were unlikely to support this proposal.

Japan's Future Role in the South China Sea

Unless Japan's sea lanes are seriously threatened or disrupted in the South China Sea, Tokyo is unlikely to move significantly beyond its present posture of attempting diplomatic initiatives to defuse regional tension within bilateral and multilateral frameworks. If these efforts fail to prevent serious strife in the Spratlys, Japan would have to rely on the United States to maintain the balance of power in the South China Sea. Although the U.S. does not support the territorial claims to the Spratlys of any particular country, it has indicated that it will not remain indifferent to any disruption of freedom of navigation in that area.[21] Any country that disrupts the sea lanes around the Spratlys cannot assume that the U.S. would not intervene militarily, and if the U.S. becomes militarily involved in a South China Sea conflict, Japan would probably provide logistics and financial assistance to its ally but refrain from direct military involvement.

The April 1996 Clinton-Hashimoto Joint Declaration called for closer coordination to include "studies on bilateral cooperation dealing with situations that may emerge in the areas surrounding Japan and which will have an important influence on the peace and stability of Japan."[22] A disruption of the sea lanes in the South China Sea would be considered an emergency in Japan's region. The Japanese media reported that "along with the planned review of the Japan-U.S. defense co-operation guideline, the government on 17 May firmed up an intention to replace "Far East emergencies" in the guideline with "emergencies in Japan's neighboring regions." The existing guideline stipulates defense co-operation between the Self-Defense Forces (SDF) and U.S. forces in case of Far East emergencies. The change would make it possible for both Japan and the U.S. to examine joint military measures so that the SDF can provide logistic support to U.S. forces not only in a Korean

20. Information received from Professor Soeya Yoshihide, a member of the Japanese delegation to the November 1995 Manila Workshop, who learned of it in discussions with Ambassador Hashim Djalal.

21. According to a U.S. Department of Defense publication: "Contested claims to islands and territorial waters in the South China Sea are a source of tension in Southeast Asia that could carry serious consequences for regional stability. . . . [T]he United States regards the high seas as an international commons. Our strategic interest in maintaining the lines of communication linking Southeast Asia, Northeast Asia, and the Indian Ocean make it essential that we *resist* any maritime claims beyond those permitted by the Law of the Sea Convention" (emphasis added). Office of International Security Affairs, DoD, *United States Security for the East Asia-Pacific Region*, February 1995, pp. 19–20.

22. Foreign Broadcast Information Service, *Daily Report: East Asia*, 96-075, 17 April 1996.

Peninsula crisis and a China-Taiwan dispute, but also in a military conflict in the Spratly Islands, pirate activities in the SLOCs, and a possible outbreak of "the second Persian Gulf War." The Japanese government considers that the regions go beyond the Far East stipulated in the Japan-U.S. Security Treaty, although "we cannot specify the extent of the regions." Specifically, the government source said that "the region includes the Middle East, the Malacca Straits, and the Spratly Islands, where a crisis could pose a serious threat to Japan."[23] If such a scenario were to take place, a segment of U.S. public and elite opinion might accuse its ally of being a free-rider and perceive that Washington was risking American lives to protect Japanese oil-tankers in the South China Sea. This would be similar to the situation during the Gulf War when some Americans claimed that their troops were shedding blood to protect Japan-bound oil in the Middle East.

Even if Beijing does not interfere with freedom of navigation while engaging in creeping advancement in the South China Sea, Tokyo would view these moves with great disquiet. Many Japanese decision-makers would view any further Chinese advancement in the Spratlys and Senkaku waters as proving their suspicions that their giant neighbor is a rising hegemon. Domestic pressure to slash Tokyo's ODA to China would arise, and it would be difficult for the government to justify to taxpayers why Beijing should remain the largest beneficiary in Japan's foreign aid program while it devotes resources to a nuclear arsenal and asserts China's claims in the Spratlys.[24] If China becomes more assertive and channels more resources to support its ambitions in the South China Sea, Japan's military and certain politicians will use the "China threat" to justify a larger increase in defense spending. Former Prime Minister Murayama, the Defence Agency, and political parties have already cited the Spratlys dispute as a prime example of instability in the Asia-Pacific that necessitates sustained defense spending in the post-Cold War era and maintenance of the U.S.-Japan alliance.[25] The Okinawa rape

23. Ibid., 96-101, 23 May 1996; also, 96-114, 12 June 1996.

24. Interview with a Japanese Foreign Ministry official, Southeast Asia Second Division, Asian Affairs Bureau, 23 June 1995.

25. A joint Defence Agency and LDP defense policy group highlighted the Spratlys as an example of conflict in the post-Cold War Asia-Pacific region that makes it difficult for Japan to reduce its defense budget (*Sankei Shinbun*, 18 July 1995). The Spratlys have also seeped into the consciousness of Japanese air force officers. When the air force conducted a poll among its officers about hardware requirements, the preference was for "AWACs that has a range that can fly to the Spratlys." The newspaper reported that this did not mean that the air force planned to expand its scope to the Spratlys (*Asahi Shinbun*, 2 December 1995). Shinshinto, the main opposition party, prepared its "Outline on Security Policy Towards the New Century," mentioning the following as issues for concern: North Korea's suspected nuclear development, instability in the Korean Peninsula, China's nuclear development, and the Spratlys problem (*Sankei Shinbun*, 28 November 1995).

incident ignited mass demonstrations against American bases and reawakened Japan's domestic debate about the role of U.S. forces in the country. In its aftermath, especially when U.S.-Japan relations are subjected to further strain, Japanese leaders can use potential instability in East Asia, including the Spratlys, to justify sustaining the alliance.

A worst-case scenario would be the end of the U.S.-Japan Alliance followed by a disruption of Tokyo's sea lanes in the South China Sea. If the alliance were to be terminated because of mutual acrimony and mismanagement, the country would have to consider seriously how to defend its sea lanes beyond the 1,000-nautical-mile range. Both Northeast and Southeast Asian countries would probably be very jittery in such a situation; greater security for Japan would mean greater perceived insecurity for its neighbors. This would have a deleterious effect on multilateral organizations such as the ARF and APEC and the vision of a peaceful and prosperous Asia-Pacific region. Paradoxically, a unilateral approach to security would probably undermine the confidence of Japan's neighbors and its own security environment.

Conclusion

Contrary to the persistent image that Japan's foreign policy is essentially reactive, even in the post-Cold War era, the country has actively addressed the Spratlys issue to enhance its quest for security and status. That Japan pursues these goals is not remarkable; no state in the international system is indifferent to such objectives. What is remarkable from a historical viewpoint is that unlike other great economic powers, Japan is not a political and strategic heavyweight. The Spratlys case study has demonstrated this imbalance in Japan's foreign policy. However, Japan's persistence in raising the issue with China has reminded Beijing that non-claimant states, especially regional great powers, also have a stake in the peaceful resolution of the Spratlys dispute. Beijing will have noted that further advances into the South China Sea at the expense of other claimants would incur the loss of political goodwill from its largest ODA donor.

The Spratlys case study has shown the limits of Japanese foreign policy. Not underpinned by autonomous military power nor forgiven by its neighbors for its militaristic past, its foreign policy is restricted to diplomacy and financial incentives that are subject to acceptance by claimant states, especially China. Ironically, the largest single recipient of Japanese ODA, Beijing, continues to exercise a veto over Tokyo's participation in the annual Workshops on the South China Sea. And unless China relents or until the sea lanes are directly threatened, Tokyo is likely to remain an interested outsider with repressed and unfulfilled ambitions to play an active role in the Spratlys dispute.

JAPAN AND GLOBAL ENVIRONMENTAL LEADERSHIP

Rowland T. Maddock

Japan is poised to take on the responsibilities of environmental leadership. The environment is a "new" issue and the assumption by Japan of an activist role will not provoke unease in Asia about Japanese intentions or be viewed in the United States as a challenge to its global hegemony. Japan more than any other country appears to have broken the link between economic growth and ecological degradation. It offers a cognitive model to other nations, especially its East Asian neighbors concerned by the nonsustainability of current growth models. Japan also deploys financial and technological resources that make a leadership bid credible.

Global environmental politics is characterized by an impoverished institutional imagination. The environment is almost the quintessential public good where actors are structurally induced to defect, often spurning opportunities for collective betterment. At the international level, the economic and political consequences of anarchy are ameliorated by regimes that structure actor expectations towards cooperation and collective benefit. Essential to effective regime creation is leadership,[1] but to date no nation (or non-state actor) has been able or willing to provide the leadership necessary for long-term environmental sustainability.

In recent years, representatives of the Japanese state at various levels have proclaimed that Japan is now ready to provide that leadership. In his letter to the 1992 UNCED conference at Rio, Prime Minister Miyazawa pressed Japan's eagerness to play "a leading role" in the international politics of the environment.[2] Former Foreign Minister Okita confirmed that unlike other countries that squandered their resources on armaments, Japan will mobilize its economic wealth and political energy for the far more important task of protecting the environment. The assumption by Japan of effective leadership cannot be made overnight, but S. Kata, director general of the Global Environmental Department at the Environment Agency, predicts that by the year 2010 Japan will be "second to none."[3] Academic political economists also, seeking to locate Japan's role in the so-called new international order, identify the environment as an issue whereby it can become a world leader.[4]

United Nations data place Japan unambiguously as the second largest economic power in the world, based moreover not on a large and poor popu-

Rowland T. Maddock is a senior lecturer in the Department of International Politics, University of Wales, Aberystwyth. He is the author of *The Political Economy of the Arms Race* (Macmillian, 1990).

lation, but on technological dynamism. Historically, the second largest power is always induced to seek a hegemonic role in the international system.[5]

With the demise of East-West ideological and great power confrontation, the single most important bilateral relationship in international politics is now that between Japan and the United States.[6] A central issue in the emerging international political economy, therefore, is the ease with which the redistribution of economic power between the hegemonic and the revisionist state can be politically accommodated. The political, economic, and technological capacities of member states change at different rates, which over time causes the international system to shift from a condition of equilibrium to one of disequilibrium. Throughout history the primary means of resolving the incompatibility between the structure of the international system and the redistribution of power has been war between the hegemonic and the rising revisionist state.[7] Some futurologists predict a similar outcome for American-Japanese bilateral relationships. Chronic economic imbalance will, they argue, inexorably collapse into political and eventually military conflict.[8] Others, however, argue that although war cannot be entirely ruled out, it is, because of the increasing disutility of the military instrument, no longer a rational means of resolving the conflict between hegemonic and revisionist states.[9] For the Japanese also hegemonic war is a "grotesque anachronism."[10] In the contemporary world system, power and influence derive more from access to and control over economic and technological resources.

The redistribution of potential economic power between the United States and Japan raises, therefore, in acute form the latter's place in the international scheme of things. For those who argue that Japan will refuse to shoulder the economic and political costs of diplomatic activism,[11] the views expressed by Mr. Miyazawa and others are little more than an orchestrated program to manage Japan's image abroad. They are designed to deflect criticism from foreign governments of its failure to play a constructive role in international affairs and from environmental groups of its destructive ecological shadow. In the Western world Japan is perceived as a neomercantilist state, exploiting the liberal trading economy but refusing to abide by the rules of the game.[12] Japanese diplomats have been shocked by the ferocity of the sometimes personal attacks made on them by environmental activists.[13] The masking function of conciliatory foreign policy statements should certainly not be underestimated but Japanese scholars argue that Japan can no longer expect to avoid the political requirements of great economic power, but must seriously confront and make a positive stand on major international issues. Its recently proclaimed public rhetoric of internationalization reflects the new political reality.[14] Moreover, the views expressed by Mr. Miyazawa and others reflect a real and growing national concern in government, the state bureaucracy, and society with ecological values and outcomes in favor of a three-fold harmony between economic growth, energy, and the environment.[15]

Despite its great wealth Japan lacks the range of economic and military resources that would enable it to mount a global challenge to American hegemony. Equally constrictive in the long run are a deep-rooted cultural exclusiveness and the dynamics of its domestic political system, which inhibit the deployment of so-called soft power. Although economic globalism has transformed the structure and dynamics of the world economy, Japanese economic progress is predicated on borderless production, the effective penetration of global markets. It is therefore not in Japan's interest to so challenge existing authority structures as to dismantle the multilateral basis of the international capitalist economy. Japan's challenge to existing hegemonic structures may therefore be constrained to "new" issues, which are not perceived by the United States and other great nations, especially its regional neighbors, as overly threatening. The environment is one such issue.[16]

Although public rhetoric is seldom matched by real economic and political commitment, there is little doubt that in the international community, the environment is bidding to rank in importance with economic welfare and national security. But as it escalates up the international agenda, it takes on the political characteristics of these traditional issues. Nations are induced to assess outcomes in zero sum terms, and less inclined to forgo their perceived national interest. It is then that leadership becomes important.

Leaders are neither altruistic actors willing and able to forgo indefinitely their own well-being for the collective good nor rational egoists seeking only to maximize unilateral welfare, security, or status. Successful political entrepreneurs are those that effectively identify their self-interest with collective values, which may, however, require both leader and follower to forego potentially available unilateral benefits.

Leaders must demonstrate to actual and potential followers, individually or collectively, the value of strategic choices that otherwise would have been rejected. The demonstration effect[17] is essentially cognitive, articulating scientific paradigms, social norms, or economic cost-benefit calculations that become preferable to available alternatives. The clarity and persuasiveness of the demonstration effect is logically unconnected to economic weight. Indeed, one way for small and otherwise uninfluential nations to make a distinctive contribution to international politics is precisely through articulating superior cognitive viewpoints, although away from the abstract realm the social paradigms associated with large states tend to carry more weight.

Knowledge of superior strategies does not of itself guarantee that they will in fact be pursued. Indeed a central problem in international political economy is the fact of, and therefore how to overcome, structural limitations to cooperation. Effective leadership therefore requires more than the articulation of a superior set of paradigms, norms, or calculations. It requires also the expenditure of real resources to translate superior possibilities into actual collective strategies. Leaders must therefore be able to transform the structural constraints and opportunities facing actual or potential followers[18] through economic plenitude, technological dynamism, or organizational innovation. The transfer of wealth, technology, and entrepreneurial skills is costly, and structural as opposed to purely cognitive leaders must be in a position to transmute structural power into bargaining leverage. This is most easily achieved if the leader can generate and mobilize a surplus beyond the immediate and legitimate demands of domestic society. (Authoritarian governments may and have squeezed a leadership surplus by holding down welfare, but in the long term this road to leadership must undermine the effectiveness of the demonstration effect.) The surplus not only facilitates the mobilization of domestic resources for foreign policy purposes, but enables the gains that derive from collective decisions to be distributed in proportions quite different from initial distributions. The exercise of structural power may take the form of a reward for cooperation or a penalty for noncooperation; access to or denial of markets, aid, technology, or innovation. It is especially critical for the supply of international public goods such as the environment where the incentive to defect is particularly pervasive.

In the business world entrepreneurs often outperform their rivals by identifying and then filling gaps in the market through the provision of new goods. Although the analogy between economic and political entrepreneurship should not be stretched too far, the environment, especially in its most recent manifestation of sustainable development, can be conceived as a "new" issue, offering opportunities for actors seeking new roles in international affairs by filling gaps left by established actors slow to respond to changing opportunities and challenges. The timing of leadership bids, matching structural power to a new cognitive *zeitgeist* is important in determining the success of those bids. There is little doubt that Japan offers a seductive model to the dynamic East Asian nations increasingly concerned by unassailable evidence of the nonsustainability of traditional growth.

Japan's recent environmental record is by international standards exemplary. One recent World Bank report described it as an environmental paragon.[19] Most OECD countries have in the past decade or so managed to reduce emissions of sulphur dioxide, one of the two acid rain gases. Japan alone has reduced emissions of nitrogen oxide, the other acid rain gas. Exceptional response to the energy crisis in the 1970s has decreased its energy coefficient such that it is by far the most energy-efficient country in the world and, as a consequence, its emissions of CO_2 per unit of GNP fall well below those of other nations. Whereas Japan accounts for 14 percent of world GNP it emits less than 5 percent of carbon dioxide emissions. Inland water quality of

TABLE 1
Man-Made Emissions of Air Pollution Per Unit of GDP

	Japan	U.S.	OECD/Europe
Sulphur oxides (KG/$1000)	0.6	4.1	4.0
Nitrogen oxide (")	0.8	4.5	4.1
Particulate Matter (")	0.1	1.9	1.1
Carbon Monoxide (")	4	15	13

Source: OECD, *The State of the Environment*, Paris, 1991, p.35.

Japanese rivers as measured by Biological Oxygen Demand and Nitrate concentration are amongst the best of all OECD nations.[20]

Japan's record is important in its own right, but it also serves to meet the first obligation of a leader, to provide a model attractive to potential followers. Japan, it appears, has broken the link between economic growth and environmental decay,[21] once considered almost an iron law of development. At the international level Japan has in recent years pursued an activist environmental diplomacy. It is a signatory to the important environmental conventions. Its commitment to stabilize energy-related per capita CO_2 emissions at the 1990 level by 2000 is exceptionally onerous given the level of energy efficiency already achieved. More significant from a regional hegemonic perspective has been its environmental aid and technology transfer programs. By 1990 it had become the world's largest aid donor, an increasing proportion of which is set aside for ecological improvement in recipient countries.

Japan has participated in debt-for-nature swaps, and has promised to contribute up to 30 percent of the $125 billion that Maurice Strong, the secretary general of UNCED, predicts will be necessary to reverse current ecological trends. As a practical beginning, $7.7 billion was made immediately available at Rio as part of the projected increase in environmental assistance of up to ¥300 bn per annum by 1997.[22] In 1993 Japanese officials instituted two new projects to assist Third World countries, the Green Aid Plan and the Energy Cooperation Plan to improve energy coefficients.

Financial assistance is matched by the transfer of environmental technology, financed by the public and the private sector, and has included exporting desulphurization and denitrification technologies to Mexico and to China, and environmentally efficient steel technology to China. For leader nations with mixed motives the exercise of hegemonic power by the state and its representatives is more effective if it can be organically linked to important domestic values and economic self interest. Western observers of the Japanese political process explain Japan's conversion to environmental activism almost exclusively as a response to international pressure.[23] Japanese scholars paint a more complex picture, where domestic forces are more prominent.

TABLE 2
Shares of Global Carbon-Dioxide Emission and Shares of Global GDP

	Col (1) % share Global GNP	Col (2) % share Global CO_2	Col (3) Ratio (1) (2)
Japan	14	5	2.8
U.S.	27	24	1.0
USSR	8	19	0.4
Germany	7	4	1.7
UK	3.5	3.0	1.1

Source: F. Cairncross, *Costing the Earth*, (London: Economist Books, 1991), p. 139.

Although fundamental philosophical and religious values impinge only indirectly on practical political and economic decisions, they do frame the cognitive context of public debate and policies. Western attitudes towards the environment, placing man in an exclusionary relationship with nature, have been traced back to Greek philosophers and Christian Biblical injunctions to dominate nature.[24] In Japan, environmental ethics draw from a concept of living nature formulated from traditional Japanese Buddhism.[25] The Japanese concept of nature entails an extension of ethics to include relations between humans and the land, and which may in this regard be more supportive of environmental values than Western paradigms, which place man separate from and superior to nature. Buddhism reveals a symbiotic link between man and nature, for divinity was proclaimed to reside in the very fabric of the natural universe. Nature and man are complementary elements in a world structured for cooperation rather than conflict. The human purpose in this holistic scheme was to preserve equilibrium between the various and equally legitimate spheres.[26] Traditional art, philosophy, literature, and religious beliefs attest a subtle awareness of kinship with animals, plants, even inanimate objects, and the Buddhist concept of nature welds the land ethic with a land aesthetic so that the natural world is laden with mutually supportive religious and aesthetic values. This is of course not unique to Japan. Fritjof Capra, the well known physicist and environmental philosopher, argues that a common and important characteristic of the Eastern world view is the awareness of the unity and mutual interrelation of all things and events, the experience of all phenomena in the world as manifestations of oneness.[27]

A more immediate social incentive to prioritize environmental values has been the somewhat belated response to Japan's three lethal incidents of industrial pollution; the notorious Yokkaichi asthma, the Itai-Itai and Minamata scandals.[28]

Japan's exceptional performance in reducing emissions and improving water quality can be traced to a unique mix of regulation and economic incen-

TABLE 3
Environmental Aid Data

	1987	1988	1989	1990	1991
¥ (bn)	10	30	85	90	120
%of total project aid	2	3	8.5	9	17

Source: *Far Eastern Economic Review*, March 12, 1992, p. 39.

tives such that by the mid-1970s it had in place one of the world's most comprehensive environmental legal systems.

Japanese firms have allocated up to 14 percent of industrial investment to pollution control, a proportion described by one expert as "staggering."[29] Japan has installed over 2,000 desulphurization and denitrification plants, almost 75 percent of the world total. In the energy sector this huge investment was partly a function of high prices in the 1970s and early 1980s.

Costly policies are more palatable if they can be shown to have economically profitable spill-ins, especially if the private sector is to be mobilized. Japanese business and political leaders anticipate that the environment will become a source of profit for business firms exploiting a newly emergent comparative advantage, who will therefore be more supportive of an activist environmental diplomacy. For a society accustomed to and confident in making long-term strategic decisions, export of environmental technology offers a source of foreign revenue to replace that from traditional industries made noncompetitive by nations at lower levels of development.[30] Because of its domestic investments Japan is already the world's largest exporter of environmental technology. As ecological sustainability assumes greater prominence in developed nations, in the dynamic NICs,[31] and also in less-developed nations eager to avoid the ecological costs of traditional growth models, Japan is well positioned to maximize the growth potential of this new global market. Exports of technology from private firms linked to an expanding aid program are almost certain to increase. Keidanren, the powerful industry association, plans to establish a fund for assisting Third World environmental protection,[32] building upon programs already in place.

Thirty industrial firms have joined with the powerful Ministry of International Trade and Industry (MITI) to provide the ¥8 bn necessary to establish the Research Institute of Innovative Technology for the Earth (RITE) designed to lead international research into technologies that will reduce emissions of carbon dioxide.[33]

The initiative of MITI is crucial to the credibility of Japan's leadership bid, in that foreign policy is effectively formulated and implemented by the executive branch.[34] Although MITI and the Environmental Agency disagree over priorities, MITI has acknowledged a more complex social objective appropriate to modern day Japan, modifying the "growth at all costs" strategy for one that seeks a reconciliation of economic growth, energy efficiency, and ecological protection. In addition to its participation in RITE, MITI has been instrumental in launching the New Sunshine Program aimed at developing better antipollution technologies. The research program, with a planned budget of ¥1550 bn over a 27-year period, is specifically designed to attract international participation. The MITI is also considering an additional international initiative to encourage the use of advanced pollution-reducing technologies worldwide. Technology Renaissance for the Environment and Energy (TREE) would promote Japanese technologies in Third World countries that seek to de-link economic growth and environmental decay. It is also backing an International Centre for Environmental Technology Transfer, which would train experts from Third World countries in environmental management and in so doing immerse them in Japanese ideas and Japanese technology. In 1993 MITI published a policy document, Fourteen Proposals for a New Earth, which made a powerful case for effective proposals to combat global warming and at the same time improve economic efficiency. The document is significant not only in demonstrating commitment to the idea of sustainable development, but also in its rejection of exclusive reliance on free market instruments favored by the United States and the European Community. The MITI proposals recommend state intervention with lower interest rates and tax incentives for industry, commerce, and households; an approach consistent with the Japanese style and acceptable to developing nations seeking to reconcile growth, equity, and ecological equilibrium.

The Environmental Agency has also been active in tightening regulations on the dumping of industrial waste at sea and in preparing a legal framework for a new environmental law, which would explicitly proclaim that the global environment should be left to future generations without further damage.[35]

Despite or perhaps because of this activism Japan has been accused of pursuing checkbook environmental diplomacy, which benefits primarily its own industry,[36] an accusation that official spokesmen are at pains to reject. Although the executive branch is divided between environmentally active and environmentally prudent groups, represented by the Environmental Agency and MITI respectively, there is growing consensus within the executive branch that Japan must look to a development paradigm that gives greater prominence to long-term sustainability.

The political process is also more responsive to environmental values. Recent prime ministers have been sensitive to ecological issues as have the LDP and the most important opposition parties. But in domestic policy making and execution the decisive actors are the zoku-gunn,[37] the so-called policy tribes. Zokus expedite legislation in issue areas of concern to members. Because historically the environment has not been important it has not warranted a separate zoku. This is now changing. Mr. Takeshita, the former prime minister, has drawn together a group of powerful LDP politicians to form a zoku around the environment.[38] The zoku is campaigning to upgrade the status of the Environment Agency to a full ministry, and looks to global environmental issues as a new focus for Japan's long-term strategy, citing both international prestige and economic profit.

Environmental managerialism at state and elite levels is matched by changing popular values. Although polls show Japanese people to have been less concerned with environmental issues than those of other developed nations and environmental pressure groups less effective, popular opinion, though lagging behind the state apparatus, is shifting. A recent poll shows that 49 percent of the Japanese people would be prepared to support a carbon tax for environmental reasons, compared with 44 percent against.

Finally Japanese environmental diplomacy is also informed by a strong defensive component. Like other nations, Japan cannot escape the depredation of transboundary pollution emanating outside its national boundaries, and like many developed nations it has realized it can often more effectively improve its own environment by investing abroad. Indeed joint implementation of environmental policy is specifically encouraged by the United Nations Framework Convention on climate change.[39] Acid rain depositions in Japan have recently, to the surprise and shock of many scientists, reached levels comparable to those in Europe and North America. A report by the Japanese Institute of Electric Power Industry estimates that China generates 50 percent of the sulphur emissions that cause acid rain in Japan, South Korea 15 percent, and Japan itself only 35 percent.[40] China is already the world's largest coal burner; emissions of sulphur dioxide have increased by over 5.4 percent over the past five years and by the year 2000 are expected to reach an annual average rate of two billion tons. Although Chinese officials have recently given increased priority to environmental issues, ambitious development plans, lagging technology, and financial constraints[41] cannot but increase pollution in China and, in its wake, spill-overs to countries such as Japan.

Japan will almost inevitably be contaminated by unregulated industrial expansion in eastern Russia. It is not difficult to believe that Russian environmental standards will be relaxed as it seeks economic expansion to compensate for ailing production and welfare in the wake of the privatization program. Japanese scientists are already fearful of nuclear waste dumping in the sea of Japan, and the Russian minister for environment has already suggested that Japan would have to pay for a radioactive waste reprocessing plant at an estimated cost of $8m.[42]

In the light of transboundary pollution, Japan is already modifying its aid program to its Asian neighbors. In particular its next loan package to China will focus on environmental issues, and it has budgeted a program to speed up the transfer of desulphurization technology, financed in part by MITI.

There are good structural and political reasons that give substance to Japanese claims to eventual environmental leadership. The transition to leadership is, for the moment however, partial and incomplete. Conservative forces tying Japan to traditional values and policies remain powerfully entrenched in the Japanese state and society.

Japanese people fail to understand the psychological impact of traditional preferences on perceptions outside the country. It may objectively be the case that whale meat is just another food source. But hunting and killing whales is an emotive and high profile issue, which can be exploited by environmental activists to bring approprobium on an entire national style. Japanese timber interests remain entrenched in the business/politics complex, and despite fine words to the contrary the International Tropical Timber Association, which Japanese interests dominate, remains committed to its traditional objective of unrestricted trade.[43]

In the state bureaucracy the Environment Agency remains a weak player, which has not yet attained the status of a ministry. Many key regulatory components have been removed from its control, and in the opinion of some experts it is not powerful enough to thwart the powerful pro-growth lobby, which is in any case weakened by the acceptance by MITI and others of a more environmentally conscious social welfare function.

Japanese environmentalism cannot of course be separated from the long-entrenched inhibitions to leadership *per se.* State and society have not resolved the conflicting demands on Japan's place in the community of nations and its habitual cultural exclusiveness makes it difficult for spokesmen to articulate transcendental values that would appeal to the non-material instincts of other peoples. It has failed to build upon its Buddhist ethical foundations to articulate a modern theory of environmental sustainability (but then neither has any other nation). The domestic political process of compromise and compacts cannot produce strong independent leaders capable of confidently proclaiming a Japanese vision of the new world order and Japan's role in it and, as Oran Young shows, personal leadership is important to success in environmental politics.[44] The progressive forces in Japanese state and society must overcome such conservative forces if Mr. Miyazawa's vision is to be realized. Although the outcome is far from forgone there are strong reasons to concur with Dr. Kata's prediction that by 2010 Japan will indeed have assumed the mantle of environmental leader.

NOTES

1. O. Young, "Political Leadership and Regime Formation," *International Organization,* vol. 45, no. 3 (1991), p. 285.
2. Y. Peng, "The Earth Summit and Japan's Initiative in Environmental Diplomacy," *Futures* (May 1993), p. 381.
3. A. Coughlin, "The Green Empire," *New Scientist*, October 2, 1993, p. 48.

4. H. Sato, "The Japanese Role in the Post Cold War World," *Current History*, vol. 90, no. 555, (1991), p. 147.
5. R. Gilpin, *War and Change in World Politics* (New York: Cambridge University Press, 1981).
6. S. Cohen, "USA-Japan Relations," *Current History*, vol. 90, no. 555, 1991, p.152.
7. R. Gilpin, op cit, p. 197.
8. J. Friedman and M. Leband, *The Coming War with Japan* (New York: St. Martins, 1992.)
9. S. Huntington, "Why International Primacy Matters," *International Security*, vol. 17, (Spring 1993), p. 93.
10. K. Taira, "An Imminent Hegemon," *Annals of the American Academy of Political and Social Science*, vol. 153, (January 1991), p.153.
11. B. Emmott, "The Economic Sources of Japan's Foreign Policy," *Survival*, vol. 84, no. 2, (Summer 1992), p. 56.
12. E. Olsen, "Target Japan as America's Economic Foe," *Orbis* (Fall 1992).
13. J. Hollimand, "Environmentalisms with a Global Scope," *Japan Quarterly*, vol. XXXVII, no. 3, (July 1990).
14. A. George, "Japan as America's Global Partner," *Journal of Northeast Asian Studies*, vol. XI, no. 4 (Winter 1992), p. 5.
15. T. Tomitate, "Japan's Climate Policy: A Rejoinder," *Security Dialogue*, vol. 24, no. 3 (1989), p. 288.
16. H. Sato, *op cit.*, p. 148.
17. R. Malnes, *Leader and Entrepreneur in International Negotiations: A Conceptual Analysis*, Fridjof Nausen Institute, Oslo EEC Publication, no. 9, 1992, p. 3.
18. *Ibid*, p. 2.
19. P. Kennedy, *Preparing for the Twentyfirst Century* (New York: Harper Collins, 1992), p. 160.
20. *The State of the Environment*, OECD, 1991, p. 60.
21. H. Sato, *op cit*, p. 148.
22. L. do Rosario, "Green at the Edges," *Far Eastern Economic Review*, vol. 155, no. 10, (March 12, 1992), p. 39.
23. H. Hollimand, *op cit.*
24. L. White, "The Historical Roots of our Ecological Crisis," *Science*, vol. 155, no. 3767, (March, 10, 1967).
25. S. Odin, "The Japanese Concept of Nature in Relation to the Environmental Ethics and Conservation Ethics of Aldo Leopald," *Environmental Ethics*, vol. 13, Winter 1991.
26. D. Kelly, et al., *The Economic Superpowers and the Environment* (R. Freeman, 1980), p. 25.
27. F. Capra, *The Tao of Physics* (London: Flemring, 1989), p. 141.
28. G. Ferman, "Japan's 1990 Climate Policy Under Pressure," *Security Dialogue*, vol. 24, no. 3 (1993), p. 288.
29. F. Cairncross, *Costing the Earth* (London: Economist Books, 1991), p. 247.
30. "Leading the Energy Race," *Far Eastern Economic Review*, vol. 155, no. 24, (June 18, 1992), p. 48.
31. D. Chan, "The Environmental Decline in Taiwan," *Journal of Northeast Asian Studies*, vol. XII, no. 1 (Spring 1993).
32. Y. Peng, *op cit*, p. 385.
33. A. Coughlin, *op cit*, p. 49.
34. A. Motofumi, "Democracy: An Unintended Victim," *Japan Quarterly*, vol. XXXVII, no. 1 (1990), p. 4.
35. Quoted in *Japan Quarterly*, vol. XXXIX, no. 4 (1992), p. 522.
36. A Coughlin, *op cit*, p. 50.
37. A. Motofumi, *op cit.*
38. *Far Eastern Economic Review*, vol. 154, no. 6, (June 18, 1992), p. 48.
39. R. Laske, and S. Oberthur, "Joint Implementation Under the Climate Change Convention," *International Environment Affairs*, vol. 6, no. 1 (Winter 1994).
40. R. Delfs, "Poison in the Sky," *Far Eastern Economic Review*, vol. 156, no. 5, (February 4, 1993), p. 16.

41. Y. Hao, "Environmental Protection in Chinese Foreign Policy," *Journal of Northeast Asian Studies*, vol. XI, no. 1 (Spring 1993).
42. "Aid Necessary to Stop Russian Dumping," *The Environmental Digest*, no. 79 (January 1994), p. 11.
43. "Tropical Forest Agreement Signed," *The Environmental Digest*, no. 79 (January 1994), p. 8.
44. O. Young and G. Osherenko, "Testing Theories of Regime Formation," V. Rittberger (ed), *Regime Theory and International Relations* (New York: Clarendon, 1993), p. 232.

ASIAN PERSPECTIVE, Vol. 20, No. 1, Spring-Summer 1996, pp. 5-50

THE PARTICIPATION OF JAPANESE MILITARY FORCES IN UNITED NATIONS PEACEKEEPING OPERATIONS

*Milton Leitenberg**

Since their establishment in 1954, the Self Defense Forces (SDF) of Japan have been a contentious issue in Japanese domestic politics. The legitimacy of their existence was opposed by the Japanese Socialist Party, which warned, in addition, of the dangers inherent in their existence or expansion. Nevertheless, as early as 1958 and again in 1961, there were requests from UN Secretary General Dag Hammarskjold to the Japanese government that Japan commit members of the SDF for service with United Nations peacekeeping missions. Such proposals were supported by the Japanese ambassador to the United Nations, by U.S. diplomats, and by a series of Japanese commissions established to examine the nation's national security issues.

These suggestions were rejected for decades by successive Japanese governments of the ruling Liberal Democratic Party. Under the pressure of the 1990-1991 Gulf War, however, authorizing legislation was finally passed in June 1992. Additionally, a rapid and large increase in UN peacekeeping operations after the end of the cold war, and the complete reversal of the positions of the Japanese Socialist Party when

*The author would like to thank several people who read the paper, as well as Mel Gurtov, for helpful suggestions. The research for this study was carried out as a portion of the work done under a J.D. and C.T. MacArthur Foundation grant.

Tomiichi Murayama became prime minister in June 1994 in a coalition government, have totally altered Japan's stance on international peacekeeping.

Members of Japan's SDF have now been successfully deployed with UN peacekeeping missions in Cambodia, Mozambique, Zaire, and most recently in the Golan Heights. Asian countries that had expressed qualms and reservations about Japan's participation beforehand now evidently accept it. All of these deployments have so far been under the provisions of Chapter 6 of the UN Charter, which excludes participation in combat. The 1992 legislation, however, permits eventual expansion of Japan's participation, if the Japanese parliament approves the extension.

This article reviews the history of these developments, and particularly the events that have taken place since 1990. It then assesses the desirability and potential benefits that may result from the participation of Japanese military forces in UN peacekeeping operations, as well as the fears that have been expressed to the effect that such expansion of the roles of the SDF could ultimately lead to a resurgence of Japanese "militarism." Finally, the article discusses in some detail the major source of reservation regarding the future conduct of Japanese governments once the threshold of SDF service beyond Japan's shores has been crossed.

Introduction

In September 1992, Japanese military forces were for the first time committed to participation in a United Nations peacekeeping mission, the United Nations Transitional Authority in Cambodia (UNTAC). This occurred under new Japanese legislation enacted in June 1992. It was followed by other short-term deployments with UN contingents: in Mozambique in May 1993; in Zaire in 1994; and most recently with UN peacekeeping forces on the Golan Heights in 1996. In September 1994, the Japanese Socialist Party (JSP) reversed decades-old policies, accepting all that they had before opposed in regard to the Japanese Self Defense Forces (SDF), including its constitutionality and legitimacy. However, the constitutional question has always been a proxy for less symbolic and more basic issues:

How can the Japanese public and political leadership guard against a resurgence of "militarism"—the enlargement of forces and the accretion of political influence that would permit the use of the Japanese military for aggressive purposes?

Has the discussion of this question been realistic? Could the growth and use of military power any longer take place without the approval and direction of the government? Does any incremental step toward the involvement and integration of the Japanese military in international collaborative activities, such as UN peacekeeping, mean the start of unavoidable and inevitable military independence, and the loss of control over the military by Japanese civil society and government? What would be the most desirable policies to follow so that the Japanese military behaved in accordance with international norms for the indefinite future? After fifty years of isolation, is the most likely deterrent against future misbehavior the SDF's integration with Asian and other militaries; or should attempts to maintain that total isolation continue indefinitely? Does the thoroughgoing and heretofore essentially absent Japanese national understanding of the practices of its armies in Asia between 1931 and 1945 place an added burden on these questions?

This paper reviews the record of the proposals, over many decades, for Japanese participation in UN peacekeeping operations; its evolution under the pressure of the Gulf War in 1990-1991; and from then to the present. Japanese legislation presently permits SDF forces to participate in UN missions authorized by the United Nations Security Council under the provisions of Chapter 6 of the UN Charter. The paper then examines whether that should be extended to UN or other international coalition operations authorized or delegated under Chapter 7 of the UN Charter—that is, permitting Japanese forces to engage in combat. It also speculates on the nature of the positions that Japanese policymakers might take when military actions are debated in the UN Security Council, if Japan were to gain a permanent seat on the Council.

History

A Framework for SDF Activity

The first discussion of Japanese participation in UN peacekeeping forces took place as early as 1946, when the Imperial Diet debated what came to be called "the pacifist clauses" of the draft constitution.[1] With the U.S. military occupation just begun and Japan not yet a member of the UN, the issue was considered much too abstract and irrelevant to the prevailing circumstances. When the constitution, drafted by American Occupation officials, was ratified in 1947, Article 9, the basis of so much contention for the next 45 years, stated:

> Aspiring sincerely to an international peace based on justice and order, the Japanese people forever renounce war as a sovereign right of the nation and the threat or use of force as a means of settling international disputes. In order to accomplish the aim of the preceding paragraph, land, sea, and air forces, as well as other war potential, will never be maintained. The right of belligerency of the state will not be recognized.

The Japanese public was strongly opposed to any significant rearmament, and it was an extremely popular initiative. When North Korea invaded South Korea in June 1950, however, the U.S. government's idealism vanished and its position changed. A large portion of U.S. ground forces moved to Korea, and with the occupation still in force, a National Police Reserve of 75,000 men was organized in the summer of 1950. In August 1952, shortly after the 1951 peace treaty went into effect, the Reserve was upgraded to the National Safety Force, and in February 1954, the Japanese "Self Defense Forces" (SDF) were established.[2]

Since that time, Japan has had an army, navy, and air force, whatever they may be called. Japanese governments have successively reinterpreted Article 9, first to permit the establishment of the SDF, and in successive decades to sanction defense cooperation with the United States under the U.S.-Japan Mutual Security Treaty as well as in other ways. In fact, during the Korean War, Japan—then still under U.S. military occupation—sent minesweepers to operate off the Korean coast to assist UN forces in response to a request from the United States. The ships were technically part of the Japanese coast guard: The deployment was made secretly, and even incurred casualties.[3] At present Japan's military expenditure is the fourth highest in the world, and the three branches of the SDF—ground, sea, and air—are among the world's best trained and equipped military forces.[4]

The 1954 SDF legislation was accompanied, however, by a resolution in the House of Councilors (Japan's upper legislative house) stipulating that the SDF could not be sent overseas to any other country. The major motive behind this resolution was reportedly not to counter the possibility of sending troops abroad for UN missions, but to prohibit any attempt to send troops outside the country for collective self-defense purposes under U.S.-Japan security arrangements. Although the Mutual Security Treaty became the bedrock of Japanese national-security policy, Japan was forbidden to participate in other collective-security arrangements. Defense cooperation was limited to that with the United States. The SDF could be used only for the defense of Japan against an armed attack on Japanese territory.

Basic contradictions inherent in the existence of Japanese military forces, the country's nominal obligation to UN peacekeeping as a member-state, Japan's national legislation, and the direct utilization of Japanese military forces in UN peacekeeping, were all explicitly joined in the mid- and late 1950s. They would not be resolved, however, until the early 1990s. The very first statement of "Basic Policies for National Defense," adopted by the Japanese National Defense Council and the Cabinet on May 20, 1957, had as its initial principle: "To support the activities of the United Nations, and promote international cooperation, thereby contributing to the realization of world peace"; while the fourth and last principles read: "To deal with external aggression on the basis of the Japan-U.S. security arrangements pending more effective functioning of the United Nations in future in deterring and repelling such aggression."[5] The conundrum was established immediately: How could Japan cooperate with the United Nations to maintain international peace and security if it did not participate in UN peacekeeping operations?

Before Japan was accepted as a member of the United Nations in 1956, debates took place in the Diet regarding the constitutionality of Japan's participation in a UN force when

Japan did become a UN member:

> The government answered that Article 43 of the Charter could be interpreted to suggest various possible ways of contributing to UN activities, the exact nature of which would be determined by "a special agreement or agreements" to be concluded between the member state and the Security Council. Thus, Japan's constitution would not necessarily be an obstacle to Japanese membership in the United Nations. Japan's application for UN membership accordingly included a statement that Japan would fulfill all obligations of a UN member "by all means at its disposal." Since no such "special agreements" have been made in the entire history of the United Nations, this question was a highly hypothetical and theoretical one.[6]

Testing the Limits

All the abstract discussion was tested almost immediately, however, and continued to be tested for the next twenty years. In July 1958, then UN Secretary General Dag Hammarskjold asked the Japanese government to send officers of the SDF to participate in the UN Observer Group in Lebanon. The Japanese government turned his request down on the argument that the mission might violate existing laws, if not the constitution. Hammarskjold didn't wait long to repeat his request for Japanese participation, which he did in February 1961, during the Congo crisis. The Japanese ambassador to the United Nations at the time supported his request. Notably, the UN operation in the Congo was authorized under Chapter 7 of the Charter, and involved combat:

> In early 1961, the statement by Japan's then Ambassador to the United Nations aroused a controversy; Ambassador Koto Matsudaira was reported to have stated that he was in trouble when Japan refused Mr. Hammarskjold's request and that "it is not consistent for Japan to adhere to UN cooperation on the one hand and to refuse all participation in the UN armies." The opposition parties demanded Ambassador Matsudaira's resignation. In the end, Mr. Matsudaira withdrew his statement. In response to criticisms by the opposition parties, the Director General of the Cabinet Legislation Bureau, Shuzo Hayashi, summarized the position of the government in the Diet in 1961. He said: "If the UN police activities are conducted in an ideal form, in other words, when a country that disrupted order within the UN system is to be punished, or in the case of establishing a police corps to maintain order, and

> if a unitary force under the United Nations is created with the participation of personnel dispatched by member states, then [Japan's participation in such a force] would not be an act of a sovereign nation. Also there is the possibility of a peaceful police force which does not conduct military activities. These possibilities would not pose problems relating to the First Clause of Article 9."[7]

This was meant to establish the framework of government policy.

In 1968, U.S. ambassador to the United Nations George Ball raised the issue again in Tokyo, remarking that "the UN's ability to send observers and armed contingents on peace-keeping missions to the world's danger spots would be vital to future peace." But Chief Cabinet Secretary Toshio Kimura responded by ruling out the possibility of contributing Japanese SDF forces to UN peacekeeping missions. "Our constitution does not allow it," he said, "but Japan might consider sending civilian personnel should a request for such a contribution be made."[8] The Japanese government also rejected a U.S. request to send minesweepers to Southeast Asian waters during the Vietnam War (an operation that bore no relation to UN peacekeeping efforts). Nevertheless, the idea of SDF peacekeeping participation apparently percolated at some level within the Japanese Foreign Ministry bureaucracy in the mid-1960's. In June 1992, during the debate on the UN PKO bill, a Japanese Foreign Ministry spokesman claimed that the initiative "has been a long-standing age-old proposal, particularly on the part of the Ministry of Foreign Affairs. It has been put forward on the table of national discussions since some 20 to 30 years ago."[9]

In 1977, the Nomura Research Institute prepared a study on the future of Japanese national-security policies under a commission from the Japanese government and with the participation of senior Japanese government officials, including Takuya Kubo, then Director General of Japan's National Defense Council. One of its recommendations was that Japan should consider sending its troops abroad for the first time since World War II in the context of United Nations peacekeeping efforts.[10] In 1980, the official government position of Prime Minister Zenko Suzuki's cabinet nevertheless continued to hold the issue at arm's length:

> It is impossible to discuss the right or wrong of Japan's participation in a UN force in general because the so-called UN forces have

> different objectives and missions. If the objectives and missions of the UN force in question include the use of force, we believe that the constitution does not allow the participation of the SDF in it. On the other hand, if their objectives and missions do not include the use of force, the constitution does not prohibit the participation of the SDF. But because the current SDF law does not give such a mission to the SDF, the SDF is not allowed to participate in it.[11]

In 1983, a second group of Japanese specialists in international law and international politics urged the Japanese government to consider the possibility of participating in UN peacekeeping operations that did not involve the use of force.[12] Neither of these recommendations had any discernible effects on policy. When Prime Minister Yasuhiro Nakasone suggested in 1987 that Japan should send minesweepers to the Persian Gulf during the Western naval operations to protect Kuwaiti oil tankers, the suggestion was turned aside both by the opposition parties and by Nakasone's own Chief Cabinet Secretary. No action was taken.

The 1980s, however, brought changes of several sorts. In 1981, the government established a sea-lane defense perimeter 1,000 miles out from the Japanese coastline. The concept had been developed years earlier in the Maritime SDF and accepted by the Japan Defense Agency (JDA) by the late 1970s. The SDF's battle plans were revised from repelling an invasion at the beachhead to meeting it out at sea. This greatly expanded the Japanese Navy's area of operations. In September 1987, Japanese legislation authorizing the dispatch of Japanese Disaster Relief Teams entered into force. In May 1988, the government of Prime Minister Noboru Takeshita proposed the concept of "three pillars of international cooperation," consisting of cooperation for peace, promotion of international cultural exchange, and an increase in official development assistance (ODA). According to Takeshita, "cooperation for peace" included "positive participation in diplomatic efforts, the dispatch of necessary personnel and the provision of financial cooperation, aiming at the resolution of regional conflicts."[13]

In 1988, Japan sent one civilian to the UN Good Offices Mission in Afghanistan and Pakistan, and another civilian to the UN Iran-Iraq Military Observer Group. In February 1990, Japan assigned thirty-one civilian observers to join in monitoring the Nicaraguan elections. In 1989, exchanges of military students between Japan and several Asian states also began. But most indicative was a statement to the Diet, in November 1989, by Juro Matsumoto, the Director General of the Japan Defense Agency. He announced he was "considering authorizing the use of troops for anti-terrorist operations, protecting Japanese nationals overseas and in international peacekeeping activities." Prime Minister Toshiko Kaifu had made a similar speech to the Diet in October 1989, saying that the government wanted to "begin studying" such a step, which (as the *Far Eastern Economic Review* commented) was "the standard Japanese approach towards implementing a sensitive policy."[14]

1990: The Gulf War and Its Effects

After 1990, a combination of pressures brought about by the Gulf War, the upsurge in UN peacekeeping in the early 1990s, and the total abandonment by the JSP of positions that it had maintained for decades—once it had joined a governing coalition—altered everything in a few brief years:

> Throughout the seven months bounded by Iraq's invasion of Kuwait on August 2, 1990, and the U.S.-led defeat of Iraq in February 1991, Japanese political and intellectual life was convulsed by an intense debate over the nation's appropriate role in the crisis... Japan entered a seven-month ordeal of tepid measures, false starts, and arcane debate that did little to enhance its image as a major power.[15]

That debate centered on the constitutionality of various proposals relating to Article 9 of the 1947 constitution. Externally, Japan was severely criticized for the fact that its contribution to the allied effort was restricted to financial support and was not very forthcoming. Seventy percent of Japan's oil comes from the Middle East, and in 1980, at the onset of the Iran-Iraq War, a Japanese minister had called on the U.S. Navy to maintain the freedom of oil supplies to Japan from the Gulf. Following Iraq's invasion of Kuwait, the U.S. government called on its allies to contribute to the multinational effort in any possible form. Prime Minister Kaifu's government first pledged $100 million, and in a few days raised that to $4 billion. A United Nations Peace Cooperation Bill was first drafted, largely by the Ministry of Foreign

Affairs, in August and September 1990. It proposed sending a 1,000-member "peace cooperation team" to the Gulf, composed of a mix of civilians and unarmed SDF personnel, to perform non-combat support roles.[16]

Public opinion was closely monitored by the Japanese press for the next two years. At the time of submission of the Peace Cooperation Bill in October 1990, public opinion was about evenly split; by November polls indicated that 78.7 percent of the public opposed the bill's passage. The Cabinet Legislation Bureau, composed of legal experts, expressed doubt in October 1990 whether the inclusion of SDF personnel in the bill's provisions was constitutional. The governing Liberal Democratic Party (LDP) was split on the issue, with important factions opposing the bill's passage, while Prime Minister Kaifu was himself continually hesitant and personally against SDF participation in UN peacekeeping. Despite the lobbying of U.S. Ambassador Michael Armacost for a Japanese contribution of personnel, the government decided to let the bill die without its coming to a vote.

Following the attack on Iraq in January 1991, and the continuing stream of U.S. criticism, the Ministry of Finance responded by suggesting an increase in Japan's financial pledge to $9 billion. With the government announcement, the Defense Agency prepared a new version of the proposed legislation. Japan's financial contribution eventually totalled $13 billion. Several delegations of LDP Diet members, together with those from the two minority opposition parties, visited UN peacekeeping operations worldwide. By the spring of 1991, the LDP and the two minority parties had come around to the position that contributing Japanese civilian personnel to a multinational force, or SDF personnel for nonmilitary activities, would not violate Article 9 of the constitution. Soon after, Prime Minister Kaifu announced that he would dispatch SDF transport aircraft to help in returning Asian refugee workers from Iraq to their home countries. But when opposition to this suggestion developed, he never issued the authorization.

In April 1991, however, following the German government's decision to participate in minesweeping operations in the Gulf following the war's end, and additional urging by the United States and some Arab coalition partners, Prime Minster Kaifu utilized a paragraph in the SDF legislation that permitted him to interpret the ocean mining in the Persian Gulf as a hazard to Japanese shipping. He was thus able to send four Maritime Self Defense Force minesweepers and two support vessels to the Gulf on April 24, 1991.[17] By this time public opinion had already begun to shift on the issues, and the deployment was received favorably both domestically and internationally. Seventy-five percent of the Japanese population supported the decision to deploy the ships on the day that the minesweepers sailed, an extraordinary shift of fifty percent of the polling population between November 1990 and April 1991. One observer also noted the route that the ships took, and found this as significant as the deployment decision: The Japanese flotilla made its way slowly, taking a month to reach the Gulf, and making stops on the way in the Philippines, Singapore, and Malaysia, just as Prime Minister Kaifu was touring the capitals of the Association of Southeast Asia Nations (ASEAN).[18] The ships received a warmer welcome than Tokyo had anticipated. The South Korean foreign minister, however, expressed dissatisfaction with these developments.[19]

On June 6, 1991, the LDP convened a "Special Study Group on Japan's Role in the International Community." It was chaired by LDP General Secretary Ichiro Ozawa, and referred to as the "Ozawa Commission." Ozawa was the most vocal member of the LDP wing that supported SDF participation in Gulf War operations. The Commission's report was not released until February 20, 1992, but its conclusions were publicly known by November 1991: It recommended Japanese participation in UN peacekeeping operations.[20] However, well before this, on September 19, 1991, the Kaifu government had submitted a new "Peacekeeping Battalion" bill to the Japanese parliament. It in fact abrogated a formal agreement, signed by the LDP with Komeito and the Democratic Socialist Party (DSP) in November 1990, that had called for the creation of a separate organization composed of civilian volunteers distinct from the SDF to be used for Japanese peacekeeping participation.[21] By September 1991, all three of these parties supported the new legislative proposal, and the LDP cabinet was united in its support. Aside from the JSP and the communist party (JCP), public and party opinions had shifted sharply as a consequence of the Gulf War. In the words of a Komeito party spokesman:

> There has been a national change of mind in this country. The Gulf War had a strong impact. We watched the war on TV, with newscasters and scholars and pundits talking about what Japan's role in the world ought to be. And the new consensus that emerged is that our strong anti-war pacifism is still there. But, beyond that, shouldn't Japan have some role in helping the UN preserve peace?.... How can our country lock itself out of the world and sit here behind the closed door of anti-war pacifism?[22]

The new legislation authorized the deployment of up to 2,000 SDF personnel to carry out noncombat tasks such as refugee relief, construction, transport, medical care and clearing ocean mines—but only as part of authorized UN peacekeeping missions, and only with a ceasefire in place. Government legal advisers now found that the legislation did not violate Article 9 of the constitution. The JSP and the JCP nevertheless remained adamantly opposed to overseas deployment of Japanese forces under any circumstances. These parties also argued that Japan's financial contributions toward the costs of the war against Iraq violated the Japanese constitution as well.

New Pressures: The United Nations and Cambodia

The Lower House of the Diet approved the peacekeeping bill on December 3, 1991. It then went to the Upper House, where the opposition parties controlled a majority. During this period, Japanese diplomats carried messages to China, South Korea, and the ASEAN states saying that a Japanese role in peacekeeping operations would not lead to a rearmed Japan.[23] Discussions between Foreign Minister Taro Nakayama and his Chinese and South Korean counterparts at a UN Security Council meeting in September drew apprehensive responses, but exceedingly mild ones. In January 1992, UN Secretary General Boutros Boutros-Ghali urged Japan to join in peacekeeping operations, asking for "even a small number" of personnel. In return, the Japanese foreign minister asked for a permanent seat on the UN Security Council, and the deletion of two clauses in the UN Charter that list Japan and Germany as "enemy nations." In September, Nakayama had asked the same at the UN, and strenuously and successfully lobbied to obtain an unprecedented seventh two-year term on the UN Security Council for the rotating seat representing Asia. Japan also successfully campaigned for the appointment of Yasushi Akashi, the most senior Japanese serving in the UN Secretariat, to become the Secretary General's Special Representative in Cambodia and to head UNTAC.[24] Once appointed, Akashi urged Tokyo to support UNTAC both financially and with personnel, specifically mentioning police forces.[25] In January, Cambodia's Norodom Sihanouk also asked the chairman of the JSP, who was visiting Cambodia, "to send Japanese troops to help clear mines and restore peace."[26]

Of greater significance was a trip by Cambodian Premier Hun Sen to Tokyo in March 1992, arranged by the Japanese Foreign Ministry. He urged passage of the peacekeeping legislation in a series of meetings with the prime minister, foreign minister, cabinet secretaries, and the heads of the DSP and Komeito parties, and specifically asked that Japanese SDF forces participate in the UNTAC:

> More than 20 nations have already decided to dispatch their troops for United Nations peacekeeping operations in Cambodia. Why doesn't Japan decide to dispatch its troops? We hope that the political parties will coordinate their views in order to make it possible to dispatch Self-Defense Forces to Cambodia. Japan should play a political role commensurate with its economic status. It is known that Japan hesitates to dispatch Self-Defense Forces troops abroad because of its remorse over the nation's acts in the past. But such an attitude is behind the times.[27]

Hun Sen's visit was considered an important stimulus to the ultimate passage of the legislation.

The issue of the participation of Japanese military forces in UN peacekeeping operations continued as one of the major political issues in Japan in 1992, and through the summer of 1993. After months of debate, a bill was finally passed on June 15, 1992. It contained additional constraints that had been required to gain the approval of the Komeito and Democratic Socialist parties, without whose votes the bill could not have passed (See the appendix for details of the bill). All missions involving direct peacekeeping duties, such as monitoring a ceasefire or collecting weapons, would be postponed—"frozen"

—for an indefinite period, and no less than three years. An additional act of parliament would be necessary to end the freeze, and each subsequent deployment would have to be approved by parliament. Participation in "peacemaking" operations or any direct military action under UN Security Council resolution, such as the war against Iraq, was still out of the question. Prime Minister Miyazawa stated that such activities clearly violated Japanese constitutional provisions.[28]

Japanese public opinion was nearly divided just prior to the bill's passage, although the numbers had been significantly inverted: 42 percent favored SDF participation in UN peacekeeping, while 37 percent were opposed.[29] China and South Korea expressed public displeasure.[30] Opposition at home and abroad arose out of the fear of a "toe in the door." In the words of a Chinese official, "What we are worried about is not the present but the future. The fear is that the [peacekeeping troop dispatch] law is a start in a bad direction."[31]

In the judgment of Philip Trezise, however, the two years of debate indicated just the opposite:

> the process by which Japan made its decision confirmed that its acquired aversion to militarism continues to be, after nearly fifty years, a domestic political force.... Realistically, what the affair tells us is that Japan remains addicted to the view that a military renascence would be a bad idea. If the step toward participation in international peacekeeping has been tentative, that is what the political situation allowed.[32]

The government had also submitted an amendment to the International Relief Force Bill at the same time as the PKO legislation was submitted to the Diet. The amendment provided for the inclusion of SDF forces as participants in any Japanese relief force to be dispatched overseas at the request of another state. It encountered little objection and was passed.[33] Six weeks later, the LDP won a large majority in the parliamentary elections for the Upper House of the Diet; the JSP, which had opposed the PKO bill, suffered the greatest losses.[34]

Only two days after passage of the PKO bill, the UN Secretary General's report, *An Agenda for Peace,* was published. It had been nearly a year in preparation, and was produced in response to a request from the heads of state of the "Group of Seven." The report appeared at the height of the post-1990 expansion of UN peacekeeping missions. Most crucially, it suggested the expanded application of peace enforcement operations under Chapter 7 sanction, in effect, reverting to the full scope of options available under the original UN Charter. Coming immediately after the climax of two years of Japanese domestic political struggles, the idea of "peace enforcement units" reportedly did not excite Prime Minister Miyazawa. When Japanese Foreign Minister Watanabe addressed the full UN General Assembly in September 1992, he said:

> Japan believes that the principles and practices of peacekeeping operations upheld by the United Nations for more than 40 years are still both appropriate and valid today and will continue to be so in the future. The idea of "peace-enforcement units," proposed by the Secretary General's report, offers an interesting approach to future peace-making efforts of the United Nations, but requires further study because it is rooted in a mode of thinking completely different from past peacekeeping forces.[35]

Nevertheless, the next development was swift, following only two or three weeks after the Diet's passage of the PKO bill. On July 1, 1992, the first Japanese "fact-finding mission for international peace cooperation" left for Cambodia. On August 11, Tokyo announced that it was officially beginning preparations for an SDF deployment, and a second fact-finding mission left on the same day. The United Nations made an official request on September 3 for a Japanese contribution of personnel to serve in UNTAC, and in late September and early October the first Japanese military engineering units arrived in Cambodia.[36] Three hundred Japanese journalists were on hand when the first 200 SDF personnel landed.[37]

Six months after the passage of the peacekeeping legislation, LDP leaders decided to initiate a process that at the time might have been expected to take years to complete, but may now be bypassed entirely due to subsequent changes in the position of the JSP on the constitutionality of the SDF. They suggested amending Article 9 of the Japanese constitution to permit participation of Japanese forces in UN peacekeeping, and they proposed establishing a commission to consider the question. They also called for the "unfreezing" of the restricted portions of the

1992 legislation, but also, and avoidably, the procurement of long-range transport aircraft and ships to move Japanese forces to peacekeeping missions.[38]

In February 1993, Boutros-Ghali unceremoniously jumped into the Japanese domestic debate, apparently with little care or preparation. In advance of a trip to Japan, he suggested that Japan should change its constitution to permit it to join peacekeeping operations, adding that such an amendment would "facilitate" Japan's "greater political role in the UN."[39] He thus joined the peacekeeping deployment issue and Japan's effort to obtain a permanent UN Security Council seat. Once in Japan, however, he felt compelled to withdraw the suggestion for constitutional change. He requested Japanese troop participation in UN forces serving in Somalia, then withdrew that idea, too, and replaced it with the suggestion that a Japanese deployment to Mozambique would be more suitable, since "there is a solid ceasefire agreement and operations are under way for rehabilitation of refugees." He also expressed the hope that Japanese forces could serve in UN missions in Latin America as well as in Africa.[40] There had been reports that at least some of the SDF military leadership and LDP "hawks" were interested in deploying personnel to both Somalia and Mozambique, but that was ruled out by both Miyazawa and the Japanese defense minister even before Boutros-Ghali made the request public.[41]

Around 1,200 SDF personnel were deployed to Cambodia overall. The mission went well, closely monitored by numerous Diet members, and with "enormous effort to micromanage Japanese involvement." Despite some calls for Tokyo to withdraw the SDF after several Japanese nonmilitary personnel serving in UNTAC were killed by Khmer Rouge ambushes, the government did not do so.[42] For a time the Japanese Foreign Ministry examined the question of cooperation with Indonesia, Thailand, and the Philippines in aiding the resettlement of Cambodian refugees, but such cooperation did not take place. The Philippine government, however, did ask the Japanese government to help transport the equipment for its forces in Cambodia from the Philippines, and Japan complied.[43]

Subsequent Developments: In Japan and Abroad

Between May 1993 and January 1995, Japan contributed 155 SDF personnel to the UN peacekeeping mission in Mozambique (ONUMOZ), for duty as staff officers and in logistics units.[44] The decision to send an SDF contingent to Mozambique was made in March 1993, and occasioned little controversy. Nevertheless, in December 1993, the head of the Japan Defense Agency (a member of the Japan Renewal Party, which favors constitutional revision) was forced to resign for commenting to party colleagues that "Japan should change its constitution to allow the Self Defense Forces to join more global peacekeeping missions."[45]

In June 1994, Tomiichi Murayama, chairman of the former JSP—now known in English as the Social Democratic Party of Japan (SDPJ)—became prime minister in a coalition government. For decades the JSP had denounced the SDF as unconstitutional, and called for the abrogation of the Mutual Security Treaty. It had also consistently opposed the peacekeeping legislation and SDF participation in UN peacekeeping operations. Even after becoming part of the ruling coalition under Prime Minister Morihiro Hosokawa in August 1993, the SDPJ had strongly objected to sending SDF troops overseas, even in a non-military capacity.

Within days of taking office, Murayama announced that his government would "firmly maintain" the security treaty. It was the precise phrase that the Socialists had not permitted to be used in the preceding coalition government of Prime Minister Tsutomu Hata, in which they had also served.[46] Furthermore, the SDPJ accepted the constitutionality of the SDF. Just over 60 percent of the SDPJ's membership approved of the new positions, and the party platform was reversed in an extraordinary convention early in September.[47] In the same week, the report of an SDPJ study group on future security policy was released. It stated that Japan needed a new basic law on national security to reconcile the constitution and the existence of the SDF. Regarding Japan and peacekeeping participation, the study group "suggested that if the SDF is to participate, a special unit should be set aside for that purpose. If a non-SDF organization is to play this role, it should be allowed to take part in military activities allowed under the framework of Japan's UN peacekeeping cooperation law."[48]

The first outcome of this policy reversal was the deployment of 401 SDF personnel to provide air transport and public health services in Zaire following the Rwandan genocide. This time it was Sadako Ogata, the United Nations High Commissioner for Refugees and the highest-ranking Japanese international civil servant, who appealed directly to Prime Minister Murayama specifically to send an SDF contingent to Zaire.[49] The PKO legislation allowed the SDF to perform humanitarian missions without Diet approval, since only peacekeeping missions required Diet approval. The SDF deployment to Zaire was the first under the humanitarian relief provisions of the PKO legislation. An SDPJ spokesman said: "Although we don't like the [peacekeeping operation] law, we should not oppose it forever. It is our job to improve it or to check to make sure the law is not abused."[50]

Toward the end of 1994, a major report produced by a national Advisory Group on Defense Issues, established some 18 months before by Prime Minister Hosokawa, was released. Its position on Japan, the SDF, and participation in UN peacekeeping was so strong as to begin with some degree of misstatement: "Japan enacted the International Peace Cooperation Law in 1992, thus making its stand clear in favor of full-scale involvement in UN peacekeeping operations, including participation of the SDF." This was not quite the case, since the PKO legislation proscribed participation in UN operations under Chapter 7 of the Charter, and permitted only those under Chapter 6. But the report was considered rather important, since it was the first in two decades commissioned by the government as a whole on defense issues. It continued as follows in regard to the SDF and UN peacekeeping:

> the fact is that the content and concept of UN peacekeeping operations are being forced to adapt to the new environment and undergo repeated experiments. There is no doubt that the United Nations is finally beginning to move in the direction of a United Nations as it should be.... Seen in this light, it should be emphasized anew that one of the major pillars of Japan's security policy is to contribute positively to strengthening the UN functions for international peace, including further improvement of peacekeeping operations. Furthermore, such contribution is important in the sense that Japan's firm commit[ment] to such an international

trend regarding security problems will strengthen its role befitting its international position.

In order that the SDF "participate as positively as possible" in all manner of UN international security activities, the report called for revision of peacekeeping legislation to provide for:

> use of SDF facilities for such purposes as training centers and advance depots for materials and equipment for peacekeeping operations, and supply by Japan of equipment necessary for peacekeeping operations conducted by other nations also merit positive consideration.... Peacekeeping operations, which are currently attracting the particular attention as a role of the United Nations, require in some cases that weapons be used to a certain extent. In view of the purposes of the United Nations already described, however, it is natural that such use of arms should be permitted. From this viewpoint, we believe that government should make efforts to obtain public understanding at home and abroad with regard to the mode of SDF participation.

The report concluded on a forceful refrain: "There is a view in some quarters that organizations other than the SDF should be dispatched to engage in peacekeeping operations. If this view is intended to evade constitutional questions, it is meaningless."[51]

The Advisory Group's report had undoubted influence on the content of the new defense policy promulgated by the Murayama administration, and announced in November 1995. It was the first major revision of Japanese defense policy since the National Defense Program Outline of 1976. It had two striking and contrasting components:

- Japanese defense forces would be cut across the board: ground, naval, and air forces. The cuts were substantial, both in manpower and in ships, tanks, and aircraft. Cuts in defense expenditure had begun as early as 1990, and the rate of growth of military expenditure was further reduced in 1994 and 1995. Now it would be cut further to produce an actual decrease when inflation rates were accounted for.
- In contrast, missions of the SDF would be increased, to include "duties beyond defense of the country, to allow them to deal with a wider range of situations, including disasters, terrorism, and peacekeeping operations."[52]

While it was suggested that "the cuts in the Japanese military may irritate the Americans, the changes are likely to reassure South and North Korea and other Asian countries that remain nervous about Japanese military intentions."[53]

Broader regional security cooperation is apparently on the agenda too. One of the more interesting developments was a report that "Japan is consulting with China about cooperation in United Nations peacekeeping operations as part of confidence building measures between the two countries." Japan had reportedly asked China to discuss "joint training and participation in UN peacekeeping activities. The Chinese government had not yet responded...."[54] Writing in December 1995, the Director of Japanese Studies at the South Korean Institute for Defense Analyses, Young-sun Song, published an article in a Japanese publication proposing South Korean-Japanese collaboration in UN peacekeeping operations. She envisaged broader forms of cooperation as theoretically possible, but for the moment suggested limiting collaboration to the kinds of operations that Japan performed for UNTAC in Cambodia. Song also expressed support for the establishment, by Japan and in Japan, of a regional multinational peacekeeping training center. She believes that it would be most feasible for South Korea and Japan to collaborate in peacekeeping operations if other Asian nations participate in the same missions. Such an idea could be discussed in the ASEAN Regional Forum, which does not have its own peacekeeping force.[55] There have also been recent suggestions by LDP officials for SDF participation in an all-Asian force, as well as in joint military exercises and personnel exchanges with Asian armed forces.[56] Conceivably, these activities could also include collaboration with Australia and New Zealand.

Discussion in the summer of 1995 centered on whether or not to send a Japanese SDF contingent to the Middle East to join a UN observer force on the Golan Heights. The result was the dispatch of a unit of 45 armed Japanese troops in February 1996, the first Japanese forces to serve in a full peacekeeping role, though only in a logistics unit.[57] Beyond these missions—Cambodia, Mozambique, Rwanda, Zaire, and the Golan Heights—Japan has not offered SDF personnel to the UN for any other peacekeeping operations. It has provided financial aid for humanitarian programs in the former Yugoslavia since 1992, and will be contributing additional funds, just as many other nations do, through its assessed peacekeeping contributions.[58] Currently, Japan's assessment is 13.95 percent of the regular UN budget and 14.01 percent of the peacekeeping budget.[59]

So far there has been only one troubling note. The suggestion by Japanese government and military sources, in January 1993, that new long-range transport aircraft and ships should be procured to move SDF forces to peacekeeping missions was patently unnecessary. Such systems could be seen as giving Japanese forces greater potential long-range offensive capability, precisely the kind of indicator that opponents of extending the missions of the SDF beyond Japanese borders fear.[60] There are no apparent difficulties at present in moving Japanese peacekeeping contributions by Japanese commercial carriers. The numbers of personnel and the size of the logistics train for the Japanese units have so far been quite limited. The Japanese sealift and airlift for its SDF deployment to Cambodia, the largest of the deployments to date, was carried out by a mix of commercial and military assets, without any significant problems. In addition, transport could be provided by other nations, in the same way that the peacekeeping contingents of military services in countries that do not have their own long-range transport are moved to the areas in which they are to serve.

In short, there is no need for Japan to acquire longer-range hardware in order to participate in UN peacekeeping operations. It was clear that the Cambodian deployment was being used opportunistically. After Japan has been contributing to the UN peacekeeping missions to everyone's satisfaction for a decade or two, and if there is then an apparent need for long-range transport, the issue can be considered at that time.

The Pros and Cons of Japanese SDF Participation in International Peacekeeping

Japan and Germany

Writing early in 1992, before legislative or judicial decisions in Germany and Japan altered the status quo on the use of military forces, Durch and Blechman commented on the post-World War II effort to "demilitarize" the two societies:

> That effort has succeeded, perhaps beyond anyone's expectations at the time and, indeed, to such an extent that both countries' governments have a difficult time convincing legislators and publics that their military participation in even so clearly a multilateral, peace-oriented, and constructive endeavor as UN peacekeeping is a good idea. Evidently there are fears in those countries that sending military units to far away lands might reawaken some atavistic imperial urge or restimulate German or Japanese forces to dominate their societies.[61]

Remarks made by former Singapore Prime Minister Lee Kuan Yew in May 1991 were put more crudely: "allowing the Japanese to participate in military operations was like giving an alcoholic liquor chocolates ... the Japanese do not know when to stop."[62] Writing in 1992, Chalmers Johnson strongly emphasized that "the Japanese political system lacks a 'checking mechanism.' ... It must be understood that most Japanese equate Article 9 of the constitution with democracy itself; to alter one is to alter the other." He quoted a Japanese academic to the effect that Japan had not arrived "at a compatibility between an army and democratic principles. In that sense, we must call modern-day Japanese democracy incomplete.... Of course, the Self-Defense Forces are going to be viewed by other countries as a threat if they are sent abroad with this present structure still intact."[63]

On the other hand, international law specialists such as Richard Gardner and John Ruggie have argued that "Japan has, like every other signatory of the United Nations charter, a solemn obligation to negotiate an Article 43 agreement with the United Nations that puts fighting forces, not simply peacekeeping troops, at the disposal of the Security Council."[64]

Both Japan and Germany are among the handful of wealthy states in the world, and both have extremely well-armed and trained military forces. On the other hand, both states invaded and conquered numerous neighboring states during World War II, and carried out military operations thousands of miles from their shores. In the case of Japan, many of its World War II and pre-war victims have in the past expressed varying degrees of apprehension or opposition to the participation of Japanese troops in peacekeeping operations. If one is interested in the surest likelihood that the armed forces of Japan should never again manifest the behavior they did during and before World

War II, is that outcome more likely to be achieved if they participate in United Nations or other international coalition peacekeeping or combat operations, or if they do not? Which carries the greatest risk of the resumption of undesired behavior 25, 50, or 100 years hence?

The resolution of the "compatibility between an army and democratic principles," and the "completion" of "Japanese democracy," would seem to have taken place in September 1994, with the complete *volte face* of the JSP. It was the JSP that had insisted for forty years that the SDF was inconsistent with Article 9 of the constitution; their total reversal of position in 1994, and the additional approval of the 1992 PKO legislation by a JSDP prime minister, signalled that in the party's view the reinterpretation of Article 9 is no longer "altering democracy itself." The Socialists renounced their long held position that Japan should pursue a permanent policy of "unarmed neutrality" exactly two years after they had fiercely fought any compromise and the enactment of the PKO legislation. One might conclude that the nature of that resolution was more than a bit ironic—perhaps even cynical—and that the polarity of the previous positions was excessive, and overloaded with clichés.

In discussions with highly informed Japanese specialists who both oppose and favor the expansion of Japanese peacekeeping operations, it was virtually impossible to obtain a description of the circumstances that could once again lead, in contemporary Japan, to a rise of "militarism" culminating (as in the 1930s) in the abrogation of civilian government, or in the aggressive use of Japanese military force for imperial conquest. When these fears are expressed they have a highly abstract quality, referring always to what came about once before, rather than to present or future conditions.[65] If one compares the international as well as the regional circumstances in Asia that existed in the 1920s and 1930s with those that obtain now, they all differ drastically:

- a China no longer fragmented, dominated by civil war and regional warlords, but instead militarily and economically powerful;
- an independent, democratizing, and economically powerful South Korea, allied to the United States, and a militarily capable North Korea;

- a Southeast Asia that is independent, has governmental legitimacy, has capable armed forces, and is organized in a respected regional group (ASEAN);
- the total absence of legitimacy to any conception of imperial conquest, at present or in the future;
- a Japan allied with the United States;
- an effective United Nations, in contrast with a completely ineffectual League of Nations;
- Japan as the second largest economy in the world, which includes its successful peacetime economic penetration of the economies of Southeast Asian states.

All of these conditions, individually and combined, make the plausibility of external military aggression extremely low. Japan's existing territorial disputes with its immediate neighbors are proximate and limited: with Russia regarding the northern islands; with China regarding the Senkaku (Diaoyutai) islands; and with South Korea regarding Tok Do (Takeshima). The likelihood of Japan's use of military force to resolve any of these disputes seems equally low.

There are, however, major differences between Japan and Germany in assessing the desirability of the participation of their military forces in international peacekeeping, and one must consider to what degree those differences should determine the policies recommended for each country. For two overriding reasons, Germany's government and military forces have gained the confidence of its neighbors in a way that Japan has not, and doubts or fears of a resurgence of German "militarism" have essentially been overcome. The first reason is that for the past forty years, German military forces have been integrated into the NATO alliance with those of its neighbors and former victims. German military forces have exercised in joint maneuvers for decades. Training is internationalized and integrated. Senior German staff officers serve in, and are incorporated into, an international command structure. German political and defense decision makers operate in an international pan-European and Atlantic setting. All of these processes, *extending over decades,* have given European countries confidence in Germany's evolution, some degree of control over both its military and foreign-policy framework, and a reasonable certainty that Germany will not again commit aggression and engage in murderous destruction.

Nothing of the sort has happened in Japan. Japanese military forces were not integrated into any larger international grouping. Although close, the bilateral Japanese-American security relationship bears no comparison whatsoever to the integrated operational functioning of NATO: There is no joint command structure, no integrated combat units, no membership by nations that Japan had invaded in World War II, and no joint decision making on the use of nuclear munitions.

There is also no way to re-do the past 40 years now. There is no "Asian NATO" on the horizon. ASEAN does not even function in that manner for its member nations in Southeast Asia. Participation by Japanese SDF forces in UN and international peacekeeping is the only mechanism at hand to initiate some semblance of the processes that German military forces have undergone, intensively, for the past decades. It is for this reason that suggestions for joint peacekeeping operations between the Japanese SDF forces and those of other Asian states seem particularly desirable.

"Packaging" the SDF's Peacekeeping Missions

It is clear from the foregoing narrative that before 1990 there had been requests to the Japanese government by UN Secretaries General and U.S. officials, to contribute personnel for United Nations peacekeeping. But besides these crucial external pressures, there were also internal ones, as Aurelia George has remarked:

> Although external pressure was decisive in inducing thē Japanese government to deliver on the PKO proposal, it was also harnessed by internal forces eager to achieve the same objective. The domestic push not only came from the small group of defense nationalists centering on the LDP's so-called "defense tribe" (*kokubo zoku*) but extended to a broad cross section of policy elites within the Ministry of Foreign Affairs and the LDP executive leadership, and to opinion leaders outside government, all of whom had their own reasons for wishing to dispatch the SDF abroad on peacekeeping missions.[66]

It is important to add that the three largest political parties—the LDP, the JSP, and Komeito—each contained factions that favored

Japanese participation in UN peacekeeping, and factions that opposed it. During the Gulf War deliberations, and during the deployment to Cambodia, the government sought to control both the internal debate and all aspects of the SDF's activity. "[E]very task, request, or other order [pertaining to the SDF] had to be sent to Japan for clearance by government bodies."[67]

For the present, the major issue is not the long-range intentions of the senior military leadership in the SDF, but of the Foreign Ministry and various political groupings. As Aurelia George emphasizes, by "packaging" the SDF's mission abroad as an international contribution, the government neutralized its opponents. A "contribution" was not the real purpose, however:

> It is true that the Ozawa vision is a nationalist vision and that he and other nationalists like him wear the cloak of internationalism, but ultimately what Ozawa and others in the LDP want is for Japan to be able to "step up to the broad array of global responsibilities ordinarily borne by major nations." For them, UN peacekeeping is the vehicle on which Japan will ride to international rehabilitation and restoration as a fully functions global power accorded an honorable place in the international community. This ultimately includes the restoration of the SDF to the status of fully fledged armed forces.... Whatever form it ultimately takes, Japanese involvement in international peacekeeping will complement a more pro-active diplomacy and higher profile in international affairs, particularly in Asia.[68]

A Japanese observer essentially agreed:

> But the true intention of the government that I sensed through contacts with government leaders in charge of the drafting of the bill was different. What really motivated the government to enact the [peacekeeping] law was a desire to become a political power. Government leaders thought that unless Japan could dispatch troops abroad, it would not be taken seriously by the international community, nor would its desire to become a permanent member on the United Nations' Security Council be given any credence.[69]

One can say, perhaps, that the "wrong" people favor Japanese UN peacekeeping participation, and for the wrong reasons, and that the "right" people oppose it. The Japanese "internationalists" are not, unfortunately, internationalists. The Socialists, who one might in the abstract assume to fit the role of internationalists, have been opposed because of their opposition to the military, both in Japan and in Germany.

The Question of Japan's Responsibility in World War II

Unlike Germany and German society, in Japan there has been no thoroughgoing national assumption of responsibility for its aggression between 1931 and 1945, and for its particularly reprehensible practices in those years.[70] The utterances of "regret" and "apologies" offered by senior Japanese political figures, isolated and symbolic, at times following months and even years of bureaucratic and interparty wrangling over the choice of a single word, only demonstrate the inability to assume responsibility all the more. It is a continuous litany of embarrassment, down to the most recent instance of Prime Minister Murayama's "apology" in the fall of 1995.

Japanese behavior during World War II was unusually and extraordinarily vicious. Estimates of the number of people killed in the Pacific theater by Japanese forces vary, but are enormous: The estimates range between 10 and 17 million for China alone.[71] There were the notorious individual massacres in Nanjing, Singapore, and Manila; and the "Three-All" campaign ("Loot All, Kill All, Burn All") carried out in North China, where as many as 250,000 Chinese were killed in a single series of reprisals related to the inconsequential U.S. air raid on Tokyo in April 1942. The Japanese used biological warfare in China. Rape by Japanese forces was extremely widespread and common, and massive in some particular instances. Prisoners of war were mistreated and killed. Chinese civilians were tortured and used for bayonet practice.[72]

Whereas a German national weekly such as *Der Spiegel* has for roughly two decades run lengthy series regarding the Holocaust and German extermination camps, a Japanese film distributor in 1988 spent three months pressuring Bernardo Bertolucci to remove 40 seconds of documentary newsreel footage of Japanese military operations in China in 1937 from the film *The Last Emperor*. When Japanese film critics publicized the fact that the film distributor had removed the newsreel sequence without Bertolucci's authorization, the producer called it "a misunderstanding."[73] In July 1992, after years of denials, including those of Japanese prime ministers, the Japanese government admitted that its army had forced as many as 200,000 women in occupied countries—including some 100,000 Korean women—into forced prostitution to serve its military.[74] It took an additional year for the Japanese government to produce an apology, and another year before it would announce a compensation scheme, entitled "Peace, Friendship and Exchange Initiative."[75] Japanese wartime reparations have in fact amounted to about one-hundredth of the tens of billions of dollars in German postwar reparations.[76]

The "textbook controversy" has always been something of an epitome of the problem.[77] For nearly the entire post-World War II period, the Japanese Education Ministry has maintained a textbook censorship policy. From the 1950s to the early 1970s, "high school textbooks referred briefly to a war between Japan and the United States, but gave students no hint that Japan had invaded neighboring countries ... government policy was to avoid going into details about the events of the war."[78] The Nanjing "incident" could not be mentioned, even in a footnote. From 1973 on, mention was allowed, but not as a "massacre" or with estimates of the numbers of people killed. In 1982, the Education Ministry insisted that the word "advance" be used for the Japanese army's invasion of China, and not "aggression." An outcry from China and South Korea forced an eventual reversal. In 1986, the Education Ministry approved a text that described Japan's war in the Pacific as a "war of liberation"; in this case Japanese Foreign Ministry intervention caused a revision.

As late as 1992, an individual sentence in textbooks, "We must not forget that Japan *caused inconvenience* to neighboring Asian countries in the past," could be altered to, "We must not forget that Japan caused unbearable suffering to neighboring nations in the past." The change was only due to Prime Minister Kaifu's having used the words, "unbearable suffering," in a speech in Singapore in May 1991. A court case challenging the Ministry of Education's censorship dragged through the Japanese courts for 28 years, ending in 1993 when the Supreme Court upheld the government's position after taking seven years to come to its judgement. The book in question had been banned by the ministry even after the author had made more than 400 revisions at the ministry's demand. The government still held that the book "stepped over the bounds of appropriate discourse," and didn't show sufficient "restraint."[79] As a German author commented:

> Indeed, there is hardly any similarity in the way Japanese and West German textbooks treat their recent history. West German history textbooks take a comprehensive, analytical and clearly moralistic approach that tries to establish cause and effect and attribute responsibility. Japanese textbooks seem to do the opposite; things are always happening as if by coincidence or *force majeure*. Major events, even whole wars, are called "incidents." Facts are lined up without interrelating them, and their impact is softened by phrases such as "it is said that" or "it was reported that." Conclusions and assessments are avoided as much as possible, and there is a great reluctance to evaluate the behavior of individuals. History is presented as a flow of events to which the Japanese were exposed with little fault of their own. Some of these differences are due to cultural patterns in general, but others seem to be more deliberate.[80]

All of this official equivocating has been reflected at the highest level of successive LDP governments. It is clear that a substantial number of senior LDP political figures see nothing wrong with Japan's behavior between 1931 and 1945, though many of them have simply refrained from commenting publicly. These officials probably accept that, in the words of a Foreign Ministry spokesman, "we should be more prudent and cautious in talking about our actions in the past." In the eight years between 1986 and 1994, no less than four Japanese cabinet ministers were forced to resign for statements that were too embarrassingly unreconstructed; cabinet members before 1986, and others subsequently, escaped by forced "withdrawals" and retractions of their remarks.[81]

- In 1986, the Minister of Education, Masayuki Fujio, was dismissed after saying that the colonization of Korea was "legitimate," and that the 1937 Japanese massacre in Nanjing did not violate international law.
- In 1988, Seisuke Okuno was forced to resign after a series of statements to the effect that Japan's invasion of China was not a war of aggression. This, despite Prime Minister Nakasone's having twice stated it as the official position, and the Foreign Ministry's insistence that it was. Prime Minister Takeshita disavowed the remarks, but did not say that they were incorrect.

Forty-one LDP Diet members signed a statement supporting Okuno.

- In 1994, Justice Minister Shigeto Nagano (a former Chief of Staff of the Ground Self-Defense Forces) was forced to resign after declaring that accounts of the Japanese Army's massacre in Nanjing were "fiction." Prime Minister Hata said that it was "improper" for his Justice Minister to deny "history as it is." Nagano also criticized former Prime Minster Hosokawa for terming Japan's invasions in Asia as "a war of aggression," and repeated the standard rightist and nationalist claim that Japan was only "liberating Asian countries from Western colonial powers."
- In August 1994, Shin Sakurai, Minister for Environmental Affairs, was forced to resign after declaring that Japan's wartime Asian invasions actually benefitted Asia.
- In October 1994, Ryutaro Hashimoto, then Minister for International Trade and Industry, stated in the Diet "that it was a matter of delicate definition whether Japan had committed aggression against Asian neighbors during the war." Hashimoto for many years led the delegation of his LDP colleagues that made an annual visit to the Yasukuni shrine to honor Japan's World War II dead. He also headed the Association of Families of War Dead, an association affiliated with the shrine that opposes Japan's apologizing for its actions during the war.[82] He did not resign his ministerial post, and was not dismissed. In January 1996, Hashimoto became the prime minister.

Even a prime minister has had to retract his remarks. In February 1989, Noboru Takeshita commented that it was "up to historians" to determine whether Japan had been an aggressor in World War II. Government officials then explained the remark as "an oversight," the Prime Minister having "been taken by surprise during questioning in Parliament. He was not prepared."[83] After two weeks, Takeshita acknowledged what had already been official policy for several years: In his slight variation, Japan was guilty of "aggression by militarism."

In the past decade there has also been a series of prime ministerial apologies, and acknowledgements of "suffering" caused by Japan during the world war. Nevertheless, they have been attended by continual dispute, highlighted by forced ministerial resignations, and seem far less than a clear and thoroughgoing acceptance of responsibility. It is significant that the two most pronounced breaks with precedent were made by the first non-LDP prime minister, Hosokawa in 1993, and the socialist Murayama in 1995, and even these were a matter of symbolic utterance of a few contested words or phrases. In the mid-1980s, Prime Minister Nakasone stated on two occasions that Japan was the aggressor in China. In 1990, Prime Minister Kaifu apologized to South Korea for its colonization by Japan, and in May 1991, he added an apology to Asian countries for Japan's wartime behavior.[84] In August and September 1993, Prime Minister Hosokawa reportedly rejected bureaucratic and political advice to maintain the "more ambiguous statements of 'regret' favored by earlier Prime Ministers." He referred to Japan's World War II role as "our great mistake"—suggesting a rejection of the lingering notion that Japan's war role had been justified—and made a few additional modifications:

> I would like to take this opportunity to express our profound remorse and apologies for the fact that Japan's actions, including acts of aggression and colonial rule, caused unbearable suffering for so many people.[85]

The following year, Prime Minister Hata more or less repeated these remarks in attempting to undo the effects of contrary remarks by one of his cabinet ministers who was forced to resign.[86] However, Hosokawa was criticized by Ryutaro Hashimoto for labeling the entire war an aggression: "I can't think that the war with the United States, England, France, and Holland was aggression," Hashimoto wrote in his book, *Vision of Japan*, that was published in 1994.[87]

One should also note that throughout the postwar period, Japanese emperors have made no reference to World War II responsibilities. In fact, one historian contended that the emperors had obstructed serious national consideration of the issue:

> The Japanese Government used Emperor Hirohito's visits to the U.S. and Europe in the 1970's to help the country rejoin the West without seriously facing questions of responsibility for the past. His hollow declarations lamenting the "unfortunate past" inoculated Japan from further discussion of its war history. More recently, Emperor Akihito performed a similar function in strengthening relations with China and South Korea.[88]

In 1994, Emperor Akihito added no more than that he felt "grief for the millions who died or suffered during World War II." [89]

When JSDP leader Murayama became prime minister, he let it be known that he would try to make 1995, the fiftieth anniversary of the war's end, "a year for self-reflection and apology to Japan's victims." He failed in his efforts and the results were quite the opposite. The Socialists had been pressing the Diet to produce a resolution apologizing for the war in general, and adding a resolve that Japan would "never again wage war," before Murayama's trip to China in May 1995. They failed, which foretold what was to come. LDP members in the coalition government would not agree, and said that Japan had done enough to make amends.[90] After months of interparty wrangling, the Diet produced a resolution in June that was a decided step backwards. The LDP would not agree to the use of the words "apology" or "regret," only to the use of the word for "reflection." Half of the Diet boycotted the final vote, and the entire enterprise was reduced to an effort to maintain the coalition by a compromise of wording.[91] When Murayama added his own "heartfelt apologies," and referred to Japan's wartime policies as a "mistake," the circumstances were again surrounded by ambiguities. The phrases were omitted by the prime minister when he spoke on the same day to a national ceremony commemorating the end of the war, and a large group of his cabinet and Diet members visited the Yasukuni shrine. Only the week before a new Education Minister again told the press that Japan "had not necessarily been the aggressor" in World War II, and questioned the utility of repeated apologies.[92]

What bearing has this issue—the inability of a very significant portion of Japan's political elite to acknowledge its World War II record—on the question of SDF involvement in UN peacekeeping? Here too, there is no way quickly to compensate for the failure of Japan to have undergone a more satisfactory evolution during the past fifty years. One might reduce the implications to an aphorism offered by a Chinese citizen's group in the United States: "A country that does not recognize its wrongs cannot do right."[93] Or, as a *New York Times* editorial noted concerning the Japanese government's admission of responsibility for its enforced prostitution program in World War II:

> The gesture was neither spontaneous nor graceful. Half a century later, Tokyo still resists acknowledging other appalling war crimes. Until it does, Japan's efforts to play a more active role in Asian affairs will provoke distrust. Some 20 million people died in the Pacific war, 17 million of them victims of Japanese aggression. Yet Japanese textbooks and popular culture still emphasize how Japan suffered.[94]

The issue, however, goes beyond "provoking" distrust. Japan's inability to assume full responsibility for the world war deserves distrust. It is perhaps the most problematical factor standing in the way of building confidence that future Japanese governments will maintain control of the SDF within international norms. Nor can one assume that the election of Ryutaro Hashimoto will lead to any improvement of the situation. What is most likely to exert a beneficial impact on Japanese behavior is the degree of influence manifested by the rest of the international community, and most particularly by other Asian nations. Japan's participation in United Nations peacekeeping, and in joint Asian peacekeeping, may well counteract the World War II experiences. At worst, such participation will not ameliorate them much; but it certainly could not aggravate them further.

A Permanent Security Council Seat?

One question remains: What positions might Japan take on peacekeeping and peace enforcement questions under Chapter 7 of the UN Charter if it were to obtain a permanent seat on the Security Council? Peacekeeping operations have become increasingly important in the work of the Security Council since 1990, and there are reasons to suspect that the Japanese position would consistently be to urge caution. Barbara Wanner commented early in 1992, before the major changes in Japanese policy enacted in June of that year:

> Some analysts ... have expressed concern that Japan's deliberative, consensus-oriented policymaking style may inhibit the country's ability to act decisively within the United Nations, particularly in the event of another crisis comparable to the one created by Iraq's aggression against Kuwait.[95]

In an interview in March 1994, Yoshio Hatana, then Japan's

Ambassador to the United Nations, said in answer to a question about the lessons that could be applied from UNTAC's experience in Cambodia:

> The first "lesson" UNTAC provided the world was the importance of restraint. UNTAC refrained from retaliating against repeated attacks and provocations from the Khmer Rouge, the rebel forces in Cambodia. Although the Khmer Rouge engaged in minor-scale military attacks in many places, UN peacekeepers kept these skirmishes from escalating into a large-scale military involvement. This certainly was commendable.[96]

Unfortunately, it was the wrong "lesson" that Mr. Akashi, head of UNTAC, took with him to Yugoslavia when he succeeded to the position of Special Representative to the Secretary General. His decisions in the face of "repeated attacks and provocations," continually shaved off portions of the Security Council's mandate to the point of appeasement of Serbian aggression. The tendency to temporize, to continually compromise and step back from confrontation always provides an advantage to the aggressor.

As regards Japan's attitude to its own participation in UN operations that require the use of military force, these may yet change should the Diet reconsider the question. However, in September 1994, Yohei Kono, president of the LDP and then foreign minister in the Murayama government, stated at the United Nations that Japan was prepared to "discharge its responsibilities as a permanent member of the Security Council," but that "Japan does not, nor will it resort to the use of force prohibited by its constitution."[97] The contradiction is plain. Although many nations do not contribute personnel to UN peacekeeping missions, there is no inherent reason that they should not. The same consideration pertains to Japan. Furthermore, Japanese military participation should have no bearing on Japan's effort to obtain a permanent seat on the UN Security Council. It is simply an obligation of all member-states of the UN, whether or not they aspire to Security Council membership.

Summary

The long history of pressure and requests from senior UN and U.S. officials for Japan to take on the task of military participation in UN peacekeeping was deferred for forty years, from the time that Japan became a full member of the United Nations. Major policy changes first took place in 1992 and 1994.

The question of Japan's World War II responsibility remains an obstacle to full-fledge participation. A single, euphemistic word or phrase, uttered once every few years by a Japanese official, does not substitute for a process of national assumption of responsibility. That national understanding seems absent in Japan, despite the apparent desire of large portions of the Japanese population to maintain their "peace" constitution. Too many senior politicians in the LDP appear so unreconstructed that they see little or nothing wrong in Japan's wartime activities.

Nevertheless, the basic question remains the same: For the long term, what process is most likely to lead to the peaceful evolution of Japan's role in the world and prevent the aggressive use of its military forces? Is it integration in UN peacekeeping operations, somewhat as a late analogue to Germany's NATO alliance experience, or should Japan be left permanently outside that structure? Either choice might work well, and either choice could lead to undesirable results. Once the precedent of overseas deployment has occurred and has been legitimized, it is obviously easier to envision the beginning of a process with untoward results, in contrast to an absolute firebreak of "*no* overseas activities," but only *if* the firebreak could be maintained forever. Nevertheless, it would seem that integrating the Japanese government and its military into the framework of collaborative UN peacekeeping stands the better chance of producing the same long-term outcome as occurred in Germany via NATO.

In addition, all the regional geopolitical developments of the past decades would appear to circumscribe the possibilities for Japanese military aggression. Since 1992, Japanese forces have participated in UN peacekeeping operations in Cambodia, Mozambique, Zaire, and, most recently, the Golan Heights. Asian nations that had expressed apprehensions before have found this development unobjectionable; some have even made public statements in its support. The past and present role of the United States in the Pacific theater is not likely to continue indefinitely, although ironically, it is desired by all the regional states: Japan, China, Korea, and Taiwan. Should a collaborative regional security regime that included Japan develop in Asia in the coming years, that would presumably aid in the same desirable evolution.[96]

APPENDIX

JAPANESE COOPERATION WITH UN PEACEKEEPING OPERATIONS

Main Features of the PKO Legislation

The PKO law authorizes the SDF's participation in two broad categories of UN operations: potentially dangerous peacekeeping duties; and supposedly less risky roles in logistical support and humanitarian assistance. For up to three years, the SDF contingents are allowed to engage only in activities in the second category, including:

- election monitoring;
- advisory functions involving civil administration;
- medical care;
- logistical support;
- bridge repairs and road maintenance;
- assistance in environmental restoration.

This "freeze" restriction aims at alleviating widely shared apprehensions in Japan about possible SDF involvement in overseas military conflicts. In order to avoid such involvement, the legislation also requires that the following safeguards be in place before and during actual deployment:

- a cease-fire among warring parties;
- the consent of those parties to Japanese deployment;
- a prior UN request for Japanese deployment;
- the impartiality of UN peacekeeping operations;
- the right of Japan to "suspend" its PKO role;
- the permission to use "light arms" (pistols and rifles) in self-defense.

In addition, to assure military accountability to civilian authority, the law requires prior Diet approval for each instance of SDF dispatch. A deployment lasting more than two years is subject to new Diet approval; if rejected, the operation must cease.

The provisions designed to assure safe PKO operations are to remain in effect for three years and can be lifted only through new legislation following parliamentary review of PKO performance during that period. Even if the "freeze" is lifted, prior Diet approval will be needed to permit an SDF dispatch on risky PKO missions. The operations put on hold include:

- ceasefire monitoring;
- patrol in buffer zones;
- monitoring of arms traffic;
- collecting and disposing of abandoned weapons;
- relocation and disarmament of warring factional forces;
- assistance in creating cease-fire lines;
- assistance in the exchange of prisoners of war.

Source: Adapted from Rinn-Sup Shinn, Congressional Research Service, 92- 665F, August 24, 1992.

The Japan Defense Agency presented a briefer, but more formal, list of Japanese PKO guidelines:

Basic Guidelines for Japan's Participation in Peacekeeping Forces (the so-called Five Principles)

I. Agreement on a cease-fire shall have been reached among the parties to the conflict.
II. The parties to the conflict, including the territorial state(s), shall have given their consent to deployment of the peacekeeping force and Japan's participation in the force.
III. The peacekeeping force shall strictly maintain impartiality, not favoring any party to the conflict.
IV. Should any of the above guideline requirements cease to be satisfied, the Government of Japan may withdraw its contingent.
V. Use of weapons shall be limited to the minimum necessary to protect the personnel's lives, etc.

Source: Japan Defense Agency, *Defense of Japan*, 1992.

NOTES

1. Takao Takahara, "Japan," in Trevor Findlay, ed., *Challenges for the New Peacekeepers*, SIPRI Research Report No. 12 (Oxford, UK: Oxford University Press, 1966), pp. 52-66.
2. Edwin O. Reishauer, *Japan: The Story of a Nation* (New York; Alfred A. Knopf, rev. ed. 1974), pp. 240-41, 275-76. For a more detailed summary of the evolution of the Japanese defense forces and defense policy, see Martin E. Weinstein, "The Evolution of the Japanese Self Defense Forces," in James H. Buck, ed., *The Modern Japanese Military System* (Beverly Hills, Calif.: Sage, 1975), pp. 41-66, and Frank C. Langdon, *Japan's Foreign Policy* (Vancouver: University of British Columbia Press, 1973), chs. 3 and 6.
3. Barbara Wanner, "Japan's 'Peace Constitution' and Its Meaning in the New World Order," *Japan Economic Institute Report*, No. 13A (April 5, 1991), p. 10; Takao Takahara, "Postwar Pacifism in Japan and the New Security Environment: Implications of Participation in UN Peacekeeping Operations," unpublished paper, April 23, 1993, p. 2.
4. Annual figures for global military expenditures, in current dollars, appear each year in *World Military Expenditures and Arms Transfers*, published by the U.S. Arms Control and Disarmament Agency (ACDA). The most current volume, for 1993-1994, provides data only through 1993. A more current estimate was provided by the compilers of the volume in a personal communication to the author.
5. Japan Defense Agency, *Boei Hakusho* [White Paper on Defense] (Tokyo: JDA, June, 1976), p. 34.
6. Akihiko Tanaka, "The Domestic Context: Japanese Politics and UN Peacekeeping," in S. S. Harrison and M. Nishihara, eds., *UN Peacekeeping: Japanese and American Contexts* (New York: Carnegie Endowment for International Peace, 1995), p. 90.
7. Ibid., pp. 90-91.
8. "Japan Rules Out UN Peace Force," *Armed Forces*, vol. XV, No. 3 (December, 1968), p. 31.
9. Splitting the difference of "20 to 30 years" at 25, this would mean around the mid-1960s. "Foreign Ministry Special Briefing on Bill on Cooperation in United Nations Peacekeeping Operations," Ministry of Foreign Affairs, Tokyo, June 5, 1992, p. 3; quoted in Aurelia George, "Japan's Participation in UN Peacekeeping Operations," *Asian Survey*, vol. XXXIII, No. 6 (June, 1993), p. 563.
10. William Beecher, "Role Abroad Urged for Japan Troops," *Boston Globe*, September 2, 1977, p. 1.
11. The government statement is dated October 28, 1980. Quoted in Takahara, "Postwar Pacifism."
12. Tanaka, "The Domestic Context," p. 91. In between these two policy

recommendations, the government had in 1980 offered another interpretation of the issue. *Defense Handbook, 1994* (Tokyo: Asagumo Shimbunsha, 1994), p. 407; quoted in Tanaka, op. cit.

13. *Ibid.*
14. Tai Ming Cheung, "Self Defense and Beyond," *Far Eastern Economic Review*, December 21, 1989, pp. 26-29.
15. Eugene Brown, "The Debate Over Japan's Strategic Future: Bilateralism Versus Multilateralism," *Asian Survey*, vol. XXXIII, No. 6 (June, 1993), pp. 543-559. See also Eugene Brown, "The Debate Over Japan's International Role: Contending Views of Opinion Leaders During the Persian Gulf Crisis," Strategic Studies Institute, U.S. Army War College, July 17, 1991.
16. Takashi Inoguchi, *Japan's Foreign Policy in an Era of Global Change* (London: Pinter, 1993), particularly pp. 99-102, 120-121; T.R. Reid, "Kaifu Abandons Bill to Send Troops to Gulf," *Washington Post*, November 8, 1990, p. A-60; Philip Trezise, "Japan's Peacekeeping Forces," *The Brookings Review*, vol. X, No. 4 (Fall, 1992), p. 56.
17. Lt. Col. A. H. N. Kim, "Japan and Peacekeeping Operations," *Military Review*, vol. LXXIV, No. 4 (April, 1994), pp. 22-33; Naoki Usi, "Japanese Politicians Debate Country's Role in Post-War Gulf," *Defense News*, March 25, 1991, p. 1; T. R. Reid, "Japan May Help Sweep Mines from Persian Gulf Waters," *Washington Post*, April 12, 1991, p. A-30.
18. Masaru Tamamoto, "Japan's Uncertain Role," *World Policy Journal*, vol. VIII, No. 4 (Fall, 1991), pp. 579-597.
19. "Seoul Concerned Over Japan's Troops Abroad," *Korea Newsreview*, August 24, 1991, p. 7.
20. Hartwig Hummel, "Japanische Blauhelme: Von der Golfkriegsdebatte zum 'PKO-Gesetz,'" INEF Report 3/1992, October, 1992, University of Duisberg. See also Barbara Wanner, "Japan Views Leadership Opportunities Through the United Nations," Japan Economic Institute Report No. 10A (March 13, 1992); and "Nakayama Conveys Japan's Peacekeeping Concerns at UN Meeting," Japan Economic Institute Report No. 37B (October 4, 1991), pp. 1-3.
21. Robert Delfs, "Japan: SDF May be Given UN Peace-keeping Role," *Far Eastern Economic Review*, June 6, 1991, pp. 12-13; Don Oberdorfer, "Japan: Searching for Its International Role," *Washington Post*, June 17, 1991, p. A-9.
22. T. R. Reid, "Japan May Let Troops Do Peace-keeping Duty," *Washington Post*, September 20, 1991, p. A-20; Steven Weisman, "Tokyo Debates Offering Troops to UN," *New York Times*, September 20, 1991, p. A-3.
23. Steven Weisman, "Japan May Send Forces Abroad," *New York Times*, December 4, 1991, p. A-5.
24. Wanner, "Japan Views Leadership Opportunities Through the United Nations."
25. Margo Grimm, "Japan Seeks Greater Role in Cambodia Reconstruction," Japan Economic Institute, Report No. 6B (February 14, 1992), pp. 6-8.

26. Chalmers Johnson, "Japan in Search of a 'Normal' Role," Policy Paper No. 3, Institute on Global Conflict and Cooperation, University of California, San Diego, July, 1992, p. 40.
27. Yoshita Sasaki, "Japan's Postwar Non-Military Diplomatic Policy at Crossroads," unpublished manuscript (September, 1992), pp. 7-8.
28. "Law Concerning Cooperation for United Nations Peacekeeping Operations and Other Operations." See also Rinn-Sup Shinn, "Japanese Participation in United Nations Peacekeeping Operations," Congressional Research Service paper No. 92-665F, August 24, 1992; "International Contribution and the SDF," ch. 3 in *Defense of Japan: 1992* (Tokyo: Japan Defense Agency), pp. 121-155; David Sanger, "Tokyo Bid to send Troops Overseas Suffers a Setback," *New York Times*, June 1, 1992, p. 1.
29. Extensive polling by the Japanese press is summarized in Inoguchi, *Japan's Foreign Policy*, p. 112, n. 9.
30. David Sanger, "Japan's Troops May Sail, and the Fear is Mutual," *New York Times*, June 21, 1992, Sec. 4, p. 4; and Stefan Wagstyl, "Public's Mistrust of Militarism is Rekindled," *Financial Times* (London), June 17, 1992, p. 4.
31. Sam Jameson, "Japanese Official Criticizes China's 'Fussing'," *Los Angeles Times*, September 8, 1992.
32. Trezise, "Japan's Peacekeeping Forces," p. 56.
33. Takahara, "Postwar Pacificism," p. 10.
34. T. R. Reid, "Japan's Ruling Party is Big Winner in National Parliamentary Election," *Washington Post*, July 27, 1992, p. A-10.
35. Quoted in Tanaka, "The Domestic Context," p. 99.
36. "Activities in Cambodia," section 2, ch. 3 in *Defense of Japan, 1993* (Tokyo: Japan Defense Agency), pp. 134-154. In September-October 1992, under the provisions of the International Peace Cooperation Law, the Japanese government also sent three civilian election observers to serve in UNAVEM II, The United Nations Angola Verification Mission II.
37. Peter McKillop, "Japan's G-Rated Adventure: Tokyo Sends Peacekeepers on Their First Mission," *Newsweek*, October 19, 1992, p. 47.
38. Charles Leadbeater, "Tokyo to Review Future of Peace Constitution," *Financial Times*, January 14, 1993; David Sanger, "Japanese Debate Taboo Topic of Military's Role," *New York Times*, January 17, 1993, p. 9; T. R. Reid, "Miyazawa Faces Revolt in Party," *International Herald Tribune*, February 3, 1993.
39. David Sanger, "UN Chief's Advice Stirring Japanese Criticism," *New York Times*, February 7 1993, p. 17.
40. "Boutros-Ghali Asks Miyazawa to Send Troops to Africa," *Financial Times*, February 17, 1993; T. R. Reid, "Boutros-Ghali Recruits Soldiers in Japan," *Washington Post*, February 19, 1993. See also *New York Times*, February 19, 1993, p. A8 and *Financial Times*, February 19, 1993.
41. *International Herald Tribune*, February 3, 1993.
42. David Sanger, "Japan Grows Wary of Cambodia Role," *New York Times*,

April 29, 1993, p. A-3; William Branigan, "Japanese Killed During Ambush in Cambodia," *Washington Post*, May 5, 1993, pp. 1, A-3; Paul Bluestein, "Japan: Is Cambodia Too Costly?" *Washington Post*, May 8, 1993, p. A-15; Victor Mallet, "Cambodia Shatters Myth of Japanese Warrior," *Financial Times*, May 25, 1993; *Japan Times*, June 21-27, 1993.

43. Masashi Nishihara, "Trilateral Country Roles: Challenges and Opportunities," in John Roper et al., eds., *Keeping the Peace in the Post-Cold War Era: Strengthening Multilateral Cooperation* (New York: A Report to the Trilateral Commission, 1993), pp. 49-66.
44. "Paths to Peace; Japan's Cooperation for World Peace," Japan Economic Education Center Foundation (Tokyo), March, 1995. See also Barbara Wanner, "Japan Tested by Peacekeeping Responsibilities," Japan Economic Institute Report, No. 25A, July 9, 1993.
45. Teresa Watanabe, "Japan Defense Agency Chief Quits Over Peacekeeping Remark," *Los Angeles Times*, December 3, 1993.
46. T. R. Reid, "Japan's New Socialist Leader Promotes Conservative Economic Program," *Washington Post*, July 19, 1994, p. A-13.
47. William Dawkins, "Politicians Catching up with Japan's Military," *Financial Times*, July 26, 1994.
48. Mari Koseki, "SDPJ Proposes New Policy Curbing SDF Capability," *Japan Times Weekly*, September 5-11, 1994. See also Barbara Wanner, "Japan Explores Restructuring Its Self-Defense Capabilities," Japan Economic Institute, Report No. 38A (October 7, 1994), and "Clinton Administration Refuses Asian Pacific Security Strategy," JEI Report No. 11A, March 24, 1995.
49. *Japan Times Weekly*, August 29-September 4, 1994, pp. 1, 5; "Japanese Land in Zaire," *New York Times*, September 24, 1994, p. A-3.
50. *Japan Times Weekly*, August 29-September 4, 1994, p. 1.
51. "The Strengthening of UN Peacekeeping Operations and the Role of the SDF" and "Missions of the SDF and Peacekeeping Operations," in *The Modality of the Security and Defense Capability of Japan: The Outlook for the 21st Century*, Advisory Group on Defense Issues, Tokyo, pp. 12-13.
52. *Japan Times*, November 30, 1995; Reiji Yoshida, "New Defense Outline Adapted by Cabinet," *Japan Times*, November 30, 1995.
53. Nicholas D. Kristof, "Japan to Cut Own Military, Keeping GI's," *New York Times*, November 29, 1995, p. A-9.
54. *Japan Times Weekly*, December 4-10, 1995. There had apparently been some possibility of joint operations with a Chinese engineering battalion assigned to UNTAC in 1992; however, the Chinese unit moved its location, and the opportunity was lost. A. H. N. Kim, "Japan and Peacekeeping Operations," p. 29.
55. Young-sun Song, "The Prospect of Cooperation Between South Korea and Japan in Peacekeeping Operations," manuscript; published as "*Nikkan wa PKO de renkei o*" ("Japan and Korea should Work Together for PKO"), *This is Yomiuri*, December, 1995, pp. 80-85.
56. See Kenneth B. Pyle, "Japan and the Future of Collective Security," in

Danny Unger and Paul Blackburn, eds., *Japan's Emerging Global Role* (Boulder, Colo.: Lynne Rienner, 1993), p. 111.

57. "Japanese Troops Join UN Golan Forces," *New York Times*, February 13, 1996, p. A-6.
58. *Japan Times Weekly*, December 4-10, 1995, pp. 1, 5. Japan also suggested that "its support for Bolkan peace efforts should be balanced [by] the European Union's assistance with efforts to provide stability in East Asia," specifically, EU contributions to the costs of procuring nuclear reactors for North Korea.
59. Since Japan's GNP is about 85 percent of the U.S. GNP, and the U.S. assessments for the UN regular and peacekeeping budgets are in the range of 25 percent, it is not clear why Japan's financial contribution should not be substantially higher.
60. Yoshitaka Sasaki, "Japanese Politics: Sailing into Stormy Seas," *Asahi Shimbun*, March 25 1993 and Sasaki, "View from Nagatacho; Showdown Nears on Landing Craft Procurement," *Asahi Shimbun*, May 6, 1993. It did not take the initiation of SDF participation in UN peacekeeping for JDA officials to call for seaborne strike systems. In 1988, the head of the Defense Agency said that Japan "had the right to possess aircraft carriers, provided they were the smaller, defensive type and were equipped only with helicopters." And in 1989 one of his deputies claimed that Japan has "the right to possess aircraft carriers equipped with combat jets." "The Politics of Defense," *Pacific Research*, vol. II, No. 3 (August, 1989).
61. William Durch and Barry M. Blechman, *Keeping the Peace: The United Nations in the Emerging World Order* (Washington, D.C.: The Henry L. Stimson Center, March, 1992), p. 90.
62. Quoted in Tamamoto, "Japan's Uncertain Role," p. 584, and attributed to *Asahi Shinbun*, May 5, 1991.
63. Johnson, "Japan in Seatch of a 'Normal' Role," pp. 23-24. Johnson is quoting Jiro Yamaguchi, in the *Journal of Japanese Studies*, Winter 1992.
64. John Ruggie, letter to the editor, *New York Times*, June 18, 1992, p. A-26. Gardner expressed the same position in a monograph on peacekeeping.
65. Writing in 1993, Frank McNeil could also only offer the "worst-case scenario, the sum of all fears in Asia, [which] sees the intimidating power of the far Right on the rise, pushing the clock back to an aggressive *remilitarized Japan*. The fears are understandable, and they have been heightened by the recent call of a Japanese military officer for a military coup to end corruption. That would require, inter alia, a radical change in the peaceful temper of the Japanese." (McNeil, *Japanese Politics: Decay or Reform; the Consequences of Political Stagnation and the Prospects for Change* (Washington, D.C.: Carnegie Endowment for International Peace, 1993), p. 6. In his foreword to the book, Ezra Vogel comments that "Japan is today in no danger of slipping into a prewar-style military or totalitarian government" (p. v).
66. Aurelia George, "Japan's Participation in UN Peacekeeping Operations:

Radical Departure or Predictable Response," *Asian Survey*, vol. XXXIII, No. 6 (June, 1993), pp. 560-575.

67. A. H. N. Kim, "Japan and Peacekeeping Operations," pp. 24, 28.
68. George, "Japan's Participation," pp. 568, 573-574.
69. Sasaki, "Japan's Postwar Non-Military Diplomatic Policy at Crossroads," p. 5.
70. The most recent extended examination of the difference between Japan and Germany in this regard is the book by Ian Buruma, *The Wages of Guilt: Memories of War in Germany and Japan* (New York: Farrar Strauss Giroux, 1994). See also the review essay by Gordon A. Craig, "An Inability to Mourn," *New York Review of Books*, July 14, 1994, p. 43.
71. For the most detailed compilation of Chinese deaths in the Sino-Japanese war, see Rudolf J. Rummel, "Japanese Mass Murder in China, 1937-1945," manuscript, and R. J. Rummel, *China's Bloody Century: Genocide and Mass Murder Since 1900* (New Brunswick: Transaction Publishers, 1991), chs. 5-6. Rummel arrives at a figure of over 10 million. The 17-million figure appears frequently in Chinese sources, and in press quotations.
72. Meirion and Susie Harries, *Soldiers of the Sun: The Rise and Fall of the Imperial Japanese Army* (New York: Random House, 1994).
73. *Washington Post*, January 23, 1988, p. C-21; Ian Buruma, "Bertolucci's Epic Tale Tiptoes Through History," *Far Eastern Economic Review*, February 18, 1988, p. 40.
74. David E. Sanger, "Japan Admits it Ran Army Brothels During War," *New York Times*, July 7, 1992, p. 1; Paul Blustein, "New Clash Over Comfort Women," *Washington Post*, July 10, 1992, p. 1; George Hicks, *The Comfort Women: Japan's Brutal Regime of Enforced Prostitution in the Second World War* (New York: Norton, 1995).
75. "An Apology from Japan, Finally, to War's Sex Slaves," *New York Times*, August 8, 1993, Sec. 4, p. 2. Paul Blustein, "Japan Sets New Plan to Aid WWII Victims," *Washington Post*, September 1, 1994, p. A-31.
76. Larry A. Niksch, "Japan's World War II Reparations: A Fact Sheet," Congressional Research Service, No. 910216F, March 7, 1991. These consisted of payments to Burma, in 1954, of $200 million; to the Philippines, in 1956, of $550 million; and to Indonesia, in 1958, of $223 million plus the cancellation of a $177 million loan.
77. Ienaga Saburo, "The Historical Significance of the Japanese Textbook Lawsuit," *Bulletin of the Concerned Asian Scholars*, vol. II, No. 4 (Fall, 1970), pp. 2-12; Hata Ikuhiko, "When Idealogues Rewrite History," and "History and National Sensibilities," *Japan Echo*, vol. VIII, No. 4 (Winter, 1986), pp. 71-78; David Sanger, "Political Editing in Japan," *New York Times*, November 22, 1992, sec. 4, p. 5; T. R. Reid, "Regrets and Resistance," *Washington Post*, August 28, 1994, p. C-2.
78. Charles Smith, "The Textbook Truth: Children Finally Exposed to Wartime Facts," *Far Eastern Economic Review*, August 25, 1994, pp. 38-39.

79. David Sanger, "Tokyo Journal," *New York Times*, May 27, 1993, p. 4.
80. Gebhard Hielscher, "Nobody Asks: What did you do in the War Daddy," *Far Eastern Economic Review*, February 19, 1987, pp. 46-47. A very similar assessment was made by a Japanese historian in 1995; see Daikichi Irokawa, *The Age of Hirohito: In Search of Modern Japan* (New York: Free Press, 1995), pp. 137-38.
81. Clyde Haberman, "Japanese Official Fires New Furor on the War," *New York Times*, May 11, 1988, p. A-14; Margaret Shapiro, "Minister Forced Out Over Defense of Japan's War Role," *Washington Post*, May 14, 1988, p. A-28; Sam Jameson, "Japanese Official Criticizes China's 'Fussing'," *Los Angeles Times*, September 8, 1992; David E. Sanger, "New Tokyo Minister Calls 'Rape of Nanking' a Fabrication," *New York Times*, May 5, 1994, p. A-9.
82. William Dawkins and Tony Walker, "Tokyo Minister Under Pressure to Quit After War Comments," *Financial Times*, October 27, 1994; Andrew Pollack, "Japan Wonders if Premier's Tie to Rightists is Ended," *New York Times*, January 15, 1996, p. A-7. Hashimoto did resign the post as head of the association shortly after he was elected president of the LDP in the fall of 1995.
83. David E. Sanger, "Takeshita Now Admits World War II Aggression," *New York Times*, March 7, 1989, Sec. 1, p. 12.
84. Paul Blustein, "Japan Issues Apology for War Actions," *Washington Post*, May 3, 1991, p. A-18. In 1990 the Mayor of Nagasaki for the first time acknowledged and offered an apology to Korean forced laborers working in Mitsubishi armaments factories in Nagasaki who died in the second atomic bombing; see "Emotions Vary after Memorial Apology," *The Japan Times*, August 10; 1990.
85. Policy Speech by Prime Minister Morihiro Hosokawa, to the 127th Session of the National Diet, August 23, 1993, Foreign Press Center, Japan; Text of the Prime Minister's Policy Speech, September 21, 1993; Statement by H. E. Mr. Morihiro Hosokawa, Prime Minister of Japan, at the 48th Session of the General Assembly of the United Nations, Permanent Mission of Japan to the United Nations, New York September 27, 1993; James Sterngold, "For Japan, the Old Slurs are the New Party Line," *New York Times*, August 15, 1993, Sec. 4, p. 5.
86. Sam Jameson, "Hata Restates Regret for Past Japanese Acts of Aggression," *Los Angeles Times*, August 16, 1994.
87. Sam Jameson, "Premier Tells of Regret for WWII Acts," *Los Angeles Times*, August 16, 1994.
88. Andrew Gordon, "My Student, the Princess," *New York Times*, March 17, 1993, p. A-21.
89. T. R. Reid, "Emperor Silent on Pearl Harbor," *Washington Post*, June 4, 1994, p. A-12.
90. *New York Times*, May 4, 1995, p. A-9; Gerard Baker, "Murayama to Express Remorse to China Over Wartime Record," *Financial Times*, May 2, 1995.

91. The operative paragraph in the resolution reads, "Recalling many acts of aggression and colonial rule in modern world history, we recognize and express [deep remorse] for these kinds of actions carried out by our country in the past. They brought unbearable pain to people abroad, particularly in Asian countries." Nicholas D. Kristof, "Japan Expresses Regret of a Sort for the War," *New York Times*, June 7, 1995, p. 1; Charles Smith, "Japan Sort of Sorry; War Apology Resolution Falls Short, Upsets Many," *Far Eastern Economic Review*, June 22, 1995, p. 21.
92. Sheryll Wu Dunn, "Japanese Apology for War is Welcomed and Criticized," *New York Times*, August 16, 1995, p. 3; Emily Thornton, "Final Mea Culpa? Prime Minister's Apology Pleases Some Asian Leaders," *Far Eastern Economic Review*, August 24, 1995, p. 18.
93. Advertisement, *New York Times*, June 17, 1994.
94. "Japan's Other War Crimes," *New York Times* editorial, July 12, 1992. See also Irokawa, *The Age of Hirohito*, pp. xiii-xv.
95. Wanner, "Japan Views Leadership Opportunities."
96. Barbara Wanner, "Japan Pursues Leadership Role in the United Nations: An Interview with Yoshio Hatano, Japan's Ambassador to the United Nations," Japan Economic Institute, Report No. 12A (March, 1994), p. 3.
97. "Statement by H. E. Mr. Yohei Kono, Deputy Prime Minister and Minister for Foreign Affairs of Japan at the 49th Session of the General Assembly of the United Nations," September 27, 1994, Press Release, Permanent Mission of Japan to the United Nations; quoted in Tanaka, "The Domestic Context," p. 101.
98. Paul Blustein, "Japan Nudges Asia to Assume Larger Regional Security Role," *Washington Post*, January 17, 1993, p. A-41.

YELTSIN'S VISIT AND THE OUTLOOK FOR JAPANESE-RUSSIAN RELATIONS

Hiroshi Kimura

The article clarifies a major misunderstanding prevalent among Americans, who tend to regard Japan's request for the return of the Northern Territories as a narrow-minded, national-egoistic demand. Instead, the issue has become a global one. The author evaluates Yeltsin's December 1992 visit to Tokyo, which has set a basic framework for further negotiation over the territorial disputes. Predicting optimistically the possible resolution of the dispute in the future, the author proposes concretely what may be done by the Japanese and the Russians.

MISUNDERSTANDINGS AMONG AMERICANS

The Northern Territories Syndrome?

Americans, as well as other non-Japanese people in the world, do not seem to have a correct understanding of the significance of the Northern Territories issue for Japan and the Japanese. What the Japanese call the "Northern Territories" problem concerns the question of sovereignty of the Northern Territories—the Habomai group of islets and the islands of Shikotan, Kunashiri, and Etorofu off the northern coast of Hokkaido. Tokyo has long been demanding the return to Japan of these islands, which Soviet troops occupied immediately after the end of World War II. For its part, Moscow has intransigently been rejecting such a request. The following three views are typical examples of the misunderstandings Americans have on this issue. These views, superficially, seem to be persuasive, but closer examination reveals the misunderstandings.

Some Americans criticize the Japanese for putting too much emphasis on the Northern Territories issue in their position on Russo-Japanese relations. Tsuyoshi Hasegawa, a Japanese-American professor at the University of California (Santa Barbara), labels such a Japanese tendency as "Japan's Northern Territories syndrome."[1] Hasegawa argues: "In an ordinary state a specific policy on specific issues toward the Soviet Union and Russia stems from a general and comprehensive Soviet/Russia policy, which in turn is

---

Hiroshi Kimura is a professor at the International Research Center for Japanese Studies in Kyoto and serves as first vice president of the International Council for Central and East European Studies (ICSEES). Dr. Kimura's publications include *Beyond Cold War to Trilateral Cooperation in the Asia-Pacific Region: Scenarios for New Relationships Between Japan, Russia, and the United States* (Cambridge, MA, 1992).

determined by the general framework of the international system the state wishes to promote and by a definition of the Soviet/Russian role in it. In Japan, the Northern Territories issue has constituted almost *the entirety* of Japan's Soviet policy."[2] Hasegawa's criticism is, to a certain extent, correct insofar as it points out the narrow-minded view that some Japanese people hold. Yet, it is an exaggeration to conclude, as Hasegawa and other American scholars are inclined to, that "Japan does not have a Soviet/Russian policy, only a Northern Territories policy."

Such a conclusion shows both a misunderstanding of the Northern Territories issue and ignorance concerning Japan's Russian policy. It especially fails to realize the fact that the Japanese demands for the return of the islands are based on Japan's concern for its national security. The Soviet Union under Stalin seized the four above-mentioned islands in the period of August 28 through September 5, 1945, which was *after* Japan had surrendered to the Allies and accepted the Potsdam Declaration. Thus, the Soviet occupation of the islands was, and remains, completely illegal. What would have happened if the Japanese had not protested against such an illegal action by the Soviet Union? If Japan had not protested the seizure of the islands, Japan would certainly have generated the impression to the world that the Japanese would easily succumb to a *fait accompli* produced by force. Such a misleading signal could even lead to the extreme situation in which Japan could not be relied upon to ensure the security of its four main islands, let alone that of the four small disputed islands. This situation would have to be taken very seriously, in view of the fact that it was Stalin's intention in 1945 to put the northern half of Hokkaido under Soviet control.[3] Japan's failure to protest would also have generated the impression that Japan tacitly recognizes the victor can take any unlawful action against the vanquished nation.

Japan's persistent demands for the reversion of the islands have also contributed to the correction of the impression prevailing in the world that the Japanese are "economic animals" solely intent on pursuing and realizing their material interests. The Japanese have been devoting an enormous amount of financial and human resources to their national movement for the return of the Northern Islands. Peter Berton, professor of international relations at the University of Southern California, once joked that from the vantage point of an economic calculation of costs and benefits, Japan would be better off purchasing or investing in land on Hawaii or other richer, warmer islands, instead of spending so much money and other resources for the return of these tiny, barren islands. Why, then, has Japan been so stubbornly pursuing something that may not necessarily pay off for it in economic terms?

For one thing, the return of territory concerns the most important task for any state, as its sovereignty and national prestige are at stake. Furthermore, in the case of Japan the following additional reasons and motivations exist. First, there is a need to get rid of the deep distrust of and feeling of threat from Russia that has built up over the years and still prevails among many Japanese. Second, Japan's desire to establish a new friendly and neighborly relationship with Russia is much stronger than the feeling of distrust and threat. Third, Japan feels it is necessary to adhere to the ideal prescribed in the postwar Japanese Constitution that an international conflict ought to be resolved not by force, but by peaceful negotiation, no matter how long or how hard the negotiation process may be. In short, even if Moscow could somehow succeed in concluding a peace treaty with Tokyo, while circumventing and shelving the thorny Northern Territories issue, the Japanese would never come to entertain heartfelt trust toward and build up friendly relations with Russia. If such a peace treaty were signed, Japan would also suffer a loss of respect among the nations of the world for pursuing an inconsistent foreign policy.

The conclusion of a peace treaty between Japan and Russia that includes a resolution of the territorial dispute would serve not only the objective of rectifying *past* mistaken actions taken by the Soviet Union after World War II, but also the objective of establishing and building a *future* relationship between the two countries. Thus, Japan's persistent pursuit of the return of the Northern Territories should be regarded as an embodiment of important needs and desires among the Japanese people and even some Russians. The shallow view in the West that Japan's pursuit of the return of the islands is simply an expression of Japan's egocentric desire to reclaim lost territory needs to be corrected.

Internationalization

Another common misunderstanding among Americans and other non-Japanese observers is that Japan tends to look at the Russian question solely from the view of its bilateral relations with Russia, not from the much wider, international, global perspective. Some have even gone so far as to argue that Japan is not willing to provide economic assistance to Russia, and so is exploiting its territorial conflicts with Russia as a convenient excuse for providing less aid to Russia. This argument is also flawed.

On the contrary, Japan very much considers the problems facing Russia and other CIS member states as a global issue and not simply an issue between Japan and Russia. Japan, as a member of the Group of Seven advanced capitalist nations, has seriously undertaken the task of providing assistance to Russia, and, in terms of volume of aid, Japan ranks third, next to Germany and the United States.[4] Tokyo has also provided Kazakhstan, Kyrgyzstan, and other Central Asian states with ODA (Official Development Aid). The fact that Japan has been giving economic aid of approximately US$5 billion to Russia despite the unresolved dispute over national borders means that Japan's government has obviously changed or even virtually abandoned its previous strategy toward Russia of "inseparability of politics and economics (*seikei fukabun*)." It also means that Tokyo sees the Russian problem as global, not simply bilateral. Tokyo is well aware that a possible threat to world security exists not due to Russia's strength but rather its weakness.

Thus Russia's problems are no longer problems for Russia alone, but have now become *international* problems. Japan continues to offer aid to Russia, and will be obliged to do so more in the future, particularly as the United States, Germany, and other G-7 member states find it hard to increase their share of assistance to Russia. However, Japan will also have to take into consideration the feelings of the Japanese people, who are not fully convinced of Japan's obligation to provide more aid than other G-7 member states to a country that has seized and kept their territory. Therefore, if the other G-7 states wish Japan to undertake a major role in financial assistance to Russia, they must make efforts in urging Russia to solve its territorial dispute with Japan. At G-7 summit meetings in Houston (1990), London (1991), and Munich (1992) both Russia and Japan were requested to make efforts to fully normalize their relations and resolve their territorial disputes. Thus, Russo-Japanese relations and the Northern Territories issue have also become an *international* issue. This is a development that Japan, as well as other G-7 countries, whether they wish to or not, must recognize. In conclusion, therefore, it is not a reasonable argument to say that "Tokyo looks at Russo-Japanese relations only through a lens of bilateral relations" or that "Tokyo exploits the Northern Territorial problem as a pretext to excuse its obligation in assisting Russia." Tokyo considers its relations with Russia from an international perspective and has committed a huge volume of aid to Russia.

No Pandora's Box?

Another example of American scholars' misunderstanding concerning the territorial conflict between Japan and Russia is the "Pandora's box" theory of setting a precedent. If Russia meets Japan's demand for the return of the Northern Territories, it will inevitably face similar claims from other nations, which is a situation Russia could not possibly endure. We are tired of hearing this theory of a situation that will not develop.

It is true that, despite the "Non-Expansion Principle" proclaimed in the Atlantic Charter, and the Cairo Declaration, the Soviet Union, taking advantage of the turmoil and confusion just before and even after the Second World War, seized by force the total land area of 6,700,000 sq. kilometers from 11 countries: three Baltic states, Finland, Poland, Germany, Czechoslovakia, Hungary, Rumania, Outer Mongolia, and Japan. However, the Baltic nations have already declared their independence, which Boris Yeltsin himself recognized. It was the Baltic countries that set the precedent for readjustment of a unilateral demarcation of national borders by the former Soviet Union. No other countries except Japan out of the above-mentioned 11 countries have officially demanded a redemarcation of the border to the Russian Federation under Yeltsin. Russia's borders with Germany and Finland are now established in the Helsinki Accords, and confirmed by CSCE Agreements. The border dispute covering 2,200 kilometers between China and Russia in the Far East has also largely been solved except for a 4–6 kilometer stretch at the confluence of the Amur and Ussuri Rivers, including two river islands and an island suburb of Khabalovsk. The Russo-Chinese dispute is quite distinct from the Russo-Japanese dispute because it involves the *re*alignment of an existing border, whereas the Russo-Japanese dispute concerns the establishment of a *new* border. Thus, our conclusion is that, even if Moscow decides to return the Northern Islands to Japan, this would not mean that a "Pandora's box" would be opened and that Russia would lose all the land it seized.

Any validity to the "Pandora's Box" or "Domino" theory could be seen only in boundary demarcation disputes between Russia and other CIS member countries. However, current border disputes between Russia and these states (such as the Baltic states, Ukraine, and Kazakhstan) are quite a different matter compared to Japan's dispute with Russia. Post-Soviet borders are based on former administrative practice, a number of subsequent bilateral joint declarations, and the December 21, 1991, Alma-Ata declaration of the CIS that agreed to "recognize and respect each other's territorial integrity and the inviolability of the existing [Soviet] borders" within the framework of the CIS.

It is true, however, that Russia and Ukraine have confronted each other over the Crimea. Some critics thus say that Russia's concession toward Japan on the Northern Territories issue may hurt Russia's position on the Crimea. From a political point of view it may be true, but from a legal point of view, it is quite the opposite. Joseph Stalin ordered his troops to seize the Northern Islands in 1945 and allowed the decree of the Supreme Soviet's Presidium of the RSFSR to declare in 1946 that the Soviet Union incorporated these islands into the territory of the USSR. In almost the same vein Nikita Khrushchev, in 1954, allowed a decree of the Supreme Soviet's Presidium of the RSFSR to declare that the RSFSR gave the Crimea to Ukraine as a gift. True, that, since 1992 under the Yeltsin leadership, the Supreme Soviet of the Russian Federation has been trying to get the Crimea back from Ukraine, arguing that the decree issued under the Khrushchev leadership was illegal. But if the Parliament of the Russian Federation declares Khrushchev's decree of 1945 invalid, it should declare Stalin's decree of 1946 invalid as well.[5] If both decrees were not declared invalid, Russia would be criticized for not being consistent and employing double standards.

RECENT DEVELOPMENTS

Yeltsin's Visit to Tokyo

Boris Yeltsin's visit to Japan in October 1993, marked two steps forward for Japan. The first step was the fact that the Russian president clearly apologized for the detention of Japanese POWs (Prisoners of War) in Siberia after World War II.[6] Unlike Gorbachev, who expressed *soboleznobanie* ("sympathy," or "condolence"), Yeltsin repeatedly (even five times!)[7] employed the word *izbinenie* ("apology"). This no doubt was one of Yeltsin's well prepared *ad-libs,* but nevertheless it represents a major overcoming of the past, something that is demanded of the top Russian leader as the inheritor of the old Soviet Union. Yeltsin's words laid to rest the ideology of the infallibility of the Communist dictatorship—the argument that the Soviet Union could do no wrong. This had the corollary effect of demonstrating to the world that Russia is more and more becoming an ordinary, normal country.

No doubt there are those who take the antipathetic view that his apology for the retention of prisoners in Siberia, in addition to being far too late in coming, was nothing more than a strategy on Yeltsin's part to circumvent demands for the return of the Northern Territories and should not be regarded as progress for Japan. Our view, however, is that the demands for an apology for the Siberian POWs and the return of the Northern Islands are not only interrelated but stem from the same principle. If a victor in war is allowed to get away with whatever illegal acts it commits, the international community would degenerate into a dark world of inhuman criminality. If Japan did not protest, it would be tacitly conceding to Russia what Russian jurist Sergei Punzhin calls "the victor's right (*pravo pobeditelia*)."[8] This would encourage Russia and other countries to violate international law again. If the new Russia under Yeltsin is to adopt "law and justice" as principles of its foreign relations, it must demonstrate palpably that it has abandoned Stalinist totalitarianism and its characteristic violence and disregard for law. Only then will Japan and other countries regard Russia as a normal country, and feel ready to engage in relations with it.

The second step forward concerns the Northern Territories. First of all, the Tokyo Declaration signed by Yeltsin in Tokyo, together with then Japanese Prime Minister Morihiro Hosokawa, confirmed that "*All* treaties and other international agreements" [emphasis added] concluded between Japan and the Soviet Union will form the basis for negotiations." The declaration also refers to the *Joint Working Documents Concerning the History of Japan-Russia Territorial Questions.* This means that some 35 documents contained in the *Joint Working Documents,* tracing back not only to the *post*-1956 Soviet Union (e.g., the Japan-USSR Joint Declaration of 1956 and the letters exchanged between Shunichi Matsumoto and Andrei A. Gromyko of 1956), but right back to Tsarist Russia (e.g., the Treaty of Shimoda of 1855, and the Treaty of St. Petersburg of 1875), will be used in future negotiations between Russia and Japan. Furthermore, at his press conference with Hosokawa, Yeltsin hinted that the treaties that would form the basis for future negotiation would include the 1956 Joint Declaration, which promises the transfer of Habomai and Shikotan from the Soviet Union to Japan upon the conclusion of a peace treaty.[9] The letters exchanged between Matsumoto and Gromyko promise continued negotiation of a formal peace treaty, which would "include the territorial issue," after normalization of relations. The fact that Yeltsin, by underlining the 35 Joint Working Documents, acknowledged the validity of both the Joint Declaration, which promises the transfer of Habomai and Shikotan, and the Matsumoto-Gromyko letters, which promise further continuation of negotiation on the territorial issue, may be interpreted to mean Yeltsin has agreed that future territorial negotiations will be for the return of Kunashiri and Etorofu.

The question may be raised as to whether the victory of Vladimir V. Zhirinovsky in the December 1993 election has prevented the Yeltsin leadership from fulfilling the promises he made during his October trip to Tokyo concerning the territorial dispute with Japan. The Russian ultranationalist Zhirinovsky, who wishes not only to restore the former Soviet Union's borders but also to expand them, will most probably never agree to return the Northern Territories to Japan. The extent of Zhirinovsky's influence on Russian domestic and foreign policies depends greatly upon the political, economic, and social developments in Russia, which no one can accurately predict at the present moment. Zhirinovsky's influence should be neither overestimated nor underestimated. It would be playing into his hands to take at face value his extreme right-wing statements, which are made partially for publicity purposes. The Russian Foreign Ministry has in fact issued a statement emphasizing that the Russian government does not share Mr. Zhirinovsky's views.

We should not forget that in the summer of 1993, before Yeltsin's visit to Tokyo, Russian Prime Minister Viktor Chernomyrdin repeatedly made statements that Moscow would not negotiate with Tokyo on the Northern Territories issue, which, in his view, had already been resolved and therefore did not exist.[10] These statements led to the pessimistic prediction among some Japanese that the Russian president, influenced by the prime minister, would not take a flexible position on the territorial dispute during his trip to Tokyo. This prediction, however, turned out to be entirely groundless. In Tokyo, Yeltsin, almost completely ignoring Chernomyrdin's statements, went his own way and did negotiate with the Japanese side on the Northern Territories issue, thereby acknowledging clearly the existence of the territorial dispute with Japan. This taught us that we should not be overly disturbed by any extreme comments. During his meeting with Tsutomu Hata, then Japanese minister of foreign affairs and later Japanese prime minister, on March 21, 1994, Chernomyrdin did confirm Yeltsin's accords with Hosokawa, saying that: "Japan and Russia would conclude a peace treaty, but one of the prerequisites for the conclusion of such a treaty was the settlement of the territorial dispute over the Kuril islands."[11] It is more important to look at the main direction in which things are moving. What then is the main direction with regard to the Northern Territories issue?

OUTLOOK FOR FUTURE RELATIONS

Optimistic Prospect of Resolution

At the risk of being criticized for injecting a rather optimistic view into the picture, I consider that the Northern Territorial issue between Japan and Russia is moving steadily forward and will be resolved in the long term. There are three reasons for this optimistic view.

First, the military-strategic value of the Northern Territories has been rapidly diminishing. In the past, one of the reasons that the Russians rebuffed requests to return the four islands was that these islands formed a vital gateway to the Sea of Okhotsk, which, in the Soviet bastion strategy, was the exclusive sanctuary for Soviet nuclear submarines. If the islands were returned to Japan, with Japan's ties to the United States through the Japan-U.S. Security Treaty, it would be easy for U.S. forces to track Soviet nuclear submarines. With the cold war over, and Yeltsin calling Japan and the United States "partners" and even "quasi-allies," the military-strategic significance of the Sea of Okhotsk, and the four islands, has diminished.[12] Furthermore, shortages of oil and other fuels, soaring transportation costs, and poor troop morale will make it increasingly difficult in the future to supply and maintain materials and troops on these small islands. Moreover, the value of the islands has become redundant in the wake of progress in military technology.

Reflecting this changed reality, Yeltsin proclaimed an acceleration of the schedule for reducing the Soviet military presence on the Northern Islands. In May 1992, he announced to Michio Watanabe, then Japanese foreign minister, that he would speed up plans for complete demilitarization of the islands except for the border patrol.[13] This step was an implementation of the third stage (demilitarization stage) of "Yeltsin's Five Stage Proposal for the Solution of the Northern Territories Issue." Although the timetable that the Russian president proposed has been delayed, due partly to resistance from the Russian military, in general developments will unquestionably move in the direction of demilitarization. In May 1993, Russian Foreign Minister Andrey Kozyrev informed Watanabe that the Russian forces in the Northern Territories had been cut by 30 percent to 7,000 troops. Major-General Alexander Shibkov, first subcommander of the troops assigned to Sakhalin Province and the four Northern Islands, explained how troop cuts in the Northern Islands were taking place "naturally": "Non-commissioned officers who have completed their term of duty are being returned to civil life. Since we are not replenishing these with personnel from other brigades, new personnel are now outnumbered by retirees."[14] In May 1993, it became known that the approximately 40 MIG-23s that had been stationed at Tennei (*Burevestnik*) Airfield in Etorofu had been completely withdrawn.[15]

Our second reason for an optimistic view is that the Russian people currently living on the Northern Islands are increasingly inclined in favor of a return of the islands to Japan. Except for Habomai, where the only inhabitants are border patrol troops, support for the return of the islands now predominates among the residents of the islands. In an opinion poll conducted in September 1993 on the three islands of Shikotan, Kunashiri, and Etorofu, following the announcement of Yeltsin's intended visit to Japan, it was found that support for reversion was far in excess of opposition: 28.9 percent supported the "two islands plus alpha" formula and 43.4 percent supported the return of all four islands, giving a total of 72.3 percent in favor of some form of reversion, while only 21.3 percent were opposed.[16] One of the reasons for this rapid change in the opinions held by current Russian residents is the deteriorating economic situation on the islands.[17] Oleg Bondarenko, Shikotan-based journalist for *Free Sakhalin,* stresses that "only the Kuril people, no one else, has the right to make a decision over the question of their stay on the Kurils. Precisely over this issue their opinion must be unconditional and obligatory (to others)."[18]

On July 21, 1993, the Sakhalin Regional People's Deputies Council, which administers the four islands, requested emergency relief for the Kuril Islands. In their letter addressed to President Yeltsin, the Congress of People's Deputies, and the Russian government, the Assembly declared: "We are forced to conclude that the central government is neglecting the present situation on the islands, in which the people are no longer able to carry on their lives. If this situation continues, the island people will be forced to consider relocating in Russia or other territories. If we cannot receive assistance from the Russian government, we will be forced to seek assistance from Japan or the United Nations."[19]

The third reason for our optimistic view is that, for the time being, Russia's economy is likely to continue deteriorating, and, thus, Japanese economic aid is becoming increasingly important. I need not elaborate further on that topic.

For these reasons, I believe that the Northern Territories issue will eventually be resolved, with Russia making major concessions to Japan.

Chto Delat'?

Even if my prediction that the Northern Territories issue will be resolved in the future is accepted, it does not necessarily lead to the conclusion that we should sit back idly and wait for this to occur. There are many things Japan can and should do in order to make sure of, and even accelerate the process for, the solution of this issue. I will examine here some measures Japan should undertake for this purpose.

Negotiation over the territorial dispute constitutes a zero-sum game, in which one party's gain is possible only at the expense of the other party. This zero-sum nature makes negotiations of the territorial dispute extremely difficult. The key to the solution of the Northern Territories conflict lies thus in the *transformation* of its zero-sum situation into a plus- or positive-sum game, in which all the parties become net winners with some benefits. How can this be accomplished? William Zartman, an expert on negotiations, has proposed a useful way of achieving such a transformation: "To yield a non-zero sum, either *things must be valued differently by the different parties or there must be side payments that are newly available* because of the agreements"[20] (emphasis added). I will apply these two valuable suggestions to the Northern Territories conflict between Japan and Russia.

Fortunately, Japan and Russia value the Northern Territories differently. For Japan, the sovereignty of the disputed lands in itself is far more important than anything else. For Russia, the security of the Sea of Okhotsk, the development of trade and economic relations with Japan, and maintenance of its prestige and dignity as a large Russian state appear to be becoming increasingly more important than the legal ownership of the tiny Northern Islands. In the case of the Okinawa reversion, Japan and the United States made a compromise, obtaining the most important thing for each party—for Japan the sovereignty of the islands, and for the United States the right to retain military bases on the islands. Likewise, in the case of the Northern Territories, each party needs to give up its less valued items in exchange for what it values more.

Another proposal by Zartman for transforming a zero-sum situation into a non-zero-sum situation is creative problem-solving by way of discovery of *new* alternatives. The Russian Federation, Japan, and the United States should make an effort to create an entirely *new* arrangement and relations among themselves.

In a new arrangement, Russia may lose the tiny Northern Islands to Japan while becoming a beneficiary of significant net gains, which may include the following:[21]

(1) *Military* gains in national security from guarantees that the disputed four islands will remain demilitarized; reciprocal reductions in U.S. and Japanese forces in the area in exchange for Russia's current and inevitable future

reductions; and a new role for Russia as a "cooperation partner" with Japan and the United States in the U.S.-Japan Security Treaty.

(2) *Political* gains from the guarantee that Russia will retain all current rights to free and safe passage of ships through the straits between Etorofu and Kunashiri, and between Etorofu and Urup.

(3) *Economic* gains from Japanese payment for all costs of relocating troops now stationed on the Islands; Japan's assumption of a lead role in a massive program of long-term G-7 aid for Russian reform, beginning with a Japanese contribution of US$5 billion per year over the next decade; a guarantee that Russia will retain all present rights to fishing and natural resources, and to the 200 mile economic zone around the disputed islands.

(4) *Social* guarantees will be most probably provided from the Japanese government that the Russian inhabitants on the islands could decide of their own free will whether they remain there, obtaining Japanese citizenship, or leave for the Russian mainland with Japanese financial and other assistance for their move.

(5) *Territorial* gains from Japan's recognition of Russia's sovereignty over southern Sakhalin and the eighteen Kuril islands, thereby renunciating in perpetuity all claims to this Russian territory; denunciation of revanchist elements in Japan who assert such claims, including the Japanese Communist party.

In this task of creating a *new* trilateral relationship, the United States should take the lead. The United States is not merely an observing third party. On the contrary, it is responsible for creating the impasse in the Northern Territories conflict. (Recall the roles Franklin D. Roosevelt and John F. Dulles played respectively in the 1945 Yalta secret agreement, the 1951 San Francisco Conference, and the 1956 Soviet-Japanese Normalization talks.) The United States should serve as an honest broker and guarantor in exploring ways to submerge this anomaly in a comprehensive agreement that produces net security, economic, and political benefits for all parties.[22]

NOTES

1. Tsuyoshi Hasegawa *et al.*, eds., *Russia and Japan: An Unresolved Dilemma Between Distant Neighbors* (Berkeley, CA: University of California Press, 1993), pp. 422–425.
2. *Ibid.*, p. 423 (italics original).
3. Graham Allison, Hiroshi Kimura, Konstantin Sarkisov, *Beyond Cold War to Trilateral Cooperation in the Asia-Pacific Region: Scenarios for New Relationship between Japan, Russia, and the United States* (Cambridge, MA: Strengthening Democratic Institutions Project, John F. Kennedy School of Government, Harvard University, 1992), p. 93; Dmitrii Volkogonov, then director of the Institute of Military History, USSR's Ministry of Defense, revealed that Stalin, even after facing U.S. President Harry Truman's rejection of Stalin's request for Soviet occupation of half the island of Hokkaido, did not easily give up his plan for seizing it. *Hokkaido Shimbun (evening edition)*, December 25, 1990.
4. Bilateral assistance provided by G-7 member states to the Russian Federation/New Independent State (NIS) is as follows (in June 1993) (U.S.$billion): (1) Germany-54.088; (2)

U.S.A.-17.669; (3) Japan-4.998; (4) Italy-4,713; (5) France-3.044; (6) Canada-1.837; (7) United Kingdom-1.386.

5. A. V. Zagorskii, "Rossiisko-iaponskie otnosheniia: B. N. El'tsin pereg dramaticheskim vyborom," in *Znakom'tes'—Iaponiia : k visitu B. N. El'tsina* (Moskva : Nauka, 1992), pp. 13–14.
6. *BBC Monitoring Summary of World Broadcasts (SU), Part 1 Former USSR,* no. 1818, October 13, 1993, p. B18.
7. *Komsomol'skaia pravda,* October 14, 1993.
8. S. M. Punzhin, "SSSR-Iaponiia: morhno Li pri pomoshch prava reshit' problemu 'severny kh territorii'?" *Sovetskoe gosudarstvo i pravo,* no. 7, 1991, p. 115.
9. Interfax (October 13, 1993) quotes Yeltsin as saying: "We will absolutely fulfill all the agreements and treaties between Japan and former [Soviet] Union. It is understandable that the [Joint Russo-Japan] Declaration of 1956 is also included in them."
10. *Moscow News,* no. 35, August 27, 1993, p. 2.
11. *BBC Monitoring (SU),* no. 1953, March 23, 1994, p. B16.
12. For more details, see an excellent study by Geoffrey Jukes, professor at the Australian National University: *Russia's Military and the Northern Territories Issue* (Working Paper no. 277) (Canberra: Strategic and Defence Studies Centre, The Australian National University, October 1993), 42 pp.; esp. pp. 7–18.
13. *Mainichi Shimbun, Hokkaido Shimbun,* May 5, 1992.
14. *Yomiuri Shimbun,* July 3, 1993.
15. *Ibid.,* May 30, 1993.
16. *Ibid.,* October 11, 1993.
17. For details of incredibly deteriorating economic situations on the disputed islands, see Leg Bondarenko, *Neizbestnye Kurily* (Moscow: VIT-Deita Press, 1992), pp. 125–215; See also *Gubernskie vedomosti3, 1993. 8. 14, p. 5.*
18. *Ibid.,* p. 255.
19. *Yomiuri Shimbun (evening edition),* June 19, 1993; See also *Guberskie vedomosti,* August 14, 1993, p. 5. Interfax of December 4, 1993, reported that during the ten-month period of 1993 as many as 826 residents left the southern Kuriles.
20. I. William Zartman, ed. *The 50% Solution* (New Haven: Yale University Press, 1987), p. 10.
21. Allison, Kimura, Sarkisov, op. cit., pp. x–xi.
22. *Ibid.,* p. 36.

Diplomacy and Security in the Twenty-first Century

KŌSAKA MASATAKA

The sorts of issues we identify as security problems today will persist well into the twenty-first century and will continue to be major concerns for Japan's government and people, though the vocabulary with which we discuss them may change. The very term we now use for "security" in Japanese—*anzen hoshō*—has not been current all that long. Previously people generally used terms like "national defense" (*kokubō*), "defense of the empire" (*teikoku no bōei*), and even "empire building" (*teikoku no kensetsu*).

However the words may change, security involves a set of dilemmas most fundamental to the human condition. First is the fact that people must at times risk their lives to defend what they, as living human beings, consider important. Without the desire to do so, they would not be human. To regard survival as the only objective is not the human way. Raymond Aron examined this contradiction in the context of an extreme case. If, he asked, a country is threatened by another, much more powerful one and it is clear that in normal circumstances resistance is hopeless, can the first country ensure survival by surrendering and allowing its people to be enslaved? This he considered dubious. Can a country be said to have survived if it has lost its collective pride and its language? If things have reached this pass, eventually even physical survival is questionable, as historical examples attest.[1]

In short, the objectives of security go beyond survival. Some may say this is irrelevant in today's world. But let us look at an example from nineteenth-century Europe that illustrates Aron's extreme case in reverse, as it were. As A. J. P. Taylor observes, all the wars around the middle of the century were initiated by countries destined to lose. It is superficial to attribute this merely to gross miscalculation. Austria, for example, had no realistic hope of victory when it challenged the French-backed Sardinian army in 1859, when Italy was on the verge of independence. Austria chose to fight because it found concessions forced through defeat in a contest of arms preferable to those extracted through diplomacy. Why, then, did it fight? Clearly not to gain territory or augment national power. Austria fought for honor. Austrians believed that if ever the time came that honor ceased to be important the nation would have lost something precious.[2]

This brings us to the next dilemma: The end of defending what is valued does not justify the use of any means whatsoever. The pursuit of something more than life is what makes us human. At the same time, however, life is if categorical importance to us. Thus, while there may be tacit acceptance of war as a necessary evil, it cannot be affirmed as a good. Faced with this antinomy, human beings have devised a variety of ploys to get around it—the simplest being to label their enemies "barbarians." Other ruses include making distinctions between combatants and noncombatants, between just and unjust wars.[3] The supreme example is the way the law of war sanctions certain forms of slaughter while condemning others. Advances in technology, however, have greatly limited the significance of such ploys. Moreover, the entire validity of the exercise of military force is now subject to harsh questioning. This obliges nations to rethink the means used to de-

1. Cited in Stanley Hoffman, ed., *Contemporary Theories of International Relations* (Englewood Cliffs, N.J.: Prentice-Hall, 1960)

2. A. J. P. Taylor, *The Struggle for Mastery in Europe, 1848–1918* (Oxford: Clarendon Press, 1954).

3. Some scholars still consider the distinction between combatants and noncombatants important. See, for example, Michael Walzer, *Just and Unjust Wars* (New York: Basic Books, 1977).

fend that which deserves defending, and also alters the character of what is regarded as worth defending.

The nature of international relations has also changed substantially. As John H. Herz noted in his landmark work *International Politics in the Atomic Age*, at the beginning of the modern age sovereign states were rigidly encased in carapaces, and interaction consisted of military contacts in the name of nations and diplomacy based on the assumption of such contacts.[4] Now, however, national borders are riddled with holes; when it comes to the flow of information, there are no borders. This gives rise to the question whether the nation is the basic unit of human existence. I myself continue to regard nations as important, but they have lost the absolute, unquestioned mastery they once enjoyed.

The multilateral, diverse nature of international relations today changes the kinds of problems that arise between nations and the means used to resolve them. And this necessarily alters the definition of what is to be defended. But let us not be too hasty in redefinition. Some maintain that the importance of military security has diminished and that from now on economic security will be the paramount concern. "Economic security" is a phrase often used to suggest that this is somehow a more realistic or pragmatic concern than military security. That, I believe, is one of great delusions of the late twentieth century. What does "economic security" seek to protect? A nation's status as the world's leading economic power? Its people's jobs? Its basic industries? Minimum supplies of natural resources? None of these are worthless objectives, but I cannot help feeling that the phrase is used to justify the pursuit of particular interests—either that or it is the shabbiest kind of tactic for winning votes.

Finally, we face the dilemma that today's sophisticated technology creates new risks of accidental disaster. Of course risk has always been part of the human condition, and that has never stopped people from adventure. But they knew they were courting danger and were prepared for a certain amount of risk. This is quite different from being caught up in some event that has only a billion-to-one chance of occurring. In terms of probability the risk may be negligible, but it is one we cannot shrug off. There is no denying that nuclear reactor accidents, earthquakes, sudden epidemics, and the like are responsible for much of people's anxiety over security today.

KŌSAKA MASATAKA
Born in 1934. Graduated from Kyoto University, where he majored in the history of European diplomacy. Did graduate work in political science at Harvard University. Taught at Kyoto University from 1971 to 1996. His books include *Saishō Yoshida Shigeru* (Prime Minister Yoshida Shigeru) and *Koten gaikō no seijuku to hōkai* (The Maturation and Fall of Classical Diplomacy). Died in May 1996.

THE RAMIFICATIONS OF NUCLEAR WEAPONS

Needless to say, nuclear weapons will have the biggest impact on future security, because they have made war, in the historical sense of a struggle for power, inherently absurd. Of course the advent of nuclear weapons alone is not responsible for this. World War I was absurd, which is why the British military strategist Basil Liddell Hart maintained that the Clausewitzian definition of war as the imposition of one's will on the enemy by destroying its military power was a Napoleonic fallacy that was no longer workable.[5] And various methods were devised for affecting the enemy's will before destroying its military power, such as destroying its central chain of command and breaking up its organizational cohesion. Nevertheless, the exercise of military power was still seen as being within the scope of rationality.

The emergence of nuclear weapons, however, made the idea of decisive war patently absurd. The formulation and implementation of nuclear strategy from the 1950s through the 1980s confirms this. In the 1950s the United

4. John H. Herz, *International Politics in the Atomic Age* (New York: Columbia University Press, 1959).

5. This is a motif running through a number of Liddell Hart's writings.

States espoused the doctrine of "massive retaliation," under which it promised to respond to a Soviet attack with a nuclear barrage. Some people felt that the threat of the use of nuclear weapons alone was a sufficient deterrent. But the use of nuclear weapons was all but eliminated as a realistic option by the inefficacy of massive destructive power as a means of attaining minor objectives and fear of the consequences of the use of nuclear weapons against such prime targets as cities, together with the realization that escalation of conflict could make governance impossible. The doctrine of massive retaliation was followed by that of limited war, the notion that the use of tactical nuclear weapons was feasible, depending on circumstances, objectives, and diplomatic ability. Nevertheless, the view that a universally obvious, unmistakable line separated nuclear and nonnuclear war prevailed.

Another example makes the same point in reverse. In the early 1960s, when the Soviet Union developed intercontinental nuclear weapons capable of striking the U.S. mainland, France used the argument that the U.S. nuclear deterrent could not be relied on to justify developing its own *force de frappe*. Proponents of an independent nuclear capability frequently asked whether America would be prepared to sacrifice New York or San Francisco to defend Paris. This was expanded into the argument that the United States could not use nuclear weapons to defend Europe and that therefore the Soviet Union could exercise military force if it had the advantage in conventional power. Of course it was unreasonable to believe America would be prepared to sacrifice New York by using nuclear weapons to defend Paris. But the French were asking the wrong question. What they should have focused on was Moscow's thinking. The Soviets might find it easy to overrun Western Europe; the Americans might quickly choose to withdraw their troops in the face of the Soviets' superior conventional strength, and they probably would not use tactical nuclear weapons in response to such an offensive. But none of this was certain. If warfare escalated, one side or the other might resort to nuclear weapons. Once events began to move in that direction, the upshot would be a world of utter chaos.

The U.S.-Soviet nuclear arms race from the late 1970s to the mid-1980s finally confirmed the absurdity of war. That, at least, was my perception. When the Soviet Union deployed SS-20 intermediate-range missiles, the West countered with intermediate-range nuclear forces. Some observers even regarded the Soviets' construction of huge missiles as setting the stage for a preemptive strike. But even if detailed technical studies revealed that one side or the other was somewhat ahead, it was senseless to augment what was already, in effect, unlimited destructive power.

This brief review demonstrates that nuclear arms had rendered impossible a decisive war or the kind of war that could lead to a final showdown. It is also safe to say that the existence of the nuclear umbrella is a concomitant of the existence of nuclear weapons. If the scenario for retaliation were clear-cut and unilateral, this umbrella would probably have a major deterrent effect, but it exists even in the absence of such a scenario. The existence of nuclear weapons has made people think that there is a very real danger that almost any major military conflict can escalate to nuclear war, and this constitutes a nuclear deterrent in the most basic sense—"existential deterrence," as it has been called.[6] The French and the Chinese justify their own nuclear capability by pointing to the U.S. nuclear umbrella that shelters Japan, but this is less a reasoned argument than emotionalistic political propaganda. They consider their independent nuclear forces worthwhile and want to publicize them, but I wonder what the judgment of history some decades down the line will be.

The only meaning the possession of an independent nuclear capability can have, under conditions in which conventional force has to be used for anything but pure self-defense, is to make it hard for other countries to engage in nuclear saber rattling. Even then, if the objectives sought by the use of conventional arms are overambitious, the danger of escalation will mount and self-restraint will be necessary. This being the case, will China's nuclear arms be effective in bringing about the forcible unification of Taiwan with the mainland?

CONTROLS ON WEAPONS OF MASS DESTRUCTION

The impossibility of a decisive war means massive, and probably fundamental, changes in international politics. Hegemonism is of little use when thinking about future international politics, nor is "neorealism," which defines international political struggles in narrow military terms. Neorealists believe that sooner or later Japan will acquire a nuclear arsenal, because they see nations as entities contending for power and take the line that lack of nuclear capability would put Japan at too great a disadvantage. I cannot relate such arguments to the real world, however. I wish to make it quite clear that I believe human beings will always vie for power and influence, and that for better or worse they will always clash over principles. Military strength plays a part in all this. But is there no alternative to pouring energy into things that are basically absurd? Moreover, since nothing lasts forever, one hegemon will eventually give way to another—not as the result of a war for hegemony but because a decisive war is a patently absurd proposition.

Let me make the point in pragmatic terms. Nuclear weapons have meaning only as an irrational expression of will. Undeniably this is an important factor in defense and security. But can it be maintained that the actual possession or lack of nuclear weapons is of decisive importance?

6. In the 1980s a certain Catholic clerical organization took the stance that while the possession of nuclear weapons is permissible, their use can never be justified. Unsophisticated though it was, this was the first expression of the concept of existential deterrence.

The nuclear powers have already gone off alert status; they are no longer poised to launch nuclear missiles at a moment's notice. What is more, if there is almost no chance that nuclear arms will be used and their only effect is to deter other countries from using them, how much difference is there between countries that possess nuclear weapons today and those that may possess them in two weeks, two months, or a year? Even the potential possession of nuclear arms has a deterrent effect. It may be virtually certain that such weapons will never be used, but the clock cannot be turned back to the prenuclear good old days—or the bad old days—of war.

This is not an argument for nuclear disarmament. Even if nuclear arms were eliminated, the ability to make them would remain. Anyone who felt the need to manufacture them would probably do so. We would need either to wipe all knowledge of how to make them from human memory or to impose stringent controls with severe penalties on all countries, including the major powers. Neither can be done. Our only options are to have a number of nuclear powers keep their weapons and maintain international order or deprive all countries of their nuclear arsenals and maintain order on the understanding that nuclear weapons could be brought back at any time.

At the moment, the latter option is academic, since the United States and Russia possess huge stockpiles of nuclear warheads, and reducing them and arranging for safe disposal will take time and money. Even then, difficulties will remain. For the time being, it should be enough if Russia and the United States reduce their stockpiles to 3,000 warheads, which they will probably agree to do. But if further cuts are made—say to 1,000 warheads or fewer—how are the three other nuclear powers to be dealt with, not to mention the three other countries that are believed to possess nuclear arms, though they have not declared so? Most fundamentally, as zero is approached "critical stability" could be compromised, resurrecting the specter of a preemptive strike. Thus we cannot say with assurance that 500 warheads are preferable to 1,000.

Nevertheless, there are certain merits to virtual as opposed to actual nuclear deterrence—the use, so to speak, of "virtual nuclear armories."[7] These would lessen the danger of nuclear proliferation. The major powers have the responsibility to reduce, even if not abolish, their nuclear arms under the terms of the nuclear-nonproliferation regime. Unless they follow through, they will not be in a position to censure countries that flout the rules. Progress in reduction will also cause nuclear weapons to recede psychologically from human society. It is true that often only the sword of Damocles prevents people from committing wrongs, but living with the possibility of devastation warps human nature. We must control weapons of mass destruction, including biological and chemical weapons, and clearly enunciate the goal of de facto eradication. Fortunately, nuclear weapons have not been used for 50 years. If they are not used for another 50 years, the image of nuclear weapons and the view of orderly international relations will alter greatly. For this reason the control—and possibly abolition—of nuclear arms and other weapons of mass destruction will be a major security task for the beginning of the twenty-first century.

7. For one argument in favor of this position, see Michael J. Mazarr, "Virtual Nuclear Arsenals," *Survival*, vol. 37, no. 3 (autumn 1995).

CIVIL WAR AND UNREST

I am not, obviously, presenting an optimistic argument. That we hardly need worry about war among developed countries is certainly a good thing. But two problems remain. One is the fact of warfare, especially civil war, in peripheral regions. The other is the fact that even if war disappears, struggles for power and influence will not.

The first problem will probably remain with us for considerable time to come, since warfare in peripheral regions is not yet clearly absurd. Of course huge numbers of people are killed and wounded in civil wars; the misery involved defies description. Still, most of the casualties are caused by starvation and disease—an age-old historical pattern. The important point is that conditions are not such that everyone can perceive the absurdity of civil war before embarking on it. In addition, most peripheral regions are poor. People are not satisfied with the status quo. Why should they want to shore up the present order?

This issue has been explored with the most rigorous realism in the conservative French journal *Le Point*. Around the time that Iraq was going down in defeat in the gulf war, *Le Point* predicted that an imperial age would follow. And, as had been the case with every empire in the past, a boundary would be drawn dividing the empire from the "barbarians." While establishing a kind of stability, this ill-defined boundary would also create an arena of conflict. The Middle East, the journal concluded, is a classic example.

With characteristic French clarity *Le Point* articulated a number of truths. It is true, for example, that bloodshed in regions regarded as peripheral often goes unreported and unheeded in the wider world. But in this day of rapidly proliferating information, there are no real peripheries. Any area penetrated by television cameras ceases to be peripheral and sometimes even becomes the focus of international politics. Less often, economic interdependence invests such regions and adjacent areas with importance. Intervention becomes necessary, which raises yet another security issue.

A fairly classical approach is probably the best way of dealing with such situations. Conditions in the region are the decisive factor. If the parties to a civil war have no desire to make peace, or if the balance of power—or the balance of fatigue—crucial to conflict resolution does not exist, peacemaking efforts will be unproductive or counterproductive. In such cases, efforts from the sidelines to prevent the conflict from expanding or to open channels for dialogue serve an important function. A noteworthy example in this context is the almost 10 years of careful groundwork by the Association of Southeast Asian Nations preceding the Cambodian peace agreement signed in Paris in 1991.

As past approaches to civil war and unrest reveal, fairly long-term intervention by a single nation in a conflict affecting the stability within its recognized sphere of influence—as with Syria in Lebanon or India in Sri Lanka—while distant from the ideal, is undeniably effective in imposing a certain order and stability.[8] The opposite approach is intervention by an authorized international organization. When there is a high probability that the exercise of military power will be needed, this takes the form of intervention by a multinational force comprising troops from a limited number of major powers. When the task is ensuring the momentum of a situation that is basically on the way to resolution, it takes the form of a United Nations peace-keeping force. In the circumstances, however, almost all attempts to invest U.N. peace-keeping forces with the ability to enforce peace have ended in failure.

The question we need to ask here is, Even if an international organization grants authority to intervene, what country or countries will send in troops in cases where there is a strong prospect of combat? One possibility is to rely on a geographically close power with a stake in the affected region, but this approach carries with it the risk of dividing the world into spheres of influence. Still, that is probably preferable to inaction. In regard to U.N. peace-keeping forces, there is also the problem of how they are to be funded. The old system under which nations policed their own spheres of influence was both unfair and inherently risky, but from the standpoint of security the fact that spheres of influence are no longer openly recognized poses its own dangers, such as refusal to intervene from the most cynical motives cloaked in the rhetoric of lofty idealism, as well as opposition to such behavior.

THE NORTH-SOUTH PROBLEM

If decisive military contests are out of the question, will future power struggles in international politics focus mainly on economic strength? This is the view espoused by Paul Kennedy and quite a few others, including so-called geo-economists. But I think they are mistaken.

Kennedy demonstrates that for the past several hundred years the nation with the greatest economic power became the hegemon. His discussion of the economic balance between the Allied Powers and the Central Powers during World War I, especially the effect of America's entry on the side of the Allies, is impressive. His discussion of the way in which the hegemon succumbed to the temptation to intervene excessively in other nations' affairs and how this weakened its power is also persuasive, especially in the light of the way U.S. President Ronald Reagan's military buildup in the 1980s worsened America's fiscal deficit.[9]

The present, however, differs definitively from the periods Kennedy discusses in that decisive war has become unfeasible. What, then, is the meaning of economic power? Adam Smith, in his 1776 *Inquiry into the Nature and Causes of the Wealth of Nations*, wrote that a wealthy neighboring nation provides commercial opportunities in peacetime but is a formidable foe,in time of war. Thus wealth is a two-edged sword. That is precisely why at the turn of the twentieth century, when British-German rivalry was heating up, German Social Democratic Party leader Eduard Bernstein pointed out that the problem was whether international economic relations were to be seen as a struggle over finite resources or a mutually beneficial competitive game. Unfortunately, the twentieth century has been dominated both internationally and nationally by ideologies emphasizing struggle.

That there will be no more decisive wars does not necessarily validate this view, though it is true that the grounds for feeling threatened by economic strength because of its identification with military power have disappeared or at least greatly diminished. The American scholar of international politics Robert Jervis stresses this point. He notes that whereas before World War I there was some truth in the observation of a contemporary English traveler to Germany that every new German factory smokestack was a cannon pointed at England, this is no longer true. He is quite right in declaring that when nations can be expected to remain at peace fear of dependence and concern over relative gains diminish.[10]

Now that there is no possibility of war, industrial countries' economic relations include a considerable degree of shared benefit inasmuch as other countries' growth cannot be seen as an unalloyed threat. Competition exists, but no threat that needs to be addressed by security policy. Conflict between the rich does not lead to bloodshed as long as private feuds are out of the question. The real threat is the North-South problem. When there are extreme disparities between rich and poor, desperation and the sense of justice can trigger fierce struggles. Moreover, terrorist techniques have become sophisticated and modern societies have few defenses, partly because of the anonymous nature of terrorism. In my view, the French are most keenly sensitive to this peril. Pierre Lellouche's masterly *Le nouveau monde* in particular is worth reading in this context.[11]

8. In both cases intervention was clearly undertaken to serve national interests, but it should be noted that this created sustainability, an important element. See, for example, Pierre Hassner, "Beyond Nationalism and Internationalism," *Survival*, vol. 35, no. 2 (summer 1993).

9. Paul Kennedy, *The Rise and Fall of the Great Powers: Economic Change and Military Conflict from 1500 to 2000* (New York: Random House, 1987).

10. Robert Jervis, *The Meaning of the Nuclear Revolution* (Ithaca: Cornell University Press, 1989).

11. Pierre Lellouche, *Le nouveau monde* (The New World) (Paris: Bernard Grasset, 1992).

The Japanese have little awareness of the gravity of the North-South problem because most countries in their vicinity have enjoyed economic growth for the past decade or two. Poverty has been greatly alleviated, and creeds of desperation have all but disappeared. This suggests that economic growth over a wide area of the South is an extremely important way of nipping in the bud the conviction that the world is divided into Northern haves and Southern have-nots. It is no exaggeration to say that this, in fact, has been Asia's greatest contribution to the world.

International cooperation in such areas as environmental problems is also useful. There is much that we do not understand about the environment, which leads to irresponsible propaganda wars. Unquestionably the burden on the global environment is excessive, but because the effects cannot be accurately predicted, exaggerated expectations are counterproductive and even violate the principle of fairness. For example, the selection of the 1990 carbon dioxide emission levels as the basis for future targets was not well thought through. Nonetheless, it is important that the major powers agree to do what is necessary for the sake of the global environment and that they draw the countries of the South into the process, which will render it more difficult to divide the world rigidly along North-South lines. Peace-keeping operations, too, should be based on tried-and-true wisdom, and should aim to show that global efforts are being undertaken. Nations, especially major powers, stand to gain a great deal from cooperation.

THE DOCTRINE OF COMPETITIVENESS

Advanced industrial nations' economic relations will, however, probably continue to be conducted on a highly adversarial basis, even if this approach flies in the face of historical lessons. We can easily call to mind cases in which a government, believing economic power to be the basis of national strength, has mobilized all the country's resources in a concerted but fruitless effort to boost the economy artificially.

Nineteenth-century Britain's economic power was the source of its diplomatic strength, but that was not the reason industrialization was promoted in the seventeenth and eighteenth centuries. In the twentieth century U.S. economic strength was the foundation of the Pax Americana, but the nation's nineteenth-century economic growth was not underwritten by an aggressive national industrial policy. I think the same observation can be made about Japan's economic growth after World War II.

This is because, basically, economic relations are not a zero-sum game but a plus-sum game. Trade is not possible unless others have the desire and means to buy what one wants to sell—unlike military relations, in which one can to some extent force others to do what one wants. It is a great mistake to think that if one country's exports rise another country's will fall. If exports increase, eventually imports will, as well. What Paul Krugman calls "the doctrine of competitiveness" is, as he states, erroneous—and, I may add, highly dangerous.[12] But since there are sociological reasons for the widespread acceptance of this mistaken theory, it may be useless to point out its fallacy.

The doctrine of competitiveness appears aggressive on first sight, but it is actually the product of a defensive mentality in two senses. First, it assumes that nations must and will continue to play an important role. Precisely because we are so accustomed to this way of thinking, we find it reassuring. But when we start thinking about what nations will do in future international relations, we have no sure answers and feel a nagging anxiety. Believing that the world's major powers will continue to vie on the basis of economic competitiveness and that this will determine the shape of international politics provides us with a clear-cut worldview. Human beings prefer a wrong answer to no answer at all. When France recently pushed ahead with nuclear tests despite widespread criticism, its decision seemed to me to reflect a pathetic determination to reaffirm the fast-dwindling functions of the state.[13]

Perhaps it would be better not to carry my discussion this far. The people of the industrial countries are aware of being caught up in truly momentous change, and this makes them uneasy. After a long respite, anxiety over falling standards of living and over unemployment have again become facts of life. People do not really understand the reasons, however, let alone have solutions. At such a time there is a great temptation to blame everything on competition with foreign countries, which is a partially accurate explanation. People know that specific industries have lost out in international competition and that bankruptcies have caused unemployment. It is harder to perceive the less tangible fact that international trade generates wealth and thus employment.

Second, the doctrine of competitiveness reflects a psychological reaction to the perception that governments no longer possess the control they used to. The notion that such control once existed may, however, be an illusion. There were indeed times when governments could regulate the currency and administer domestic economic policy on that basis, but there were also times when individual countries could not set exchange rates and central banks could not determine interest rates. Nonetheless, loss of control makes nations feel tempted to manage their domestic economies on their own.

This is, no doubt, a genuine feeling; but to believe that all would be well if one could manage the economy without being influenced by interdependence is to evade the facts of economic life. Despite growing interdependence,

12. Paul Krugman, "Competitiveness: A Dangerous Obsession," *Foreign Affairs*, vol. 73, no. 2 (March/April 1994).

13. Jean-Marie Guéhenno, in *La fin de la démocratie* (Paris: Flammarion, 1993; tr. *The End of the Nation-State*, 1995), reveals a perception that the era of a world and nations that were easy to understand, a time of strong governments and bureaucratic institutions, has ended, and betrays a mild nostalgia for that bygone age.

citizens' economic welfare depends on their country's domestic efforts to a greater extent than once thought. This can be understood if we consider that less than 20% of the Japanese and American economies depend on foreign trade. The bulk of the economic activity is generated at home, and whether the domestic economy is sound is thus of decisive importance.

According to one study, it is impossible for an individual government to control exchange rates; it is at the mercy of natural, sometimes severe, fluctuations; but what actually exerts the most pernicious influence on a national economy is the government's failure to act where it can and should: allowing fiscal deficits to pile up, failing to tighten money when the relative value of the currency drops, and letting consumption grow without restraint. Just as we cannot control heat and cold, so it is all but impossible for us to control the international economic climate. But that does not mean we are helpless; we can, after all, dress warmly when the weather is cold.[14]

SECURITY POLICY OBJECTIVES

The kind of self-determination I have been discussing differs from that of the past. For one thing, some measures have to be decided in coordination with other countries, and some have to be implemented jointly. For another, self-determination must take into account the external environment, as well as the impact of one's actions on it. Nations today, facing the contradictory demands of cooperation and autonomy, could be torn asunder. Of course such contradictory demands have existed for a long time in the international community, comprising as it does numerous independent political units, but in the past diplomacy was the province of a small elite. Today we live in an age of the masses (of which mass democracy is one manifestation) and of information. The dilemma of cooperation versus autonomy can no longer be resolved through subtle and complex maneuvers (I am reminded of the definition of diplomacy as "the art of protocol") but must be dealt with openly, even if the overly open debate is sometimes little better than a shouting match.

The safest way to justify international collaboration at home is to explain that everyone has to share the pain for the sake of international harmony. This is the rationale for many compromises in economic negotiations. To give a recent example, it was the way the Japanese government explained to the public the partial liberalization of rice imports in 1994. This explanation was not altogether correct; after all, the Japanese themselves stood to benefit from being able to buy cheaper rice. When Britain repealed its protectionist Corn Laws in 1846, the government defended the move as both advantageous to Britain and beneficial to international cooperation.

The way in which measures are justified is extremely important. If governments feel obliged to say they have made concessions when actually they have not, what are they to say when they really have made concessions? Sometimes the bargaining partners can trade off concessions in totally different fields. Fortunately, many economic problems are amenable to this kind of trading off. But there are some that do not lend themselves to this approach, that involve something close to a zero-sum game, such as issues of rules and principles.

Traditionally, Japan has handled almost all economic friction with the United States by compromising—sometimes pretending to make concessions without actually giving up anything substantive, sometimes wriggling off the hook by focusing on niggling technicalities, sometimes making concessions with strings attached. Just think of the reasons Tokyo gave in the 1994 negotiations over imports of automobile parts for refusing as a matter of principle to accept Washington's insistence on "numerical targets." The first argument was that numerical targets violate the principles of free trade and of business as a whole. This was because the Japanese believed the Americans had publicly demanded such targets on the grounds that the Japanese market was closed and that extraordinary measures were permissible to pry it open. Accepting numerical targets would be tantamount to confessing that Japan was in the wrong, and would pave the way for further U.S. pressure. It would also mean recognizing the American definition of open markets, which, taken to its logical conclusion, would oblige Japan to adopt the same economic system as the United States.

Few Japanese would have agreed to this. Furthermore, the Americans' position was itself faulty, as we can see if we look at the criticism of the Japanese corporate groups known as *keiretsu*. Of course they have flaws; they tend to operate as closed systems and to stagnate because of the difficulty of injecting new blood. Many Japanese recognize the need to rectify such aspects. More fairness and greater openness would be good for the *keiretsu* themselves. But not everything about them is bad. They are loosely linked groups, and this flexibility is widely credited as being one of Japan's strengths. No one in Japan would want to change that totally.

Let me give another example, Japan's collectivism. Many, including me, recognize its evils, especially the danger of squelching individuality. Recognizing individual initiative is fine. But is it fine for those who succeed to enjoy wealth in geometric proportion to their success, while those who fail are doomed to a wretched existence? The overwhelming majority of Japanese would say no. Actually, I think Japan can be justifiably proud of its equitable distribution of wealth and its low crime rate; it may be said to lead the world in both respects. The naturally evolved institutions that have brought this about are at the nation's core. While also upholding the principle of international cooperation, we should defend these institutions. Doing so should be seen as the objective of Japanese security policy.

Security can never be reduced to considerations of hu-

14. Peter Drucker, *Post-capitalist Society* (New York: Harper Business, 1993).

SHOULD WE TURN A BLIND EYE TO SUCH PHENOMENA AS GENOCIDE AND APARTHEID ON THE GROUNDS OF NONINTERVENTION?

man life or property or territory. The objective of security is to protect the institutions, customs, and system of common knowledge that make the Japanese what they are and Japan what it is. Automobile accidents are far and away the leading cause of sudden death in Japan, killing one person in ten thousand every year, but they cannot be considered to jeopardize security. It would be a security problem, however, if even a fraction of this number of people were seized and murdered in their own country, because this would represent a challenge to the system, that is to say, to the government's basic role of protecting citizens' life and property.

DUTIES BEYOND BORDERS

Problems involving economic institutions are a relatively minor headache. In most cases compromise is possible, and the futility of going to war over the stakes is all too clear. There may be bloodless economic "wars," but who would engage in actual combat over less than $10 billion worth of auto parts? John Maynard Keynes's remark that the good thing about the economic field is things do not become excessively serious is highly significant.

Political institutions, which directly involve government legitimacy, pose much graver problems. Consider the impact of America's human-rights diplomacy and its handling of the Taiwan problem on its relations with China. In regard to human rights, the most cynical assessment would be that America is engaged in a futile exercise. Whether human rights are respected within China has no impact on America itself, and it is doubtful that America can exert any influence on conditions within China for better or for worse. The conclusion this view leads to is that Washington should leave events in China to take what course they will, in accordance with the principle of noninterference.

The principle of noninterference, however, must not be perceived simplistically, because order and stability in the international community are not the only values at stake. I do not think this principle means that one must refrain from any involvement whatsoever in other countries' affairs or, conversely, that governments are free to run their own countries any way they like. What Stanley Hoffman calls "duties beyond borders" also exist.[15] In principle, other countries' governments should not assist people fighting to free themselves from an oppressive regime, but individuals are permitted to help at their own risk, and are even praised for doing so. As a rule political exile is recognized, and aiding people who are fleeing tyranny is considered heroic.[16] Nor is it realistic to expect governments to be indifferent to humanitarian imperatives. We must not overlook the fact that increased information and interchange are leading more and more scholars of international law to endorse the concept of humanitarian intervention. Should we turn a blind eye to such phenomena as genocide and apartheid on the grounds of nonintervention?

The Taiwan problem is thornier, since it involves government legitimacy. There is no question that the government of the People's Republic of China in Beijing represents China. But how far China extends is moot. Beijing holds that it embraces the Chinese cultural sphere. That is the only way to explain the position that Mongolia, Manchuria, and Tibet are part of China. This view is based on the belief in a line of legitimate rule stretching from the legendary Xia dynasty down to the present; when a regime loses the "mandate of Heaven" it is replaced through revolution, but the legitimate line remains unbroken.[17] Thus, belief in the identity of culture and state and the ideology of "approved history" are the basis of legitimate power in China. It would be difficult, otherwise, to explain how Manchuria, which was not part of China until less than 400 years ago, has been so since the Manchus conquered China and established the Qing dynasty (1644–1912). Naturally, there can only be one legitimate regime.

Added to this traditional way of thought is the experience of recent history. China's position is that the imperialistic powers encroached on its territory for over a century, when it was feeble and divided. This stance is well grounded in fact. Still, the extent of China's legitimate territory is very difficult to determine. Nationalism had a great deal to do with the success of the communist revolution. The Chinese Communist Party regards the restoration of "lost territories" as a sacred mission, and most Chinese support this. Thus, in Beijing's view Taiwan is an integral part of China, and unification is the only option.

A case can also be made for Taiwanese independence, however. In accordance with the principle of self-determination, the people of a particular region are entitled to declare themselves independent, establish their own government, and conduct political activities on that basis, as long as they do so by lawful means. The principle of self-deter-

15. Stanley Hoffman, *Duties Beyond Borders* (Syracuse: Syracuse University Press, 1981).

16. See Hedley Bull, *The Anarchical Society* (New York: Columbia University Press, 1977).

17. Okada Hidehiro, *Sekaishi no tanjō* (The Birth of World History) (Tokyo: Chikuma Shobō, 1992).

mination is more widely accepted today than in the past. But in reality, declaring independence is a more delicate and difficult proposition. There are no clearly defined criteria for recognition. America, for example, declared independence from Britain in the eighteenth century, but when part of the United States wanted to break away in the mid-nineteenth century, it was not allowed to do so. At the beginning of the 1990s the Soviet Union split fairly easily into a number of sovereign states, but this I think reflects a difference in the Soviet and Chinese perceptions of national territory. At the time of its formation the Soviet Union did not claim to be perpetuating the tradition of czarist Russia. (In fact, Ukraine and some other republics declared independence shortly after the Bolshevik revolution, though they eventually lost it.)

The most reasonable approach to problems like that of Taiwan is probably to reinforce the principle of self-determination by doing everything possible to avoid head-on collisions over principles while urging the avoidance of the exercise of military power even in regard to matters regarded as internal problems. There is in fact a trend in this direction. For example, Chechnya is legally part of Russia, and therefore Russia is justified in using military force to counter the Chechen independence movement, but its doing so has elicited no little international criticism.

THE MANIPULATION OF SYMBOLS

Nonetheless, the Taiwan problem could grow into a clash of principles that would pose a major security problem. The major reason is that the manipulation of symbols will become increasingly significant in international politics. Military force will continue to be important to maintain order on the periphery, but decisive war between developed countries is out of the question. If we assume this, we can also expect contests of economic one-upmanship to lose their verisimilitude. Of course nations will behave as if their actions are important, and will insist that they are defending their national economic interests. This will not be a totally pointless exercise, but the kinds of results that governments today consider important will become almost meaningless. The value of prying open other countries' markets is negligible when compared with the value of putting one's own economy on a sound basis.

Politicians have to do something, though, to make an impression on people. In most countries governments are elected, which means that leaders have to win votes. Diplomatic performance is an ideal means of appealing to the public. Governments have always sought diplomatic successes to compensate for unpopularity due to domestic failures. There are many cases in which foreign adventures have hastened a government's decline.

Today, precisely because confrontation does not lead to out-and-out conflict, the diplomatic card can be played more easily than before. Thus the manipulation of symbols to sway people takes on added importance. Aside from the fact that the results are not determined by voting, international politics has come to resemble domestic politics in this respect. The last couple of years provide any number of examples, including the recent round of Japan-U.S. trade talks. As anyone could see, the specific issues were hardly weighty. The U.S. negotiators were aware that Japan's opening its market in accordance with American demands would barely reduce the bilateral trade imbalance. The point was not to reap substantive benefits but to impress upon the world the closed nature of Japanese market—and, more important, to impress upon the American public how hard the administration was working to open it up. Likewise, the Japanese government's major objective was to demonstrate that it could not agree to the U.S. demands because it was defending free trade.

Opposition to French and Chinese nuclear tests is another example. In my opinion, almost none of those opposed were thinking about such matters as the nuclear balance among the major powers or nuclear deterrence. In the case of France, they were objecting to what they saw as a symbol of anachronistic big-power arrogance. For France, too, the putative impact of the tests on the stability of nuclear deterrence was secondary, at least after the protest movement gained steam. France pushed ahead with the tests to demonstrate the weight of government decisions and to display its resolve to remain a major power.

I am not saying that manipulating symbols is meaningless or mistaken. To sway people's minds and influence societal trends in this way has always been a major concern of politics. Nor does just anything become a contentious issue. Even if we cannot say flatly that the French and Chinese nuclear tests were wrong, however, they were certainly problematic. Commencing such tests after the Nuclear Nonproliferation Treaty was indefinitely extended in 1995—in other words, right after the nonnuclear powers had committed themselves to its regime—showed an arrogant disregard for less powerful nations. It is not surprising that France and China lost face with other countries as a result.

The success or failure of international conferences and nations' popularity at such forums has also grown in importance, and this is no bad thing. ASEAN and the Asia-Pacific Economic Cooperation forum that evolved from it are almost powerless to directly resolve "hard" problems like North Korean nuclear armament or the territorial dispute over the Spratly Islands in the the South China Sea, but no major power can afford to disregard totally the mood of such forums. International criticism of China's hard-nosed stance over the Spratlys, for example, should act as a brake of sorts on Beijing.

THE CASE FOR QUIET BUT FIRM DIPLOMACY

In formulating security policy in the twenty-first century, we must understand both the importance and the limitations of symbol manipulation and be aware of its functions and dynamics. We need to ponder the meaning of Greenpeace's ability to mobilize public opinion. The age of gentlemanly, businesslike diplomacy may be at an end. My own preference, however, is for quiet diplomacy. Certainly it is possible to make points by manipulating symbols, but the impact of doing so tends to be greater at home than internationally, partly because of the kind of rhetoric used to appeal to local voters. In other words, the process may deteriorate into one of domestic self-satisfaction.

That is not all. An even greater danger is that when manipulation of symbols develops into a clear-cut conflict of principles, compromise becomes extremely difficult and a crisis of proportions no one wanted can result. The distinctions between the real-world phenomena of democracy and empire, individualism and collectivism, self-determination and stability, are not black and white; but the words have diametrically opposed meanings, which makes rapprochement difficult. The ability to smooth over rather than accentuate real conflicts of principle, to handle problems as though no such conflict existed, is a valuable skill.

A few years ago Samuel Huntington advanced the thesis of "the clash of civilizations."[18] I am skeptical of his Eurocentrism (more precisely, his New England–centrism) and his narrow equation of conflict with armed conflict. This is not to say that clashes of civilizations will never occur. The Asia-Pacific region has the potential to become a prime focal point of such conflict. Precisely for that reason, however, Japan should behave as though such a clash could not occur or, if it does, in such a way as to alleviate it. Clearly articulated principles may raise morale, as does a battle cry; but if this is what it takes to raise morale, it is often a sign either of spiritual poverty or of domestic instability. Building up a solid record of achievement and continuing to speak reasonably, even if in a small voice, evokes trust over the long run.

In this context, I would like to add that Japan may find itself caught between the strident universalism of America and the fundamentalism of China, backed by its long history and huge size and population. Contemplating such an eventuality, I believe that even if it may be anachronistic in the information age, a businesslike approach, not seeking popularity or prestige or leadership in the international arena, is a wise stance. Of course it will not be easy. Sticking to specifics rules out ambiguity and beating around the bush. It means enunciating extremely clear opposition to the forcible unification of Taiwan with China and making it clear that this is of concern to a sizable segment of the international community.

Is Japanese diplomacy up to the task? The roots of "inarticulate Japan" go deep. For one thing, managing the Japan-U.S. alliance has led to decades of equivocation and sophistry; straight talk has become all but impossible. To give a prime example, for all intents and purposes the two nations are engaged in joint defense, and yet the government maintains that even if Japan has the right of collective self-defense, it cannot be exercised. This sort of verbal fog reminds me of the opaque utterances of the court nobles of medieval Japan, which had almost no relation to the language of people in the world of action.

Most Japanese probably agree that the bilateral alliance is important. More than the quantity and quality of weapons, the amount of national wealth, or the extent of national territory, a country's security is determined by its diplomatic relations: what countries it allies itself with, how many countries it counts as friends, what countries it can somehow accommodate. America is Japan's sole ally and is central to our international relations. Moreover, this relationship is contributing to regional stability and is acknowledged by most countries. If so, we should be able to talk about it with confidence. Why then do we indulge in sophistry and excuses? Old habits die hard, they say, but I think this has gone on far too long.

Another problem is that we still have not come to terms with World War II in our relations with either ourselves or others. In 1995, the fiftieth anniversary of the war's end, many countries demanded apologies from Japan, putting the government in a tight spot. Certainly there are specific areas in which Japan should accept responsibility, but insistence that Japan keep shouldering the burden of the past after half a century, and after Japan has made restitution for its wartime actions (a fact recognized by both sides) is basically odd. It flies in the face of humanity's intelligent distinction between war and peace. The German historian Sebastian Haffner states that once those who have violated the law of war have been punished, their victims compensated, other war-related issues settled, and borders redrawn, it is time to let bygones be bygones and build new relationships of cooperation. Historically, he says, this has always been people's wise approach. He also declares that eternally branding one side a villain is wrongheaded.[19]

The responsibility for this ongoing condemnation lies not only with the victors but also with the vanquished. More fundamentally, however, a past war is a highly effective symbol to manipulate. Breast-beating over the past is extremely political behavior. Perhaps the present ambience is conducive to this sort of thing. Certainly a past war serves in some sense as a surrogate for the war we do not have today. I believe this is dangerous, and may even be the weakest point of the postwar order. To face the issue of war responsibility firmly rather than finesse it may be the key task of Japan's security policy. If the Japanese spirit is corroded by continued evasion and equivocation, no amount of power, wisdom, or money will help.

Translated from "21 seiki no kokusai seiji to anzen hoshō no kihon mondai," in Gaikō Forum, *Special Issue, 1996, pp. 4–23. (Courtesy of Toshi Shuppan, Publishers)*

18. Samuel P. Huntington, "The Clash of Civilizations?" *Foreign Affairs*, vol. 72, no. 3 (summer 1993).

19. Sebastian Haffner, *Anmerkungen zu Hitler* (Munich: Kindler, 1978; tr. *The Meaning of Hitler*, 1979).

Acknowledgments

Minear, Richard H. "Orientalism and the Study of Japan." *Journal of Asian Studies* 39 (1980): 507–17. Reprinted with the permission of the Association for Asian Studies Inc.

Gluck, Carol. "The People in History: Recent Trends in Japanese Historiography." *Journal of Asian Studies* 38 (1979): 25–50. Reprinted with the permission of the Association for Asian Studies Inc.

Garon, Sheldon. "Toward a History of Twentieth-Century Japan." *Monumenta Nipponica: Studies in Japanese Culture* 45 (1990): 339–52. Reprinted with the permission of *Monumenta Nipponica*.

Dower, John W. "The Useful War." *Daedalus* 119:3 (1990): 49–70. Reprinted by permission of *Daedalus*, Journal of the American Academy of Arts and Sciences.

Bix, Herbert P. "Japan's Delayed Surrender: A Reinterpretation." *Diplomatic History* 19 (1995): 197–225. Reprinted with the permission of *Diplomatic History*.

Bernstein, Barton J. "Understanding the Atomic Bomb and the Japanese Surrender: Missed Opportunities, Little-Known Near Disasters, and Modern Memory." *Diplomatic History* 19 (1995): 227–53. Reprinted with the permission of *Diplomatic History*.

Sadao, Asada. "The Mushroom Cloud and National Psyches: Japanese and American Perspectives of the A-Bomb Decision, 1945–1995." *Journal of American-East Asian Relations* 4 (1995): 95–116. Reprinted with the permission of Imprint Publications.

Moore, Ray A. "Reflections on the Occupation of Japan." *Journal of Asian Studies* 38 (1979): 721–34. Reprinted with the permission of the Association for Asian Studies Inc.

Williams, Justin, Sr. "American Democratization Policy for Occupied Japan: Correcting the Revisionist Version." *Pacific Historical Review* 57 (1988): 179–202. Reprinted with the permission of the University of California Press. Copyright by the Pacific Coast Branch, American Historical Society.

Schonberger, Howard. "A Rejoinder." *Pacific Historical Review* 57 (1988): 209–18. Reprinted with the permission of the University of California Press. Copyright by the Pacific Coast Branch, American Historical Society.

McNelly, Theodore. "The Japanese Constitution: Child of the Cold War." *Political Science Quarterly* 74 (1959): 176–95. Reprinted with the permission of the author and the Academy of Political Science.

Schonberger, Howard. "U.S. Policy in Post-War Japan: The Retreat from Liberalism." *Science & Society* 46 (1982): 39–59. Reprinted with the permission of *Science & Society*.

Koschmann, J. Victor. "The Debate on Subjectivity in Postwar Japan: Foundations of Modernism as a Political Critique." *Pacific Affairs* 54 (1981–1982): 609–31. Reprinted with the permission of the University of British Columbia.

Carlile, Lonny E. "Party Politics and the Japanese Labor Movement: Rengo's 'New Political Force.'" *Asian Survey* 34 (1994): 606–20. Reprinted with the permission of the University of California Press.

Garon, Sheldon M. "The Imperial Bureaucracy and Labor Policy in Postwar Japan." *Journal of Asian Studies* 43 (1984): 441–57. Reprinted with the permission of the Association for Asian Studies Inc.

Anderson, Stephen J. "Japan: The End of One-Party Dominance." *Current History* 92 (Dec. 1993): 406–12. Reprinted with the permission of Current History Inc.

Hirsh, Michael, and E. Keith Henry. "The Unraveling of Japan Inc.: Multinationals as Agents of Change." *Foreign Affairs* 76:2 (1997): 11–16. Reprinted by permission of *Foreign Affairs*, (March/April 1997). Copyright 1997 by the Council on Foreign Relations, Inc.

van Wolferen, Karel. "Japan's Non-Revolution." *Foreign Affairs* 72:4 (1993): 54–65. Reprinted by permission of *Foreign Affairs*, (Sept./Oct.) Copyright 1993 by the Council on Foreign Relations, Inc.

Mukae, Ryuji. "Japan's Diet Resolution on World War Two: Keeping History at Bay." *Asian Survey* 36 (1996): 1011–30. Reprinted with the permission of the University of California Press.

Kasuya, Kazuki. "A Journalist's Perspective on Postwar Japan." *Japan Review of International Affairs* 10 (1996): 55–69. Reprinted with the permission of the Japan Institute of International Affairs.